A·N·N·U·A·L E·D·I·T

M000011794

Educational Psychology
02/03

Seventeenth Edition

EDITORS

Kathleen M. Cauley
Virginia Commonwealth University

Kathleen M. Cauley received her Ph.D. in educational studies/human development from the University of delaware in 1985. Her research interests center on applying cognitive developmental research to school learning. Currently, she is studying children's mathematical understanding.

Fredric Linder
Virginia Commonwealth University

Fredric Linder received an A.B. in American civilization from the University of Miami, Florida, an M.A. in psychology from the New School for Social Research, and a Ph.D. in educational psychology from the State University of New York at Buffalo. His research focuses on the values and cognitive learning styles of students.

James H. McMillan
Virginia Commonwealth University

James H. McMillan received his bachelor's degree from Albion College in 1970, an M.A. from Michigan State University in 1972, and a Ph.D. from Northwestern University in 1976. He has reviewed and written extensively in educational psychology.

McGraw-Hill/Dushkin
530 Old Whitfield Street, Guilford, Connecticut 06437

Visit us on the Internet
http://www.dushkin.com

Credits

1. **Perspectives on Teaching**
   Unit photo—Courtesy of Pamela Carley/McGraw-Hill/Dushkin.
2. **Development**
   Unit photo—United Nations/DPI photo by Shelley Rotner.
3. **Exceptional and Culturally Diverse Children**
   Unit photo—United Nations/DPI photo by Y. Nagata.
4. **Learning and Instruction**
   Unit photo—© 2002 by Cleo Freelance Photography.
5. **Motivation and Classroom Management**
   Unit photo—© 2002 by Cleo Freelance Photography.
6. **Assessment**
   Unit photo—United Nations/DPI photo by O. Monsen.

Copyright

Cataloging in Publication Data
Main entry under title: Annual Editions: Educational Psychology. 2002/2003.
1. Educational psychology—Periodicals.   2. Teaching–Periodicals.   I. Cauley, Kathleen M., *comp.*;
Linder, Fredric, *comp.*; McMillan, James H., *comp.* II. Title: Educational psychology.
ISBN 0–07–250681–4   370.15'05   82-640517   ISSN 0731–1141

Seventeenth Edition

Cover image © 2002 PhotoDisc, Inc.
Printed in the United States of America   1234567890BAHBAH5432   Printed on Recycled Paper

Editors/Advisory Board

Members of the Advisory Board are instrumental in the final selection of articles for each edition of ANNUAL EDITIONS. Their review of articles for content, level, currentness, and appropriateness provides critical direction to the editor and staff. We think that you will find their careful consideration well reflected in this volume.

To the Reader

In publishing ANNUAL EDITIONS we recognize the enormous role played by the magazines, newspapers, and journals of the public press in providing current, first-rate educational information in a broad spectrum of interest areas. Many of these articles are appropriate for students, researchers, and professionals seeking accurate, current material to help bridge the gap between principles and theories and the real world. These articles, however, become more useful for study when those of lasting value are carefully collected, organized, indexed, and reproduced in a low-cost format, which provides easy and permanent access when the material is needed. That is the role played by ANNUAL EDITIONS.

Educational psychology is an interdisciplinary subject that includes human development, learning, intelligence, motivation, assessment, instructional strategies, and classroom management. The articles in this volume give special attention to the application of this knowledge to teaching.

Annual Editions: Educational Psychology 02/03 is divided into six units, and an overview, which explains how the unit articles are related to the broader issues within educational psychology, precedes each unit.

The first unit, *Perspectives on Teaching,* presents issues that are central to the teaching role. The authors of the articles provide perspectives on the value of educational psychology, describing effective teaching and the standards movement. Additionally, how teachers can help students who have been affected by the national tragedy of September 11, 2001, is explored.

The second unit, entitled *Development,* is concerned with child and adolescent development. It covers the biological, cognitive, social, and emotional processes of development. The essays in this unit examine the issues of parenting, moral development, the social forces affecting children and adolescents, as well as the personal and social skills needed to cope with school learning and developmental tasks.

The third unit, regarding exceptional and culturally diverse students, focuses on the learning disabled and the gifted and on multicultural education. Diverse students require an individualized approach to education. The articles in this unit review the characteristics of these children and suggest programs and strategies to meet their needs.

In the fourth unit, *Learning and Instruction,* articles about theories of learning and instructional strategies are presented. The different views of learning, such as information processing, behaviorism, and constructivist learning, represent the accumulation of years of research on the way humans change in thinking or behavior due to experience. The principles generated by each approach have important implications for teaching. These implications are addressed in a subsection on instructional strategies, covering such topics as instructional methods, authentic instruction, and learning styles.

The topic of motivation is perhaps one of the most important aspects of school learning. Effective teachers need to motivate their students both to learn and to behave responsibly. How to manage children and what forms of discipline to use are issues that concern parents as well as teachers and administrators. The articles in the fifth unit, *Motivation and Classroom Management,* present a variety of perspectives on motivating students and discuss approaches to managing student behavior.

The articles in the sixth unit review assessment approaches that can be used to diagnose learning problems and improve instruction. The focus is on how alternative assessments, such as performance assessments and portfolios, can be integrated with instruction to enhance student learning. Approaches to grading are also reviewed.

This seventeenth edition of *Annual Editions: Educational Psychology* has been revised in order to present articles that are current and useful. Your responses to the selection and organization of materials are appreciated. Please complete and return the postage-paid *article rating form* on the last page of the book.

Kathleen M. Cauley
Editor

Fredric Linder
Editor

James H. McMillan
Editor

Contents

UNIT 1
Perspectives on Teaching

Five selections discuss the importance of research and the value of scientific inquiry to the teaching process.

Unit Overview   xvi

The concepts in bold italics are developed in the article. For further expansion, please refer to the Topic Guide and the Index.

UNIT 2
Development

Five articles examine how social interaction in the classroom influences child and adolescent development.

UNIT 3
Exceptional and Culturally Diverse Children

Seven articles look at the problems and positive effects of educational programs for learning disabled, gifted, and culturally diverse children.

The concepts in bold italics are developed in the article. For further expansion, please refer to the Topic Guide and the Index.

UNIT 4
Learning and Instruction

Ten selections explore the important types of student/teacher interaction.

Unit Overview 72

The concepts in bold italics are developed in the article. For further expansion, please refer to the Topic Guide and the Index.

The concepts in bold italics are developed in the article. For further expansion, please refer to the Topic Guide and the Index.

UNIT 5
Motivation and Classroom Management

Eight selections discuss student control and motivation in the classroom.

The concepts in bold italics are developed in the article. For further expansion, please refer to the Topic Guide and the Index.

UNIT 6
Assessment

Four articles discuss the implications of educational measurement for the classroom decision-making process and for the teaching profession.

The concepts in bold italics are developed in the article. For further expansion, please refer to the Topic Guide and the Index.

Topic Guide

This topic guide suggests how the selections in this book relate to the subjects covered in your course. You may want to use the topics listed on these pages to search the Web more easily.

On the following pages a number of Web sites have been gathered specifically for this book. They are arranged to reflect the units of this *Annual Edition*. You can link to these sites by going to the DUSHKIN ONLINE support site at *http://www.dushkin.com/online/*.

ALL THE ARTICLES THAT RELATE TO EACH TOPIC ARE LISTED BELOW THE BOLD-FACED TERM.

Accountability
38. Fighting the Tests: A Practical Guide to Rescuing Our Schools

Aggression
8. Raising a Moral Child

Aggressive behavior
32. Reinforcement in Developmentally Appropriate Early Childhood Classrooms

Alternative assessment
37. Teaching About Performance Assessment

Assessment
11. Chaos in the Classroom: Looking at ADHD
14. Gifted Students Need an Education, Too
31. Teaching Students to Regulate Their Own Behavior

Attachment
6. Wired for Thought

Behaviorism
21. Caution—Praise Can Be Dangerous
32. Reinforcement in Developmentally Appropriate Early Childhood Classrooms
33. Another View on "Reinforcement in Developmentally Appropriate Early Childhood Classrooms"

Benefits
18. In Search of … Brain-Based Education

Brain-based education
18. In Search of … Brain-Based Education
19. Educators Need to Know About the Human Brain

Brain development
6. Wired for Thought

Career development
18. In Search of … Brain-Based Education

Character development
18. In Search of … Brain-Based Education

Classroom assessment
36. Fundamental Assesment Principles for Teachers and School Administrators

Classroom climate
20. Ability and Expertise: It's Time to Replace the Current Model of Intelligence

Classroom management
31. Teaching Students to Regulate Their Own Behavior

Cognition
6. Wired for Thought
18. In Search of … Brain-Based Education

Cognitive development
6. Wired for Thought
7. Play an Endangered Species
18. In Search of … Brain-Based Education

Cognitive learning
1. What Good Is Educational Psychology? The Case of Cognition and Instruction
18. In Search of … Brain-Based Education
19. Educators Need to Know About the Human Brain
24. Concept Mapping as a Mindtool for Critical Thinking

Concept mapping
24. Concept Mapping as a Mindtool for Critical Thinking

Constructivism
22. The Challenges of Sustaining a Constructivist Classroom Culture

Critical thinking
24. Concept Mapping as a Mindtool for Critical Thinking

Culture
8. Raising a Moral Child

Development, child-adolescent
6. Wired for Thought
7. Play an Endangered Species
8. Raising a Moral Child
9. The School and the Child and the Child in the School
10. Differing Perspectives, Common Ground: The Middle School and Gifted Education Relationship

Developmentally appropriate practice
32. Reinforcement in Developmentally Appropriate Early Childhood Classrooms

Differentiated instruction
25. Mapping a Route Toward Differentiated Instruction
26. Reconcilable Differences? Standards-Based Teaching and Differentiation

Disabilities
11. Chaos in the Classroom: Looking at ADHD
32. Reinforcement in Developmentally Appropriate Early Childhood Classrooms

World Wide Web Sites

The following World Wide Web sites have been carefully researched and selected to support the articles found in this reader. The easiest way to access these selected sites is to go to our DUSHKIN ONLINE support site at *http://www.dushkin.com/online/*.

AE: Educational Psychology 02/03

The following sites were available at the time of publication. Visit our Web site—we update DUSHKIN ONLINE regularly to reflect any changes.

General Sources

American Psychological Association
http://www.apa.org/psychnet/

By exploring the APA's "PsychNET," you will be able to find links to an abundance of articles and other resources that are useful in the field of educational psychology.

Educational Resources Information Center
http://www.eric.ed.gov

This invaluable site provides links to all ERIC sites: clearinghouses, support components, and publishers of ERIC materials. Search the ERIC database for what is new.

National Education Association
http://www.nea.org

Something—and often quite a lot—about virtually every education-related topic can be accessed at or through this site of the 2.3-million-strong National Education Association.

National Parent Information Network/ERIC
http://npin.org

This is a clearinghouse of information on elementary and early childhood education as well as urban education. Browse through its links for information for parents.

U.S. Department of Education
http://www.ed.gov/pubs/TeachersGuide/

Government goals, projects, and grants are listed here, plus many links to teacher services and resources.

UNIT 1: Perspectives on Teaching

The Center for Innovation in Education
http://www.center.edu

The Center for Innovation in Education, self-described as a "not-for-profit, non-partisan research organization" focuses on K–12 education reform strategies. Click on its links about school privatization.

Classroom Connect
http://www.classroom.net

This is a major Web site for K–12 teachers and students, with links to schools, teachers, and resources online. It includes discussion of the use of technology in the classroom.

Education World
http://www.education-world.com

Education World provides a database of literally thousands of sites that can be searched by grade level, plus education news, lesson plans, and professional-development resources.

Goals 2000: A Progress Report
http://www.ed.gov/pubs/goals/progrpt/index.html

Open this site to survey a progress report by the U.S. Department of Education on the Goals 2000 reform initiative. It provides a sense of the goals that educators are reaching for as they look toward the future.

Teacher Talk Forum
http://education.indiana.edu/cas/tt/tthmpg.html

Visit this site for access to a variety of articles discussing life in the classroom. Clicking on the various links will lead you to electronic lesson plans, covering a variety of topic areas, from Indiana University's Center for Adolescent Studies.

UNIT 2: Development

Association for Moral Education
http://www.wittenberg.edu/ame/

AME is dedicated to fostering communication, cooperation, training, curriculum development, and research that link moral theory with educational practices. From here it is possible to connect to several sites on moral development.

Child Welfare League of America
http://www.cwla.org

The CWLA is the United States' oldest and largest organization devoted entirely to the well-being of vulnerable children and their families. This site provides links to information about issues related to morality and values in education.

Coping With Traumatic Events
http://www.childtrauma.org/Traumatic_events_teachers.htm

Dr. Bruce D. Perry offers these special comments for teachers and personnel who are dealing with children who have been experiencing trauma caused by the terrorist attacks on the United States.

Guidelines for Developmentally Appropriate Early Childhood Practice
http://www.newhorizons.org/naeyc.html

Here is a 23-page excerpt from a report, edited by Sue Bredekamp, that covers every aspect of appropriate programs that serve children from birth through age 8, published on the Web by the National Association for the Education of Young Children.

The National Academy for Child Development
http://www.nacd.org

This international organization is dedicated to helping children and adults reach their full potential. Its home page presents links to various programs, research, and resources into such topics as ADD/ADHD.

National Association of School Psychologists (NASP)
http://www.nasponline.org

The NASP offers advice to teachers about how to help children with special needs cope with terrorism. The site includes tips for school personnel as well as parents.

Scholastic News Zone
http://www.scholasticnews.com

At this site, Scholastic Classroom magazines provide up-to-date information to children, teachers, and parents online to help explain the war on terrorism.

www.dushkin.com/online/

UNIT 3: Exceptional and Culturally Diverse Children

The Council for Exceptional Children
http://www.cec.sped.org/index.html

This page will give you access to information on identifying and teaching gifted children, attention-deficit disorders, and other topics in gifted education.

Global SchoolNet Foundation
http://www.gsn.org

Access this site for multicultural education information. The site includes news for teachers, students, and parents, as well as chat rooms, links to educational resources, programs, and contests and competitions.

International Project: Multicultural Pavilion
http://curry.edschool.virginia.edu/curry/centers/multicultural/ papers.html

Here is a forum for sharing of stories and resources and for learning from the stories and resources of others, in the form of articles on the Internet that cover every possible racial, gender, and multicultural issue that could arise in the field of multicultural education.

Let 1000 Flowers Bloom/Kristen Nicholson-Nelson
http://teacher.scholastic.com/professional/assessment/100flowers.htm

Open this page for Kristen Nicholson-Nelson's discussion of ways in which teachers can help to nurture children's multiple intelligences. She provides a useful bibliography and resources.

Multicultural Publishing and Education Catalog
http://www.mpec.org

This is the home page of the MPEC, a networking and support organization for independent publishers, authors, educators, and librarians fostering authentic multicultural books and materials. It has excellent links to a vast array of resources related to multicultural education.

National Attention Deficit Disorder Association
http://www.add.org

This site, some of which is under construction, will lead you to information about ADD/ADHD. It has links to self-help and support groups, outlines behaviors and diagnostics, answers FAQs, and suggests books and other resources.

National MultiCultural Institute (NMCI)
http://www.nmci.org

NMCI is one of the major organizations in the field of diversity training. At this Web site, NMCI offers conference data, resource materials, diversity training and consulting service information, and links to other related sites.

UNIT 4: Learning and Instruction

Education Week on the Web
http://www.edweek.org

At this page you can open archives, read special reports, keep up on current events, and access a variety of articles in educational psychology. A great deal of material is helpful in learning and instruction.

Online Internet Institute
http://www.oii.org

A collaborative project among Internet-using educators, proponents of systemic reform, content-area experts, and teachers who desire professional growth, this site provides a learning environment for integrating the Internet into educators' individual teaching styles.

Teachers Helping Teachers
http://www.pacificnet.net/~mandel/

This site provides basic teaching tips, new teaching-methodology ideas, and forums for teachers to share their experiences. It features educational resources on the Web, with new ones added each week.

The Teachers' Network
http://www.teachnet.org

Bulletin boards, classroom projects, online forums, and Web mentors are featured on this site, as well as the book *Teachers' Guide to Cyberspace* and an online, 4-week course on how to use the Internet.

UNIT 5: Motivation and Classroom Management

Canada's Schoolnet Staff Room
http://www.schoolnet.ca/home/e/

Here is a resource and link site for anyone involved in education, including special-needs educators, teachers, parents, volunteers, and administrators.

National Institute on the Education of At-Risk Students
http://www.ed.gov/offices/OERI/At-Risk/

The At-Risk Institute supports a range of research and development activities designed to improve the education of students at risk of educational failure due to limited English proficiency, race, geographic location, or economic disadvantage. Access its work and links at this site.

UNIT 6: Assessment

Awesome Library for Teachers
http://www.neat-schoolhouse.org/teacher.html

Open this page for links and access to teacher information on everything from assessments to child development topics.

Phi Delta Kappa International
http://www.pdkintl.org

This important organization publishes articles about all facets of education. You can check out the online archive of the journal, *Phi Delta Kappan,* which has resources such as articles having to do with assessment.

Washington (State) Center for the Improvement of Student Learning
http://www.K12.wa.us/reform/

This Washington State site is designed to provide access to information about the state's new academic standards, assessments, and accountability system. Many resources and Web links are included.

We highly recommend that you review our Web site for expanded information and our other product lines. We are continually updating and adding links to our Web site in order to offer you the most usable and useful information that will support and expand the value of your Annual Editions. You can reach us at: *http://www.dushkin.com/annualeditions/.*

UNIT 1
Perspectives on Teaching

Unit Selections

1. **What Good Is Educational Psychology? The Case of Cognition and Instruction**, Richard E. Mayer
2. **Good Teachers, Plural**, Donald R. Cruickshank and Donald Haefele
3. **What I Hope for in My Children's Teachers: A Parent's Perspective**, David Boers
4. **Helping Children Cope with Loss, Death and Grief: Response to a National Tragedy**, *National Association of School Psychologists*
5. **The Standards Juggernaut**, Marion Brady

Key Points to Consider

- What questions would you like to see educational psychologists study?

- Describe several characteristics of effective teachers.

- As we move into the twenty-first century, what new expectations should be placed on teachers and schools? What expectations will fade?

 **Links: www.dushkin.com/online/**
These sites are annotated in the World Wide Web pages.

The Center for Innovation in Education
http://www.center.edu

Classroom Connect
http://www.classroom.net

Education World
http://www.education-world.com

Goals 2000: A Progress Report
http://www.ed.gov/pubs/goals/progrpt/index.html

Teacher Talk Forum
http://education.indiana.edu/cas/tt/tthmpg.html

The teaching-learning process in school is enormously complex. Many factors influence pupil learning—such as family background, developmental level, prior knowledge, motivation, and, of course, effective teachers. Educational psychology investigates these factors to better understand and explain student learning. We begin our exploration of the teaching-learning process by considering the characteristics of effective teaching.

In the first article, Richard Mayer describes the contributions of educational psychology to our understanding of how students learn. The next two articles present perspectives on effective teaching—the variety of professional perspectives as well as a parent perspective.

The next article discusses the range of reactions that children and adolescents have experienced in response to the terrorism attacks of September 11, 2001, and suggests ways that educators can help them to cope and continue their schooling.

Finally, we look toward the future and the educational issues that may ultimately change the teacher's role. The fifth article, "The Standards Juggernaut," suggests that schools ought to be forward-looking institutions. The author asks us to think more carefully about the goals of education and what should be in the curriculum to prepare students for the future.

Educational psychology is a resource for teachers that emphasizes disciplined inquiry, a systematic and objective analysis of information, and a scientific attitude toward decision making. The field provides information for decisions that are based on quantitative and qualitative studies of learning and teaching rather than on intuition, tradition, authority, or subjective feelings. It is our hope that this aspect of educational psychology is communicated throughout these readings, and that, as a student, you will adopt the analytic, probing attitude that is part of the discipline.

While educational psychologists have helped to establish a knowledge base about teaching and learning, the unpredictable, spontaneous, evolving nature of teaching suggests that the best they will ever do is to provide concepts and skills that teachers can adapt for use in their classrooms. The issues raised in these articles about effective teaching, and the issues facing teachers in the twenty-first century, help us understand the teaching role and its demands. As you read articles in other chapters, consider the demands they place on the teaching role as well.

What Good is Educational Psychology?
The Case of Cognition and Instruction

Research on cognition and instruction has made considerable progress in recent years, in terms of contributions both to cognitive theory and to educational practice. Two important contributions are psychologies of subject matter, which specify how people learn school subjects such as reading and mathematics, and teaching of cognitive strategies, which fosters improvements in how students learn and think. In short, the thesis of this essay is that psychology and education are good for one another. When it comes to the role of psychology in education, there is nothing as beneficial to practice as a good theory. When it comes to the role of education in psychology, there is nothing as beneficial to theory as a good practical problem. Although much has been accomplished, the promise of educational psychology in the 21st century rests in the development of an educationally relevant science of how people learn.

Richard E. Mayer
Department of Psychology
University of California at Santa Barbara

It is not easy being an educational psychologist these days. To our colleagues in psychology, we are too educational, a disparaging label reflecting our interest in studying educationally relevant problems rather than contrived laboratory tasks. To our colleagues in education, we are too psychological, a disparaging label reflecting our interest in basing educational practice on scientific research methods and theories rather than relying on popular opinion and doctrine. We disturb psychology by failing to accept contrived artificial laboratory research as the ending-point for psychological research. We disturb education by failing to accept good intentions, expert opinions, and doctrine-based claims as the rationale for educational practices. Yet, it is precisely the juxtaposition of these two criticisms that create the unique potential of educational psychology to advance both psychological theory and educational practice. Educational psychology refuses to turn its back on the study of practical educational problems as a source of rich research questions, and educational psychology refuses to turn its back on the role of scientific research methods and theory in answering educational questions.

THE MUTUAL DEPENDENCE OF PSYCHOLOGY AND EDUCATION

The pages of educational research periodicals have been filled with obituaries cheering the death—or at least the diminished strength—of psychology as a force in education (see Levin & O'Donnell, 1999; Mayer, 1993). To some in the educational research community, psychology has become an irrelevant and troublesome irritation. My goal in this article is to provide examples showing that educational psychology—far from being dead or irrelevant—is a vibrant field that has been experiencing unprecedented success in understanding educational issues. It is ironic, and for me, frustrating, that at a time when educational psychology has matured to the point where its promise for contributing to both education and psychology has never been greater, this is the time that it is in jeopardy of being rejected by both fields. Now that psychologists and educators finally have something worthwhile to talk about, it would be unfortunate for both fields if the conversation was closed.

What Does Education Have to Offer Psychology?

Psychology is a field that has been amazingly successful in studying important human issues within highly artificial, perhaps sterile, environments. The result is the development of research-based theories that are so limited that they are widely recognized as trivial. By the 1950s, the grand theories of learning had died because of their inability to account for learning beyond rats running mazes and pigeons pecking keys. By the 1970s, cognitive psychology, with all of its precisely measured reaction times down to the millisecond, was about to die of its own irrelevance (Neisser, 1976). What saved cognitive psychology from its demise was a shift in focus to realistic situations, including educational ones (Mayer, 1992, 1996, 2001). Today, in some research centers, educational and cognitive psychology appear to be merging.

What cognitive psychology needs is the challenge of explaining learning and cognition in realistic situations. To develop theories of learning and cognition that are relevant, psychologists need to examine realistic learning situations. Educational venues offer exactly what cognitive psychology needs: questions about how people learn to read, to comprehend what they read, to write, to compute, to solve mathematics problems, to think scientifically, to think historically, to learn a second language, and so on. Cognitive psychology is enriched by the challenge of developing theories that account for educationally relevant learning and cognition. An example is Chi, Bassok, Lewis, Reimann, and Glaser's (1989) research on how successful and unsuccessful problem solvers study worked-out examples in science textbooks—research that contributes to cognitive theories of analogical reasoning as well as educational practice in science teaching.

What Does Psychology Have to Offer Education?

Education is a field facing monumental practical problems that are often addressed through well-intended fads, expert opinions, and doctrine-based agendas (Levin & O'Donnell, 1999). The result is educational practice that has advanced very little over the last century and still is rarely based on proven instructional techniques. Yet, there is no more important societal task than the education of youth.

What education needs is a set of scientifically valid methods of instruction based on research evidence and tested theory. Help in meeting this need is precisely what psychology has to offer. The scientifically sound research methods of psychology constitute one of the greatest inventions of the 20th century and hold great promise for improving educational practice. Instead of being embarrassed by a commitment to examine educational issues using scientific research methods, educational psychologists should be proud to be able to extend the domain of science into education. Research-based psychological theory can help guide the design of instructional methods and materials.

In short, psychology needs something real to study, and education provides it; education needs a scientific methodology for addressing its problems, and psychology provides it. It is a match made in heaven that has had a somewhat difficult history here on earth. As Mayer (1992) showed, the relation between psychology and education has moved through three phases in the 20th century: (a) a one-way street from psychology to education in which psychology was supposed to develop theories of learning and education was supposed to apply them, (b) a dead-end street for psychology and education in which psychology focused on noneducational issues and education focused mainly on practical issues, and (c) a two-way street between psychology and education in which both disciplines work together for their mutual benefit. Will the two-way street endure as we enter the 21st century or will psychology and education again fall back into their former noncommunicative stance? The thesis of this brief essay is that much is to be gained by continuing the conversation between psychology and education.

WHAT CAN HAPPEN WHEN COGNITION AND INSTRUCTION MEET?

What can happen when psychology and education meet? In this section, I briefly summarize some of the productive results of the collaboration between cognitive psychologists—who aim to understand how people learn—and educators—who aim to understand how to help people learn. Two important contributions of this collaboration between cognition and instruction are the development of psychologies of subject matter, and the teaching of cognitive strategies.

Psychologies of Subject Matter

One of the most productive accomplishments of educational psychology has been the development of psychologies of subject matter (Bruer, 1993; Mayer, 1999; Shulman & Quinlan, 1996). Psychologies of subject matter concern learning and instruction within specific school subjects such as reading, writing, mathematics, science, and history. Instead of examining how people learn in general, psychologies of subject matter examine topics such as how people learn to read, learn to write, learn to think mathematically, learn to think scientifically, and learn to think historically.

One of psychology's original goals—throughout the first half of the 20th century—was the development of a single all-encompassing general theory of learning (Mayer, 2001). In its search for the one true theory of learning, psychology generated several of them ranging from Thorndike's connectionism to Hull's mathematical learning theory to Skinner's behaviorism to gestalt theory. By midcentury, it had become clear that psychology's search for a general theory of learning was a failure, and eventually the grand theories of learning melted away. Education offered the challenge of understanding how people learn in real school content areas; having failed to establish general theories based on contrived laboratory learning tasks, psychology finally accepted the offer. In short, education rescued psychology from its fruitless search for a general theory of learning. In place of educationally irrelevant general theories, educational psychologists began to develop specific theories tailored to specific subject areas.

In this section, I provide brief examples of the contributions of educational psychology in reading, mathematics, and history.

Psychology of learning to read. What does a child need to know to be able to read? Researchers have shown that one important prerequisite cognitive skill is phonological awareness (or phonemic awareness): awareness that words can be broken down into sound units and that sound units can be combined to form words. For example, phonological awareness involves being able to discriminate the sounds of each of the three letters in the spoken word, "cat"; and being able to produce and blend the sounds of /c/ and /a/ and /t/ to say "cat." Common tests for phonological awareness include being able to (a) tell if two words rhyme (e.g., "cat" and "hat"), (b) recite a list of words (e.g., "hat, fir, led"), (c) tap out the number of sounds in a word (e.g., giving three taps for "cat"), (d) add a sound to a word (e.g., adding "c" to "at" to get "cat"), (e) delete a sound from a word (e.g., taking away the first sound in "cat" to get "at"), or (f) substitute a sound in a word (e.g., given the spoken word "park," change the last would to /t/ yielding the word "part").

What is the evidence that phonological awareness is related to being able to learn how to read? First, students who have difficulty in learning to read in elementary school score lower on tests of phonological awareness than students who are good readers (Bradley & Bryant, 1978; Stanovich, 1991). Second, students who lack phonological awareness when they enter elementary school are more likely to fail to become strong readers later in elementary school than are students who enter school with phonological awareness (Bradley & Bryant, 1985; Juel, Griffith, & Gough, 1986; Wagner & Torgesen, 1987).

An important educational implication is that students who enter elementary school without skill in phonological awareness could benefit from phonological awareness training. For example, Bradley and Bryant (1983, 1985, 1991) provided phonological awareness training to 5- and 6-year-olds in 40 10-min sessions spread over 2 years. In one session, a student was shown a picture of a bus and asked to pick out another picture of a word that started with the same sound. In another session, a student was shown four pictures and asked to choose the one that began with a different sound from the others. In yet another session, a student was asked to tell whether two spoken words rhymed. A comparison group received 40 10-min lessons involving the same words, but the tasks involved things like sorting pictures based on their semantic category.

Does phonological awareness training work? Students in the trained group showed a strong improvement on tests of phonological awareness, whereas the comparison group did not. Importantly, on a reading test administered after the training, the trained group was five times more likely than the comparison group to be able to read words containing two or three sounds. On a standardized reading test given at the end of the school year, five times as many students were classified as readers in the trained group as in the comparison group. These studies demonstrate that targeted instruction in phonological awareness can have a strong effect on a student's ability to learn to read.

In a recent review, Goswami and Bryant (1992) concluded the following: "There can be little doubt that phonological awareness plays an important role in reading... There is also evidence that successful training in phonological awareness helps

children learn to read" (p. 49). By carefully analyzing the specific knowledge needed to become a reader, by carrying out rigorous longitudinal studies, and by conducting well-controlled intervention experiments, researchers have pinpointed a potentially important factor in early reading instruction—namely, phonological awareness. This line of research is a little gem of educational research because it represents a powerful example of how educational psychology can contribute to education and psychology.

Psychology of mathematics learning. What does a student need to know to learn basic arithmetic, such as how to add and subtract single-digit numbers? One concept targeted by researchers is number sense, which includes the concept of the mental line and the ability to use it. Number sense can be tested by asking questions such as, "What number comes after 7?", "Which is closer to 5—6 or 2?", "Which number comes first when you are counting—8, 5, 2, or 6?", and "Which number is bigger—5 or 4?".

What evidence is there that a child's knowledge of the mental number line is related to learning arithmetic? Case and his colleagues developed a test of students' knowledge of the mental number line (Case & Okamoto, 1996; Griffin, Case, & Capodilupo, 1995; Griffin, Case, & Siegler, 1994). When they administered the test to 6-year-old children, they found that most of the children from low socioeconomic status (SES) homes lacked an adequate knowledge of the mental number line, and also most could not solve simple arithmetic problems such as, "2 + 4 = __." In contrast, most of the high SES children demonstrated adequate knowledge of the mental number line and also most could solve simple arithmetic problems. This line of research suggests that an obstacle to learning basic arithmetic may be that some students enter school without a conception of a mental number line.

Does number line training work? If knowledge of a mental line is a cognitive prerequisite for learning arithmetic, then students who lack this knowledge could benefit from instruction that is specifically targeted at helping them develop it. For example, the "Rightstart" program consists of 40 half-hour sessions in which students learn how to use a mental number line by playing various games (Griffin & Case, 1996; Griffin et al., 1994, 1995). The games give students experience in comparing two dice to see which number is higher, moving a token along a number-line path based on the number on the die, moving a token backwards along a number-line path for a certain number of steps, and so on.

Low SES first graders who received the training showed large improvements on tests of number-line knowledge, whereas a comparison group that received traditional mathematics instruction did not. More importantly, on an arithmetic test given at the end of the year, twice as many of the trained students mastered basic arithmetic as did students in the comparison group. Griffin and Case (1996) concluded that "a surprising proportion of children from low-income homes in North American families—at least 50% in our samples—do not arrive in school with the central conceptual structure in place that is necessary for success in first grade mathematics"

(p. 102). This knowledge deficiency can be remedied through careful, focused instruction activities. Number-line training is an important example of how educational psychology can contribute to education and psychology. It is another little gem in the crown of educational psychology.

Psychology of history learning. As a final example, let's consider the knowledge that is needed for upper-elementary school students to understand their history textbooks. Research on reading comprehension has demonstrated that people understand a passage by relating the presented material to their relevant prior knowledge. If a student lacks relevant prior knowledge, the student will have difficulty in understanding a textbook passage.

For example, Beck, McKeown, Sinatra, and Loxterman (1991) asked fourth and fifth graders to read a U.S. history passage about the French and Indian War that began with the following sentence: "In 1763, Britain and the colonies ended a 7-year war with the French and Indians." Based on interviews with students, McKeown and Beck (1990) determined that most students lacked useful background knowledge such as the idea that Britain and France both wanted the same piece of land in North America, that the conflict over this land resulted in a 7-year war called the French and Indian War, and that the colonies belonged to Britain and so they sided with Britain, whereas the Indians sided with France.

Beck et al. (1991) rewrote the passage so that it would help students use appropriate prior knowledge, including their knowledge that two people wanting the same object can lead to conflict. For example, the first sentence was expanded to include the following:

> About 250 years ago, Britain and France both claimed to own some of the same land here in North America…. In 1756, Britain and France went to war to see who would get control of the land. Because the 13 American colonies belonged to Britain, the colonists fought on the same side as Britain. Many Indians fought on the same side as France. (p. 257)

In this way, Beck et al. (1991) helped students prime their "conflict schema"—their prior knowledge that conflicts occur when two people both want to possess the same object. Activating this schema is intended to help students organize the material in a meaningful way.

Does schema activation help students learn? Students who read a revised version of the textbook passage scored more than 50% higher on an essay test than did students who read the original version of the passage (Beck et al., 1991). These results show that a prerequisite to meaningful learning of history is that students possess and activate appropriate prior knowledge. This line of research on schema activation is another example of the contribution of educational psychology to education and psychology. It is yet another little gem of educational psychology research.

Teaching of Cognitive Strategies

Another important development in educational psychology is the teaching of cognitive strategies (Pressley & Woloshyn, 1995; Weinstein & Mayer, 1986). Cognitive strategies are cognitive processes that the learner intentionally performs to influence learning and cognition. Examples include basic processes such as using a rehearsal strategy to memorize a list and metacognitive strategies such as recognizing whether one comprehends a passage.

In this section, I briefly summarize research on teaching of strategies for learning lists, strategies for comprehension of test, and strategies for solving problems.

List learning strategies. Belmont and Butterfield (1971) found that special-education students performed more poorly on learning a list of six letters than did regular-education students. In addition, the special-education students generally did not spontaneously engage in any rehearsal strategies (such as repeating the list aloud), whereas the regular-education students often did rehearse. However, when special education students were explicitly taught to rehearse, by stating the list aloud, their performance on remembering lists increased to the level of the regular-education students.

Reading comprehension strategies. Brown and Palinscar (1989; Palinscar & Brown, 1984) showed that it is possible to teach seventh graders how to use reading comprehension strategies such as questioning, in which the student creates an appropriate question for a passage; clarifying, in which a student detects and corrects any potential comprehension difficulties such as definitions of unfamiliar words; summarizing, in which a student produces a concise summary for a passage; and predicting, in which a student suggests what will come next in subsequent text. In some studies, students who were given focused and sustained training in these strategies showed substantial gains in their reading comprehension performance, whereas comparison students who received conventional instruction did not.

Problem-solving strategies. Covington, Crutchfield, Davies, and Olton (1974) developed a program intended to teach elementary school students how to generate and test hypotheses within the context of detective stories. Students who received training over an extended period of time were better able to solve detective-like problems than were equivalent students who had not received training (Mansfield, Busse, & Krepelka, 1978; Olton & Crutchfield, 1969).

In each case, students learned specific learning strategies that improved their performance on new tasks. Research on teaching of cognitive strategies represent a landmark contribution of educational psychology. For example, Pressley and Woloshyn (1995) argued that "cognitive strategies… represent the most important instructional advance of the past 15 years" (p. iii). Armed with a solid research base, it is now possible to improve how students learn and think, by helping them develop and use appropriate cognitive strategies.

The work I highlighted represents only a few examples of educational psychology's contributions to education and psychology. Furthermore, psychologies of subject matter and teaching of cognitive strategies represent just two fruitful areas of contribution. Other important areas of contribution include the development of new conceptions of intellectual ability, new ways of assessing learning outcomes, and new ways of designing computer-based (or Web-based) instruction. Research on cognitive strategies contributes to cognitive theories of learning by pinpointing the knowledge that learners build, and contributes to educational practice by specifying the knowledge that students need for various tasks.

Development of an Educationally Relevant Science

Perhaps the most enduring outcome of the meeting of cognition and instruction is the development of educationally relevant theories of learning and cognition (Bransford, Brown, & Cocking, 1999; Bruer, 1993; Lambert & McCombs, 1998; Mayer, 1999). The development of an educationally relevant science fulfills the century-old dream of the world's first educational psychologist, E. L. Thorndike, in which teachers "direct their choices of methods by the results of scientific investigation rather than general opinion" (Thorndike, 1906, p. 257). After 100 years of progress, educational psychology faces the new century with research methods and theories that have the potential for improving both educational practice and psychological theory (Mayer, in press).

Our challenge is to get psychologists and educators to work together to solve the dilemmas of education. A potentially useful solution is to encourage teachers to skillfully teach learners cognitive strategies in specific subject areas and to encourage psychologists to skillfully study educationally relevant problems.

In short, psychology and education are good for one another. When it comes to the role of psychology in education, my argument is that there is nothing as beneficial to practice as a good theory. When it comes to the role of education in psychology, my argument is that there is nothing as beneficial to theory as a good practical problem. Although much has been accomplished, the promise of educational psychology remains great in the new century.

REFERENCES

Beck, I. L, McKeown, M. G., Sinatra, G. M., & Loxterman, J. A. (1991). Revising social studies text from a text-processing perspective: Evidence for improved comprehensibility. *Reading Research Quarterly, 26,* 251–276.

Belmont, J. M., & Butterfield, E. C. (1971) Learning strategies as determinants of memory deficiencies. *Cognitive Psychology, 2,* 411–420.

Bradley, L., & Bryant, P. (1978). Difficulties in auditory organization as a possible cause of reading backwardness. *Nature, 271,* 746–747.

Bradley, L., & Bryant, P. (1983). Categorizing sounds and learning to read: A causal connection. *Nature, 301,* 419–421.

Bradley, L., & Bryant, P. (1985). *Rhyme and reason in reading and spelling.* Ann Arbor: University of Michigan Press.

Bradley, L., & Bryant, P. (1991). Phonological skills before and after learning to read. In S. A. Brady & D. P. Shankweiler (Eds.), *Phonological processes in literacy* (pp. 37–45). Hillsdale, NJ: Lawrence Erlbaum Associates, Inc.

Bransford, J. D., Brown, A. L., & Cocking, R. R. (Eds.). (1999). *How people learn.* Washington, DC: National Academy Press.

Brown, A. L., & Palinscar, A. S. (1989). Guided, cooperative learning and individual knowledge acquisition. In L. B. Resnick (Ed.), *Knowing, learning, and instruction* (pp. 393–451). Hillsdale, NJ: Lawrence Erlbaum Associates, Inc.

Bruer, J. T. (1993). *Schools for thought.* Cambridge, MA: MIT Press.

Case, R., & Okamoto, Y. (1996). The role of central conceptual structures in the development of children's thought. *Monographs of the Society for Research in Child Development, 61,* 246.

Chi, M. T. H., Bassok, M., Lewis, M. W., Reimann, P., & Glaser, R. (1989). Self-explanations: How students study and use examples in learning to solve problems. *Cognitive Science, 13,* 66–71.

Covington, M. V., Crutchfield, R. S., Davies, L. B., & Olton, R. M. (1974). *The productive thinking program.* Columbus, OH: Merrill.

Goswami, U., & Bryant, P. (1992). Rhyme, analogy, and children's reading. In P. B. Gough, L. C. Ehri, & R. Treiman (Eds.), *Reading acquisition* (pp. 49–63). Hillsdale, NJ: Lawrence Erlbaum Associates, Inc.

Griffin, S., & Case, R. (1996). Evaluating the breadth and depth of training effects when central conceptual structures are taught. *Monographs of the Society for Research in Child Development, 61,* 83–102.

Griffin, S. A., Case, R., & Capodilupo, S. (1995). Teaching for understanding: The importance of central conceptual structures in the elementary school mathematics curriculum. In A. McKeough, J. Lupart, & A. Marini (Eds.), *Teaching for transfer: Fostering generalization in learning* (pp. 123–151). Hillsdale, NJ: Lawrence Erlbaum Associates, Inc.

Griffin, S. A., Case, R., & Siegler, R. S. (1994). Rightstart: Providing the central conceptual prerequisites for first formal learning of arithmetic to students at risk for school failure. In K. McGilly (Ed.), *Classroom lessons: Integrating cognitive theory and classroom practice* (pp. 25–49). Cambridge, MA: MIT Press.

Juel, C., Griffith, P. L., & Gough, P. B. (1986). Acquisition of literacy: A longitudinal study of children in first and second grade. *Journal of Educational Psychology, 78,* 243–255.

Lambert, N. M., & McCombs, B. L. (1998). *How students learn.* Washington, DC: American Psychological Association.

Levin, J. R., & O'Donnell, A. (1999). What to do about educational research's credibility gaps? *Issues in Education, 5,* 177–229.

Mansfield, R. S., Busse, T. V., & Krepelka, E. J. (1978). The effectiveness of creativity training. *Review of Educational Research, 48,* 517–536.

Mayer, R. E. (1992). Cognition and instruction: On their historic meeting within educational psychology. *Journal of Educational Psychology, 84,* 405–412.

Mayer, R. E. (1993). Outmoded conceptions of educational research. *Educational Researcher, 22*(9), 6.

Mayer, R. E. (1996). Learners as information processors: Legacies and limitations of educational psychology's second metaphor. *Educational Psychologist, 31,* 151–161.

Mayer, R. E. (199). *The promise of educational psychology.* Upper Saddle River, NJ: Prentice Hall.

Mayer, R. E. (2001). Changing conceptions of learning: A century of progress in the scientific study of education. In L. Corno (Ed.), *Yearbook of the National Society for the Study of Education* (pp. 34–75). Chicago: University of Chicago Press.

Mayer, R. E. (in press). E. L. Thorndike's enduring contributions to educational psychology. In B. J. Zimmerman and D. H. Schunk (Eds.), *Educational psychology: A century of contributions.* Mahwah, NJ: Lawrence Erlbaum Associates, Inc.

McKeown, M. G., & Beck, I. L. (1990). The assessment and characterization of young learners' knowledge of a topic in history. *American Educational Research Journal, 27,* 688–726.

Neisser, U. (1976). *Cognition and reality.* San Francisco: Freeman.

Olton, R. M., & Crutchfield, R. S. (1969). Developing the skills of productive thinking. In P. Mussen, J. Langer, & M. V. Covington (Eds.), *Trends and issues in developmental psychology* (pp. 68–91). New York: Holt, Rinehart & Winston.

Palinscar, A. S., & Brown, A. L. (1984). Reciprocal teaching of comprehension-fostering and monitoring strategies. *Cognition and Instruction, 1,* 117–175.

Pressley, M., & Woloshyn, V. (1995). *Cognitive strategy instruction that really improves children's academic performance* (2nd ed.). Cambridge, MA: Brookline.

Shulman, L. S., & Quinlan, S. S. (1996). The comparative psychology of school subjects. In D. C. Berliner & R. C. Calfee (Eds.), *Handbook of educational psychology* (pp. 399–422). New York: Macmillan.

Stanovich, K. E. (1991). Discrepancy definitions of reading disability: Has intelligence led us astray? *Reading Research Quarterly, 26,* 7–26.

Thorndike, E. L. (1906). *The principles of teaching based on psychology.* Syracuse, NY: Mason-Henry Press.

Wagner, R. K., & Torgesen, J. K. (1987). The nature of phonological processing and its causal role in the acquisition of reading skills. *Psychological Bulletin, 101,* 192–212.

Weinstein, C. E., & Mayer, R. E. (1986). The teaching of learning strategies. In M. C. Wittrock (Ed.), *Handbook of research on teaching* (3rd ed., pp. 315–327). New York: Macmillan.

Good Teachers, Plural

What makes a teacher good? Looking at the ways we have answered that question in the past century may place the current evaluation craze in perspective.

Donald R. Cruickshank and Donald Haefele

There are as many kinds of good teachers in our schools as there are varieties of good apples in supermarkets. Unfortunately, we tend to recognize and honor only one kind of teacher at a time. We currently glorify teachers whose students pass standardized tests (Bradley, 2000). In the 1990s, we admired those who had proven they could bring about greater student achievement. In the 1980s, good teachers were those who followed Madeline Hunter's prescriptions for teaching success (Garman & Hazi, 1998). And the list goes on.

For the first half of the 20th century, school principals, supervisors, and education professors determined the attributes of good teachers.

Let us identify some of these visions of good teachers. Only then can we begin to explore how we can value them all and how school districts can support the development of many kinds of teachers and create ways to evaluate them.

Visions of Good Teachers

Ideal teachers. For the first half of the 20th century, school principals, supervisors, and educational professors determined the attributes of good teachers. Schools, school districts, and colleges cranked out checklists and rating scales that scored such traits as professional attitude, understanding of students, creativity, control of class, planning, individualization, and pupil participation. During this period, scholar Dwight Beecher (1953) developed the popular Teaching Evaluation Record, and Arvil Barr and his associates (1961) drew up a comprehensive list of ideal attributes that included buoyancy, emotional stability, ethical behavior, expressiveness, forcefulness, and personal magnetism.

Thus, an ideal teacher met subjective standards of excellence determined by selected, significant others. Because the standards were subjective, many disagreements developed over what the standards meant and which teachers met them (Mitzel, 1960; Morsh & Wilder, 1954).

Analytic teachers. By the early 1960s, administrators encountered problems associated with measuring the attributes of ideal teachers (Cruickshank, 1990). In a search for some other way to judge teacher quality, experts soon began describing good teachers as analytic.

Analytic teachers methodically inspected what they did in the classroom. They recorded and examined their classroom practice using a variety of observation techniques (Simon & Boyer, 1968). Many teachers and observers used the Flanders System of Interactional Analysis (Flanders, 1960) to make a detailed record of the teacher-student interactions occurring during a lesson: how much and about what the teacher talked, how much and about what students talked, and the extent and nature of student silence or confusion. Teachers modified their practice on the basis of these analyses. Becoming an analytic teacher required being investigative and self-correctional. Over time, the work involved in being analytical seemed to overwhelm even proponents of this vision of good teachers.

Effective teachers. In 1966, the influential Coleman Report asserted that students' socioeconomic backgrounds influenced their learning more than their teachers did (U.S. Department of Health, Education, and Welfare). Immediately, dozens of educational researchers set out to show that teachers made a crucial difference in student achievement. First, researchers identified teachers whose students scored higher on tests than did comparable students taught by others. Next, they examined these overachieving teachers, referred to as *outliers* or *effective teachers*, to determine exactly what they were like and what they did so that other teachers might benefit from such knowledge.

The findings of many studies (Rosenshine, 1971; Rosenshine & Furst, 1971) consistently found that effective teachers carefully monitor learning activities and are clear, accepting and supportive, equitable with students, and persistent in challenging and engaging them. Nonetheless, researchers disagreed about the methods used in the studies and about whether student gain is the most important outcome of teaching (Cruickshank, 1990).

Paralleling the development of the concept of the effective teacher has been a significant increase in the amount of student-achievement testing. As a result, we have become more focused on the product—better student scores on standardized tests—and on rewarding teachers who succeed in teaching to the test. In many states, teachers and principals are deemed effective and are rewarded monetarily when students demonstrate satisfactory gains on standardized tests. Opposition to this narrow definition of teacher effectiveness is mounting (Hoff, 1999; Kohn, 1999).

Dutiful teachers. Those less than satisfied with the attributes originally assigned to effective teachers argued that teachers who do not display the typical attributes of effective teachers, such as enthusiasm, may yet bring about student learning. They asserted that studying the attributes of effective teachers can be useful, especially for guiding preservice and inservice development, but these attributes should not be used as standards for judging teacher quality. Rather, we should evaluate teachers according to how well they understand and perform their duties: knowledge of the subject matter, school, and community; demonstrated classroom skills, including testing and grading; personal characteristics that encourage learning; and service to the profession (Scriven, 1990).

Competent teachers. The U.S. accountability movement in the 1970s spurred an effort in education to identify competencies that teachers should possess. Specifically, the public wanted to know what teachers needed to know and be able to do.

To identify teacher competencies, scholars studied the early research on teacher effectiveness, analyzed what teachers do, and obtained the opinions of expert teacher practitioners and other educators. The most thorough compilation (Dodl et al., 1972) organized competencies in the areas of planning instruction, implementing instruction, assessing and evaluating students, communicating, and performing administrative duties.

The public also wanted to make certain that teachers used their knowledge and performed well in the classroom. Consequently, the teacher-testing movement was born, soon to be given a boost by the 1983 publication of *A Nation At Risk* (National Commission on Excellence in Education). Thereafter, teachers or teachers-to-be had to pass tests developed by state education departments or by such national organizations as the Educational Testing Service and the National Board for Professional Teaching Standards.

The Educational Testing Service developed the Praxis teacher competency series of tests for use in teacher preparation programs and entry into the teaching profession. Praxis assesses three areas: reading, writing, and math skills near the beginning of a preservice teaching program; professional academic and pedagogical knowledge near the end of a teaching program; and on-the-job classroom performance. Thirty-eight states currently require some Praxis testing.

The National Board for Professional Teaching Standards provides national certification for experienced teachers who meet competencies set forth by discerning teachers (King, 1994). Teachers seeking National Board certification submit portfolios that include lesson plans, videotapes of lessons taught, and samples of student work. They also come to regional sites for further inspection and testing. States now offer incentives for teachers to obtain Board certification. For example, in Massachusetts, the Veteran Teachers Board offers up to $50,000 over 10 years to any public school teacher who receives National Board certification (Bradley, 1998).

Even the National Council for Accreditation of Teacher Education is moving toward assessing the competence—the knowledge and skills—of preservice teachers and away from merely reviewing their programs of study (Bradley, 1999).

Expert teachers. In the 1980s and into the 1990s, many scholars decided that what makes a teacher good is expertise. Expert teachers are different from nonexperts in three ways: they have extensive and accessible knowledge that is organized for use in teaching; they are efficient and can do more in less time; and they are able to arrive at novel and appropriate solutions to problems (Sternberg & Horvath, 1995). Thus, expertise is more than experience. Teachers could be experienced and have less expertise than some novices.

Reflective teachers. The definition of the reflective teacher was developed at Ohio State University in the late 1970s. Reflective teachers are students of teaching, with a strong, sustained interest in learning about the art and science of teaching and about themselves as teachers (Cruickshank, 1987, 1991). Reflective teachers are introspective, examining their own practice of teaching and seeking a greater understanding of teaching by reading scholarly and professional journals and books, including teachers' autobiographies. Because they want to be thoughtful practitioners, they constantly monitor their teaching—for example, by using videotape or audiotape.

Satisfying teachers. Satisfying teachers please students, parents or caregivers, teaching colleagues, administrators, and supervisors by responding to their needs. In Rochester, New York, for example, parents rate their children's teachers on the basis of 20 questions that inquire about such qualities as the teacher's accessibility, clarity, responsiveness, and optimism (Janey, 1997).

School or parent organizations recognize satisfying teachers by presenting them with awards for good teaching. More often, however, admiration shows up in daily responses to the teacher: students advise one another to take this teacher's courses, fellow teachers look to this teacher for guidance and inspiration, most parents want their children in this teacher's class, and administrators trust this teacher to respond positively to difficult students.

Of course, knowing and meeting the expectations of others is a daunting task, and considerable disagreement can develop about what expectations are appropriate. We can all think of instructors who did or did not satisfy us or others but who were nonetheless effective teachers.

Diversity-responsive teachers. Diversity-responsive teachers take special interest in and are particularly sensitive to students who are different culturally, socially, economically, intellectually, physically, or emotionally. For example, Jacqueline Irvine and James Fraser (1998) believe that African American students are best served by "warm demanders" (p. 56). Warm demanders use a culturally specific pedagogical style that is substantively different from the approaches described in effective teaching research. Such teachers perceive themselves as parental surrogates and advocates, employ a teaching style filled with rhythmic language and rapid intonation, link students' everyday cultural experiences to new concepts, develop personal relationships with the learners, and teach with authority.

Diversity-responsive teachers are also dedicated to bettering the lives of students both inside and outside the classroom. Often working with children who have special needs, this kind of teacher demonstrates great tenderness, patience, and tact. A well-known exemplar is Annie Sullivan, Helen Keller's teacher (Peterson, 1946).

Respected teachers. Respected teachers, real and fictional, sometimes are idolized in books and films. Some of the real ones include LouAnne Johnson in *Dangerous Minds*, Jaime Escalante in *Stand and Deliver*, and Marva Collins in *The Marva Collins Story*. Fictional, virtuous teachers have been crafted in *Mr. Holland's Opus; The Prime of Miss Jean Brodie; Up the Down Staircase; To Sir, with Love;* and *Goodbye, Mr. Chips*.

Historian Richard Traina (1999) explored the autobiographies of some 125 prominent Americans to determine what qualities in teachers they valued. He notes that three attributes stand out: subject-matter competence, caring about students and their success, and distinctive character. Respected teachers possess and demonstrate virtuous qualities, including honesty, decency, fairness, devotion, empathy, and selflessness. Most such teachers also have determination, overcoming great odds to ensure student success.

Moving Forward

None of these categories is mutually exclusive. And no variation, by itself, has proven or is proving to be just right: None satisfies all education stakeholders. In a utopian world, teachers would demonstrate all aspects of teacher "goodness" and possess the attributes of all 10 visions. In the real world, we must learn how to recognize and appreciate the many models that teachers can follow to be good teachers.

Further, we need to answer some questions. Have we identified all of the possible exemplars of good teaching?

Variations of a Good Teacher

IDEAL teachers meet standards set by school principals, supervisors, and education professors.

ANALYTIC teachers use observation techniques to record how well they are meeting their instructional intentions.

EFFECTIVE teachers bring about higher student achievement.

DUTIFUL teachers perform assigned teaching duties well.

COMPETENT teachers pass tests that indicate they possess requisite teacher attributes.

EXPERT teachers have extensive and accessible knowledge and can do more in less time.

REFLECTIVE teachers examine the art and science of teaching to become more thoughtful practitioners.

SATISFYING teachers please students, parents or caregivers, colleagues, supervisors, and administrators.

DIVERSITY-RESPONSIVE teachers are sensitive to all students.

RESPECTED teachers possess and demonstrate qualities regarded as virtues.

To what extent do the exemplars overlap? Are some models more valuable than others? Who decides which exemplar is more valuable? Should all teachers be good teachers according to at least one of the 10 or so models? What should be the standard for good teachers within each vision of a good teacher? How can we prepare teachers and help them become good by some criteria? How can teachers document what kind of good teachers they are? How can we reward good teachers?

Tests for teachers were a direct result of the push to describe the competent teacher and to determine to what extent teachers measure up.

In addition, we need to conduct research. To what extent do various education stakeholders agree on what makes teachers good? How do perceptions of good teachers differ by age, gender, socioeconomic background, educational level, geographic area, and political persuasion? Which exemplars of good teachers are related to which educational outcomes? To what extent can good teachers be readily distinguished from bad teachers?

Evaluating Different Kinds of Teachers

School districts that appreciate multiple kinds of good teachers need to create teacher evaluation systems corresponding to the full range of teaching exemplars. To meet legal requirements, an evaluation system must be both formal (guided by public, written policies and procedures) and standardized (applied evenly and fairly). For example, all teachers must meet the criteria of one of the exemplars. Evaluations of *effective teachers* should require that teachers demonstrate such attributes as clarity and enthusiasm—qualities associated with student achievement. *Dutiful teachers* should be judged on such criteria as knowledge of subject matter and classroom skills.

Clearly, to judge each vision of a good teacher, we must use valid criteria that are related to the particular exemplar that the teacher strives to emulate. A good teacher evaluation system should also have predictive validity and make the desired impact on students; an evaluation of a *satisfying teacher*, for example, should include surveys of students and parents. Of course, any teacher evaluation system should require that evaluators—administrators, supervisors, teaching peers, or others—receive training so that each evaluation is objective and would result in approximately the same outcome if done by another evaluator.

Accepting Many Exemplars

Substantiating that there are all kinds of good teachers serves several useful ends. First, it dispels the traditional notion that there is only one kind of good teacher. Second, it permits teachers to describe which kind of good teacher they are and, when necessary, submit evidence to that effect. Third, it provides positive direction for teachers and persons responsible for teachers' continuing development. Finally, such knowledge enables the teaching profession to identity and remove teachers who are unable to meet any definition of what makes teachers good.

Meanwhile, Wyoming Governor Jim Geringer, chairman of the Education Commission of the States, whose membership consists of governors and top state education officials, reports that he hopes to work with the states to define what it means to be a good teacher (Sandham, 1999). Is the time right for educators, educational researchers, and elected officials to join hands in broadening the scope of this ambitious and important task?

References

Barr, A., Worcester, D., Abell, A., Beecher, C., Jenson, L., Peronto, A., Ringness, T., & Schmidt, J. (1961). Wisconsin studies of the measurement and predictability of teacher effectiveness. *Journal of Experimental Education, 30*, 1–156.

Beecher, D. (1953). *The teaching evaluation record.* Buffalo, NY: Educators Publishing Company.

Bradley, A. (1998, February 25). A better way to pay. *Education Week, 17*(24), 29–31.

Bradley, A. (1999, January 13). NCATE unveils a plan for aspiring elementary teachers. *Education Week, 18*(18), 5.

Bradley, A. (2000, March 22). L.A. proposes linking teacher pay to tests. *Education Week, 19*(28), 3.

Cruickshank, D. (1987). *Reflective teaching: The preparation of students of teaching.* Reston, VA: Association of Teacher Educators.

Cruickshank, D. (1990). *Research that informs teachers and teacher educators.* Bloomington, IN: Phi Delta Kappa Educational Foundation.

Cruickshank, D. (1991). *Reflective teaching.* Bloomington, IN: Phi Delta Kappa Educational Foundation.

Dodl, N., Elfner, E., Becker, J., Halstead, J., Jung, H., Nelson, P., Puriton, S., & Wegele, P. (1972). *Florida catalog of teacher competencies.* Tallahassee: Florida State University.

Flanders, N. (1960). *Teacher influence, pupil attitudes, and achievement: Final report.* Minneapolis: University of Minnesota.

Garman, N., & Hazi, H. (1998, May). Teachers ask: Is there life after Madeline Hunter? *Phi Delta Kappan, 69*(9), 669–672.

Hoff, D. (1999, September 22). Standards at crossroads after debate. *Education Week, 19*(3), 1, 9.

Irvine, J., & Fraser, J. (1998, May 13). Warm demanders. *Education Week, 17*(35), 56, 42.

Janey, C. (1997, October 1). Seeking customer satisfaction. *Education Week, 17*(5), 39.

King, M. (1994). Locking themselves in: National standards for the teaching profession. *Teaching and Teacher Education, 10*(1), 95–108.

Kohn, A. (1999, September 15). Confusing harder with better. *Education Week, 19*(2), 68, 52.

Mitzel, H. (1960). Teacher effectiveness. In C. Harris (Ed.), *Encyclopedia of educational research* (3rd ed.) (p. 1481). New York: MacMillan.

Morsh, J., & Wilder, E. (1954). *Identifying the effective instructor: A review of quantitative studies.* Lackland Air Force Base, TX: Air Force Personnel and Training Center.

National Commission on Excellence in Education. (1983). *A nation at risk.* Washington, DC: U.S. Department of Education.

Peterson, H. (1946). *Great teachers.* New York: Random House.

Rosenshine, B. (1971). *Teaching behaviors and student achievement.* London: National Foundation for Educational Research.

Rosenshine, B., & Furst, N. (1971). Research on teacher performance criteria. In B. O. Smith (Ed.), *Research in Teacher Education* (pp. 37–72). Englewood Cliffs, NJ: Prentice-Hall.

Sandham, J. (1999, August 4). ECS members take closer look at the teaching profession. *Education Week, 18* (43), 23.

Scriven, M. (1990, September). Can research-based teacher evaluation be saved? *Journal of Personnel Evaluation in Education, 4*(1), 19–32.

Simon, A., & Boyer, E. (1968). *Mirrors for behavior: An anthology of classroom observation instruments.* Philadelphia: Research for Better Schools.

Sternberg, R., & Horvath, J. (1995, August/September). A prototype view of expert teaching. *Educational Researcher, 24*(6), 9–17.

Traina, R. (1999, January 20). What makes a teacher good? *Education Week, 18*(19), 34.

U.S. Department of Health, Education, and Welfare. (1966). *Equality of educational opportunity: Summary report* (The Coleman report). Washington, DC: U.S. Government Printing Office.

Donald R. Cruickshank (cruickshank1@osu.edu) is Professor Emeritus and **Donald Haefele** (haefele@osu.edu) is Associate Professor of Education at Ohio State University, 2817 Wickliffe Rd., Columbus, OH 43221.

What I Hope for in My Children's Teachers

A Parent's Perspective

DAVID BOERS

Teaching today may be more difficult than it has ever been. Children still go through the critical stages that children have always gone through to attempt to establish who they are and to grow into what they can become (Santrock 1987). The difference these days is that children go through these stages at faster paces and with different types of adult guidance (Elkind 1994). Whether it is because of the media, the lack of parent involvement, the dearth of traditional families, or simply an adult-centered society, teachers often end up with classes filled with too many students with too many problems. Students seem to have difficulty in personal and logical progression through normal child developmental stages, such as the realization of self-worth, productivity, and the establishment of identity. Teachers end up trying to deal with this difficult situation. In this article I will share what, in spite of all of the above, many parents still hope for in their children's teachers.

Let us begin with the premise that parents and guardians do care deeply about their children's success in school. The myth of a lack of caring parents in America today often overshadows, perhaps obliterates, the fact that in all communities many, if not most, parents want to work with teachers for the benefit of their children (Willis 1993). And these parents genuinely want to go beyond fundraising and cheerleading to serious relationships with teachers about their children. They do not all have the "My kid's gotta go to Harvard" mentality; they just care about their children having a good experience in school.

As a parent of school-aged children, I have attempted to be supportive of my children's school experience. In doing this, I have attempted to be supportive of teachers, administrators, school programs, district initiatives, and education in general. To this end, I have regularly communicated with teachers, administrators, program coordinators, school board members, and other parents regarding educational progress in our community and for my children. After ten years, dozens of teachers and administrators, and a number of curricular and cocurricular programs, I have experienced both the extreme joy of a genuine sense of partnership and an empty sense of detachment. I have come to care deeply about strengthening the connection between teacher and parents in a way that achieves the mutual goal of providing children with the greatest chance for school and life success. For I have learned that the key to my children's success in school is the competence and professionalism of classroom teachers and the communication that develops between my children's teachers and me. In an effort to define this issue more clearly, I offer the descriptions below to form a portrait of what I hope for in my children's teachers.

Enthusiastic, Energetic, Happy, Positive

Nothing works better to get students excited about school than a teacher who loves teaching and learning. I want my children's teachers to be enthusiastic about school, about learning, and about what goes on in class so they can carry on the joy of learning we have already started and continue at home. And I want the enthusiasm to be overt and obvious, genuine, not feigned.

It takes energy to be enthusiastic. It takes energy to teach. Teaching is an active profession, and I hope my children's teachers are healthy enough both physically and mentally to have the energy for planned and spontaneous enthusiastic activity, because this energy is conveyed to the students.

In school, if the teachers are happy, my children will be happy (Boers 1995). Conversely, if the teachers are not happy, negative things can happen. The mission of all teachers should center on fostering happy, well-adjusted children who will grow up to be happy, well-adjusted adults. If my children's teachers are not happy at school,

I worry about their working with my children. If my children's teachers are happy at school, I see unlimited potential for all kinds of spontaneous learning.

Enthusiasm, energy, and happiness contribute to creating a positive environment, one in which children's basic needs—physiological needs, safety and security, love and belonging, self-esteem, and self-actualization (Santrock 1987)—are met, as are additional needs for power, freedom, and fun (Glasser 1990). A positive environment leads to greater curiosity, greater production, and higher levels of thinking. When students are empowered as valued decision makers in the classroom, the classroom is much more conducive to achievement and retention because it is a positive place to be (Glasser 1993). For those reasons, I hope my children's teachers are positive leaders.

Competent, Research-Based, Well-Read, Confident

I hope my children's teachers have a high degree of competency in the knowledge of human growth, development, and learning. I hope that they can appropriately apply methods and strategies for dealing with children in all ways, not just academically. For example, teachers know full well that children grow, develop, and learn in different ways and through individual processes. Teachers must then have the competence to perceive student levels and provide direction and instruction beginning at those levels. If my children are developmentally more immature than the others in the class, then the teacher's behavioral directions and instructional techniques need to be different for them. In this case, perhaps my children would need more specific directions and more direct instruction.

I hope my children's teachers teach from a reputable base of qualified research—that at any time, they can cite notable researchers and theorists to justify what they are saying or doing. For example, if methods such as assertive discipline (Canter 1986) or control theory (Glasser 1986) were used, I would be interested in knowing that teachers understand the research that supports those methods and are able to explain the psychology of the process that leads to the expected results. Academically, if teachers use theories of multiple intelligences (Gardner 1983), they ought to know and understand and be able to explain the human growth, development, and learning principles that are inherent in the strategies. In other words, I would prefer that teachers know what they are doing and understand why they are doing it.

Teaching is a profession, and I hope that my children's teachers read professional journals and books so that they can understand, use, and talk about current knowledge and practice. Understanding current knowledge about the brain (Jensen 1998) or quality school teaching (Glasser 1993) is vital to the effective delivery of instruction. Children, schools, and teaching are very widely studied and written about, with the hope that what occurs at school makes sense for student progress. There are no professions left that can "do it the way we've always done it." Therefore, it is important that teachers regularly read, understand, and apply ideas that work, as reported in contemporary professional writings.

I hope that my children's teachers are confident enough to listen and respond professionally to my questions and challenges, not in grudge-match fashion, but as a matter of two-way intellectualizing for the benefit of students. If my children's teachers can confidently (not brashly) carry on a two-way conversation, they will model the same in the classroom. Confidence leads to open-mindedness and a willingness to learn and share knowledge and will serve as a good model for my children's learning.

Personable, Communicative, Respectful, Welcoming

I hope my children's teachers get to know who we are as a family. They should understand our family's lifestyle and goals. For example, I'd like teachers to know that we take learning and school seriously, expect to do difficult work, and want to be challenged constantly. I will willingly share our family's joys, happiness, and sorrows with my children's teachers if given the chance. From this, I hope that my children's teachers know how my children think and act and live their lives, so they can avoid jumping to conclusions and help find possibilities and connections for my children. Teachers teach my children best when they personally know my children.

I hope my children's teachers communicate with me eagerly, early, and regularly via notes, telephone calls, e-mail. I want to know how my children are doing and how things are going. I'd like to hear teachers' opinions, comments, and advice regarding my children's growth and progress. When teachers know and care about my children and me personally, they should be eager to share whatever they know about us. Teachers have the advantage of being in school, a place where my children spend a tremendous amount of time, so they know what is going on in that part of my children's life. Teachers' communicating what they observe is an important learning tool for parents.

I hope my children's teachers are respectful of me as a parent partner. If my ideas and values are different from the teachers', they can still be heard, pondered, considered, and perhaps implemented.

In the best-case scenario my children's teachers would know me well enough to seek me out and use me as a resource. I will hang bulletin boards and supervise game day activities but would also ask that teachers use me as a guest teacher in areas of curriculum in which I have appropriate knowledge. When I take the initiative to make myself available, I would hope the teachers would follow up on the offer and even consider creating situations where I might be involved.

Student-Centered, Differentiating, Homework-Efficient, Work-Responsive

I hope my children's classrooms are student-centered, as opposed to teacher-centered or even subject-centered. My children are more important to me than social studies, foreign language, or any academic area. But I also know that when a teacher focuses on the student as a learner (rather than on the teacher as teacher), more achievement and more retention in academic endeavors occur. This is a result of increased ownership of academic material on the part of students. Student-centered classrooms have the additional advantage of increasing the opportunities for developing caring, compassionate students who see every person as a valuable individual (Kohn 1996, 101–19). I want my children and all the children they are with to be caring, compassionate people.

When my children's teachers use a multiple-modality approach that allows for different approaches to instruction (Holloway 2000), it gives my children options of different ways to achieve the class goals. If my children can convey key concepts graphically rather than in writing, they should have that opportunity. One-dimensional teaching will not accommodate my children's learning styles. This includes differentiation through assessments that are meaningful and authentic.

I hope teachers will call on my children and expect them to perform every day as a natural part of being in school. If homework is assigned, I hope that it is worth doing, clearly explained, and connected to the curriculum. Otherwise, homework can become drudgery that makes school unpleasant and unappealing (Gratz 2000). My children's teachers can encourage, via meaningful homework, my children's love for school.

Effective time management is critical for teachers. It permits them to return work in a timely fashion with specific, meaningful teacher comments. I know that my children have the teacher in mind when they do the work. They want and need to know soon whether they have met the requirements, exceeded the requirements, or have work left to do. If in fact teachers are abiding by an integrated, connected curriculum, my children need to know in a timely fashion how they are doing to better connect it to where they have been and where they are going.

Well-Planned, Conferencing-Complete, Honest, Holistic

My children's teachers need to know where they are going and how that fits into everything else taught and learned in previous years, as well as all that will follow in ensuing years. If that is too much to ask, then teachers should at least have a clear set of goals and strategies for the entire school year and for each day of that year. This does not prevent spontaneity related to course goals. Further, I hope that my children's teachers have a vision for an integrated set of school learning experiences, if not across the curriculum and cocurriculum every day in school, then at least with each teacher's own course offerings. I hope my children's teachers will not force them to learn in small, isolated, nonintegrated units, one after another, all year long. All students deserve teachers with a vision that school is good, school is meaningful, school is desired, and that every day is connected to the last one.

I hope my children's teachers have a specific, detailed plan for our conferences that goes beyond merely presenting grades. Handing out a computerized list of scores may be a start, but the teacher is so much more involved with my children's lives than to be one-dimensional in conferencing. I want to know about skill levels, academic performance, social skills, and personal happiness. I hope my children's teachers will tell me how they assess my children in those four areas.

I hope my children's teachers are honest about who they are, how they teach, and how they are working with my children. Honest teachers eliminate the see-through camouflage of teachers or systemic games that sometimes block the path to what is best for students. Honest teachers allow for an authentic discussion and a focused collaboration in educational partnerships.

I believe that my children's teachers need to have an understanding of the school experience, both as an experience unto itself and as a part of a bigger whole. Teachers should support special school events such as homecoming, harvest moon celebration, multicultural awareness week, and so on, by being involved themselves and by reducing or eliminating homework so that students are encouraged to become involved. Further, most districts have at least an unwritten agreement to reduce work on a specific evening so that children may attend religious education. It is important that teachers honor such agreements.

These are the hopes that I have for my children's teachers. I know that I am not alone in these hopes. Concerned parents love school. We want to be partners in education, and we very much respect the difficulties of being a teacher. In my experience, model teachers demonstrate the characteristics I have described in their professional approach to their important responsibility. I hope that all teachers reflect on their classrooms, contemplate refining their skills, and ponder their attitudes in making the educational experiences of all of their students the very best possible. Parents want the best for their children and will be there to support thoughtful, caring, and knowledgeable teachers as they work with the sometimes difficult classroom conditions that exist in our schools.

Key words: teachers, parent expectations, characteristics, student-teacher relationships

REFERENCES

Boers, D. 1995. *Happy classrooms: The CARTIE model for behavioral/academic success K–12.* Ripon, WI: WISC

Canter, L. and M. Canter. 1986. *Assertive discipline elementary resource materials workbook, grades K–6.* Santa Monica, CA: Canter and Associates.

Elkind, D. 1994. *Ties that stress: The new family imbalance.* Cambridge: Harvard University Press.

Gardner, H. 1983. *Frames of mind: The theory of multiple intelligences.* New York: Basic Books.

Glasser, W. 1986. *Control theory in the classroom.* New York: Harper and Row.

_____. 1990. *The quality school: Managing students without coercion.* New York: Harper and Row.

_____. 1993. *The quality school teacher.* New York: HarperPerennial.

Gratz, D. B. 2000. High standards for whom? *Phi Delta Kappan* 81 (9): 681–87.

Holloway, J. H. 2000. Preparing teachers for differentiated instruction. *Educational Leadership* 58 (1): 82–84.

Jensen, E. 1998. *Teacher with the brain in mind.* Alexandria, VA: Association for Supervision and Curriculum Development.

Kohn, A. 1996. *Beyond discipline: From compliance to community.* Alexandria, VA: Association for Supervision and Curriculum Development.

Santrock, J. 1987. *Adolescence: An introduction.* Dubuque, IA: Wm. C. Brown.

Willis, S. 1993. Teaching young children: Educators seek developmental appropriateness. *Association for Supervision and Curriculum Update.*

David Boers is a professor of graduate education at Marian College, Fond du Lac, Wisconsin.

From *The Clearing House,* September/October 2001, pp. 51-54. Reprinted with permission of the Helen Dwight Reid Educational Foundation. Published by Heldref Publications, 1319 Eighteenth St., NW, Washington, DC 20036-1802. © 2001.

Helping Children Cope With Loss, Death, and Grief: Response to a National Tragedy

The security and safety that was a hallmark of our American society was shattered by the events of September 11th. Never before in our nation's history have so many lives been lost in a single day. Communities are impacted by multiple losses that stretch their capacities to cope. It is difficult to predict how students, adults and schools will be able to deal with the harsh realities of life in the coming weeks, months and years. Children who have experienced the loss of one or both parents, siblings, other relatives, friends, or neighbors are now suffering from profound grief.How can caring adults help these children deal with loss of this magnitude? How can we begin to understand and respond to the depths of their suffering? One thing we do know is that this will be an extremely difficult and painful task. Children and adolescents will need all the support they can get and they will require a long time to recover. Life may not be the same for anyone in this country, but those youngsters who have sustained personal losses may require significant assistance from trained, caring adults.

Expressions of Grief

Talking to children about death must be geared to their developmental level and their capacity to understand the related facts of the situation. Children will be aware of the reactions of significant adults as they interpret and react to information about death and tragedy. The range of reactions that children display in response to the death of significant others may include:

- *Emotional shock* and at times an apparent lack of feelings, which serve to help the child detach from the pain of the moment;
- *Regressive (immature) behaviors*, such as needing to be rocked or held, difficulty separating from parents or significant others, needing to sleep in parent's bed or an apparent difficulty completing tasks well within the child's ability level;

- *Explosive emotions and acting out behavior* that reflect the child's internal feelings of anger, terror, frustration and helplessness. Acting out may reflect insecurity and a way to seek control over a situation for which they have little or no control;
- **Asking the same questions over and over**, not because they do not understand the facts, but rather because the information is so hard to believe or accept. Repeated questions can help listeners determine if the child is responding to misinformation or the real trauma of the event.

Helping Children Cope

The following tips will help teachers and parents support children who have experienced the loss of parents or loved ones. Some of these recommendations come from Dr. Alan Wolfelt, Director of the Center for Loss and Life Transition in Fort Collins, Colorado.

- *Allow children to be the teachers about their grief experiences*: Give children the opportunity to tell their story and be a good listener.
- *Don't assume that every child in a certain age group understands death in the same way or with the same feelings*: All children are different and their view of the world is unique and shaped by different experiences. (Developmental information is provided below.)
- *Grieving is a process, not an event*: Parents and schools need to allow adequate time for each child to grieve in the manner that works for that child. Pressing children to resume "normal" activities without the chance to deal with their emotional pain may prompt additional problems or negative reactions.
- *Don't lie or tell half-truths to children about the tragic event*: Children are often bright and sensitive. They will see through false infor-

16

mation and wonder why you do not trust them with the truth. Lies do not help the child through the healing process or help develop effective coping strategies for life's future tragedies or losses.

- *Help all children, regardless of age, to understand loss and death*: Give the child information at the level that he/she can understand. Allow the child to guide adults as to the need for more information or clarification of the information presented. Loss and death are both part of the cycle of life that children need to understand.

- *Encourage children to ask questions about loss and death*: Adults need to be less anxious about not knowing all the answers. Treat questions with respect and a willingness to help the child find his or her own answers.

- *Don't assume that children always grieve in an orderly or predictable way*: We all grieve in different ways and there is no one "correct" way for people to move through the grieving process.

- *Let children know that you really want to understand what they are feeling or what they need*: Sometimes children are upset but they cannot tell you what will be helpful. Giving them the time and encouragement to share their feelings with you may enable them to sort out their feelings.

- *Children will need long-lasting support*: The more losses the child or adolescent suffered, the more difficult it will be to recover. This is especially true if they lost a parent who was their major source of support. Try to develop multiple supports for children who suffered significant losses.

- *Keep in mind that grief work is hard*: It is hard work for adults and hard for children as well.

- *Understand that grief work is complicated*: When death results from a terrorist act, this brings forth many issues that are difficult, if not impossible, to comprehend. Grieving will also be complicated by a need for vengeance or justice and by the lack of resolution of the current situation: Perpetrators may still be at large and our nation is at war. The sudden nature of death and the fact that many individuals were considered missing rather than dead further complicates the grieving process.

- *Be aware of your own need to grieve*: Focusing on the children in your care is important, but not at the expense of your emotional needs. Adults who have lost a loved one will be far more able to help children work through their grief if they get help themselves. For some

families, it may be important to seek family grief counseling, as well as individual sources of support.

Developmental Phases in Understanding Death

It is important to recognize that all children are unique in their understanding of death and dying. This understanding depends on their developmental level, cognitive skills, personality characteristics, religious or spiritual beliefs, teachings by parents and significant others, input from the media, and previous experiences with death. Nonetheless, there are some general considerations that will be helpful in understanding how children and adolescents experience and deal with death.

- *Infants and Toddlers*: The youngest children may perceive that adults are sad, but have no real understanding of the meaning or significance of death.

- *Preschoolers*: Young children may deny death as a formal event and may see death as reversible. They may interpret death as a separation, not a permanent condition. Preschool and even early elementary children may link certain events and magical thinking with the causes of death. As a result of the World Trade Center disaster, some children may imagine that going into tall buildings may cause someone's death.

- *Early Elementary School*: Children at this age (approximately 5–9) start to comprehend the finality of death. They begin to understand that certain circumstances may result in death. They can see that, if large planes crash into buildings, people in the planes and buildings will be killed. However, they may over-generalize, particularly at ages 5–6—if jet planes don't fly, then people don't die. At this age, death is perceived as something that happens to others, not to oneself or one's family.

- *Middle School*: Children at this level have the cognitive understanding to comprehend death as a final event that results in the cessation of all bodily functions. They may not fully grasp the abstract concepts discussed by adults or on the TV news but are likely to be guided in their thinking by a concrete understanding of justice. They may experience a variety of feelings and emotions, and their expressions may include acting out or self-injurious behaviors as a means of coping with their anger, vengeance and despair.

- *High School*: Most teens will fully grasp the meaning of death in circumstances such as the

World Trade Center or Pentagon disasters. They may seek out friends and family for comfort or they may withdraw to deal with their grief. Teens (as well as some younger children) with a history of depression, suicidal behavior and chemical dependency are at particular risk for prolonged and serious grief reactions and may need more careful attention from home and school during these difficult times.

Tips for Children and Teens with Grieving Friends and Classmates

Many children and teens have been indirectly impacted by the terrorists' attacks. They have learned of the deaths of people close to their friends and classmates—parents, siblings, other relatives and neighbors. Particularly in areas near the World Trade Center or Pentagon, it is not unusual to find several children in a given classroom who lost a family member—or even multiple family members. Additionally, all over the country, children have been impacted by the death of a family member at either the attack site or on board one of the four hijacked planes. Seeing their friends try to cope with such loss may scare or upset children who have had little or no experience with death and grieving. Some suggestions teachers and parents can provide to children and youth to deal with this "secondary" loss:

- Particularly with younger children, it will be important to help clarify their understanding of death. See tips above under "helping children cope."

- Seeing their classmates' reactions to loss may bring about some fears of losing their own parents or siblings. Children need reassurance from caretakers and teachers that their own families are safe. For children who have experienced their own loss (previous death of a parent, grandparent, sibling), observing the grief of a friend can bring back painful memories. These children are at greater risk for developing more serious stress reactions and should be given extra support as needed.

- Children (and many adults) need help in communicating condolence or comfort messages. Provide children with age-appropriate guidance for supporting their peers. Help them decide what to say (e.g., "Steve, I am so sorry about your father. I know you will miss him very much. Let me know if I can help you with your paper route…") and what to expect (see "expressions of grief" above).

- Help children anticipate some changes in friends' behavior. It is important that children understand that their grieving friends may act differently, may withdraw from their friends for a while, might seem angry or very sad, etc., but that this does not mean a lasting change in their relationship.

- Explain to children that their "regular" friendship may be an important source of support for friends and classmates. Even normal social activities such as inviting a friend over to play, going to the park, playing sports, watching a movie, or a trip to the mall may offer a much needed distraction and sense of connection and normalcy.

- Children need to have some options for providing support—it will help them deal with their fears and concerns if they have some concrete actions that they can take to help. Suggest making cards, drawings, helping with chores or homework, etc. Older teens might offer to help the family with some shopping, cleaning, errands, etc., or with babysitting for younger children.

- Encourage children who are worried about a friend to talk to a caring adult. This can help alleviate their own concern or potential sense of responsibility for making their friend feel better. Children may also share important information about a friend who is at risk of more serious grief reactions.

- Parents and teachers need to be alert to children in their care who may be reacting to a friend's loss of a loved one. These children will need some extra support to help them deal with the sense of frustration and helplessness that many people are feeling at this time.

Resources for Grieving and Traumatized Children

At times of severe stress, such as the trauma of the terrorist attacks on our country, both children and adults need extra support. Children closest to this tragedy may very well experience the most dramatic feelings of fear, anxiety and loss. They may have personally lost a loved one or know of friends and schoolmates who have been devastated by these treacherous acts. Adults need to carefully observe these children for signs of traumatic stress, depression or even suicidal thinking, and seek professional help when necessary.

Resources to help you identify symptoms of severe stress and grief reactions are available at the National Association of School Psychologist's website—*www.nasponline.org*. See also:

For Caregivers

Deaton, R.L. & Berkan, W.A. (1995). *Planning and managing death issues in the schools: A handbook*. Westport, CT: Greenwood Publishing Group.

Mister Rogers Website: *www.misterrogers.org* (see booklet on Grieving for children 4–10 years)

Webb, N.B. (1993). *Helping bereaved children: A handbook for practitioners*. New York: Guilford Press.

Wolfelt, A. (1983). *Helping children cope with grief*. Bristol, PA: Accelerated Development.

Wolfelt, A. (1997). *Healing the bereaved child: Grief gardening, growth through grief and other touchstones for caregivers*. Ft. Collins, CO: Companion.

Worden, J.W. (1996). *Children and grief: When a parent dies*. New York: Guilford Press

For Children:

Gootman, M.E. (1994). *When a friend dies: A book for teens about grieving and healing*. Minneapolis: Free Spirit Publishing.

Greenlee, S. (1992). *When someone dies*. Atlanta: Peachtree Publishing. (Ages 9–12).

Wolfelt, A.(2001). *Healing your grieving heart for kids*. Ft. Collins, CO: Companion.

The Standards Juggernaut

It is hard to resist the notion that what is important is whatever we and our peers happen to know. But if we buy that simplistic idea, the clones we create will be poorly prepared to cope with changing reality, Mr. Brady points out.

BY MARION BRADY

WHAT should the young be taught? No question we can ask ourselves is more important. Nothing less than the survival of humankind hinges on our choice of answers.

Perhaps surprisingly, the question rarely generates "deep" debate. Of course, there have been long-running arguments about creationism versus evolution, phonics versus whole language, the acceptability of certain novels for classroom use, and whether or not some textbooks encourage socialist or other "anti-American" perspectives.

But these are arguments over details. There has been very little dialogue focusing on fundamental curricular issues—little debate about the ultimate goals of education, little debate about what new knowledge belongs in the curriculum, little debate about what old content can be abandoned, little debate about whether or not the traditional disciplines are the best organizers of knowledge, and little debate about the appropriateness of the arbitrary boundaries that separate fields of study.

We have had no comprehensive national conversation about these questions. Hands are wrung about almost everything else connected with the schools—discipline, standardized test scores, teacher qualifications, funding, vouchers, charters, and so on—but the most important questions about schooling are not being answered. Indeed, they are not even being asked.

There is almost no dialogue about fundamental curricular issues because it seems to be widely assumed that there are no serious problems with the traditional curriculum. What should the young be taught? Without hesitation, policy makers and politicians answer, "They should be taught what those of us who are educated know." This is the philosophical underpinning of the latest educational fad: the standards movement.

Enter, center stage, the people Susan Ohanian has called the "Standardistos." No need, in the Standardisto view, to identify and clarify an overarching reason to educate. No need to decide what new knowledge belongs in the curriculum. No need to agree on what old knowledge to discard to make room for the new. No need to weigh the merit of alternative ways of organizing knowledge. No need to introduce students to the integrated, mutually supportive nature of all knowledge. From the Standardisto perspective, all that is necessary is to determine what most "well-educated" people know, organize it, distribute it to the schools, and demand that teachers teach it and students learn it. In the name of reform, the Standardistos are freezing in bureaucratic place the worst aspects of traditional education.

The standards movement has a lot going for it. Its promoters are true believers who have ready access to the media because they are considered authorities. The movement has massive political and corporate backing. Educators who oppose the movement are not well organized. It enjoys an inspired label—who can reasonably oppose the setting of standards? Perhaps most important, it meshes well with simplistic, popular views of what educating is all about.

Every day, across America, committees are at work embedding and reinforcing the standards fad. Sadly, because the consequences of their actions will take so long to manifest themselves, the causal link between what they are doing and its ultimately calamitous consequences may not become apparent in time to do anything about it. The perspectives of the Standardistos demand much closer scrutiny than they are getting.

Your Facts or Mine?

It hardly needs to be said that we are experiencing an information explosion that is unprecedented in human history. We can teach only the tiniest fraction of all there is to know, and that fraction grows smaller by the hour.

To the question "What should the young be taught?" the Standardisto answer is the one noted above: that body of general knowledge that those of us who are educated already know. That generations should share a large body of general knowledge makes good sense. Every society needs a "language of allusion" in order to function. Such statements as "The Monroe Doctrine is still a sensitive issue for many Latin Americans" or "He has the patience of Job" have meaning only if the speaker and the listener share some level of understanding of the Monroe Doctrine and of the Biblical story of Job's troubles.

A shared language of allusion provides a significant means of holding a society together. However, it is a mistake to assume that whatever members of the dominant elite know should determine what is taught to the young. The importance of a fact has nothing whatsoever to do with either the status of the people who know it or their number. What

counts, finally, is societal survival, from which it follows that *the relative importance of a bit of knowledge depends on the long-term effects of its being generally known*. That is a very different criterion.

A fact-based curriculum that teaches students about ancient Rome's battles with Carthage but fails to explore the differing value systems that underlie most conflict is missing a significant learning opportunity. A curriculum that requires students to learn the names of major rivers or mountain ranges but leaves them unaware of the implications of a gradual drop in the level of their region's water table tacitly invites eventual disaster.

Determining the probable or possible long-term consequences of knowing or not knowing something is, of course, no easy task. The process requires looking at the world as a system, and traditional schooling does not encourage that. Ordinary experience may tell us, say, that medical research increases life expectancy; that increased life expectancy expands the total population; that increased population expands the demand for food, water, and living space; and that those needs are on a collision course that could have disastrous consequences.

But what ordinary experience tells us is not addressed by the traditional curriculum that the Standardistos are so eager to reinforce. Tracing even a simple causal sequence like the one above touches on physiology, technology, geography, economics, and sociology. In our schools, such subjects are taught, if at all, at different levels and at different times, as if they had little or nothing to do with one another. Standards are written for disciplines. It is a rare standards document that tries to promote the exploration of relationships *between* or *beyond* the familiar disciplines.

It is hard to resist the notion that what is important is whatever we and our peers happen to know. But if we buy that simplistic idea, the

clones we create will be poorly prepared to cope with changing reality.

Depth or Breadth?

Two theories about how students learn best have long been in competition. One of them is summarized by the old saying "Throw enough mud on the wall, and some of it is bound to stick." This view acknowledges that not everything taught is learned, but it suggests that there is nevertheless merit in bombarding students with information because at least some of it will be remembered.

The second theory is summarized in the statement "Less is more." Early in the 20th century, mathematician, teacher, and philosopher Alfred North Whitehead maintained that dumping vast amounts of information on students was counterproductive. He argued that humans are simply not mentally equipped to handle a great deal of random, "inert knowledge." The young, Whitehead said, need to study in great depth a relatively few really powerful ideas, ideas that encompass and explain major aspects of human experience.

For example, Whitehead probably would have approved studying the concept of polarization. This process, by means of which minor differences between humans become major ones, touches almost every dimension of life. Polarization gradually turns complex, "gray" issues into ever simpler "black and white" ones, attaches to those issues ever greater significance, and loads them with ever more emotion until effective communication becomes impossible, and conflict becomes all but inevitable. A shared, thorough understanding of the process of polarization sheds light on the dynamics of friendship, marriage, neighborhood incidents, labor/management relationships, barroom brawls, religious schisms, international relations, and much more.

There are concepts even broader than polarization, concepts that cut across all fields of knowledge and disclose their inherent interrelations.

For example, concepts such as "pattern," "structure," "relationship," and "system" are central to all disciplines, including those not yet developed. By focusing on these kinds of large-scale mental organizers, students will be equipped to expand existing fields of study and to explore intellectual territory of which we currently have little or no knowledge.

Such organizers are essential. Give adults the exams they took a few years earlier in high school or college, and their poor performance will prove that facts that are not made part of an often-used larger scheme of meaning are soon forgotten.

The Standardistos pay lip service to the necessity for both breadth and depth, but nowhere in evidence in their efforts are "big" ideas that organize the myriad facts they demand that students remember. Indeed, most are convinced that the young cannot handle big ideas, that facts must come first, and that, given enough facts, some master pattern will eventually emerge to bind them together in a way that makes useful sense.

Here or There?

Effective teachers of the young are much concerned with what, in educational jargon, is called "developmentally appropriate material." Certain sequences are taken for granted. The simple is taught before the complex, the tangible before the intangible, the concrete before the abstract.

Most Standardistos have little use for such ideas. E. D. Hirsch, Jr., surely a closet Standardisto, asks, "What, exactly, does 'developmentally appropriate' mean?... Must children in the second grade have their horizons bounded by the local mall, as opposed to... learning about China and India, ancient Greece, and the Civil War?"[1]

The question, of course, is whether reach equals grasp. Learning about China, India, and ancient Greece involves learning about extremely complex cultural systems

that are shaped by deep-seated assumptions about life, death, the individual, significant others, nature, causation, the good life, the supernatural, and much more. The assumptions that undergird these cultural systems manifest themselves in myriad social institutions and physical productions and arrangements. There is no doubt some merit in teaching second-graders how to locate China and India on a globe, but it is surely naive to think that an ability to recall rehearsed answers to a few carefully chosen and phrased questions about those countries is of value.

What's more, the local shopping mall to which Hirsch gives such short shrift deserves more respect than most Standardistos give it. To those who have not thought much about the matter, it might seem too mundane to merit the attention of second-graders. But choose any field of study—physics, language, economics, art, sociology, even history—and any randomly selected mall will provide enough raw study material to keep a team of graduate students occupied indefinitely. It is only the extreme familiarity of shopping malls that keeps their inherent complexity below our threshold of awareness.

The same could be said for the study of a student's school. There is no concept appropriate for the general education curriculum that does not manifest itself in some teachable way within the physical boundaries of a school.

To the casual observer, attempting to teach the young about China or India might seem to indicate more respect for the intellectual capabilities of the young than does a focus on the mall or other topics drawn from student experience. In fact, just the opposite is the case. Because they know little or nothing about things remote in time and space other than what they are told, second-graders have few options other than to parrot such information back. But make their own experience a legitimate focus of study, and their insights and

critical powers can begin to be displayed, sometimes in startlingly impressive ways that demand genuine respect.

I do not mean to suggest that schoolwork should be confined to the study of immediate reality. Even the very young have imaginations that can transport them almost anywhere. But surely, given the difficulties inherent in dealing in a systematic way with the complex, the abstract, and the remote, immediate reality is the place to begin to build the descriptive and analytical conceptual models that will eventually take students to wider experience. Standardistos, unaccustomed to the instructional use of what students know rather than what they themselves know, rarely write standards that exploit the teaching power of a student's own experience.

There is yet another reason for focusing primary attention on the student's "here and now" rather than on preprocessed, canned information. Back in the 1960s, the education establishment's thinking about thought became somewhat more sophisticated. "Thinking" began to be seen as actively engaging in a wide range of mental processes. Recalling was just one of those processes. Categorizing, translating, hypothesizing, valuing, generalizing, and synthesizing were others. Even the very young, it became apparent, use a great many thought processes in the course of ordinary experience.

When teaching is seen primarily as telling by means of teacher talk or textbook reading, the mental processes available to students dwindle down to just one: recall. Students may not be able to put their fingers on the reason schoolwork so often frustrates and bores them, but its lack of genuine intellectual challenge is surely a major factor.

Here, again, is why the study of immediate, firsthand experience—the mall, the school, the street—can be so engaging. Its inherent complexity demands the use of every known thought process, and the level of difficulty automatically adjusts to that which is most appropriate for the individual student.

The Appeal of the Simplistic

In times of uncertainty, easy answers have great appeal. This is such an era, and well-meaning politicians and policy makers are quick to supply them.

Unfortunately, more often than not, behind legislation and new initiatives lies a gross lack of understanding of education. Many share the view of Standardisto Louis Gerstner, Jr., CEO of IBM, who apparently believes that educating has to do primarily with "the distribution of information." If only it could be that simple. Teaching, real teaching, involves the altering of the images of reality in the minds of others, a challenge inherently far more complex than those presented by rocket science.

The educational establishment has itself to blame for the fact that so many who do not know what they are doing are promoting simplistic approaches to educating. The establishment has drifted along thoughtlessly, assuming that the major curricular issues have been solved and that all that is needed now is a bit

of touching up of what was taught last year, a task that can be handled by the subject-matter specialists.

In eras when knowledge changed little from generation to generation, that view was probably an acceptable one. Today, it is not. The perspectives of subject-matter specialists are too narrow; their interest in the whole, of which their specializations are parts, is too restricted; the rate of societal change is too rapid for reform of the "touching up" sort. Freezing the status quo in place, assuming that what the young should be taught is merely what the educated happen to know, ensures that, as the years pass, school curricula will bear less and less relationship to reality.

There are other wrongheaded views shared by many Standardistos—that somehow just "raising the bar" increases students' ability to clear it, that before the standards movement there were no standards, that the talent wasted by one-size-fits-all programs is not worth developing, that students who will be turned into "failures" by the standards will not present a serious problem, that standardized tests tell us something really important, that market forces have a magical ability to cure the ills of education, that ex-

trinsic rewards are dependable motivators, and so on. However, behind the standards juggernaut and impelling it forward is the single, primary, simplistic, and unexamined assumption that what the next generation most needs to know is what this generation knows. Surface that assumption and carefully examine it, and every other Standardisto assumption will begin to show itself in a different light.

Teaching to lists of what is "important" that have been devised by the elders is the ultimate "back-to-basics" program. If we proceed down the road we are now on and succeed in replicating ourselves, we will have an America in which everyone understands and is comfortable with everyone else—as we slide toward oblivion.

Note

1. E. D. Hirsch, Jr., *Cultural Literacy: What Every American Needs to Know* (Boston: Houghton Mifflin, 1987).

MARION BRADY (mbrady@digital.net) is an education consultant living in Cocoa, Fla.

From *Phi Delta Kappan*, May 2000, pp. 649-651. © 2000 by Phi Delta Kappan International, Inc. Reprinted by permission.

UNIT 2
Development

Unit Selections

6. **Wired for Thought**, Sharon Begley
7. **Play an Endangered Species**, Sheila G. Flaxman
8. **Raising a Moral Child**, Karen Springen
9. **The School and the Child and the Child in the School**, Debra Eckerman Pitton
10. **Differing Perspectives, Common Ground: The Middle School and Gifted Education Relationship**, Hilda C. Rosselli and Judith L. Irvin

Key Points to Consider

• How do biology and environment interact to produce an intelligent human being?

• Why is an accurate perception of self important to children's self-esteem?

• How can schools and teachers provide an environment that is conducive to adolescent development?

 **Links: www.dushkin.com/online/**
These sites are annotated in the World Wide Web pages.

Association for Moral Education
http://www.wittenberg.edu/ame/

Child Welfare League of America
http://www.cwla.org

Coping With Traumatic Events
http://www.childtrauma.org/Traumatic_events_teachers.htm

Guidelines for Developmentally Appropriate Early Childhood Practice
http://www.newhorizons.org/naeyc.html

The National Academy for Child Development
http://www.nacd.org

National Association of School Psychologists (NASP)
http://www.nasponline.org

Scholastic News Zone
http://www.scholasticnews.com

The study of human development provides us with knowledge of how children and adolescents mature and learn within the family, community, and school environments. Educational psychology focuses on description and explanation of the developmental processes that make it possible for children to become intelligent and socially competent adults. Psychologists and educators are presently studying the idea that biology as well as the environment influence cognitive, personal, social, and emotional development and involve predictable patterns of behavior.

The perceptions and thoughts that young children have about the world are often quite different than those of adolescents and adults. That is, children may think about moral and social issues in a unique way. Children need to acquire cognitive, moral, and social skills in order to interact effectively with parents, teachers, and peers. Human intelligence encompasses all of the above skills and reflects the child's intelligent adaptation to the environment.

Today the cognitive, moral, social, and emotional development of children takes place in a rapidly changing society. A child must develop positive conceptions of self within the family as well as at school in order to cope with the changes and become a competent and socially responsible adult. In "Wired for Thought," Sharon Begley discusses the interaction of biology and environment, while Karen Springen describes "Raising a Moral Child." The article "Play: An Endangered Species" discusses the cognitive and social skills of children. Adolescence brings with it the ability to think abstractly and hypothetically and to see the world from many perspectives. Adolescents strive to achieve a sense of identity by questioning their beliefs and tentatively committing to self-chosen goals. Their ideas about the kinds of adults they want to become and

the ideals they want to believe in sometimes lead to conflicts with parents and teachers. Adolescents are also sensitive about espoused adult values versus adult behavior. The articles in this unit discuss the unique needs of young adolescents and also suggest ways in which schools and teachers can help meet these needs.

Wired for Thought

Babies know more, and know it sooner, than researchers ever suspected. There is a mind in the crib, requiring stimulation to thrive.

By Sharon Begley

WHEN ALISON GOPNIK GOT HOME from the lab one day, she was overcome with the feeling that she was a lousy teacher, an incompetent scientist and a bad mother. A student had argued with a grade, a grant proposal had been rejected and the chicken legs she'd planned for dinner were still in the freezer. So the University of California, Berkeley, developmental psychologist collapsed on the couch and started to cry. Her son, almost 2, sized up the situation like a little pro. He dashed to the bathroom, fumbled around for what he needed and returned with Band-Aids—which he proceeded to stick all over his sobbing (and now startled) mother, figuring that eventually he would find the place that needed patching. Like most 2-year-olds, the little boy had just reached the point where he could not only exhibit empathy (even babies bawl when they hear another baby cry), but also try to soothe another's pain.

For decades scientists studying the blossoming of children's minds had been pretty much blind to this and other talents of the sandbox set. That's changing: researchers today have a lot more respect for what a child's mind is capable of. Babies know more, and know it earlier, than

the founders of the field of child development ever guessed. Even 1-month-olds learn whether their parents respond to them quickly or slowly. From 4 to 6 months, babies come to understand that some things (Dad's clothes) change, but others (his face) do not. Between 7 and 10 months they may learn to carry out sequences of actions to reach a goal, like piling up pillows so they can clamber up and see onto Mom and Dad's bed. By 18 months they can form intentions and understand the intentions of others.

Pint-size scientists
Babies actively seek out information through observations and experiments, changing their brains

---

How children come to achieve these and other cognitive milestones has proved the real revelation. The sequence of brain development is genetically programmed, with the brain stem coming online first to control basic bodily func-

tions like respiration. The cerebellum and basal ganglia follow, to control movement. The limbic system, for emotion and memory, comes next, and the cerebral cortex, for higher-order thinking, matures last. "The *quality* of neural development, however, is shaped by a child's experiences," says neurobiologist Lise Eliot of Chicago Medical School. Like miniature scientists, babies are sponges for information, learning through "mini-experiments with pots and pans, and by playing peekaboo and other everyday games," says developmental psychologist Andrew Meltzoff of the University of Washington. "A baby doesn't just grow into a 3-year-old without external stimulation, like a caterpillar into a butterfly. A baby contributes to cognitive growth by actively seeking information, through observations, play and baby-size experiments. This information changes the baby's mind."

Literally. Brains change as a result of the experiences they live. At birth the brain is packed with an estimated 100 billion neurons. But newborn brains should be labeled SOME ASSEMBLY REQUIRED. Although genes rough out where the brain's visual centers will be and where the auditory centers will nestle, where the regions that govern emotion will lie and where the center of higher thought will sit, the fine details are left to experience. This discovery of the importance of experience led in the 1990s to a proliferation of products and services offering "brain stimulation" for babies, marketed to parents frantic that failing to introduce number concepts in infancy will doom their child to a 400 on the SAT. But the formative experiences scientists have in mind don't involve flashcards. A new report from the National Academy of Sciences called "The Science of Early Childhood Development" puts it this way: "Given the drive of young children to master their world... the full range of early childhood competencies can be achieved in typical, everyday environments. A cabinet with pots and pans... seems to serve the same purpose as a fancy, 'made for baby' musical instrument."

How powerful are everyday interactions? Scientists have recently found that the way a parent talks to children can make them better at some tasks than others. It is a peculiarity of the Korean language that verb endings convey so much information that a mother can talk about the world to her baby without using many nouns. English, in contrast, uses comparatively more nouns and fewer verbs. The result? Korean babies use more verbs in their speech, and English-speaking babies more nouns. But the effects go beyond language. Korean babies, scientists at UC, Berkeley, found in a recent study, learn to solve action problems, like using a long-handled rake to retrieve out-of-reach objects, months before English-speaking kids do. But English hearers learn the concept of categories before Korean-speaking children do, apparently reflecting a language that emphasizes objects. The difference between the languages that babies hear seems to make one kind of problem easier than another.

No one is suggesting that parents adopt a different language depending on how they want their child to think: playing to children's strengths is enough to nurture little minds. Scientists learned how badly they had underestimated babies when Meltzoff discovered that just

40 minutes after birth, babies can imitate facial expressions. That might not seem like such a big deal, but it's actually pretty impressive. A newborn has never seen her own face, yet still knows that she has cheeks she can raise to mimic Dad's smile, and a tongue she can poke out to match what her brother is doing. From the first, babies know that they are like other people, an insight they will build on as they play imitating games with you.

36% of parents of young children say they plan to start sending their child to school by the age of 3; an additional **29%** say they'll do so at 4

It is babies' capacity for "abstract mental representation," as Eliot calls it, that has really taken scientists by surprise. At the tender age of 4 weeks, many babies can transfer data taken in by one sense over to another sense. After they have been sucking on a nubby pacifier, for instance, they can pick it out of a lineup: shown a smooth one and the nubby one, they look longer at the nubby one, an indication that they recognize how something should look from how it feels. Their capacity for abstract thinking extends even to physics. When scientists rig things so a block appears suspended in midair, even 3-month-olds stare at it as if in disbelief that the law of gravity has been repealed. Perhaps the most dramatic evidence of infants' capacity for abstract thinking comes from a 1992 experiment in which 5-month-olds watched scientists place dolls one by one behind a screen. If six dolls went in, but the screen was raised to reveal only four, the babies appeared startled. The kid can't sit, but she's caught you in a mathematical error.

Babies have an innate understanding of the world of things that the simplest games can encourage. A 5-month-old will follow a ball with his eyes as it rolls behind a screen, then scan ahead to the far edge, expecting the ball to emerge.

But his grasp of where and when an object should be found has limits. If you show a 6-month-old a little toy, then cover it with a cloth, his face is a mask of befuddlement. A 9-month-old, though, can find the toy, and loves playing hide-and-seek games with objects.

When babies turn 1, they begin to look where people point. This suggests that their minds grasp not only the physical world but other minds. "Like imitation, pointing implies a deep understanding of yourself and other people," says Gopnik, coauthor with Meltzoff and Patricia Kuhl of the 1999 book "The Scientist in the Crib." The baby now grasps that two minds can share an intention—to turn the eyes in the indicated direction. At this age, pointing games are not only a blast but a way to encourage the neural connections underlying this nascent understanding.

Also by their 1st birthday, babies begin to grasp the idea of shared feelings. If Mom peeks into one box and looks disgusted, then peeks into another box and looks delighted, and next pushes the two boxes toward her baby, the child will shun the first box and gleefully reach into the second. He is learning to judge what is good and bad in the world by others' reactions, which means that a look of disgust when your in-laws arrive can leave a lasting impression. Even a 9-month-old can learn how the world works by watching how others make it work. When Meltzoff ran an experiment in which he touched his forehead to a box rigged to light up when touched, babies were mesmerized. When the kids returned to the lab a week later, they immediately touched their own foreheads to the box and turned the lights on.

This is not just a "stupid baby trick." It shows, rather, that "babies can use other people to figure out the world," says Meltzoff. This is the age when they are adept little mimics, an age when parents have a clear shot at teaching babies how the world works by holding books, hugging older siblings and otherwise acting as they hope their children will.

Before they are 1, most babies can grasp only broad categories. If a blue ball rolls behind a screen and a yellow truck comes out, they're not surprised: the category "rolling object" covers both ball and truck. Once children reach their 1st birthday, though, a blue truck's turning into a yellow duck elicits definite surprise. This is about the age when kids sort objects into sensible groups, like grouping toy horses with toy horses and pencils with pencils. At 2 or 3, children go beyond superficial appearances. They know that baby tigers, though they look like kittens, belong to the same category as grown tigers. And, showing that they are ready for the era of the genome, they seem to know about heredity: ask a preschooler if a pig raised by cows will have a curly tail or a straight one, and he doesn't hesitate to answer curly. Young children take to category games like pigs to pokes.

Fun with physics
Even a 3-month-old stares in disbelief at objects that defy gravity, like balls dangling in midair

It was only a generation ago that psychologists proclaimed that newborns have no cortex, the thinking part of the brain. They thought of babies as slightly mobile vegetables—"carrots that cry." Now we know that babies come prewired to learn. Although many parents (and marketers) have interpreted that as a clarion call to bombard them with "stimulation," in fact the best science we have today says that children learn about causes and categories, self and other, through listening and watching, and through games no fancier than hide-and-seek and peekaboo. "If you make a child feel loved, connected, purposeful and inquisitive, brain development will follow," says Peter Gorski of Harvard Medical School. "Our role as parents is not to perfect brain circuitry, but to foster the development of healthy, sane and caring human beings." We are a social species. Our babies learn in social environments, from people who love them, who delight in their little triumphs and pick them up when they slip, who recognize the mind behind the brain.

Play
An Endangered Species

In their rush to increase teaching hours, many districts are eliminating recess and free time—and something valuable is being lost

By Sheila G. Flaxman

Children know a simple truth that many administrators seem to have forgotten: Play is a necessary part of growing up.

Unfortunately, in their frantic quest to raise standardized test scores and give children a competitive advantage at ever-earlier ages, many school districts have targeted "nonessential" activities as cutting into crucial instructional time. The result: Recess and nonacademic free time are being shortened and even eliminated. A widespread belief is that schools should be solely devoted to academics and play can occur outside of the educational system.

I believe that this is a dangerous proposition. Playtime—recess play or unorganized inside play—is a vital educational activity all its own. It allows children at all ages to use initiative and imagination, to be creative and social. Children left to their own devices will explore, experiment, test, err, and try again, all at their own pace. They will use their bodies and expend energy that might otherwise erupt when they need to be focused and alert.

The Value of Free Playtime

Free play is a critically important factor in normal development from birth through childhood. Early in the 20th century, pioneer child-development specialists such as Switzerland's Jean Piaget and Russian psychologist Lev Vygotsky recognized the value of such activity. Vygotsky believed that play leads directly to the development of a child's conceptual abilities, enabling him or her to master abstract thought, among other skills. Piaget, who developed a widely accepted theory of intellectual development, noted that through the joys of recreation "knowledge arises

neither from objects nor the child, but from interactions between the child and those objects."

Play Involves Free Choice

A lot of what is passed off as "play" in schools—the use of games, toys, and puzzles that teach academic concepts—does not promote the enriching qualities of play that involves free choice, that is nonliteral and self-motivated. Nonliteral, by definition, is nonrealistic. Children direct and invent this kind of play—no one presents them with a task or a set of standards to follow. This means that the use of materials, the environment, the rules of the game, and the roles of the participants all flow from the children's imaginations and their sense of reality.

Children engage in such play because they enjoy it—it's self-directed. They do not play for rewards; they enjoy the doing, not the end result. Once they get bored, they go on to do something else—and continue to learn and grow.

But is this activity really as important as traditional academic areas of the curriculum? Teachers of young children are often obligated to explain and justify the value of play to administrators and parents anxious to know why their children aren't learning at a faster rate. Such critics believe that play takes valuable time away from more important activities and allows children to hide in a fantasy world instead of facing the realities of the here and now.

Preparation for Adulthood

The view held by critics of play is countered by the work of experts such as Piaget. He maintained that infants and

Free Play:
10 Benefits to Children

1 Muscular development and control of large muscles, fine motor skills, and eye-hand coordination.

2 Speech development through social interactions during play.

3 Social development: parallel play leading to cooperative play.

4 Language-skill development through dramatic play to clarify ideas.

5 Problem solving and creative thinking—probably the most important skills for living in the world today.

6 Increased consciousness of the cause-and-effect involved in a sequence of events.

7 Therapeutic value in providing opportunities for "safe" acting-out behaviors.

8 Opportunities for self-talk, a useful tool for teachers as they listen to children at play.

9 Development of self-confidence while trying new things in a nonjudgmental environment.

10 Learning cooperation and values by putting themselves in the "shoes" of others.

young children learn new concepts through a two-part method: discovering a process and then practicing it. Seen in this light, play is the best preparation for adulthood, especially in our highly technological, competitive society. That's because play, whether in the classroom, at recess, or outdoors, is all about discovering and practicing. It allows children to form an understanding of the social, emotional, moral, and intellectual concepts to which they are being introduced at every turn as they rapidly develop.

This is especially important today, when children are being exposed to so much, so early. Play helps them make sense of and internalize all the stimuli by which they are being bombarded; it provides emotional release from the increasing stress of modern life.

Many recess activities, especially those that require coordinated efforts, teach children how to work together, how to take turns, and how to reciprocate. They offer concrete evidence that, by following some basic rules for the good of the group, the children can keep playing and having fun. If we allow children the freedom to experiment with language, higher-order thinking skills, and new ways of sharing a toy, they will make discoveries that help them throughout life.

The social skills learned during free recreation are also closely related to the establishment of moral guidelines. We bemoan the fact that children do not have appropriate role models. Yet moral development arises from the ability of a child to put him- or herself in the other child's shoes—a lesson of play.

It's Good for the Body, Too

The most forward-thinking workplaces today recognize the need for employees to stretch, exercise, and move around—many provide a designated space in which to do so. If adult workers are happier, healthier, and more productive thanks to such respite, imagine the benefits for young students.

Daily media stories of out-of-control young people should be a warning that kids need safe, healthy outlets for physical energy. Plus, there is an ever-increasing amount of research documenting the poor physical condition of children today. Yet schools persist in curtailing the time allotted for children to run, skip, stretch, jump—play. Why don't more administrators realize that active play develops healthy bodies while teaching children to enjoy exercise?

In your classroom and school, take the opportunity to fight for free play as an integral part of a child's day. When playtime is threatened, so is a child's chance to grow.

Sheila G. Flaxman has been an early-childhood teacher and administrator for 35 years. She lives and works in Little Rock, Arkansas.

Raising a Moral Child

For many parents, nothing is more important than teaching kids to know right from wrong. But when does a sense of morality begin?

By Karen Springen

NANCY ROTERING BEAMS AS she recalls how her 3-year-old son Jack recently whacked his head against a drawer hard enough to draw blood. It's not that she found the injury amusing. But it did have a silver lining: Jack's wails prompted his 2-year-old brother, Andy, to offer him spontaneous consolation in the form of a cup of water and a favorite book, "Jamberry." "Want 'Berry' book, Jack?" he asked. Nancy loved Andy's "quick-thinking act of sympathy." "I was thrilled that such a tiny person could come up with such a big thought," she says. "He stepped up and offered Jack refreshment—and entertainment—to take his mind off the pain."

All parents have goals for their children, whether they center on graduating from high school or winning the Nobel Prize. But for a great many, nothing is more important than raising a "good" child—one who knows right from wrong, who is empathetic and who, like Andy, tries to live by the Golden Rule, even if he doesn't know yet what it is. Still, morality is an elusive—and highly subjective—character trait. Most parents know it when they see it. But how can they instill and nurture it in their children? Parents must lead by example. "The way to raise a moral child is to be a moral person," says Tufts University psychologist David Elkind. "If you're honest and straightforward and decent and caring, that's what children learn." Humans seem innately inclined to behave empathetically; doctors talk about "contagious crying" among newborns in the hospital nursery. And not all children of murderers or even tax cheats follow in their parents' footsteps. "What's surprising is how many kids raised in immoral homes grow up moral," says New York psychiatrist Alvin Rosenfeld.

81% of mothers and 78% of fathers say they plan eventually to send their young child to Sunday school or some other kind of religious training

Parents have always been preoccupied with instilling moral values in their children. But in today's fast-paced world, where reliable role models are few and acts of violence by children are increasingly common, the quest to raise a moral child has taken on new urgency. Child criminals grow ever younger; in August, a 6-year-old California girl (with help from a 5-year-old friend) smothered her 3-year-old brother with a pillow. Such horrific crimes awaken a dark, unspoken fear in many parents: Is my child capable of committing such an act? And can I do anything to make sure that she won't?

There are no guarantees. But parents are increasingly aware that even very young children can grasp and exhibit moral behaviors—even if the age at which they become "morally accountable" remains under debate. According to the Roman Catholic Church, a child reaches "the age of reason" by 7. Legally, each state determines how old a child must be to be held responsible for his acts, ranging from 7 to 15. Child experts are reluctant to offer a definitive age for accountability. But they agree that in order to be held morally responsible, children must have both an emotional and a cognitive awareness of right and wrong—in other words, to know in their heads as well as feel in their hearts that what they did was wrong. Such morality doesn't appear overnight but emerges slowly, over time. And according to the latest research, the roots of morality first appear in the earliest months of an infant's life. "It begins the day they're born, and it's not complete until the day they die," says child psychiatrist Elizabeth Berger, author of "Raising Children with Character."

It's never too early to start. Parents who respond instantly to a newborn's cries lay an important moral groundwork. "You work to understand what the baby's feeling," says Barbara Howard, a specialist in developmental behavioral pediatrics at the Johns Hopkins University School of Medicine. "Then the baby will work to understand what other people are feeling." Indeed, empathy is among the first moral emotions to develop. Even before the age of 2, children will try to comfort an upset child—though usually in an "egocentric" way, says Marvin Berkowitz, professor of character education at the University of Missouri-St. Louis: "I might give them *my* teddy even though your teddy is right there." To wit: Andy Rotering brought his brother his own favorite book.

Morality consists of not only caring for others but also following basic rules of conduct. Hurting another child, for instance, is never OK. But how you handle it depends on your child's age. If a 1-year-old is hitting or biting, "you simply say 'no' firmly, and you remove the child from the situation," says Craig Ramey, author of "Right From

Birth." But once a child acquires language skills, parents can provide more detail. "You can say, 'We don't hit in this family'," says David Fassler, chairman of the American Psychiatric Association's council on children, adolescents and their families. "You can say, 'Everyone feels like hitting and biting from time to time. My job is to help you figure out what to do with those kinds of feelings'." Suggest alternatives—punching a pillow, drawing a sad picture or lying quietly on a bed.

Children grow more moral with time. As Lawrence Kohlberg of Harvard University has said, kids go through progressive stages of moral development. Between 1 and 2, children understand that there are rules—but usually follow them only if an adult is watching, says Barbara Howard. After 2, they start obeying rules—inconsistently—even if an adult isn't there. And as any adult who has ever driven faster than 65mph knows, people continue "circumstantial" morality throughout life, says Howard. "People aren't perfect, even when they know what the right thing to do is."

Though all children are born with the capacity to act morally, that ability can be lost. Children who are abused or neglected often fail to acquire a basic sense of trust and belonging that influences how people behave when they're older. "They may be callous because no one has ever shown them enough of the caring to put that into their system," says Howard. Ramey argues that "we come to expect the world to be the way we've experienced it"—whether that means cold and forbidding or warm and loving. According to Stanford developmental psychologist William Damon, morality can also be hampered by the practice of "bounding"—limiting children's contact with the world only to people who are like them—as opposed to "bridging," or exposing them to people of different backgrounds. "You can empathize with everyone who looks just like you and learn to exclude everyone who doesn't," says Damon. A juvenile delinquent may treat his sister gently—but beat up an old woman of another race. "The bridging approach ends up with a more moral child," says Damon.

No matter how hard you try, you can't force your child to be moral. But there are things you can do to send him in the right direction:

If you're honest, straightforward, decent and caring, that's what children learn'

• Decide what values—such as honesty and hard work—are most important to you. Then do what you want your children to do. "If you volunteer in your community, and you take your child, they will do that themselves," says Joseph Hagan, chairman of the American Academy of Pediatrics' committee on the psychosocial aspects of child and family health. "If you stub your toe, and all you can say is the F word, guess what your child is going to say when they stub their toe?"

Always help your child see things from the other person's point of view

• Praise children liberally. "You have to ignore the behaviors you don't want and highlight the behaviors you do want," says Kori Skidmore, a staff psychologist at Children's Memorial Hospital in Chicago. Rather than criticizing a toddler for his messy room, compliment him on the neat corner, recommends Darien, Ill., pediatrician Garry Gardner. Use "no" judiciously, otherwise "a child starts to feel like 'I'm always doing something wrong'," says the APA's Fassler. "If you're trying to teach a child to share, then praise them when they share. Don't just scold them when they're reluctant to."

• Take advantage of teachable moments. When Gardner's kids were 3 and 4, they found a $10 bill in front of a store. Gardner talked to them about the value of the money—and they agreed to give it to the shopkeeper in case someone returned for it. They mutually decided "finders keepers" shouldn't apply to anything worth more than a quarter. "Certainly you wouldn't go back and say, 'I found a penny'," says Gardner. Parents can also use famous parables, like "The Boy Who

Cried Wolf," or Bible stories to illustrate their point.

• Watch what your child watches. TV and computer games can glorify immoral behavior. "If children are unsupervised, watching violence or promiscuity on TV, they're going to have misguided views about how to treat other people," says Karen Bohlin, director of Boston University's Center for the Advancement of Ethics and Character. "Children by nature are impulsive and desperately need guidance to form good habits. That can come only from a loving caregiver who's by their side, teaching them how to play nicely, safely, fairly, how to take turns, how to put things back where they belong, how to speak respectfully."

• Discuss consequences. Say, " 'Look how sad Mary is because you broke her favorite doll'," explains Berkowitz. Parents can also ask their children to help them pick fair punishments—for example, no TV. "They're learning that their voice is valued," says Berkowitz. Allowing kids to make choices—even about something as trivial as what to have for lunch—will enable them to make moral ones later. "If they don't learn peanut butter and jelly at 2, how are they going to decide about drinking when they're 14?" asks family physician Nancy Dickey, editor in chief of Medem, an online patient-information center.

• Always help them see things from the other person's point of view. If a child bops his new sibling, try to reflect the newborn's outlook. Say, " 'Oh, my, that must hurt. How would you feel if someone did that to you?'" says Howard. Gardner encourages parents whose kids find stray teddy bears to ask their children how sad they would feel if they lost their favorite stuffed animal—and how happy they would be if someone returned it. "It's one thing to hear about it at Sunday school," he says. And another to live the "do unto others" rule in real life.

In the end, the truest test of whether a parent has raised a moral child is how that young person acts when Mom or Dad is not around. With a lot of love and luck, your child will grow up to feel happy and blessed—and to want to help others who aren't as fortunate. Now, *that's* something to be proud of.

Reinventing the Middle School

The School and the Child and the Child in the School

Middle school students are still open to new ideas, still undecided about who they are and what they will ultimately be, thereby creating a wonderful opportunity for teachers to be a part of their journey into adulthood.

By Debra Eckerman Pitton

S itting in a meeting with a group of teachers who were discussing plans for the conversion of their district's junior high into a new middle school, I overheard one 8th grade teacher say, "I don't know about expecting all of this interdisciplinary teaching stuff and flexible scheduling to really make a difference. It was so much easier back a few years ago… the kids listened to you and did what you asked. Now it seems that the kids don't care, they don't do the work, or they just aren't as capable. There is so much need for discipline and…"

One of the administrators cut her off. "The kids who come in our doors are the kids we need to teach. The parents aren't keeping all the good ones at home. We have to find ways to meet students' needs, whatever they are, not pine for the 'good old days.' Yes, students are different today; our society has changed. With technology and the impact of the media, very little is the way it was 10 or 15 years ago, so why would you expect the students to remain the same?"

Unconvinced, the teacher just shook her head. I listened to the rest of the discussion, but thought for a long time about those comments. I am aware of the challenges involved in the process of moving a junior high towards a middle school philosophy, yet I wondered why this was so. I wondered if the difficulty of embracing a middle school approach was related to this perception that kids today are somehow not as capable and bright as their predecessors.

Who Are the Students in Our Schools?

Behind all of the concepts espoused by middle level philosophy lies the premise that we need a different structure for children of this age because they are developmentally different from elementary and high school students. If teachers do not recognize the impact of these developmental differences, then they will not be able to respond accordingly. Eccles, Lord, Roeser, Barber, & Josefowicz (1996) state that middle school students require different types of educational environments in order to meet each individual's developmental needs at that particular time, as well as to help them continue to develop. Students at this transitional period, between grade school and high school, need schools and classrooms that help them move through this period of adjustment.

If we know that students of this age need teaching and classroom interactions that provide them with meaning and address their developmental issues, why do many middle school classrooms still reflect a teacher focused, content directed, autocratic approach? Perhaps it is because we, as educators, have not been willing to give any real credence to the insights provided by developmental theory. As adults, we know that we work harder on things we enjoy, we learn more when we choose to do something and are involved in the decision making, and we strive to do our work well when it means something to us. Yet when we face a classroom full of young adolescents, it is easy to pull rank and dictate what *we* think is important, what *we* think is relevant and meaningful. Why is it so easy to tell young people what to do rather than to ask them?

As adults, most of us would never think of forcing another individual to follow our directives. We ask for input, we work in committees, we gather multiple perspectives and we build consensus. Even without reviewing the research on group dynamics (Johnson & Johnson, 1991), adults are aware that a higher quality work product is produced when individuals have a say in what is completed and how it is accomplished. At least here in the United States, it is a commonly held belief that if someone has a voice in a decision they are more likely to support it. Our democratic society demands active participation in making decisions that affect us as individuals. As research into group interaction and the effects of group participation identifies, being a part of group decision-making, rather than being dictated to, results in a more productive worker (or learner) and a higher quality product (Johnson, 1990; Johnson & Johnson, 1991). Well intentioned adults strive to positively interact and give everyone a voice in our communities, in the work place, and in government. So why does this not occur in many classrooms, when our purpose is to develop future citizens?

Perhaps teachers find a classroom of hormonally charged young people innately threatening, so keeping control becomes paramount. We know that all of the changes young people are going through at this time creates anxiety and often confusion and hostility. It is scary to think about unleashing all of that emotional energy in a classroom. It feels more comfortable to keep things under control, to manage all aspects of the classroom. Middle school philosophy suggests that teachers give up much of that control and begin to work with their students as they would other adults. This is asking for change that is too much for many teachers to handle. They are moving out of their comfort zones if they let go of their control of the curriculum and ask students what they would like to learn. Teachers let go of their control if they ask other teachers with differing perspectives to share in the development of curriculum. They let go of their control when they have to teach in areas that stretch them beyond current levels of knowledge and preparation. Finally, they let go of their control if they give the students opportunities to express themselves freely.

Structural changes such as teaming flexible schedules, exploratory options, interdisciplinary curriculum, and advisory groups have been identified as critical elements in creating a supportive learning environment for middle schoolers. However, several studies indicate that teachers may need to adjust the way they interact with their students for these changes to be effective. Eccles and Midgley, (1989); and Eccles, Midgley, Buchanan, Wigfield, Reuman and Mac Iver, (1993), identified that despite awareness of the physical, social, emotional and cognitive changes occurring in young people, classrooms for students between the ages 10–14 often reflect strong teacher centered control and emphasis on discipline along with limited input from students in the way the class is run. Decisions about curriculum and learning opportunities are most often left solely to the teachers. Eccles and Wigfield (1997) refer to Mac Iver and Reuman's (1988) work which concluded that this mismatch between the emerging adolescent's need for self-management and the opportunities provided for them in the classroom results in the students' lack of motivation and interest in school. These studies point out that for many young adolescents there seems to be no purpose to being in school, nor any feeling that they are being allowed to develop and have a voice. Therefore, they choose to act out.

Middle school students are at a crossroads in their educational development; failing to sense a purpose to schooling will create feelings of apathy

Middle school students are at the crossroads in their educational development, and for many, the sense that there is no purpose to their schooling creates a feeling of apathy and disinterest. This can result in failure or dropping out of school altogether. Teachers must recognize that adolescent changes cannot be downplayed. The incorporation of student choice and proactive accommodation for the young adolescents' myriad physical, emotional and social stresses must be included in every classroom. While many educators can recite a litany of young adolescent needs, their own reactions to the adolescents' push for independence and self-determination is often to try to squash the emerging sense of self with control and directives. It is easier to try and control the tensions and emotional ups and downs among students than to try and help them learn to deal with such issues. It often feels more comfortable for teachers to keep a tight hold on the reins in their class-rooms, yet it is only through the sharing of decision making that students will feel invited into the learning process. Extending an invitation to students to join in the educational process says that the teacher values them as individuals.

Changing Perceptions

Just as we know middle school students are going through an adjustment period and that they need support to accomplish a successful transition to adulthood, so too do teachers moving into a middle school concept need support as they move into a new dimension of teaching. Teacher preparation programs must provide more emphasis on the links between adolescent development and best practice in the classroom. However, McEwin and Dickinson (1995) reported that many issues, such as lack of program availability, interest, teacher resistance, and a dearth of advocates for the middle level concept has prevented widespread implementation of specialized middle school teacher preparation. Thus there are too few teachers who have studied to any extent the needs of young adolescents or the appropriate educational responses to those needs.

Atwell, noted middle school writing teacher, described an epiphany she experienced after working with a student who did not follow her prescribed writing program. Atwell wrestled with ideas from experts who suggested that she needed to let go of her extensive writing curriculum. At first she resisted, but after observing her students at work, she stated, "I saw that my creation (the curriculum) manipulated kids.... Students either found ways to make sense of, or peace with, the language arts curriculum, or they failed the course." (Atwell, 1998, p. 4.). Here was a teacher who had created a very thoughtful, detailed curriculum, and who struggled to identify what would make her teaching better. "I ratio-nalized… what I needed were even more creative, more open topics (for writing).... I needed better students—kids who consistently made my assignments their own,… who came to me prepared by their teachers to write well. I needed better colleagues." (Atwell, 1998, p. 11).

I find it interesting that Atwell also complained about the students and felt that if only somehow the kids were different and their prior classrooms were more effective—she would be successful, just like the teacher in the planning meeting mentioned at the beginning of this article. The fact was that Atwell needed to change, just as many teachers have to change before they can truly help middle school students learn. Atwell went on to say "I didn't know how to share responsibility with my students and I wasn't too sure I wanted to. I liked the vantage of my big desk. I liked being creative, setting topic and pace… taking charge. Wasn't that my job? If responsibility for their writing shifted to my students, what would I do?" (Atwell, 1998, p. 13).

Atwell articulated the unspoken fear that many educators hold—what will my role be if I no longer dictate every move in the classroom?

Atwell articulated the unspoken fear that many educators hold—what will my role be if I no longer dictate every move in the classroom? We know what the research says about development and the needs of students. As teachers, we have to change our selves to be able to create classrooms and schools where students can learn. We need to let go of the image of what teachers *used* to do and what we *thought* kids were like. Our society has changed, and those kids who, as Atwell said, "didn't make peace with the curriculum," who used to leave school or fail, can no longer be ignored or pushed out. Society is demanding that all students be given the opportunity to learn. Standards are being set, and the expectation is that teachers can and must help students learn.

It is not easy to let go of the tightly held beliefs about teaching that shape educators' perceptions about their role and responsibilities in a classroom. However, we cannot close our eyes to what we now know about how students learn. We need to overcome our fears about giving students a voice in their own learning if we want to enable all students to reach their potential.

Becoming Responsive to Young Adolescents' Needs

Specifically, what can teachers do to move out from behind the desk and work with the students to develop appropriate educational experiences? The answer has always been out there—in the concepts proposed by the middle school model. Two primary areas to start with are the advisory program and the curriculum.

In their 25-year perspective on middle schools, McEwin, Dickinson, and Jenkins (1996) described research on the implementation of the middle school concept which indicated that teacher-based guidance programs had declined slightly from 1988 to 1993. For advisory programs that were in place, there seemed to be an increase of time allotted to them, although there was some question as to what was occurring during those advisory times. Again, lip service to the concepts of supporting young adolescent needs and creating strong connections between caring adults and adolescents seems to be the common experience. Advisory is a foreign experience for many teachers, and McEwin, Dickinson, and Jenkins' work confirmed that teachers are often opposed to this role. Lack of preparation heightens teachers' feelings of inadequacy when leading advisory activities, discussions, and lessons.

Any job that makes one stretch into areas that are uncomfortable has the potential to make them a better person.

Teaching, which addresses new ideas, knowledge, and competencies that students need to develop into adulthood, is not static. Any job that makes one stretch into areas that are uncomfortable has the potential to make them a better person as they rise to meet the new challenges. Teachers will benefit from meeting this challenge.

So what should advisory look like? It is not a good option to simply use advisory time for a study hall or revert to an administrative home room model. Students at this age need opportunities to talk about issues they are concerned about, they need to feel a sense of belonging, and they need to connect with an adult who cares. If teachers view their students as emerging adults and acknowledge the needs and concerns of young adoles-cents, then it makes sense that the teacher's role must also include facilitating opportunities for student discussion and skill building in the social and emotional areas. All of these things happen in a well developed and carefully facilitated advisory program.

Once middle school teachers have embraced the effective use of advisory programs to support their students, the other area where educators need to let go of their preconceived images of middle school students is in the area of curriculum. There are two important shifts that need to occur: Content has to connect to the lives of the students in order to be meaningful, and students need to have some voice in the decisions about what they will learn.

While integrated curriculum may hook students and excite them about learning, it is a scary step for many teachers.

Inviting students to share in curriculum decision making is another difficult step for teachers. Atwell (1998), describing what she had learned about curriculum for young adolescents, stated "Learning is more likely to happen when students like what they are doing. Learning is also more likely when students can be involved and active and when they can learn from and with other students" (p. 69).

Making Connections

Giving the students a voice in deciding what they learn is only part of the curriculum shift that must happen in middle school classrooms. Interdisciplinary or integrated curriculum is another way to make the learning meaningful, but it is another middle school concept that teachers often resist. Brazee (1995) stated, "While there are numerous arguments for an integrated curriculum, perhaps the most compelling one is that an integrated curriculum best addresses the unique needs of young adolescents, yet it is the least developed in practice" (p. 16). Another curriculum expert, Beane (1995), added "Curriculum integration begins with real-life problems as themes, proceeds according to the organic integration of knowledge and serves the purpose of enhancing self and world meaning" (p. 28). George, Stevenson, Thomason, and Beane (1992) suggested that middle school curriculum needs to begin by seeking out answers to young adolescent's concerns about their world, and that teachers must discuss this with their students as a part of curriculum planning. This is very different from the traditional curriculum developed and implemented by most teachers. However, while it may "hook" students and excite them about learning, it is a scary step for many teachers.

Many of us are fearful of going somewhere where we have not been before. Descriptions of appropriate middle school curriculum suggest major shifts from the way teachers have developed their lessons in the past. "The definition of who is learning in the school should be expanded to include teachers and other adults.... Adults cannot simply provide answers to powerful questions,

but must seek them along with young people" (George, Stevenson, Thomason, & Beane, 1992, p. 97). This echoes what Atwell proposed: that we must be involved with our students in their learning. But if a teacher does not have everything all lined up and ready to go in the classroom because she wants to ask students for their input, then there are many opportunities for the teacher to "lose control." This is the heart of many teachers' fears: that the students will overwhelm them with their voices and energy and the teacher will lose control in the classroom.

Teaming provides an answer—holding hands and going together makes the process more comfortable. Teachers who are developing new curricula and seeking connections to provide adolescents with relevant learning experiences cannot make this change overnight. Working together they can structure class discussions on curriculum development to allow for student voice and yet maintain a focus. School systems should provide scheduling that supports teaming and does not undermine efforts to link content and help students make sense of the curriculum.

Teachers who struggle to let go of the control they traditionally have held over the curriculum and to shift their view of young adolescent learners need support. This support must come from school districts in the form of money and time. McEwin, Dickinson, and Jenkins state that the "lack of money to support two prep times for development of team teacher project(s) and no common planning time for teachers" (1996, p. 107) are major obstacles to the implementation of middle school concepts. Teachers need to discuss and reflect with their colleagues about their fears and frustrations as they work to move their classroom interactions in a new direction. Two prep periods give teachers time to plan for their own classes but also provide valuable interaction time for colleagues during team planning time. Common planning time underpins the concept of teaming and provides the opportunity for personal interactions that must be provided to teachers before they can model it for their students. Interdisciplinary curriculum cannot be generated and coordinated if the teachers involved never have a chance to talk. Districts that provide the financial means to support two prep times for faculty teams are doing their part to help teachers implement middle level concepts.

Support for Change

With all that we know about young adolescents, why is it that despite 25 years of discussion and study on the positive effects of middle schools, some districts still refuse to provide the resources that will enable students' needs to be met? A longitudinal study of middle schools involved in comprehensive school transformation identified that there was higher achievement by students in schools with high levels of implementation of the middle school concept (Felner, Jackson, Kasak, Mulhall, Brand, & Flowers, 1997). More than 15,000 students were involved in this study which showed increased levels of achievement in reading, mathematics, and language arts, The implication from this study is clear: Young people in schools that implemented middle school concepts at a high level "achieve a higher level academically than those in non-implemented schools and substantially better than those in partially implemented schools" (Felner, et. al., 1997, p. 544).

The more comprehensive the implementation of middle school concepts, the better the results for students.

Research such as this should not be ignored. We need to disseminate what we know about middle school teaching and learning so parents, teachers, and administrators are as aware of the best practices for middle schools as they are with medical research. As Felner's study indicated, the more comprehensive the implementation of middle school concepts, such as those in *Turning Points* (Carnegie Council on Adolescent Development, 1989), the better the results for students. Indeed, "the presence or absence of a particular element of the program may affect the levels of implementation of other components." (Felner, et. al., 1997, p. 543.) Middle schools and middle school teachers should not pick and choose which of the middle level components they want to use. All of the elements need to be present, especially those difficult for teachers to embrace—advisory and student centered curriculum. Time and money for teacher development and interaction are crucial to the effective implementation of all of the middle level concepts. Parents need to be informed that schools cannot simply consider what is efficient, but must find the resources to implement what is good for young people. Referendums that provide money to fund the operation of middle schools must be supported. In addition, those responsible for educational funding in our state governments need to be informed about the components of effective middle schools and their positive impact on young adolescents' educational experiences.

Making a Difference

For students to be supported in their middle school years, for them to be a part of the school, teachers need to be supported by district funding so they have the time, money, and other resources to develop their understandings of teaming, curriculum, and student centered learning. However, in describing barriers that can impede the movement towards implementation of middle school concepts, Lipsitz, Mizell, Jackson, and Austin (1997) stated that "A lack of individual will to persevere despite formidable obstacles has been the most persistent, albeit understandable, barrier to school reform." (1997, p. 539).

Ultimately, teachers must let go of their old perceptions of young adolescents, learn to enjoy and appreciate their students as young adults, and allow themselves to learn how to work in teams to implement concepts such as advisory and student centered curriculum.

Middle school students are still open to new ideas, still searching for answers and undecided about who they are and what they will ultimately be. This creates a wonderful opportunity for teachers to be a part of their journey into adulthood. But as with all adults, we cannot force the learning process, we must invite the students to join us on the journey. The children who are in our middle schools today are the best we have. There are none of those "perfect children" hidden away somewhere waiting for teachers to fill their heads with knowledge. Students today are a part of a world that is active, mobile, and ever-changing. We need to change our perception of students and help them deal with the issues they will have to face as adults.

This will only happen when we bring the child into our school, into our classroom, and make the school a place that reveals their world. Middle schools will never reach their potential until the human element, the teachers, stretch themselves and learn to focus on the students. Franklin D. Roosevelt once said "we have nothing to fear but fear itself"—a great quote for a middle school teacher. We cannot fear going forward, changing our world view, and inviting young adolescent learners into the classroom as partners. Through teacher commitment in the areas of advisory and student centered curriculum, coupled with district support, middle level classrooms can provide a meaningful learning experience for every child in the school.

References

Atwell, N. (1998). *In the middle: New understandings about writing, reading and learning.* Portsmouth, NH: Boynton/Cook.

Beane, J. A. (1995). Myths, politics and meaning in curriculum integration. In Y. Siu-Runyan & V. Faircloth (Eds.), *Beyond separate subjects: Integrative learning at the middle level* (pp. 25–38). Norwood, MA: Christopher-Gordon.

Brazee,E. (1995). An integrated curriculum supports young adolescent development. In Y. Siu-Runyan & V. Faircloth (Eds.), *Beyond separate subjects: Integrative learning at the middle level* (pp. 5–24). Norwood, MA: Christopher-Gordon.

Carnegie Council on Adolescent Development. (1989). *Turning Points: Preparing American youth for the 21st century.* New York: Carnegie Corporation.

Eccles, J. S., Midgely, C., Buchanan, C. M., Wigfield, A., Reuman, D., & Mac Iver, D. (1993). Development during adolescence: The impact of stage/environment fit. *American Psychologist, 48*(2), 90–101.

Eccles, J. S., Lord, S. E., Roeser, R. W., Barber, B. L., & Jozefowicz, D. M. H. (1996). The association of school transitions in early adolescence with developmental trajectories through high school. In J. Schulenberg, J. Maggs & K. Hurrelmann, (Eds.), *Health risks and developmental transitions during adolescence* (pp. 283–320). New York: Cambridge University Press.

Eccles, J. S., & Midgley, C. (1989). Stage environment fit: Developmentally appropriate classrooms for young adolescents. In C. Ames & R. Ames (Eds.), *Research on motivation in education* (pp. 139–186). New York: Academic Press.

Eccles, J. S. & Wigfield, A. (1997). Young adolescent development. In J. L. Irvin, (Ed.), *What current research says to the middle level practitioner* (pp. 15–29). Columbus, Ohio: National Middle School Association.

Felner, R. D., Jackson, A. W., Kasak, D., Mulhall, P., Brand, S., & Flowers, N. (1997). The impact of school reform for the middle years. *Phi Delta Kappan, 78*(7), 528–532, 541–550.

George, P. S., Stevenson, C., Thomason, J., & Beane, J. (1992). *The middle school and beyond.* Alexandria, VA: Association for Supervision and Curriculum Development.

Johnson, D. W. (1990). *Reaching out: Interpersonal effectiveness and self-actualization* (4th ed.). Englewood Cliffs: NJ: Prentice-Hall.

Johnson, D. W., & Johnson, F. P. (1991). *Joining together* (4th ed.). Englewood Cliffs: NJ: Prentice-Hall.

Lipsitz, J., Mizell, M. H., Jackson, A. W., & Austin, L. M. (1997). Speaking with one voice: A manifesto for middle-grades reform. *Phi Delta Kappan, 78*(7), 533–540.

McEwin, C. K. & Dickinson, T. S. (1995). *The professional preparation of middle level teachers: Profiles of successful programs.* Columbus, Ohio: National Middle School Association.

McEwin, C. K., Dickinson, T. S. & Jenkins, D. M. (1996). *American middle schools: Practices and progress—A 25 year perspective.* Columbus, OH: National Middle School Association.

Mac Iver, D., & Reuman, D. (1988, April). *Decision making in the classroom and early adolescents' valuing of mathematics.* Paper presented at the annual meeting of the American Educational Research Association, New Orleans.

Debra Eckerman Pitton is an associate professor of education at Gustavus Adolphus College, St. Peter, Minnesota, E-mail: dpitton@gustavus.edu

From *Middle School Journal,* September 2001, pp. 14-20. © 2001 by the National Middle School Association.

Differing Perspectives, Common Ground: The Middle School and Gifted Education Relationship

What Research Says

Middle school educators and advocates for the gifted share much common ground for addressing the needs of a wide variety of learners: flexible pacing, independent study, and teaching thinking skills.

By Hilda C. Rosselli & Judith L. Irvin

A curious relationship has evolved over the years between the fields of gifted education and middle grades education. On an initial glance, beliefs important to each field indicate an amazing overlap in philosophy and practices. However, when middle grades philosophy positioned heterogeneous grouping as one of the preeminent guideposts for policies and practices endorsed by the field, the common ground between the two fields lessened. Leaders in gifted education, unable to embrace a total abandonment of grouping, responded vehemently and expressed reservations regarding the ability of the middle school movement to meet the needs of high ability students (Gallagher, Coleman, & Nelson, 1995; Plucker & McIntire, 1996; Sicola, 1990; Tomlinson, 1992; 1994). The resulting differences reframed the relationship between experts from gifted education and middle grades education and fueled lively debates on the moral and efficacious nature of ability grouping. Others sought to re-examine the goodness of fit between the two movements by moving beyond the rhetoric of differences towards a healthier focus on programs and practices (Coleman, Gallagher, & Howard, 1993; Coleman & Gallagher, 1995; Mills & Durden, 1992; Rosselli, 1995). At the same time, with the advent of the National Research Center on the Gifted and Talented and federally funded Javits grants, a more defined research focus in gifted education provided a rich source for examining implications for middle level education. This article provides an overview of the literature that has historically framed the

debates between gifted education and middle grades education followed by discussion of research that seeks common ground between the two fields and implications relative to middle school education policies and practices that hold promise for considering the unique needs of high ability students.

Nature and definition of giftedness and intelligence

Although the field of gifted education has traditionally been grounded in the use of IQ scores for identification and definition purposes, the last twenty years has seen a growing interest in other views of intelligence and giftedness. On the heels of Howard Gardner's work (1983) has followed a redefining of gifted education by well-renowned experts (Gagne, 1995; Feldhusen, 1992; Renzulli, 1994; Treffinger, 1992) who are not convinced that traditional IQ measures are sufficient for identifying the unique and individual talents of capable youth. With the publication of National Excellence: A Case for Developing America's Talent (U.S. Department of Education, 1993), the term "talent" appeared liberally throughout the report and served as a cornerstone for encouraging more overlap between education reform and the development of individual gifts and talents. Furthermore, the 1990s saw growth in a researchable knowledge base regarding the diversity rather than the homogeneity within the gifted population (Betts & Neihart, 1988; Ford, 1993; Maker, 1996; Nielsen, Higgins, Hammond, & Williams, 1993). This work specifically focuses attention on the historically under-represented presence of students from culturally diverse backgrounds, from low socioeconomic environments, with limited English proficiency, and with two exceptionalities.

Characteristics and needs of gifted students

A number of developmental characteristics that apply to middle level adolescents apply to gifted adolescents as well, particularly: rapid physical growth, varying levels of cognitive operations, sporadic brain growth, affective ambivalence, and capacity of introspection. Like all adolescents, teens who are gifted must also cope with the achievement of independence, discovery of identity as a person, exploration and acceptance of sexuality, development of meaningful interpersonal relationships, and establishment of personal values and philosophy (Clark, 1988). Clearly, being gifted places some additional twists on the already difficult tasks of adolescent maturation. Wallace (1985) described the gifted adolescent as a doubly marginal individual. The obvious move is away from the family, which is part of the adolescent experience, as well as a move away from the system that perhaps supported and nurtured a specific gift or talent. This new autonomy may cause an additional burden or responsibility for the gifted adolescent, just at a time when he/she has few appropriate peer role models to emulate. Manaster and Powell (1983) reported that gifted adolescents may feel "out of stage" due to their perfectionism and focus on success, causing them to be out of touch with their immediate environment. In addition, alienation from their age-peer group may be influenced by gifted students' awareness of their unusual abilities or interests, causing them to feel "out of phase." Lastly, these students may feel "out of sync" as though they do not, should not, or cannot fit in. Buescher (1985) also found that ownership, or the simultaneous owning and questioning of the abilities of these youngsters, may compete with the beliefs that a debt is owed towards parents, teachers, and society.

To be gifted and to be under-challenged in school creates another undesirable combination. High ability students have reported school work being too easy (Tomlinson, 1995), spending little or no time studying, and group work leading to gifted students doing all the work (Clinkenbeard, 1991). In one study of high ability middle level students, Plucker and McIntire (1996) found that students exhibited a variety of nonconstructive behaviors such as interacting with peers, selected attention, and reduced effort when the level of stimulation or challenge was inappropriate. In addition, teachers in the study did not always recognize when high ability students were trying to stimulate themselves intellectually and sometimes even allowed the students to pursue nonconstructive behaviors rather than adapt or modify instruction.

Instructional implications

Middle school instruction is intended to respond to the recognized developmental needs of young adolescent students. Earlier research on brain periodicity fueled support for a movement away from abstract types of thinking. The resulting de-emphasis on academics also acknowledged that young adolescent students do not always prize school achievement and that over-challenging students at the middle school level could contribute to poor self-concept (National Association of Secondary School Principals, 1989). Tomlinson (1992) has questioned the implications of accepting findings that only 20% of 14 year-olds use even early formal operations. In her view, this finding still creates a need to explore viable options for these 20 percenters, many of whom might be identified as gifted students. In their study of talented teenagers, Csikszentmihalyi, Rathunde, & Whalen (1993) found that students seem to benefit more from a differentiated (more complex and even competitive) learning environment than an integrated (supportive and comfortable) environment. Beane and Lipka's (1986) finding that only 25% of an individual's academic school achievement is linked to IQ while 50% is related to self-concept has posed another dilemma. For gifted students, academic success plays an important role in maintaining self-esteem. This aspect of self-concept is supported by students' intellectual peers who act as "mental catalysts and who provide realistic perspective of their abilities" (Sicola, 1990). Furthermore, Bloom (1985) found in his study that "... exceptional levels of talent development require certain types of environmental support, special experiences, excellent teaching, and appropriate motivational encouragement at each stage of development" (p. 543).

To allow any student to underachieve continually can result in a negative impact on self-concept which, in turn, can impact future performance. Ironically, it was the middle school movement that reminded educators that lockstep-graded practices "force[s] many students to compromise the integrity of their individual readiness" (NASSP, 1989, p. 7). In 1988, Chapman and McAlpine conducted a study to examine the academic self-concepts of mainstreamed intellectually gifted and average students over a two-year period. They measured perceptions of ability in the areas of math, reading, spelling, general ability, penmanship, neatness, and confidence/satisfaction at the beginning and the end of the sixth grade year and then again at the end of the seventh year. These researchers found that, with the exception of penmanship, the students identified as gifted had overall higher perceptions of general ability as well as specific academic areas. However, the gifted students showed lower perceptions of school satisfaction than the average students. Chapman and McAlpine felt that lack of challenge in a mainstreamed environment may cause boredom which could explain the lower scores.

In a qualitative study conducted in a sixth grade gifted class, Clinkenbeard (1991) found that students who were identified gifted felt that their general classroom teachers and peers held sometimes unrealistic expectations of them. Teachers expected them to achieve and behave at a gifted level consistently, some days failing to acknowledge that the students' achievements were linked to effort as well as ability. Students who participated in the study also felt that they were graded harder than were other students and their age peers were sometimes jealous and insulting. Gifted adolescents appear to develop a variety of coping strategies to deal with these types of pressures, including the use of one's abilities to help others in classes, making friends with other bright students, selecting programs and classes designed for gifted/talented students, and achieving in areas outside of academics/school. In their study of gifted adolescents' adjustment, Buescher and Higharn (1989) found gender differences indicating girls to be more at risk for avoiding or walking away from their talents during early adolescence whereas boys more often select friends that provide support for their talent areas.

Equity and excellence

The greatest philosophical difference that separates advocates of gifted education and those of the middle school concept does not lend itself to traditional research methodology. As Plowman (1988) stated, "Education of the gifted and talented is consistent with the philosophical principles and basic tenets of our educational and political systems which include: concern for individuals, individualized instruction, equal opportunity, and equal access" (p. 60). Yet, services that address the needs of high ability learners are sometimes suspect and equated with social discrimination (Johnston & Markle, 1986; McKay, 1995). Helpful to this discussion is a closer look at what Salkind (1988) addressed as two other types of equity. Horizontal equity involves the equal treatment of individuals who have similar needs while vertical equity exists when children who have different needs are treated differently; otherwise referred to as the "unequal treatment of unequals." Both types of equity must guide policy and practices involving services for high ability adolescents.

Ability grouping

As mentioned previously, the main point of disagreement between the two fields often centers around the issue of ability grouping. Kulik and Kulik's

(1987) second meta-analysis coded 82 studies of between-class and 19 within-class programs and described the outcomes on a common scale. For inclusion in their analysis, the studies had to be quantitative, include both a control group and an experimental group with a similar aptitude, and involve a classroom rather than a lab setting. In 49 studies of comprehensive between-class grouping, the effect sizes were .12 for high, .04 for middle, and .00 for low groups with the difference between the high and low groups statistically significant at $p < .05$. In 25 studies dealing with special classrooms only for talented students, variation of effect size from -.27 to 1.25 led the Kuliks to believe that factors other than grouping played a role in the outcome. Two features showing significant relationships in an analysis of total class grouping within the classroom were instructor effects and flexibility/permanence of assignment. The Kuliks concluded that the strongest and clearest effects of grouping were in programs designed especially for talented students. They also concluded that programs designed for all students in a grade, rather than only for talented students, had significantly lower effects. The Kuliks noted that their results are, in some regards, similar to those of Slavin, particularly their findings that comprehensive grouping between classes has little or no effect, either positive or negative.

As the debates have ensued, Slavin (1990) has led a discussion on the practice of "regrouping" for select subject areas as an alternative to ability grouping. To be instructionally effective, Slavin believes that regrouping plans must meet two conditions: 1) instructional level and pace must be completely adapted to student performance level, and 2) regrouping should only be done for one or two subjects so that students remain in a heterogeneous setting most of the day. The National Association for Gifted Children believes that this type of flexible use of grouping will help match students' advanced abilities and knowledge while still maintaining the important social goals of the middle school movement (National Association for Gifted Children, 1994). However, many still question the practice of keeping high ability students in a heterogeneous setting for the majority of the day if their cognitive needs require more challenge.

Revisiting program organization

Over the years a wide variety of programs have been developed to meet the needs of gifted adolescents. Gifted education has rallied around options that move beyond the traditional pull-out and self-contained programs, such as early admission or acceleration options, special schools, mentorships, continuous progress, dual enrollment, and within-class individualization. As an alternative to formal grouping, Renzulli (1994) researched the use of Talent Pools which are composed of the top 15–20 percent of the general population using either general ability or one or more specific areas of ability. Students in these talent pools are then offered opportunities to learn subjects at a faster pace using "curriculum compacting"; thus, freeing up time for enrichment within the general education class. In addition, thousands of students now participate each year in Talent Searches during which seventh and eighth grade students take the SAT. The results of these talent searches can help districts identify able students who may be in need of more academic challenge. Allowing students to take Algebra as early as seventh grade permits them to be able to take more advanced math electives during high school such as: Differential Equations, Real Analysis, Linear Algebra, or Theory of Numbers.

Regardless of the delivery model employed, certain assumptions undergirding the philosophy of gifted services must be supported at the middle school level.

All children progress through challenging material at their own pace. Gifted students often reach mastery in significantly less time than other learners.

- Achieving success for all students is not equated with achieving the same results for all students.
- Most students gain self-esteem and self-confidence from mastering work that initially seems slightly beyond their grasp.
- In addition to sometimes serving as peer role models, high ability students also need to spend time learning new material and stretching to their full potential.
- Flexible grouping of gifted learners should be offered based on students' abilities and talents in these areas.
- Professionals working with gifted students require ongoing specialized training to support their ability to work with this population of students.
- Program strategies used with gifted students should address academic as well as social and personal needs.

In 1995, Coleman and Gallagher conducted a study to identify schools where the middle school movement was blended with quality program services for students who are gifted. Successful sites used instructional grouping to offer challenges to students as well as some form of enrichment. A variety of differentiation approaches were utilized, including mentoring, flexible pacing, independent studies, interdisciplinary units, and thinking skills. In addition, each site also had at least one person on staff who was knowledgeable about the needs of gifted students.

The call for more collaboration between the gifted and the middle school movements will be enhanced if schools first explore the common ground existing between the two fields (Coleman & Gallagher, 1992), namely, that both are committed to meeting the unique developmental needs of students during early adolescence. As programs for the middle school gifted student continue to evolve, the following touchstones can be useful in guiding program decisions:

1. Do the program services support excellence over mediocrity?
2. Will the program offerings help students see in themselves a strength, passion, or capability that can become a highly developed talent?
3. Do the program offerings support students' varying learning needs, e.g., pace, and style?
4. Do the program offerings eliminate an artificial ceiling for learning?
5. Do the program offerings promote depth of understanding rather than just access to quantity?
6. Do the program offerings promote the gifted student's capacities for creative and critical thinking skills?
7. Do the program offerings provide a balance of curricular and co-curricular offerings including appropriate exploratory activities?
8. Do the program offerings offer opportunities to develop an understanding for relationships within and between disciples?

References

Beane, J., & Lipka, R. (1986). *Self-concept, self-esteem, and the curriculum.* New York: Teachers College Press.

Betts, G., & Neihart, M. (1988). Profiles of the gifted. *Gifted Child Quarterly, 32*(2), 248–253.

Bloom, B. (1985). Generalizations about talent development. In B. Bloom (Ed.), *Developing talent in young people* (pp. 507–549). New York: Ballantine Books.

Buescher, T. M. (1985). A framework for understanding the social and emotional development of gifted and talented adolescents. *Roeper Review, 8*, 10–15.

Buescher, T. M., & Higham, S. J. (1989). A developmental study of adjustment among gifted adolescents. In J. Van Tassel-Baska & P. Olszcwski-Kubilius (Eds.), *Patterns of influence on gifted learners: The home, the self, and the school* (pp. 102–124). New York: Teachers College Press.

Chapman, J., & McAlpine, D. (1988). Students' perceptions of ability. *Gifted Child Quarterly, 32*(1), 222–225.

Clark, B. (1988). *Growing up gifted: Developing the potential of children at home and school* (3rd ed.). Columbus, OH: Charles E. Merrill.

Clinkenbeard, P. R. (1991). Unfair expectations: A pilot study of middle school students' comparisons of gifted and regular classes. *Journal for the Education of the Gifted, 15*(1), 56–63.

Coleman, M., & Gallagher, J. (1992). *Middle school survey report: Impact on gifted students.* Chapel Hill, NC: Gifted Education Policy Studies Program, University of North Carolina at Chapel Hill.

Coleman, M. R., & Gallagher, J. (1995). The successful blending of gifted education with middle schools and cooperative learning: Two studies. *Journal for the Education of the Gifted, 18*(4), 362–384.

Coleman, M. R., Gallagher, J., & Howard, J. (1993). *Middle school site visit report: Five schools in profile.* Chapel Hill, NC: Gifted Education Policy Studies Program, University of North Carolina at Chapel Hill.

Csikszentmihalyi, M., Rathunde, K., & Whalen, S. (1993). *Talented teenagers: The roots of success and failure*. Cambridge, UK: Cambridge University Press.

Feldhusen, J. (1992). *TIDE: Talent identification and development in education*. Sarasota, FL: Center for Creative Learning.

Ford, D. (1993). An investigation of the paradox of underachievement among gifted black students. *Roeper Review, 16*(2), 78–84.

Gagne, F. (1995). From giftedness to talent: A developmental model and its impact on the language of the field. *Roeper Review, 18*(2), 103–111.

Gallagher, J., Coleman, M. R., & Nelson, S. (1995). Perceptions of educational reform by educators representing middle schools, cooperative learning, and gifted education. *Gifted Child Quarterly, 39*(2), 66–76.

Gardner, H. (1983). *Frames of mind*. New York: Basic Books.

Johnston, J. H., & Markle, G. (1986). *What research says to the middle level practitioner*. Columbus, OH: National Middle School Association.

Kulik, J. A., & Kulik, C. L. C. (1987). Effects of ability grouping on student achievement. *Equity and excellence, 23* (1&2) 22–30.

Maker, C. L. (1996). Identification of gifted minority students: A national problem, needed changes, and a promising solution. *Gifted Child Quarterly, 40*(1), 41–50.

Manaster, G. J., & Powell, P. M. (1983). A framework for understanding gifted adolescents' psychological maladjustment. *Roeper Review, 6*(2), 70–73.

McKay, J. (1995). *Schools in the middle: Developing a middle-level orientation*. Thousand Oaks, CA: Corwin Press.

Mills, C. I., & Durden, W. G. (1992). Cooperative learning and ability grouping: An issue of choice. *Gifted Child Quarterly, 36*(1), 11–16.

National Association of Secondary School Principals. (1989). *Middle level education's responsibility for intellectual development*. Reston, VA: Author.

National Association for Gifted Children. (1994). *Position paper: Middle schools*. Washington, DC: Author.

Nielsen, E., Higgins, D., Harmmond, A., & Williams, R. (1993). Gifted children with disabilities. *Gifted Child Today, 15*(5), 9–12.

Plowman, P. (1988). Elitism. *Gifted Child Today, 56*(3), 60.

Plucker, J. A., & McIntire, J. (1996). Academic survivability in high-potential middle school students. *Gifted Child Quarterly, 40*(1), 7–14.

Renzulli, J. (1994). *Schools for talent development: A practical plan for total school improvement*. Mansfield Center, CT: Creative Learning Press.

Rosselli, H. (1995). Meeting gifted students halfway in the middle school. *Schools in the Middle, 5*(3), 12–17.

Salkind, N. (1988). *Equity and excellence: The case of mandating services for the gifted child*. Unpublished document. University of Kansas.

Sicola, P. K. (1990). Where do gifted students fit? An examination of middle school philosophy as it relates to ability grouping and the gifted learner. *Journal for the Education of the Gifted, 14*(1), 37–49.

Slavin, R. E. (1990). Achievement effects of ability grouping in secondary schools: A best evidence synthesis. *Review of Educational Research, 60*(3), 471–499.

Tomlinson, C. A. (1992). Gifted education and the middle school movement: Two voices on teaching the academically talented. *Journal for the Education of the Gifted, 15*(3), 206–238.

Tomlinson, C. A. (1994). Gifted learners: The boomerang kids of middle school? *Roeper Review, 16*(3), 177–182.

Tomlinson, C. A. (1995). Deciding to differentiate instruction in middle school: One school's journey. *Gifted Child Quarterly, 39*(2), 77–87.

Treffinger, D. (1992). Programming for giftedness: Needed directions. *INNOTECH Journal, 16*(1), 54–61.

U.S. Department of Education. (1993). *National excellence: A case for developing America's talent*. Washington, DC: Author.

Wallace, D. (1985). Giftedness and the construction of a creative life. In F. Horowitz (Ed.), *The gifted and talented: Development perspectives* (pp. 361–386). Washington, DC: American Psychological Association.

Hilda C. Rosselli is the Associate Dean for Undergraduate Programs in the College of Education at the University of South Florida, Tampa. E-mail: rosselli@tempest.coedu.usf.edu

Judith L. Irvin is a professor at Florida State University, Tallahassee. E-mail: irvin@coe.fsu.edu

Originally appeared in the January 2001 issue of *Middle School Journal*, pp. 57-62. Used with permission from National Middle School Association.

UNIT 3
Exceptional and Culturally Diverse Children

Unit Selections

Key Points to Consider

- Describe the characteristics of ADHD children, and discuss the strategies teachers can use to help.

- Who are the gifted and talented? How can knowledge of their characteristics and learning needs help to provide them with an appropriate education?

- What cultural differences exist in our society? How would multicultural education help teachers deal more effectively with these differences?

- What are some of the criticisms concerning multicultural programs?

 **Links: www.dushkin.com/online/**
These sites are annotated in the World Wide Web pages.

The Council for Exceptional Children
http://www.cec.sped.org/index.html

Global SchoolNet Foundation
http://www.gsn.org

International Project: Multicultural Pavilion
http://curry.edschool.virginia.edu/curry/centers/multicultural/papers.html

Let 1000 Flowers Bloom/Kristen Nicholson-Nelson
http://teacher.scholastic.com/professional/assessment/100flowers.htm

Multicultural Publishing and Education Catalog
http://www.mpec.org

National Attention Deficit Disorder Association
http://www.add.org

National MultiCultural Institute (NMCI)
http://www.nmci.org

The Equal Educational Opportunity Act for All Handicapped Children (Public Law 94-142) gives disabled children the right to an education in the least-restrictive environment, due process, and an individualized educational program that is specifically designed to meet their needs. Professionals and parents of exceptional children are responsible for developing and implementing an appropriate educational program for each child. The application of these ideas to classrooms across the nation at first caused great concern among educators and parents. Classroom teachers, whose training did not prepare them for working with the exceptional child, expressed negative attitudes about mainstreaming. Special resource teachers also expressed concern that mainstreaming would mitigate the effectiveness of special programs for the disabled and would force cuts in

services. Parents feared that their children would not receive the special services they required because of governmental red tape and delays in proper diagnosis and placement.

It has been more than two decades since the implementation of P.L. 94-142, which was amended by the Individuals with Disabilities Education Act (IDEA) in 1991 and introduced the term "inclusion." Inclusion tries to ensure that disabled children will be fully integrated within the classroom. Many of the above concerns have been studied by psychologists and educators, and their findings have often influenced policy. For example, research has indicated that inclusion is more effective when regular classroom teachers and special resource teachers work cooperatively with disabled children.

The articles concerning the educationally disabled confront some of these issues. David Aloyzy Zera presents "The Oppression of Inclusion," and the authors of "Chaos in the Classroom: Looking at ADHD" offer a description of attention deficit hyperactivity disorder and effective ways to treat it. Other exceptional children are the gifted and talented. These children are rapid learners who can absorb, organize, and apply concepts more effectively than the average child. They often have IQs of 140 or more and are convergent thinkers (that is, they give the correct answer to teacher or test questions). Convergent thinkers are usually models of good behavior and academic performance, and they respond to instruction easily; teachers generally value such children and often nominate them for gifted programs. There are other children, however, who do not score well on standardized tests of intelligence because their thinking is more divergent (i.e., they can imagine more than one answer to teacher or test questions). These gifted divergent thinkers may

not respond to traditional instruction. They may become bored, respond to questions in unique and disturbing ways, and appear uncooperative and disruptive. Many teachers do not understand these unconventional thinkers and fail to identify them as gifted. In fact, such children are sometimes labeled as emotionally disturbed or mentally retarded because of the negative impressions they make on their teachers. Because of the differences between these types of students, a great deal of controversy surrounds programs for the gifted. Such programs should enhance the self-esteem of all gifted and talented children, motivate and challenge them, and help them realize their creative potential. The two articles in the subsection on gifted children consider the characteristics of giftedness, and they explain how to identify gifted students and provide them with an appropriate education.

The third subsection of this unit concerns student diversity. Just as labeling may adversely affect the disabled child, it may also affect the child who comes from a minority ethnic background where the language and values are quite different from those of the mainstream culture. The term "disadvantaged" is often used to describe these children, but it is negative, stereotypical, and apt to result in a self-fulfilling prophecy whereby teachers perceive such children as incapable of learning. Teachers should provide academically and culturally diverse children with experiences that they might have missed in the restricted environment of their homes and neighborhoods. Gary K. Clabaugh in "Teaching the New Immigrants: How 'Multicultural' an Educator Are You Prepared to Be?" takes issue with some aspects of multicultural programs, while other articles in this section address these individual differences and suggest strategies for teaching these diverse children.

Chaos in the Classroom: Looking at ADHD

Diagnosing and helping students with ADHD requires the collaboration of parents, clinicians, teachers, and students.

Steven C. Schlozman and Vivien R. Schlozman

Students increasingly walk through the classroom door wearing invisible labels and prescriptions. A list of psychiatric and learning disorders that was intended to clarify the difficulties different students experience has instead bewildered teachers and administrators. Educators must make sense of their students' new diagnostic criteria and glean from this information the most effective ways to assist their pupils. Given the enormous increase in the diagnosis and treatment of attention deficit hyperactivity disorder (ADHD) among school-age children, neuropsychiatric problems characterized by inattention and hyperactivity are pressing classroom issues.

Students diagnosed with ADHD often arrive in the classroom with medication and teaching recommendations that are based on completed psychological testing. In spite of these recommendations, teachers frequently have little or no contact with their students' clinicians. Tight budgets, large classrooms, and often multiple students with the same diagnosis who require different teaching strategies substantially challenge the educator's primary objective: to teach and inspire every student dynamically and efficiently. Reaching that goal starts with an understanding of ADHD and how teachers can help students who have been diagnosed with the disorder.

Describing and Diagnosing ADHD

ADHD is a neuropsychiatric disorder that begins before 7 years of age (American Psychiatric Association, 1994). Problems in the three core domains of *inattention, hyperactivity*, and *impulsivity* characterize the disorder.

Clinicians define *inattention* as age-inappropriate poor attention span and *hyperactivity* as age-inappropriate

increased activity in multiple settings. For example, an inattentive child may pay poor attention to details or appear as though his or her mind is elsewhere. Often, the child has difficulty sustaining a single activity. One mother describes her son's bedtime difficulties: He starts to brush his teeth, follows the cat into the playroom while his mouth is full of toothpaste, notices the blocks and sits down to play, and in two minutes turns on the computer at the other end of the room.

Most children will occasionally display many of the aspects ascribed to ADHD, and this recognition may account for much of the controversy surrounding the disorder.

Hyperactive children may fidget excessively and have difficulties playing quietly. Children with ADHD display, sometimes paradoxically, a level of inflexibility that leads them to experience intense frustration when asked to break from one activity and move on to something new. The child will appear to have well-honed attentional skills, but his or her rigidity will increasingly lead to tantrums and agitation.

Impulsivity refers to the tendency to act rashly and without judgment or consideration. A child might frequently interrupt others, take other children's toys, or appear consistently impatient and frustrated.

As these descriptions suggest, the symptoms of ADHD exist along a spectrum. Most children will occasionally display many of the aspects ascribed to ADHD, and this recognition may account for much of the controversy surrounding the disorder. To standardize the diagnosis, the Diagnostic and Statistical Manual-IV (DSM-IV) lists formal criteria (American Psychiatric Association, 1994). ADHD can be characterized as three types: predominantly inattentive, predominantly hyperactive-impulsive, or a combination of the two types. To some extent, these differentiations account for the increasingly recognized population of children—often girls—who display what appear to be difficulties primarily with attention but who respond to conventional treatments.

The brief adolescent tantrum or the distraction of an 8-year-old before vacation does not constitute sufficient data for a diagnosis of ADHD.

Finally, one of the most difficult and important aspects of understanding ADHD is to consider the child's developmental expectations. Obviously, we don't expect the same judgment or attention span from a 6-year-old and a teenager. In addition, symptoms must persist over time and exist in more than one setting. The brief adolescent tantrum or the distraction of an 8-year-old before vacation does not constitute sufficient data for a diagnosis of ADHD.

In fact, the heterogeneity and developmental aspects of ADHD make the diagnosis of the disorder potentially quite complicated (Cantwell, 1996). Ideally, the clinician should take a very careful history from as many sources as possible and note such important factors as the persistence of the symptoms and the extent to which these symptoms cause problems. Because emotionally troubled children often appear inattentive or agitated, the clinician should ask about difficulties in the child's life that might account for a change in the child's behavior. We must also remember, however, that many children experience difficult life changes but do not display symptoms of agitation or inattention.

Although research addresses the efficacy of specific laboratory tests, the descriptive criteria of ADHD remain the most effective means of making an accurate diagnosis. Clinicians must take the time to speak with parents and teachers, noting that children with ADHD will often appear normal in a brief office visit or in a one-on-one situation. As evidence mounts of a strong genetic component to the disorder, clinicians should ascertain whether siblings, parents, or close relatives suffer similar symptoms. Because many parents were not diagnosed as children, simply asking whether they were diagnosed with something similar to ADHD is usually not sufficient (Biederman et al., 1992). The clinician must probe parents for their memories of their childhood behavior.

Do inattention and hyperactivity always equal ADHD? In addition to the heterogeneity of ADHD, we must note that other psychiatric processes may account for many of the disorder's symptoms. Children with intense anxiety or depression are particularly likely to have problems that appear similar to ADHD, and evidence also exists that suggests that symptoms of depression—as the child's self esteem suffers in the face of continuing social and developmental failures—can complicate ADHD (Zametkin & Monique, 1999). Clinicians should also screen for problems with substance abuse, Tourette's syndrome, and psychosocial stressors. Clinicians, parents, or teachers may mistakenly attribute symptoms of these conditions to ADHD, and the symptoms may complicate the course of a child who happens also to suffer from ADHD.

In general, younger children with ADHD are happy. The preteen diagnosed with ADHD who is not generally in good spirits should be carefully scrutinized for other or additional psychological problems. Conversely, as children with untreated ADHD age, they may develop significant self-image problems. These difficulties come about as the young people continually endure academic and social failures; simply treating their ADHD will often not meet all of their social, developmental, and learning needs.

Although we don't clearly understand the causes of ADHD, current research suggests evidence of potentially causative brain abnormalities. Many of these studies implicate problems with frontal lobe function (Rubia et al., 1999). In general, the frontal lobe region of the cerebral cortex allows for the planning and execution of complex and complicated tasks. We often refer to the activity of this portion of the brain as executive function, and we think that children with ADHD have deficits in executive functioning.

Evidence for these deficits has been generated both by neuropsychological testing and by neuroimaging studies, as well as by the observation that individuals with frontal lobe injuries display behavior similar to that of people with ADHD. As stated earlier, strong evidence for a genetic component of the disorder also exists (Biederman et al., 1992). Further, mounting evidence suggests that psychological and environmental stress can lead to the development of the syndrome (Weiss, 1996). Although we know of no clear cause for the disorder, most theorists would argue that both environmental and biological factors play substantial roles in the development of ADHD.

Treating ADHD

Treatments for ADHD include behavioral and medical therapies. Stimulants such as methylphenidate (Ritalin) and dextroamphetamine (Dexedrine) continue to be first-line medical treatments, with more than 40 years of experience confirming the relative safety and effectiveness of these medications. Although the number of stimulants on the market proliferates, response to a specific stimulant remains idiosyncratic; some children will do better on one stimulant than the other, and it is difficult to predict which medication will work best. In addition to the stimulants, tricyclic antidepressants such as desipramine can be very effective, though their use is somewhat limited in younger children. Medications such as clonidine (Catapress) and guanfacine (Tenex), both high blood pressure medications, appear to treat the impulsive symptoms of the syndrome, but are not effective for inattention.

In general, if medical therapies work and the child receives the appropriate dose and stimulant, the child's behavior should improve relatively quickly. If a child does not improve or improves only minimally, both the proposed treatment regimen (dose and/or medication) and often the diagnosis itself should be re-evaluated. Nevertheless, we need to understand the limitations of medical therapies. Although such symptoms as overactivity, attention span, impulsivity, aggression, social interaction, and academic performance will often improve, such specific skills as reading and such antisocial behavior as cheating or stealing may not show marked progress without additional interventions (Zametkin & Monique, 1999). Children still must master the fundamental developmental task of learning to focus on activities or subjects that are not of immediate interest. No medication can take the place of the mastery of skills and attainment of maturity necessary for academic and social success.

Behavioral treatments of ADHD include daily report cards, positive reinforcement, social skills groups, and individual therapy (Barkley, 1990). As the child matures, these treatments may also address the child's self-image. Although psychodynamic therapies (play or talk therapies) may not be directly effective, we have found that the relationship between a child and an effective therapist often ameliorates many of the problem behaviors associated with ADHD.

Finally, when deciding on treatment, the parents and the child must take part in the decision-making process. Some families prefer behavioral remedies; others may request medications. Attention to such details as the meaning of each treatment modality, as well as the hopes and concerns of both the parents and the child, will have enormous benefits. Adolescents may not wish to take medications, for instance, but may be willing to implement equally effective study and behavioral strategies. Conversely, both time and financial constraints may limit the efficacy of psycho-therapy. Clinicians must educate families about ADHD and its treatment and help the families make informed decisions. Clinicians should leave time at the end of an appointment for questions—if families cannot ask questions, their understanding of and compliance with treatment is severely threatened.

The issue of alcohol and drug abuse and ADHD deserves special mention. Because stimulants are addictive substances, we often worry that prescribing these medica-tions will predispose children to addictive problems. Although caution is always necessary when using stimu-lants, recent research suggests that, in fact, the number of children developing substance abuse problems is substan-tially higher in those with ADHD who do not receive adequate treatment (Biederman, Wilens, Mick, Spencer, &

Faraone, 1999). Nevertheless, in adolescents with pre-existing problems with substances, clinicians often prefer treatment with medications other than stimulants.

ADHD in the Classroom

Just as diagnosing and treating children with ADHD is complex, working with the inattentive and hyperactive child challenges all teachers. The problems that children with ADHD experience may lead to chaotic classrooms, missed and incomplete assignments, and miserable teachers and students alike. Educators have found, however, a number of useful classroom techniques.

To assist the student with ADHD, educators need to exercise caution, creativity, and vigilance.

First, teachers must view the child as a whole person. The child is not a person with ADHD, or an "ADHDer," but a complete and unique individual. Although seemingly obvious, teachers must resist the tendency to label a child with unfair expectations. Most important, teachers can remind students that they are capable of learning and of enjoying the learning process. Many students diagnosed with ADHD will arrive in the classroom severely demor-alized, having gleaned from their parents and peers that they are unable to excel academically. On the other hand, telling students that they can learn as easily as students without attentional deficits might reintroduce a pattern of failure and disappointment.

Educators, therefore, should be proactive when they suspect a psychiatric reason for a student's difficulties. Studies have demonstrated that teachers are valuable sources of clinical information. At the same time, teachers should be aware of their own biases. Many of the studies, for instance, suggest that teachers frequently suspect ADHD in boys more often than in girls (Dulcan, 1997).

To assist the student with ADHD, educators need to exercise caution, creativity, and vigilance. Teachers must employ all of their professional skills to structure class-rooms and make assignments clear. Educators should let students with ADHD know that they will work creatively with the students to explore learning and organization strat-egies. An honest relationship between teacher and student is essential.

To be most effective, teachers should discuss the strat-egies with the student outside of class so that the student understands the teacher's expectations and the kinds of support the teacher will offer. Specific strategies might include nonverbal reprimands for out-of-control behavior. A simple and silent hand on the student's shoulder incon-spicuously tells the student that his or her behavior is inappropriate. Similarly, relying on such cues as lost eye contact between a student and teacher might help a teacher recognize wavering attention. If a child is persistently unable to focus, move his or her seat to a less distracting part of the room. Some other strategies include the following:

Require meticulously organized assignment books. For every class, the student with ADHD must have each day's homework recorded. When the teacher doesn't assign homework, the student writes "no homework" in the appropriate place. If the student fails to keep the log current, he or she must get the teacher's signature in the assignment book at the end of class. The teacher should also both write the assignment on the board and repeat the assignment aloud. This time-honored teaching technique of appealing to multiple senses works well for children with ADHD.

Teach students with ADHD to break down assignments into smaller, less overwhelming components. When reading textbooks, for example, we have found a variation of Robinson's SQ3R method to be effective (Robinson, 1961). The student surveys each section of the text by first reading the boldfaced print, looking at the visuals, and reading the captions under the visual displays. The student then generates a general statement about what he or she will be reading, allowing him or her to focus on the content of the reading material. After each section, the student stops to recap the main idea of the completed segment. This strategy helps the student become actively engaged with and focused on the text.

Use flash cards. After students give themselves a pretest to determine what they have already mastered, they make flash cards of all of the material that they don't know. They then can separate the cards into three piles: mastered material that they know without hesitation, material that they've guessed correctly but without confidence, and material that they don't know. In this way, the students gain a sense of control over the learning situation and learn to transfer these strategies to other academic and non-academic learning settings. The corresponding sense of accomplishment for both teacher and students can be enormously rewarding.

Experienced teachers will note that many of these strategies have been around for years—long before we reached our present understanding of ADHD. We know now that ADHD leaves the student with deficits in executive functioning and that the time-honored classroom techniques create for the student a kind of external frontal lobe. Good teachers have simply hit upon these techniques in their quests to engage and teach their students.

Teachers need not be overwhelmed by the growing complexity of psychiatric and psychological diagnoses that follow their beleaguered students. As always, good educators remain central to a child's development.

Teachers should never hesitate to contact a child's clinician. If a student appears different or suffers a behavioral change, a physician or psychologist will use this valuable information to determine a diagnosis and treatment. Although clinicians and teachers have just begun to work together, educational and clinical collaborations need to evolve and prosper. The teacher, the clinician, and most important, the student, will benefit enormously.

References

American Psychiatric Association. (1994). *Diagnostic and statistical manual for mental disorders* (4th ed.). Washington, DC: Author.

Barkley, R. A. (Ed.). (1990). *Attention deficit hyperactivity disorder: A handbook for diagnosis and treatment.* New York: Guilford.

Biederman, J., Faraone, S. V., Keenan, K., Benjamin, K., Krifcher, B., Moore, C., Sprich-Buckminster, S., Ugaglia, K., Jellinck, M. S., & Steingard, R. (1992). Further evidence for family-genetic risk factors in attention deficit hyperactivity disorder: Patterns of comorbidity in probands and relatives in psychiatrically and pediatrically referred samples. *Archives of General Psychiatry, 49,* 728–38.

Biederman, J., Wilens, T., Mick, E., Spencer, T., & Faraone, S. V. (1999). Pharmacotherapy of attention deficit hyperactivity disorder reduces risk for substance use disorder. *Pediatrics, 104,* e20.

Cantwell, D. P. (1996). Attention deficit disorder: A review of the past 10 years. *Journal of the American Academy of Child and Adolescent Psychiatry, 35,* 978–87.

Dulcan, M. (1997). Practice parameters for the assessment and treatment of children, adolescents and adults with attention deficit/hyperactivity disorder. *Journal of the American Academy of Child and Adolescent Psychiatry, 36* (Suppl. 10), 85S–121S.

Robinson, F. P. (1961). *Effective study.* New York: Harper and Row.

Rubia, K., Overmeyer, S., Taylor, E., Brammer, M., Williams, S. C., Simmons, A., & Bullmore, E. T. (1999). Hypofrontality in attention deficit hyperactivity disorder during higher order motor control: A study with functional MRI. *American Journal of Psychiatry, 156,* 891–6.

Weiss, G. (1996). Attention deficit hyperactivity disorder. In M. Lewis (Ed.), *Child and adolescent psychiatry: A comprehensive textbook* (pp. 544–63). Baltimore, MD: Williams and Wilkins.

Zametkin, A. J., & Monique, E. (1999). Current concepts: Problems in the management of attention deficit hyperactivity disorder. *New England Journal of Medicine, 340,* 40–46.

Steven C. Schlozman, M.D., is Clinical Instructor in Psychiatry, Massachusetts General Hospital/Harvard Medical School, 15 Parkman St., WACC-725, Boston, MA 02114; and Lecturer in Education, Harvard Graduate School of Education; 617-724-6300, ext. 133-1114; sscholzman@partners.org. **Vivien R. Schlozman** is a private practice educator at the Pembroke Hill School. She may be reached at 6600 Overhill Rd., Shawnee Mission, KS 66208.

The Oppression of Inclusion

David Aloyzy Zera and Roy Maynard Seitsinger

Adherence to Federal and state guidelines drives the least-restrictive environment (LRE) clause and the free appropriate public-education (FAPE) mandate for all students with disabilities in school systems. However, many school systems have taken the requirements one step further by implementing full-inclusion classroom models in which all services such as special education and speech are provided in the general-education classroom. Children are often forced to fit within an existing program rather than enter a program designed to meet their particular needs. The U.S. Department of Education, Office of Special Education and Rehabilitative Services, indicates that between 1986 and 1996 the percentage of students with disabilities educated in regular classrooms increased by 19.9 percent. Children with specific learning disabilities experienced the greatest increase in service in regular classrooms—27 percentage points.

Questions arise about the efficacy of these inclusion practices and the moral and ethical components associated with them. Teachers and parents who wish to implement what *they believe* is an appropriate program for the child (which may be a resource room or even a self-contained class) often find that their hands are tied by limited resources: monetary, psychological, and otherwise.

The authors utilized a critical theory perspective in their questioning process to foster active dialogue about the nature of inclusionary practices. If we wish to understand more completely the tacit and overt relationship between the individual (teacher, parent, child) and the school, we must frame our investigation using a dialogical reference point that examines the nature of this relationship.

Critical theorists scrutinize the framework of the way we organize "our lives and the way our lives are organized for us" (Foster 1982, 72). Unique and sublet differences within existing frameworks are explored and questions of import are asked. In our exploration of inclusionary classroom practices we focused on two significant questions:

a. Why is inclusion the preferred model of so many educational systems? and
b. Should full inclusion be a goal for the American public education system?

As a result of our questioning and reflective process, we concluded that the inherent power structures of school systems are often unproductive and the voice of the individual goes unheard. Although inclusionary practices assume a high moral purpose, the implementation of the practice frequently goes awry. Services are not provided, resources are not always available, and truly individualized programs are not designed to meet student needs.

We believe... that many current inclusionary practices directly violate the intent of the laws that were designed to help children with disabilities.

We believe not only that many current inclusionary practices directly violate the intent of the laws that were designed to help children with disabilities, but also that the practice is an oppressive one in the way that it is currently implemented in many schools.

Why Inclusion?

The very purpose of educational agencies is to overtly support the students they serve. Hiring support personnel such as special educators, speech and language pathologists, and psychologists is one avenue in which systems portray their intent to provide specialized services. However, the result is often literally oppressive when these services are not provided in the most valuable setting or in the least-restrictive environment for the individual student. It is important, therefore, to examine the stated intents of legal mandates and the underlying messages and ideas that bureaucracies ask practitioners to implement.

Why have systems moved away from providing individual special education instruction in small-class settings (resource rooms) and decided instead to provide services within mainstream settings? How did school systems make the leap from adhering to the "least restrictive environment" (LRE) clause of Federal law to implementing full inclusion? The LRE, ideally, means a student's placement in the setting most like the educational setting of non-disabled peers in which the student can be successful (D'Alonzo, Giordano, and Cross 1995). Specifically, the statute states that "to the maximum extent appropriate, children with disabilities, including children in public or private institutions or other care facilities, are educated with children who are not disabled" (NICHCY 3) [Section 612(a)(5)(A) of IDEA 97]. The term "inclusion" does not appear in disability law.

However, several court decisions and vocal parent groups have interpreted LRE as requiring inclusion. The emerging philosophical stances of some local educational agencies (LEAs) go a step further and mandate full inclusion that results in little or no direct instruction for students with disabilities. Some LEAs ignore the mandate that requires them to determine the LRE individually.

Why Not Inclusion?

By providing service solely within general-education classrooms, inclusion may in fact deny individuals their right to appropriate programs.

For example, it may be that speech and language services can be provided in a general-education classroom. However, some disorders are based in auditory-processing deficits—a problem that could be exacerbated in a classroom with general students. In this situation, as well as in others, it may appear that the service is being provided, but the question remains: is it being provided appropriately?

The practice of inclusion, acknowledging that all students can learn and recognizing similarities among people, can nonetheless turn LEAs into a trap that attempts to provide for all students in mainstream settings. The rights of both parents and children are violated by systems that do not adhere to governmental policies mandating a full continuum of services, from full inclusion to residential treatment facility or hospitalization.

The belief that all students are similar enough that their needs can be met in traditional classrooms fosters false hopes in students with disabilities and their parents. Further compounding the problem, parents may be misled into believing that inclusionary settings provide the appropriate services for their children. Additionally, teachers may also believe that what is being offered is the most appropriate. This recursively negative situation sets up a circumstance in which no one wins, least of all the child.

For example, parents who have faith in their child's teacher may believe everything possible is being done for the child. At the same time, the school system may continue to promote the inclusion-based model because that is what many universities are training their teachers to do.

Whatever the intent of full-inclusion policies, their implementation has been faulty. Student success in these settings is dependent on fundamental changes in the way schools treat children. They must bring a full range of resources to bear on the children's needs. But this approach has not been universal.

How can school systems be alerted that inclusionary practices, no matter how altruistic the intentions, are often far from being altruistic in action?

A few school systems refuse even to acknowledge that their inclusion practices have become oppressive. How can school systems be alerted that inclusionary practices, no matter how altruistic the intentions, are often far from being altruistic in action? The questioning process continues and we must ask ourselves: how can these systems be restructured to meet the needs of the population they purport to help?

Systems Change

Even when inclusive LEAs for students with disabilities are based on the moral high ground, failure results if processes are not examined thoroughly and procedures are not implemented properly. Consequently, the decisions of the bureaucratic system can oppress the culture and societies they are designed to benefit.

For some students, a full-inclusion setting is indeed the least restrictive one, whereas for others it may be the *most constrictive*. Was it not the intent of law to provide for students with special needs in the least-restrictive environment *in which they would be successful?*

"Success" is another key term to examine within this dialogue, for how is success determined? For some, whose primary goal is social interaction, full inclusion may be the most successful. For others, who are concerned with such skills as articulation, reading at expected age level, or performing mathematical calculations, an inclusion model may actually prove harmful.

What about the child? Student-centered, needs-based decision-making is the core of law and intentions, yet the parties to inclusion decisions all too often seem to avoid this paramount question and its obvious answer.

Perhaps eliminating special education services completely and simply training educators to understand children's development and master subject areas could resolve the inclusion quandary. Alternatively, educational bureaucracies might want to consider eliminating general education and training everyone to become a special educator. As in the inclusion debate, many persons would staunchly support one option or the other. And, just as with inclusion, the pendulum swing from one extreme to the other would probably do nothing but create further problems.

The practice of inclusion is also ripe for abuse economically. As Seymour Sarason reminds us, "The dilemmas of limited resources cannot be ignored?" (1996, 282). It is easier to add a student to an inclusionary setting than it is to create an individualized program for a child with special needs. The leap has too often been to a service-provision design, often made at the local level and driven by local economics rather than student need.

The Problem Is Already Solved

The Federal government has consistently designed plans and developed legal mandates to solve the social and educational dilemmas of inclusion. Why the mandates have not been followed consistently is difficult to answer. But it seems clear that the current practices of full inclusion can ultimately prove just as harmful as the segregatory practices of an earlier day.

Aside from legal requirements, it is ethically and morally essential for school systems to provide a full continuum of services for students with disabilities. Local education agencies must ensure that "a continuum of alternative placements is available to meet the needs of children with disabilities for special education and related services" (NICHCY 5) [34 CFR-300.551 (a)]. It is important for LEAs to review these mandates and interpret them as they are—and not misinterpret them as they wish them to be.

Our belief is that widespread, thoughtless inclusion practices are as oppressive a stance as segregation ever was.

References

D'Alonzo, B. J., G. Giordano, and T. L. Cross. 1995. Inclusion: Seeking educational excellence for students with disabilities. *Teacher Educator.* 31 (1): 82–95.

Foster, W. 1982. *Paradigms and promises: New approaches to educational administration.* Buffalo, N.Y.: Prometheus Books.

National Information Center for Children and Youth with Disabilities (NICHCY) 1998. *Office of Special Education Programs' IDEA amendments of 1997 curriculum: module 8, least restrictive environment, background text,* 1–9.

Sarason, S. 1996. *Revisiting the culture of the school and the problem of change.* New York: Teachers College Press.

U.S. Department of Education, Office of Special Education and Rehabilitative Services. *Annual Report to Congress on the Implementation of the Individuals with Disabilities Education Act, 1988–1998.*

David Aloyzy Zera, Ph.D., is an assistant professor at Fairfield University, Fairfield, Connecticut.

Roy Maynard Seitsinger, Ph.D., is Director of Curriculum and Grants for the Bristol/Warren Regional School District in Rhode Island.

From *Educational Horizons,* Fall 2000, pp. 16-18. © 2000 by Educational Horizons. Reprinted with permission of the authors.

Challenges of Identifying and Serving Gifted Children with ADHD

Lori J. Flint

How often have we, as parents and educators, watched a story about students labeled as one thing or another on the evening news and felt it was oversimplified? Those of us who regularly work with children know that we can't oversimplify like that because, like adults, children are not always what they appear to be. Children are complicated, with a variety of factors, both positive and negative, simultaneously affecting them. Many children are labeled as gifted or learning disabled or having attention-deficit hyperactivity disorder (ADHD) as though that label explains the child, when what it really does is provide appropriate educational services to that child. But what about children who bear one label and also display other tendencies?

Take, for example, the idea of gifted children. Many people probably think of children as being identified as gifted according to a single intelligence test and don't realize that giftedness today often is measured in other ways: high motivation, exceptional creativity, outstanding achievement, and fantastic products.

Whoever these children with exceptional gifts and talents are, and however their gifts are measured, they're all really good in school, and have it made in life, right? Not necessarily. Some students identified as being gifted have other exceptionalities, as well; some have exceptionalities that preclude them from ever being identified as gifted.

This article describes the special situations and needs of three children—Tony, Mikey, and Gina. As you read the first part of the article, think about your own suggestions for interventions—how you might help them in your home or classroom. Then read the rest of the article to see what others have to say about working with children who have both giftedness and attentional difficulties.

Three Children

Tony

Nine-year-old Tony is a charmer. He has an engaging smile and knows how to turn it on and off. Tony is also a challenge to have in the classroom. He blurts out answers constantly, never stops moving, and argues with the teacher and with his peers incessantly. He is of average intelligence, displays little creativity, earns low grades on both objective and project-based work, does not like school, and typically achieves at a below-average level. Tony is disorganized and distractible and is always either talking or making other noise. He is usually missing either his work or some vital component needed to do his work. He visits the office on a regular basis because he is removed from the classroom when he is so disruptive the teacher cannot continue teaching. Tony's teacher will be happy when this school year is over, but worries about where Tony will go next year and whether his new teacher will be able to handle him—he needs a teacher who is neither too permissive nor too authoritarian. Tony carries with him two labels: He has been diagnosed with ADHD and oppositional defiant disorder (ODD). Tony is one of four children in a family headed by a single parent.

Mikey

Six-year-old Mikey was referred to the schools' student support team (SST) by his classroom teacher. Why was he referred? Mikey was distractible, inattentive, fast-moving, and talkative, to the point of not functioning well in his first-grade classroom. He also displayed some aggressive behavior and poor social skills. One member of the SST was a perceptive administrator whose experience included a 14-year stint teaching gifted children. The recommendation from the team included referring the boy for testing for the gifted program.

Exercise caution in both the identification and treatment of ADHD in children identified as being gifted.

The gifted intervention specialist in the school began evaluating Mikey, first by observing him in his classroom on several occasions, then by administering a variety of mental ability, achievement, creativity, and motivation instruments; all designed to ascertain whether Mikey was gifted according to his state's multiple criteria identification law. As he sat to take a mental ability test in a one-on-one testing situation with his school's gifted specialist, the differences this child exhibited were quickly noted. Mikey was, indeed, exceptionally active; hanging off the chair, even standing, at times, during the testing. He vocalized and was impulsive in answering nearly all questions on the tests. During the administration of a mental ability test, he rushed through the verbal and quantitative sections, performing only at the 48th percentile, and slowing only when he came to something entirely new: the matrix section of the test. He barely listened to the instructions, then dove in. As soon as he was allowed to begin, he started solving the problems rapidly and accurately; thriving on the challenge. He missed none. Unfortunately, his score on this single subtest was not adequate to place him in the gifted program, so he required additional testing. Mikey's performance on the other evaluation measures was inconsistent, ranging from the 99th percentile on some instruments designed to evaluate creativity and mental ability to the 48th on others that measured achievement and motivation. The gifted intervention specialist worked with him, using movement to set the stage for optimal performance.

After several weeks of evaluation, Mikey qualified for the gifted program, identified as creatively and cognitively gifted. Why did the gifted specialist work so hard to help this child qualify? Because she saw a child with immense potential, but who needed a great deal of help channeling that potential into constructive avenues. He was also identified, soon after this, by his family doctor as having ADHD, of both the inattentive and hyperactive types. Mikey comes from a blended family with economic difficulties. He was born when his mother was 14 years of age; his mother never finished high school, and is herself identified as having ADHD, like her mother before her.

Gina

Gina is a highly gifted fifth grader whose performance on mental ability, creativity, and achievement tests regularly place her in the 99th percentile, with scores at the ceiling of the tests. She is an award-winning artist and poet, and an academically high-achieving student who has been in gifted programs since kindergarten. Gina is easily frustrated by new tasks, cries with little or no provocation, and gloats when she figures out things the others have not. She takes great delight, outwardly at least, in all of her differences. She always wants to be first and best. Gina is in nearly constant motion: swooping into a room to announce her arrival; sitting like a frog on her chair, head hanging down and hair swinging around her face; always drawing, writing, or otherwise creating with her hands.

Most foods go untasted by her because she dislikes all but a few for various reasons: too strong, too slimy, wrong color, too disgusting. Gina will only wear clothing made of soft knits and whose tags have been removed, because everything else is either too constricting, or stiff, or makes her itch. She often has her nose turned up in distaste at environmental odors, whether they are caused by someone's lunch or the remnants of some cleaning solution.

Gina's social skills are not those of a typical fifth grader, either. Because of her emotional disability, she stands out in both her gifted and general classrooms. Her propensity toward arguing with adults amazes other students and frustrates the teachers, because she is not engaging in intellectual discourse, but rather, the sort of irrationality that comes of being opinionated and not listening to instructions, as well as an unwillingness to take academic risks. Gina comes from a family of highly gifted, highly educated people.

Attention Deficit or Overexcitability?

Though these three students display many similar behaviors, in each case the behaviors are attributable to different causes. In Tony's case, ADHD is considered the underlying problem; in Mikey's case, ADHD with psychological overintensities associated with giftedness; and in Gina's case, the psychological overintensities concomitant with giftedness alone. How can such similar behaviors be assigned such different attributions, and how can they be distinguished from one another so the correct diagnosis is made in each case?

Making a correct diagnosis is not simple; it requires that educators and other professionals make thorough evaluations for both giftedness and ADHD (Cramond, 1995; Lovecky, 1994; Ramirez-Smith, 1997). According to Webb and Latimer (1993), in recent years educators have increasingly referred gifted children for ADHD evaluation. Because characteristics and behaviors are the foundation of a diagnosis of ADHD, and they can be misleading in the case of gifted people, educators and other professionals must exercise great care when conducting such evaluation (Baum, Olenchak, & Owen, 1998), with parents and teachers working closely with the diagnosing physician.

Children with ADHD *can't* stop moving, whereas children with high psychomotor behavior *love* to move.

In children with average creative and cognitive intelligence, this diagnosis can be made by a physician well versed in the characteristics of children with attention-deficit disorder (ADD) or ADHD (see box, "What is Attention-Deficit Hyperactivity Disorder?") in a fairly straightforward manner by means of thorough psychological and physical examinations. In gifted children, however, the diagnosis may be complicated by other issues, such as psychological overexcitabilities (Dabrowski, 1972; Piechowski, 1986; Piechowski & Colangelo, 1984).

Dabrowski saw these "forms of psychic overexcitability" (OEs) as contributing to individuals' psychological development, so they were a measure of developmental potential. Overexcitabilities are so often present in creatively, academically, intellectually, or otherwise gifted people that some educators are searching for ways to measure overexcitabilities as a tool for identification of gifted people. Psychological intensities are such a part of people who are considered gifted that, for the purpose of this article, the behaviors should be considered to be present when giftedness is mentioned. Researchers have categorized *overexcitabilities* into five main areas: psychomotor, emotional, intellectual, imaginational, and sensual, as follows:

- Those with *psychomotor overexcitabilities* are easy to spot: They are nearly always moving. Their behavior has been characterized as feeling driven to move, a love of movement, restlessness, superenergy, and a need for a high level of activity. Rapid speech, impulsiveness, and a need to act are also characteristic of those who

possess this overintensity. All this sounds remarkably like the hyperactivity of ADHD (Barkley, 1990; Hallowell & Ratey, 1995), though the difference appears to be that children with ADHD *can't* stop moving, whereas children with high psychomotor behavior *love* to move.

- *Imaginational overexcitabilities* are characterized by a facility for invention and fantasy, an ability to engage in detailed visualization, a well-developed sense of humor, animistic and magical thinking, and elaborate application of truth and fiction. Children who possess imaginational OEs can have rich and fulfilling inner experiences during the pedestrian activities of a typical school day. What looks like inattention could be, instead, a rich imaginational scenario unfolding within the child's mind. A creatively gifted 4th-grade student described it like this: "Social studies can be really boring when we just read it aloud and take notes, so I like to pretend I'm in whatever situation we're learning about."

- *Emotional overintensity* is one of the more outwardly visible of the overexcitabilities. Characterized by an intensity of feeling, a marked ability to empathize with others, and somatic expression of feelings, these children are the ones who can see all sides of a situation, who can find it painfully difficult to make new friends, who cry at the smallest frustration. What appears to be the emotional overreactivity of ADHD could, instead, be the expression of emotional overintensity.

- *Sensual overexcitabilities* manifest themselves as extreme sensitivity to touch; delight with the aesthetic things in life, such as art, music, fabric, surroundings, or words; extreme dislike or love for certain foods due to specific textures or tastes; sensitivity to odors or chemicals in the environment; or any other sensory-related experiences. People who experience heightened pleasure when indulging in favorite foods or drinks are displaying this sort of sensual overexcitability. Stopping to feel the fabric of every item passed in a department store, noticing the particular blue of the sky, or admiring the

shape of a flower could easily be construed as distractibility, but it could also be illustrative of being tuned in to the beauty of one's surroundings.

Researchers have categorized *overexcitabilities* into five main areas: psychomotor, emotional, intellectual, imaginational, and sensual.

Look at a classroom full of students of any age. Some are simply there, doing as they are told, whereas others display an absolute thirst for learning. These individuals possess a drive to learn that knows no boundaries—**an intellectual overintensity.** What they learn does not seem to matter as long as it is new and interesting. These are the people who think and wonder, who ask the questions instead of knowing the answers, who exhibit sustained concentration, who have excessive curiosity, and who integrate intuition and concept. They are naturally metacognitive thinkers, are detailed planners, and express early concerns about values and morality. Many of these characteristics appear only in the child's mind, so may look, again, like inattention to the outside observer. At times, this overexcitability also may be seen as similar to the hyperfocusing in people with ADHD. Intellectual OEs may also be expressed as a hyperactivity seen by outsiders as distractibility, but which may be heightened mental arousal that never stops, even during sleep.

Who Are They?

With all these similarities, how can we tell the difference between a gifted child with overexcitabilities and one with ADHD? Both children possess exceptional mental faculties, but one has greater availability of resources, while the other founders in a quagmire of disorganization and distractibility. In such cases, parents and teachers find it difficult to distinguish between the child who *won't* do his or her work and the one who *can't*. Gifted children with

ADHD are usually labeled as underachieving or lazy long before they are ever labeled as ADHD.

Studies have shown that gifted children identified as having ADHD are, generally, more gifted than their non-ADHD peers (Dorry, 1994; Zentall, 1997). Because the negative behavioral manifestations of ADHD may keep these children from performing well on group tests, many educators believe diagnostic tests uncover only the children who have extremely superlative talents or gifts. Though high intelligence can help the child overcome some of the challenges of ADHD over his or her lifetime (Barkley, 1990; Phelan, 1996), it does so only to the extent that it allows the child to compensate to the point of seeming average.

These children also tend not to be nominated for gifted testing or programs. Wolfle & French, in a presentation to the National Association for Gifted Children (1990), reported the following characteristics of a typical gifted child with ADHD excluded from gifted programs:

- Makes jokes or puns at inappropriate times.
- Is bored with routine tasks and refuses to do them.
- Is self-critical, impatient with failures.
- Tends to dominate others.
- Would rather stay by oneself.
- Has difficulty moving into another topic when engrossed.
- Often disagrees vocally with others in a loud, bossy manner.
- Is emotionally sensitive—may overreact.
- Is not interested in details, often hands in messy work.
- Refuses to accept authority, nonconforming, stubborn.

This is the portrait of a child who refuses to play the school game, has his or her own ideas about how to live, and will not compromise. Teachers do not particularly tend to like these children, thus they do not generally refer them for gifted programming because, in the teacher's mind, these students do not deserve to be there. Parents find them difficult to live with, and peers reject them, so life becomes a series of negative interactions with few opportunities for self-fulfillment. The worst part is that such children are intelligent enough to realize they are different, but may be helpless to change their behaviors at their own volition.

In his work with gifted children with ADHD, Mendaglio (1995) found that these children are painfully aware of their academic failures and misbehaviors. This awareness often manifests itself outwardly as nonspecific anger. On the positive side, he reported, when such children do qualify for and are placed into programs for gifted and talented children, they and their parents report immediate, lasting, positive increases in self-esteem and attitude.

The Creativity Link

Creativity and ADHD share many, many characteristics. Indeed, both creativity and ADHD are so difficult to define precisely and can look so much alike, one might be hard pressed to define certain characteristics as one or the other. In her study of 70 gifted children, Lovecky (1994) found that almost all of these children, even those with additional learning disabilities and exceptional hyperactivity, displayed creativity. The differences between them and their gifted/non-ADHD peers was, "organizing their creative ideas into products, and sustaining enough interest and motivation to finish a project once they had gotten past the novelty of the initial idea" (p. 3).

Hallowell and Ratey (1995) found certain characteristics of the ADHD mind beneficial to the development of creativity. These included a higher tolerance for chaos and ambiguity and no firm belief that there is one proper place for ideas or images. This can lead to unusual combinations of imagery and ideas and to new ways of seeing things.

Hyper-reactivity in the minds of people with ADHD is amazing to behold. The ideas come and come, changing from one topic to another with an awesome rapidity and proliferation. With this many ideas, new ones pop up with regularity, leading to people with creative/ADHD characteristics to think of themselves as "idea people."

Educators should place the child in classrooms where expectations are high and teaching is holistic, relevant, challenging, and meaningful.

The impulsivity of ADHD can lead to a need to create—anything. This impulse is an urge that demands satisfaction. Combined with the hyperfocusing of ADHD, this impulsivity can produce impressive results in a brief period of time. Of course, there will also be many times of distractibility to balance these periods of intense concentration and productivity.

Creative production also occurs when people spontaneously bring unlike items together in unusual ways. Creative people with ADHD do this often. They see and find amusing combinations others may never have thought of. This is a strategy others have to be taught to use, usually in expensive creativity-training workshops.

Cramond (1994), in a review paper, and Piirto (1992), in her book *Understanding Those Who Create*, noted that the defining characteristics of ADHD are also key descriptors in the biographies of highly creative people. Inattention, hyperactivity, and impulsivity were frequently mentioned as characteristic of many writers, artists, authors, inventors, and composers. These characteristics transferred across disciplines and were found in every area of creativity.

How Can You Tell Whether It Is Truly ADHD?

When we see ADHD-type behaviors, in combination with giftedness of either intellect or creativity, how can we tell if we need to take action to label and treat the ADHD? This is a question asked in nearly every article on the topic. The overwhelming primary response is this: Exercise caution in both the identification and treatment of ADHD in children identified as being gifted. Beyond that, research has identified several characteristics of gifted children with ADHD—characteristics that are not generally present in the child who is gifted but not identified as having ADHD.

The first is inconsistency in performance. Non-gifted ADHD children are known for inconsistency in school performance that occurs at any time in any subject (Barkley, 1990). Being gifted does not exempt children from these sorts of academic inconsistencies (Webb & Latimer, 1993). If children are functioning at a high level in a subject one day, then failing in the same subject days later, there may be reason to suspect a problem. A thorough history of the child's performance will reveal a pattern of variability of task performance over time. These children's performance may also be linked to the teacher's characteristics and teaching style; these students will not produce quality work for a teacher they do not like or respect.

There is a movement in the field now to find a means of measuring overexcitabilities as a tool for identification of gifted people.

A visit to a gifted resource classroom, otherwise known as a gifted "pullout" program, will generally reveal a higher than normal activity level, a great deal of talkativeness, and a high level of enthusiasm and task commitment for challenging, interesting tasks. The enthusiasm, movement, talkativeness, and high activity levels are desirable, though can be exhausting for the teachers involved, because these behaviors correspond to the ways gifted children are identified today. Gifted resource classrooms generally exist to serve gifted students in elementary schools, but sometimes can be found at higher grade levels. Wherever they are found, they are often the high point of a gifted students' day or week—time away from their general education classrooms to be spent with intellectual peers. While children with ADHD tend toward inattention, and distraction in nearly every situation, gifted children with ADHD will retain the hyperactivity and problems with sustained attention, except during certain highly stimulating, novel, motivating tasks, such as those to be found in the gifted resource classroom. Those gifted children who are unresponsive to even those tasks stand out among their peers and should be investigated.

Gifted children with ADHD, like all children, not only deserve, but *require* highly stimulating and mentally and psychologically challenging environments to be successful, something few schools provide. Many gifted children have problems with school environments that provide few opportunities for creativity, provide only concrete, linear-sequential instruction, teach only at the lower levels of the taxonomy, require excessively rote and repeti-

tive work, and do not allow learners to progress at their own rate (Baum et al., 1998; Cramond, 1995; Lovecky, 1994; Zentall & Zentall, 1983). This type of learning environment can be a disaster for any child, but you can virtually guarantee it will be for the child who has characteristics of both giftedness and ADHD. These children will frequently shut down when given repetitive tasks, even knowing that unfavorable consequences are certain to follow. When one 11-year-old gifted child with ADHD was asked about this, he responded, "It actually makes me feel sick to my stomach when they make me do the same thing over and over."

When the ADHD has gone undiagnosed for many years, the student may have developed problems with self-esteem and depression.

Whereas children with ADHD tend toward not liking school and gifted children usually do, gifted children with ADHD usually have a few subjects (particularly science) they really love and may not care about the rest (Zentall, 1997). This can lead to incredible power struggles in the home and school when parents and teachers see that the child can attend in some situations but won't (or can't) in others. In children like this, underachievement begins early, with the ADHD not generally identified until at least 6th grade (Lovecky, 1994). By then the child has set up a pattern of inconsistent performance and failure to complete work, leading to frequent negative feedback, leading in turn to diminished academic self-esteem and anger. This pattern of underachievement and the negative response it generates create a cycle within the school and the family that is difficult to break.

Though gifted children frequently display mental ages and social functioning well above those of their chronological peers, they still may exhibit some discrepancies within themselves between these developmental strands, while the gifted child with ADHD may exhibit a much wider and debilitating discrepancy between intellectual age and social and emotional ages. This can cause the child to be

out of sync with everyone (Lovecky, 1993). Social skills are usually underdeveloped in these children; as a result, they may have few friends, with those few generally being younger. Again, these children are aware of their differences and lack of friends, so may become depressed or oppositional in response.

How Do We Help These Paradoxical Children Become Achievers?

Research on underachievement in general, and in gifted people with ADHD specifically, has given us ideas on how to help these children become achievers. As far back as 1959, Passow and Goldberg provided insight in their landmark study on how to reverse underachievement. Their studies revealed that if teachers wish to reverse underachievement, they should place students in a stimulating, rich environment with a teacher who is kind and accepting, who values each of them as individuals, and who maintains high expectations. In addition, the researchers found that students needed further, intensive instruction in study and organizational skills; a characteristic shared by many underachievers, and nearly all children diagnosed with ADHD (Dorry, 1994; Maxwell, 1989). In today's world, gifted children with ADHD can be taught word processing and computer skills that will allow them to compensate for their inability to write quickly or neatly, or to keep their thoughts while writing (Ramirez-Smith, 1997).

Medication works most effectively when coupled with stable parental support at home.

Teachers who have successfully worked with gifted children with ADHD recognize that cognitive therapy is helpful. It is beneficial to talk openly with students about expectations and problems and include them in developing plans of action (Mendaglio, 1995). Contracts, with student-chosen rewards, are helpful in some cases. Because gifted children tend to be primarily intrinsically motivated, external rewards and punishments have little effect unless they are selected by the children themselves. Students need to be convinced that failure is not an option, that today's work will pay off in the future, and that hard work will benefit them personally. Goal setting is another useful strategy in this area, because it helps remove the child from the impulsivity of the moment and develop focus on the future.

What About Parents?

Parenting gifted children with ADHD can be an extremely frustrating experience. There is an awareness of the child's precocity and talents that leads to higher expectations, but that, when coupled with the ADHD behaviors, leads to frustration with the child's self-destructive behaviors. Parents need to deliberately educate themselves about how to deal appropriately with these children (see box, "Tried and True Strategies for Parents") and be advocates for them, while not being rescuers available to bail the children out of every jam (Zentall, 1997). Negativity and power struggles are common in families with gifted children with ADHD. On a more positive note, a child with ADHD who is gifted, who has a supportive family, and who is taught specific ways to compensate for his or her deficits has a much greater chance of becoming a productive adult (Phelan, 1996). Though the gifted child with ADHD may for many years demand an inordinate amount of the family's re-sources, it appears that early intervention and long-term support eventually pay off.

Home-school communication is essential for the success of gifted children with ADHD (Baum et al., 1998; Ramirez-Smith, 1997; Wolfle & French, 1990). Teachers need to be informed about these children's specific needs, and most are not. How could they be? In teacher education programs, there has traditionally been little room for teaching about gifted children at all, let alone those with additional exceptionalities. Parents can be useful in providing materials that inform educators about the characteristics and needs of a gifted child with ADHD. There should be ongoing, open communication between parent and teacher, with the child included as needed.

Tried & True Strategies for Parents of Gifted Children with ADHD or Overexcitability

- **Love your children for who they are**, not for what they do or don't do; obvious, but not always easy with these extremely challenging children.
- **Set standards and *insist* they be met**. Do what it takes to communicate that failure is *not* an option, and that every action has its consequences. If there are no natural consequences, design some specific to the situation.
- **Use humor to defuse stress and anger**. An advanced sense of humor is a characteristic many gifted children share. Take advantage of it.
- **There are no quick fixes**. Know that gifted children with ADHD require intensive, long-term, interventions. Be consistent over time.
- **Communicate regularly with your child's teachers** in a positive fashion, no matter what grade your child is in, and do so *before* problems surface. Remember, your mutual goal is to help the child be successful.
- **Impose organization on your children until they prove they can do it themselves**. Find a good system and teach and reteach it. Expect backsliding from time to time, all the way through school.
- **Provide opportunities for your child to express his or her creativity**. When things get really bad, this may be his or her lifesaver.
- **Nothing breeds success like success**. Find some way to show your child that he or she can be successful at something meaningful, if only he or she tries. Provide a choice of opportunities and insist he or she chooses one and sticks with it until successful completion.
- **Make sure your child is provided with appropriate curriculum and teachers from the start**. Positively but honestly present your child and his or her needs to school administrators *before* the end of this school year for next year's placement, then trust the school personnel to do the work of placing the child appropriately.

Because of the myriad needs generated by having a gifted child with ADHD in the classroom, administrators and teachers must hold discussions about classroom placements and include both current and former teachers, administrators, and parents. Educators should place the child in classrooms where expectations are high and teaching is holistic, relevant, challenging, and meaningful (DeLisle, 1995), and where teachers are willing to teach to the child's strengths while remediating the weaknesses. Multi-modal approaches allow the gifted child with ADHD to play to his or her strengths and express creativity (Lovecky, 1994). Several successful research projects have employed talent development and attention to students' specific intelligences, talents, or gifts as means to promote academic success for at-risk students (Baum, Owen, & Oreck, 1996; Baum, Renzulli, & Hebert, 1994; Olenchak, 1994). It is clear that proper curriculums, instruction, and pacing can make a great deal of difference in the school lives of gifted children with ADHD.

In some cases, physicians may prescribe medication for students to help control the ADD/ADHD symptoms, allowing the giftedness to emerge more fully. According to many researchers, doctors should not prescribe medication unless educators, parents, and other professionals have explored all other possible avenues because medication may have some detrimental effects on creativity, imagination, and intellectual curiosity (Baum et al., 1998; Cramond, 1995). That, of course, is a question to be decided by the doctors, parents, and children; and they should make such decisions on an individual basis. Wolfle & French (1990) stated that medication works most effectively when coupled with stable parental support at home. A review of literature on the effects of stimulant medication and children with ADHD has reinforced that medication alone provides only short-term effects; people should not expect it to improve long-term adjustment in either social or academic areas (Swanson et al., 1993).

Finally, researchers have suggested counseling for some of these children, especially when the ADHD has gone undiagnosed for many years, because the child may have developed problems with self-esteem and depression. When counseling is undertaken, however, educators, parents, and others must be careful to select counselors familiar with both the social and emotional needs of gifted children and children with ADD/ADHD (Webb & Latimer, 1993).

Now What?

The literature has little to say about children doubly blessed with giftedness and ADHD, even less of the literature is research based. In a search for materials on the subject, I found no information on this topic in traditional educational literature; I found some in the social sciences literature; and the rest in the gifted literature. Because most teachers have a hard enough time keeping up with information in their own area of expertise and seldom have the opportunity to examine the gifted literature, it seems logical that this information must be disseminated into mainstream education.

Educators need to do more to improve the quality of identification of these high-potential, though terribly at-risk children and to reduce the likelihood of misdiagnosis of children who are gifted and creative and overexcitable as having ADHD. On the other hand, writers and researchers can heighten our awareness of the existence of this segment of the population so that gifted children who actually *do* have ADHD are not missed in diagnosis. Misdiagnoses can cut some students off from services that they may need. Teachers who are educated on this topic can be of immense help when it comes time to work with doctors in diagnosing possible medical conditions such as ADHD.

Finally, we must learn to value these children; they have much to offer. Though the learning environments and teaching practices discussed earlier are desirable for all children, gifted or not, these doubly-blessed students possess the creative potential to produce great ideas and make wonderful contributions to our society. With appropriate curriculums; informed teachers and administrators; and educated, involved parents working together, we can reclaim a segment of our population who currently underachieve at a high rate. Most of all, we can teach these young people that in working to show their strengths and overcome their deficits, they make themselves even better. As educators, we need to help them learn who they are, what they are capable of, and how to reach their potential.

References

American Psychiatric Association (1994). *Diagnostic and statistical manual of mental disorders* (4th ed.: DSM IV). Washington, DC: Author.

Barkley, R. (1990). *Attention deficit hyperactivity disorder: A handbook for diagnosis and treatment.* New York: Guilford Press.

Baum, S., Olenchak, F., & Owen, S. (1998). Gifted students with attention deficits: Fact or fiction? Or, can we see the forest for the trees? *Gifted Child Quarterly, 42*(2), 96–104.

Baum, S., Owen, S., & Oreck, B. (1996). Talent beyond words: Identification of potential talent in dance and music in elementary students. *Gifted Child Quarterly, 40*(2), 93–102.

Baum, S., Renzulli, J., & Hebert, T. (1994). Reversing underachievement: Stories of success. *Educational Leadership, 52*(3), 48–53.

Cramond, B. (1994). Creativity and ADHD: What is the connection? *Journal of Creative Behavior, 28*(3), 193–210.

Cramond, B. (1995). The coincidence of attention deficit hyperactivity disorder and creativity. *Monograph of the National Research Center on the Gifted and Talented, RBDM 9508, United States Government: Connecticut.* (ERIC Document Reproduction Service No. 388 016)

Dabrowski, K. (1972). *Psychoneurosis is not an illness.* London: Gryf.

DeLisle, J. (1995). ADD gifted: How many labels can one child take? *Gifted Child Today, 18*(2), 42–43.

Dorry, G. (1994). The perplexed perfectionist. *Understanding Our Gifted, 6*(5), 3, 10–12.

Hallowell, E., & Ratey, J. (1995). *Driven to distraction.* New York: Simon & Schuster.

Lovecky, D. (1993). Out of sync with everyone. *Understanding Our Gifted, 5*(5A), 3.

Lovecky, D. (1994, July/August). The hidden gifted learner. *Understanding Our Gifted, 3 & 18.*

Maxwell, V. (1989). Diagnosis and treatment of the gifted student with attention deficit disorder: A structure of intellect approach. *Reading, Writing & Learning Disabilities, 5,* 247–252.

Mendaglio, S. (1995, July/August). Children who are Gifted/ADHD., *Gifted Child Today, 18,* 37–38.

Olenchak, F. (1994). Talent development: Accommodating the social and emotional needs of secondary gifted/learning disabled students. *Journal of Secondary Gifted Education, 5*(3), 40–52.

Passow, H., & Goldberg, M. (1959). Study of underachieving gifted. *Educational Leadership, 16,* 121–125.

Phelan, T. (1996). *All about attention deficit disorder.* Minneapolis, MN: Child Management Press.

Piechowski, M. (1986). The concept of developmental potential. *Roeper Review, 8*(3), 190–197.

Piechowski, M., & Colangelo, N. (1984). Developmental potential of the gifted. *Gifted Child Quarterly, 28,* 80–88.

Piirto, J. (1992). *Understanding those who create.* Dayton: Ohio Psychology Press.

Ramirez-Smith, C. (1997). *Mistaken identity: Gifted and ADHD.* Reston, VA: The Council for Exceptional Children. (ERIC Document Reproduction No. ED413690)

Swanson, J., McBurnett, K., Wigal, T., Pfiffner, L., Lerner, M., Williams, L., Christian, D., Tamm, L., Willcutt, E., Crowley, K., Clevenger, W., Khouzam, N., Woo, C., Crinella, F., & Fisher, T. (1993). Effect of stimulant medication on children with attention deficit disorder. A "review of reviews." *Exceptional Children, 60,* 154–162.

Webb, J., & Latimer, D. (1993). *ADHD and children who are gifted (ERIC Digest No. 522).* Reston, VA: The Council for Exceptional Children.

Wolfle, J., & French, M. (1990). *Surviving gifted attention deficit disorder children in the classroom.* Paper presented at the meeting of the National Association for Gifted Children, Little Rock, AR.

Zentall, S. (1997, March). *Learning characteristics of boys with attention deficit hyperactivity disorder and/or giftedness.* Paper presented at the annual meeting of the American Educational Research Association, Chicago, IL. (ERIC Document Reproduction No. 407791)

Zentall, S., & Zentall, T. (1983). Optimal stimulation: A model of disordered activity and performance in normal and deviant children. *Psychological Bulletin, 94,* 446–471.

Lori J. Flint, *Doctoral Candidate, Department of Educational Psychology, The University of Georgia, Athens.*

Address correspondence to the author at Department of Educational Psychology, The University of Georgia, 325 Aderhold Hall, Athens, GA 30602-7143, (e-mail: LJFSTAT@AOL.COM)

From *Teaching Exceptional Children,* March/April 2001, pp. 62-69. © 2001 by The Council for Exceptional Children. Reprinted by permission.

Gifted Students Need an Education, Too

Gifted children have the right to an education that takes into account their special needs. Here are suggestions for how to provide it.

Susan Winebrenner

Math time is beginning in Kate Ahlgren's primary grade classroom. Her objective is to teach several concepts relating to the base 10 method of counting and computing. Her first task is to assess her students' previous mastery of these concepts. She plans to allow those students who already have a clear understanding of this week's work to spend their math time applying what they have mastered about base 10 to learning about base 5.

Kate conducts a hands-on assessment by giving all students several tasks to complete with Cuisenaire rods. As she directs students to demonstrate what happens when they count past 10, she watches specifically for students who complete each directed task quickly and correctly. Fifteen minutes later, she has identified four children who clearly need more challenging content for the rest of this week's math work. She assigns a base 10 application task for most of the students to complete with partners and takes those four youngsters aside to briefly teach them the essential elements of base 5.

The four students practice excitedly for a few minutes under Kate's supervision. She explains that they will be working together for the rest of this week on learning about base 5 because that will challenge them. She assures them that all students should be working on challenging learning tasks.

Kate gives the four advanced students several tasks similar to those she has demonstrated. They practice together while she works with the rest of the students for the duration of the math period. Just before her instruction ends, she explains to the whole class that they will notice that not all students are working on the same tasks in math. She reassures them that this is perfectly all right and that her job is to make sure that all students are working on tasks that will help them move forward in their own learning. In this way, Kate makes differentiation the normal and acceptable condition of her classroom. She

knows that when her students know something is all right with her, it will generally be all right with them, too.

Differentiated learning for high-ability students in heterogeneous classrooms is as important as it is for other children, yet the needs of the gifted are often misunderstood. Here are reasons why and suggestions for how teachers and administrators can differentiate the prescribed grade-level curriculum to meet the needs of high-ability students.

Why Provide Differentiated Learning for Gifted Students?

For the past 10 years, students who were not learning successfully were targeted for special attention. Sadly, during that same time, the needs of our most capable students have been overlooked. One reason for this neglect is the ability of gifted students to score high on assessments, which has led to the erroneous assumption that they must be learning. Another reason for ignoring their needs is that many educational leaders have misunderstood research on role modeling to mean that some gifted students should be present in all classrooms to facilitate forward progress for other students. Although students who struggle to learn can benefit from mixed-ability classes, they have plenty of positive role models in students who function well at the appropriate grade level, who are capable but not gifted learners. The discrepancy in learning ability between students who struggle to learn and gifted students is simply too wide to facilitate positive role modeling (Schunk, 1987).

Consider the range of abilities present in most classrooms. Visualize that both extremes of a learning curve are equally far removed from the norm. Students who fail to achieve the designated standards have received unprecedented attention during the past several years. They are identified for special services before they start kindergarten, experience lower student-teacher ratios, and may even have a full-time aide assigned to them for the entire school day. School districts spend much more money educating this population than they designate for the usual per-pupil expenditure.

© SUSIE FITZHUGH

Teachers are expected to create numerous differentiation adjustments for low-achieving students by modifying the amount of work, depth, complexity, and content of the curriculum and by linking students' learning styles and interests to the prescribed learning tasks. Politicians, community members, and teachers avidly follow the progress of these students' learning for evidence that these students are indeed moving forward.

Contrast this with the situation for gifted students, whose natural learning abilities place them as far from average as their classmates who struggle to learn. In September, many of these youngsters could take the assessments that all students in their grade will take at the end of the year and still score at or above the 95th percentile. Simply in the interests of equity, these students are as entitled to receive the same types of differentiation so readily provided to the students who struggle to learn.

To assume that gifted students are learning because they achieve acceptable standards on state assessments is unrealistic. In Colorado, Oregon, and several other states,

educators have realized that the learning progress of gifted students cannot be adequately measured simply because the students meet or exceed minimum standards, so these states have specified learning expectations at exemplary levels. By setting exemplary standards, they can document the learning progress of gifted students.

Does the Promise of Education for All Apply to Gifted Students?

Every school district's mission statement promises its parents that "[a]ll students, including those who are exceptional, are entitled to a public-supported education in which instruction is geared to their needs, interests, and developmental levels" (Reis, Burns, & Renzulli, 1992, p. 3). Unfortunately, those at greatest risk of learning the least in classrooms are those at the top range of ability. Because a sense of confidence comes primarily from being successful at something perceived to be difficult (Rimm, 1990), gifted students who rarely undergo demanding learning experiences may lose confidence in their ability to perform well on challenging learning tasks. Many of these students learn to find the easiest way out, postponing their exposure to challenge in many patterns of underachievement (Rimm, 1990; Schmitz & Galbraith, 1985).

Either we must explain to parents that the promise of the school's mission statement does not apply to high-ability students, or we must commit ourselves to providing these students with appropriate and differentiated learning experiences. Whatever has been designated as suitable for students who are learning at a level commensurate with their age is not equally appropriate for students who learn at levels more typical of students several years older.

What Are the Characteristics and Needs of Gifted Students?

Gifted students learn differently from their classmates in at least five important ways. They learn new material in much less time. They tend to remember what they have learned, making spiral curriculums and reviewing previously mastered concepts a painful experience. They perceive ideas and concepts at more abstract and complex levels than do their peers. They become passionately interested in specific topics and have difficulty moving on to other learning tasks until they feel satisfied that they have learned as much as they possibly can about their passionate interest. Finally, gifted students are able to operate on many levels of concentration simultaneously, so they can monitor classroom activities without paying direct or visual attention to them.

Gifted students have already mastered much of the grade-level work, so they should have opportunities to function at more advanced levels of complexity and depth and to tie their own passionate interests into their schoolwork.

Why Are Many Educators Reluctant to Help Gifted Students?

Many teachers are reluctant to facilitate the needs of gifted students because of the lack of teacher training in this type of differentiation, a concern that other students or parents will accuse them of unfairness, or their belief that providing differentiation for this population is elitist.

Most preservice teachers take at least one course about meeting the needs of special–education students, but few states require teachers to take any courses in how to recognize and teach gifted students. Many teachers assume that gifted kids are highly productive, always complete their work on time, get consistently high grades, and will make it on their own without much assistance. Many educators believe that a student who is unproductive in school could not possibly be gifted.

Such misconceptions about how gifted students do their work are sources of great frustration for the students, their parents, and their teachers. Most teachers in my workshops are surprised when I tell them that gifted students often resist doing their assigned work because it is designed for age-appropriate learners and usually cannot provide the challenge and sense of accomplishment that would keep gifted learners motivated to work.

Another part of the problem is confusion about whether the mandated goals must actually be *taught* to students. Realistically, teachers are only required to demonstrate that all their students have *learned* the designated standards. Students who have already mastered the required content should be allowed to demonstrate their mastery before test-preparation sessions begin and to work on alternative activities because they already know the required content. When teachers learn how to plan and provide these alternative activities routinely to students who demonstrate prior mastery, these students can make progress in their own learning during more of their time in school.

How Can Teachers Provide Differentiation for Gifted Students?

The typical approach to differentiation for gifted students in heterogeneous classes has been to offer extra credit, an expectation that doesn't work because the only students eligible for extra credit are those who often have more than enough earned credit. The practice of offering extra credit should be replaced with approaches that can motivate gifted students to become enthusiastic learners.

Compact the curriculum. The most important needs of gifted students are to have regular opportunities to demonstrate what they already know, to receive full credit for content they have already mastered, and to spend their own learning time on challenging activities that accelerate and enrich the regular curriculum (Reis, Burns, & Renzulli, 1992). Compacting the curriculum can answer these needs.

To ascertain who would benefit from a compacted curriculum for a specific topic, teachers will want to provide interested students with pre-assessment opportunities for all learning activities. Teachers should use the same methods of assessment that they plan to use at the end of a learning unit, including written tests or observed performance on designated tasks. Because the preassessment is open to all students, the learning task itself can identify those who could benefit from the specific differentiated tasks regardless of whether particular students have been designated as gifted.

Students who can demonstrate previous mastery of upcoming content are expected to pay attention to direct instruction only when instruction includes concepts they have not yet mastered. On days when the lesson content is based on what these students have already mastered, they work instead on extension activities provided by the teacher or suggested by the students themselves. They receive full credit for what they have already mastered and earn daily credit for following the teacher's expectations about on-task behavior and productivity and by developing alternative projects and activities.

Design alternative learning experiences. As part of their regular lesson planning, teachers design alternative learning experiences. These provide differentiation opportunities in terms of *content, learning processes, products, learning environment*, and *assessment*.

The *content* is different because it moves students beyond grade-level standards or is connected to students' passionate interests. The *learning processes* called upon are different because they provide depth and complexity appropriate to these students' learning abilities. *Products* differ in that they demonstrate the students' learning at advanced levels, moving beyond typical research activities to the development of individual students' talents and curiosities and the presentation of their findings to appropriate audiences. Sometimes the *learning environment* is also different; students may pursue interests outside the regular classroom, work more independently on self-directed projects, or collaborate with other students. Even the *assessment process* is different because students receive full credit for what they have already mastered and do not have to complete all the work assigned to the rest of the class.

One particularly striking opportunity to provide alternative learning experiences presented itself when I discovered that James, one of my exceptionally gifted 6th graders, was writing a book at home on the anatomy and physiology of the human body. I pretested him and other interested students at the beginning of all language arts, reading, and writing units. James experienced differentiation in *content* because he wrote his book in class, in *learning processes* because he used sophisticated writing techniques, and in *assessment* because his grades for each unit were earned at the time of the pretest rather than at the end of the unit, with an overall grade that included an evaluation of his on-task behavior and project.

Allow differentiated pacing. For a curriculum that cannot be assessed beforehand because it is unfamiliar to all, gifted students work at their own pace to learn the required concepts and spend more time developing an expertise on a related topic of their choice.

Agree on expectations. Teachers and students work together to set up standards for evaluating productivity, behavior, and differentiated products and then agree to these standards in writing. Teachers should arrange to spend time with these students. It is important that gifted students not feel abandoned by the teacher and that they learn that everyone needs help on challenging tasks.

What Can Administrators Do to Facilitate Differentiation for Gifted Students?

Acknowledge the needs of gifted students. Acknowledge that the precedent for differentiation has been firmly set by the differentiation opportunities always available for students who struggle to learn. Because gifted learners are just as far removed from average as are children with learning problems, the differentiation that gifted students need is highly defensible and equitable.

Facilitate gifted education training for staff. Any strategies teachers learn for the benefit of their gifted students are applicable to many other students and tend to raise the learning bar for all students. One strategy, for example, is to allow students to get credit for an entire assignment by answering correctly at least four of the five most difficult problems first. This challenge motivates many students to listen more carefully to instructions so they can also qualify.

Investigate cluster grouping. Look into the practice of cluster grouping for gifted students. Cluster grouping is the practice of purposefully placing four to six gifted students together in an otherwise heterogeneous class. Their teacher must have some training in how to differentiate the curriculum for students who demonstrate previous mastery or who can learn new content faster than their classmates. Studies have demonstrated that cluster grouping can lead to improved achievement for many

students at all levels of learning ability (Gentry, 1999; Winebrenner & Devlin, 1996).

Communicate your expectations. Make clear your pledge that all students, including the most capable, will be able to learn something new and challenging every day. Clarify your commitment to the goal that all students will be expected to make continuous progress in their own learning. To that end, expect gifted students to demonstrate competencies that exceed those designated as basic.

Keep the Promise

Parents of gifted learners have a right to expect that schools will fulfill the promise made to all students that children will have consistent and daily opportunities for challenging learning experiences and will demonstrate continuous forward progress in their learning. This expectation requires providing gifted students with differentiation of the regular curriculum. To complacently accept their performance at regular competency levels is to deny their equal right to an appropriate education.

References

Gentry, M. L. (1999). *Promoting student achievement and exemplary classroom practices through cluster grouping: A research-based alternative to heterogeneous elementary classrooms.* Storrs, CT: National Research Center on the Gifted and Talented.

Reis, S. M., Burns, D. E., & Renzulli, J. S. (1992). *Curriculum compacting: The complete guide to modifying the regular curriculum for high ability students.* Mansfield Center, CT: Creative Learning Press.

Rimm, S. (1990). *How to parent so children will learn.* Watertown, WI: Apple Publishing.

Schunk, D. H. (1987). Peer models and children's behavioral change. *Review of Educational Research, 57,* 149–174.

Schmitz, C., & Galbraith, J. (1985). *Managing the social and emotional needs of the gifted.* Minneapolis, MN: Free Spirit Publishing.

Winebrenner, S., & Devlin, B. (1996). *Cluster grouping of gifted students: How to provide full-time services on a part-time budget.* Reston, VA: ERIC Clearinghouse on Disabilities and Gifted Education (ERIC Digest Document Reproduction Service No. 397618).

Susan Winebrenner is an educational consultant and author of *Teaching Gifted Kids in the Regular Classroom* (Free Spirit Publishing, 2000). She may be reached at P.O. Box 398, Brooklyn, MI 49230–0398 (e-mail: ecsfirst @aol.com)

Teaching the New Immigrants:
How "Multicultural" an Educator Are You Prepared to Be?

Gary K. Clabaugh

Immigrant children are flooding into our schools in record numbers. And unlike previous immigrants, they herald from every niche and cranny of the globe. Consequently they bring with them a bewildering and often-conflicting variety of cultural beliefs and practices.

This development weighs heavily on teachers. The world's first truly cosmopolitan culture is struggling to life in their classrooms, generating many new and difficult problems.

What help do besieged frontline teachers get in the face of these difficulties? Chiefly warm, fuzzy slogans issued by pedagogical staff officers safe in the rear. It is at this rear echelon level that schools become rainbows where "you can be you and I can be me." Would that it were that simple.

Why can't our public schools be one big happy family where everyone just gets along? Because the various cultural values and behaviors brought into the schoolhouse are often at odds with one another. And because some of these values and behaviors are incompatible with basic American values, including the very tolerance that makes multiculturalism possible in the first place.

Advocates of multicultural education argue that the United States should no longer be a melting pot, but a salad bowl. The salad bowl simile has much to commend it. But it is important to remember that one doesn't make a palatable salad by just throwing whatever is at hand into the bowl willy-nilly. Some flavors and textures go well together; others do not. Remember too that the American "salad" is already well along, so we should ask if what is added complements the preexisting ingredients.

Some advocates of "multicultural education" do not seem to deeply consider what immigrants might bring with them from their native land. That's why they are so enthusiastic about the possibilities of easy tolerance. Consider, for example, that some cultures define themselves in terms of their animosity for other cultures. What happens when these antagonistic cultures collide in the classroom?

A teacher just told me of a class where children from two antagonistic cultures refused to sit together, much less work together. In fact, when she turned her back to write on the board they began hissing one another. Clearly even the most ardent multiculturalist doesn't want the teacher to respond to such behavior by saying something like, "See how these kids hate one another? They are expressing their respective cultures. Isn't that great!" At this point of mutual antagonism respect for these cultures has to give way to a non-negotiable demand for tolerance. Otherwise, multicultural education will die by its own hand. But how many advocates of multicultural education have even thought about this sort of clash?

Similarly, many cultures tolerate, even endorse, boys treating girls as inferior beings—representatives of a subordinate sex. This is part of a broader cultural pattern of regarding women as inferior members of the human race. Should the hard-won rights of U.S. females give way to a desire to accommodate cultural difference?

This is not an argument for Pat Buchanan-style jingoism. Certainly a child's native language and culture can be a wonderful resource for them as individuals—particularly if they aren't female, homosexual, or handicapped. And selected aspects of foreign cultures can be of great value for America as a nation. (We hardly have a corner on wisdom.) Nevertheless, many imported cultural beliefs and practices must be discouraged if, for example, we value free and unfettered expression, think that women's rights should equal those of men, or hold that homosexuals should at least be left alone.

And who says that cultural background is the sine qua non for classifying kids to begin with? Every one of us has many different characteristics, only some of which are linked to our culture(s) of origin. Consider a child with the following characteristics:

- Female
- Studies hard
- Self-disciplined
- Loves to play the violin
- Writes well
- Hates algebra
- Speaks limited Spanish
- Has one parent from Mexico

Why should this young lady's one-sided affiliation with Mexican culture be the characteristic educators zero in on? Is that more worthy of consideration or accommodation than her love for the violin or her talent for writing?

Besides, not all students want to be defined by their parents' cultural practices and affiliations. Some kids long to escape into mainstream America. In support of multiculturalism, should educators join forces with their parents to keep them in the Old World fold? Suppose, for instance, a young lady confides to her teacher that she is going to run away with the American boyfriend she loves, rather than marry the middle-aged man her parents picked for her, as is their culture's custom. Should the teacher tell the parents? More generally, if old ways start to die in a new land, is it the job of educators to try to keep them alive?

The hard core in all this is that multicultural education has limits. And that's the point of the table that follows. To help you explore where *you* would place those limits. Here is how it works. Rate each of the listed cultural beliefs or practices in terms of how you think educators should deal with them. Use the listed choices. If, for example, members of [a] child's native culture eat dogs and cats for food, decide if educators should:

celebrate it—have assemblies praising, provide cere-
monial expression for, favorably publicize?

support it—serve in the cafeteria, point out advantages of?

permit it—not interfere with practice of?

take no position?

discourage it—try to persuade others to abandon practice, advise against?

undermine it—provide disincentives for, support activities incompatible with?

prohibit it—bar the practice of, impose sanctions on?

OK, how about exploring your limits by filling out the survey
below? (These are actual cultural practices, not fictions.)

This brief questionnaire illustrates a very basic reality: "multicultural education" is more problematic than it first appears. With any
in-depth consideration of how different various cultures really are,
easy uninformed tolerance inevitably turns into worried reflection.

How, then, shall we deal with these youngsters who are entering our classrooms from all over the world? Respect their worth
as *individuals*, not as often-unwilling representatives of one or another culture. And insist that they do likewise when dealing with
others. If we do otherwise we risk miring our schools in incessant
and counterproductive ethnic and racial conflict.

*Gary K. Clabaugh is a professor of education at La Salle University in Phila-
delphia, Pennsylvania. He directs La Salle's Graduate Program in Education
and coordinates arts and sciences graduate programs.*

Possible School Policy Responses to Cultural Differences

Cultural Belief or Practice	Celebrate	Support	Permit	Take no position on	Discourage	Undermine	Prohibit
1. Celebrate a harvest festival by sacrificing live animals							
2. Regard the earth as one's "mother"		X					
3. Regard the elderly as having special knowledge							
4. Share wives with friends							
5. Select marriage partners for children				X			
6. Suppress female aspirations for education							X
7. Punish children corporally						X	
8. Use native language, refuse English						X	
9. Leave old people to starve if they can't work						X	
10. Make fun of disabled persons							X
11. Eat special foods				X			
12. Blame witchcraft and kill selected old women when the community suffers misfortune							X
13. Marry multiple women							
14. Seclude married women from the world							X
15. Have male tribal elders digitally deflower all 8-year-old girls as a part of their coming of age							
16. Eat the flesh of cats and dogs							
17. Take hallucinogenic drugs for religious purposes				X			
18. Require surgical removal of pubescent girls' clitorises by unlicensed practitioners							X
19. Wear decorative scars					X		
20. Hold hands with same sex in public			X				

Celebrate Diversity!

How to create a caring classroom that honors
your students' cultural backgrounds

By Mary Antón-Oldenburg, Ed.D.

"I don't want to phool around, I just want to read," writes Olivia, a young Russian immigrant, during a reading-reflection time. Zena, a child of African-American and North African descent, often misses school to help her recently widowed mother care for Zena's younger siblings. Pasha's parents, who came to the United States from India with high expectations, want their first grader to be assigned harder work, while Susie, a middle-class white child, has parents who want "a typical experience" for her—she should learn to read and write, primarily through play. Though names and some details have been changed, these are all real children—and students of mine.

As a teacher, juggling the expectations and experiences of such widely diverse youngsters and their parents can be both overwhelming and enriching. It's a challenge more and more of us need to face. The young people who fill our classrooms are increasingly diverse, which is a reflection of the United States as a whole. Nearly 8 million new immigrants settled in this country between 1981 and 1990, according to the most recent figures available from the United States Census Bureau. It is estimated that 80 percent of them came here from Latin America, the Caribbean, and Asia. Experts predict that by 2020 children of color will make up close to 46 percent of America's school-age population.

While one of our most basic goals as teachers is to support the growth of the individual child, it can become complicated when that child is from a very different background than our own, whatever our ethnic origin. We need to challenge ourselves to take steps to help our students appreciate their own cultural ways, even as we help them succeed as students.

All Learning is Culturally Constructed

The culture children bring to school can have a profound effect on how they respond. One good example of this is recounted in *Teaching Other People's Children: Literacy and Learning in a Bilingual Classroom,* by Cindy Ballenger (Teachers College Press, 1999). Puzzled by her lack of success in guiding the actions of the students in her bilingual Haitian preschool class, Cindy noticed that her Haitian colleagues seemed to be having an easier time with the youngsters. These teachers used verbal patterns, she discovered, that conveyed not only a reprimand, but linked a child's behavior to concepts of universal good and bad. These messages were delivered with affection, but without the same attention to honoring the child's individual feelings as is considered "best practice" for mainstream American children. Cindy successfully learned to adapt to this pattern of talk.

Experiences such as Cindy's suggest that we may need to reconsider our current understanding of what is good practice and move toward more culturally relevant teaching. Of course, that might not seem so easy when we are faced with 25 or more students, many with different backgrounds and sets of cultural experiences. What is a teacher to do?

Multicultural Education as a Way of Life

In caring classrooms, all children must be represented. This means that multicultural content must be seen as a way of life, not an add-on. Celebrate Black History Month, but take steps to make sure that representation of African-Americans—and all groups—occurs throughout the year. Regardless of your present school population, your students will benefit from a broad education that includes many diverse points of view and incorporates diverse cultural understanding. This goal can best be accomplished by seeing the teaching of multicultural content as a thread that runs through all your curricular areas.

Here are some other ways to celebrate student diversity:

• **Learn about the backgrounds of your students.** Educate yourself about unfamiliar cultures. When you have choices in curriculum, think carefully about underrepresented groups. Go beyond the obvious holidays, heroes, and foods. And remember: You have a greater potential to increase student understanding by in-depth coverage of a few cultures than you do by devoting a number of hurried days to many cultures.

With hardworking Pasha in my first-grade class, we embarked on a six-week study of the diversity of India. We were surprised to find that India has, for example, more than 100 official languages. Through exploration in film and language, culture and stories, museum visits and, yes, food, the students and I came to understand that just being from the same country does not mean that you are identical to others. We came to appreciate the multiple aspects of Indian culture, and this, in turn, helped us see that even groups that might look the same to us from their appearance have differences.

• **Encourage the teaching of multiple perspectives.** Resources abound to allow even young children to see the world from different points of view. For example, *The True Story of the Three Little Pigs,* by John Scieszka (Penguin, 1996), gives this well-worn tale a new spin by telling it from the wolf's perspective. Cut out some magazine pictures of a variety of people doing different things, and ask your students to imagine what these people are thinking. Older children will appreciate texts such as "The Bee," a poem found in *Joyful Noise: Poems for Two Voices,* by Paul Fleischman (HarperCollins, 1992), in which the points of view of a drone and a queen bee are presented.

• **Celebrate all kinds of stories.** Storytelling style can vary widely between cultures. Researchers have found that Japanese children tell shorter narratives than their white middle-class peers. In contrast, some African-American children may tell longer stories which include events and episodes that do nor appear, on the surface, to be related. They use elaborate wordplay and elicit greater participation of the audience. Latino children may tell stories in which personal relationships are emphasized rather than ones in which events are primary.

If you encounter a child whose narratives don't quite make sense to you, consider that you may be unfamiliar with that child's storytelling style. Investigate such styles and genres, in print and on audio- and videotape, and share them with your class. Audiotape the stories students tell, and look for patterns in them. Create a class library of stories told in the styles of different cultures. Ask parents for advice and suggestions.

To learn more, read *The Need for Story: Cultural Diversity in Classroom and Community,* by Anne Haas Dyson and Celia Genishi (National Council of Teachers of English, 1994), and *Chameleon Readers: Teaching Children to Appreciate All Kinds of Good Stories,* by Allyssa McCabe (McGraw-Hill, 1995).

• **Encourage the use of a child's primary language.** Research shows that children who develop strong vocabulary and concepts in their primary language will transfer these strengths to their secondary language. If two or more of your students speak in a non-English tongue, invite them to discuss among themselves a curricular topic in that language before completing an assignment or after they finish reading. Allow for journal writing in either language. Whenever possible, provide texts in a child's primary language, for reading during quiet times of the day. Encourage parents and other community members to help you provide resources in home languages to students. And most important, encourage parents to continue to discuss high-level concepts with their children in their home language.

Learn more about teaching students whose home language is not English in *Between Worlds: Access to Second Language Acquisition,* by David E. and Yvonne S. Freeman (Heinemann, 1994).

• **Be mindful of the books you read in class and the characters you choose for class study.** Pick books that portray boys and girls from diverse cultures—but first screen these books for stereotypic presentations. Ask yourself: Does this book present this group/person in a sensitive manner? Are the illustrations appropriate, or do they include exaggeration of cultural features or images? If I were a member of this culture, would I feel positive about my image in this book? Are the setting and illustrations appropriate to the time and place in which this story occurs?

• **Teach your students to actively critique the materials that they use, the media they view.** Ask students to be aware—in the books they read and the TV and videos they watch—of who is represented and how. I encourage my students to "talk back" to portrayals that they consider inaccurate. Sometimes, we create scripts based on these verbal critiques. Helping children to talk about and even rewrite texts that contain uncomfortable stereotypes or images teaches them that books can be challenged. It empowers them to view the world with a critical eye.

• **Help students create a classroom language for challenging stereotypic statements.** Model the caring but firm statements of "We don't talk about people in that manner here" and "The way that you are talking about that person [or group] is offensive to me and to many others. I don't think you mean to be so disrespectful." Help them take ownership in expressing personal views and beliefs. Include in your modeling modulators such as: "For me," "I believe," "I am wondering," and "I think."

• **Maintain high expectations for all children!** A teacher's attitude towards a student's potential is a powerful predictor for student achievement. Treat all your students as if they are the most capable. Work from the assumption that they bring great cultural resources with them—and you may just discover a treasure trove of experience and wisdom that will enrich everyone's learning.

Mary Antón-Oldenburg, Ed.D., is a teacher-researcher in Brookline, Massachusetts with 18 years' experience in grades K–8.

Cultural and Language Diversity in the Middle Grades

JOHN MYERS and DIANE BOOTHE

Teachers today must address the challenges presented by a diverse, multicultural population of students in U.S. middle schools. In some schools in the rapidly growing Atlanta metropolitan area, for example, more than 100 different cultures are represented—and almost as many languages spoken. In 1994, there were approximately 8,000 limited-English-proficient students (commonly referred to as ESOL students) enrolled in the public schools of Georgia (Georgia Department of Education 1994). By 1998, that figure had doubled (Georgia Department of Education 1998). The number of identified middle grades ESOL students in Texas, Florida, and California far surpasses that of Georgia. Across the nation, many middle level ESOL students remain unidentified, often because they are part of a migrant population.

At the middle level, the special physical, social, and emotional needs of learners must be taken into consideration when developing ESOL curricula and instructional strategies. Just as there is no typical middle grader, there is no typical ESOL student. One thirteen-year-old ESOL student may have spent eight years in a private school in his or her country of origin and received instruction in three languages. He or she may have a greater knowledge of mathematics than the typical American student at the same grade level. Conversely, another thirteen-year-old ESOL student may have had little formal education, perhaps having spent less than five years in a rural school. Ideal instructional strategies at the middle level for helping both students—and all those in-between—take the student where he or she is, then combine materials using language that students can understand, vocabulary development activities, cooperative learning, and positive and immediate feedback. Such activities and supportive settings reduce feelings of insecurity and isolation and motivate students to excel individually and as members of the group.

Students and a Macrocultural Perspective

How else do we address diversity in our schools? We must first acknowledge that the challenges of diversity are significant. The world is changing, and today's middle graders must be prepared for life in a multicultural society. Educators at all levels must recognize their responsibility to teach with a multicultural and multiethnic perspective, regardless of the content area. Teachers at the middle level must serve as role models by treating students from different cultures equitably and by conveying to students that a diverse population in the classroom is as much an opportunity for learning as it is a challenge.

Middle grades students often have fragile self-images; their psyches bruise easily. Yet, they are inherently curious and, when motivated, enthusiastic learners. Teachers can help them to develop personal rationales for embracing diversity and see the importance of multicultural thinking. Too often, students (and teachers) are influenced by ethnocentric misconceptions that portray members of other cultures according to stereotypes, rather than as the people they really are. Young people need to develop a macrocultural view of the world, and educators must stand ready to dispel misrepresentation and unrealistic generalizations wherever they may be found.

We must also work to preserve the cultural identity and enhance the self-concepts of our diverse (often ESOL) students. Baruth and Manning (1992), in a review of studies on the effects of minority group status on personality development during identity formation, concluded that self-concept is central to a learner's development. Minority group members' perceptions of self have a direct and significant effect on their social, psychological, and intellectual development.

Steps to Take

To foster a macrocultural perspective in all of our students at the middle level, we recommend that the following steps be taken by teachers, administrators, parents, students, and community members:

1. Develop a collaborative plan focused on celebrating diversity. The plan should draw on the resources that can be contributed by students from diverse backgrounds.

2. Set an example by welcoming new Americans, especially those who are particularly isolated because of limited English proficiency.

3. Integrate "global learning" into the curriculum when studying geography, travel, and current events. Technological

Learning can be broadly defined as a relatively permanent change in behavior or thinking due to experience. Learning is not a result of change due to maturation or temporary influences. Changes in behavior and thinking of students result from complex interactions between their individual characteristics and environmental factors. A continuing challenge in education is understanding these interactions so that learning can be enhanced. This unit focuses on approaches within educational psychology that represent different ways of viewing the learning process and related instructional strategies. Each approach to learning emphasizes a different set of personal and environmental factors that influence certain behaviors. While no one approach can fully explain learning, each is a valuable contribution to our knowledge about the process and the improvement of student performance.

The discussion of each learning approach includes suggestions for specific techniques and methods of teaching to guide teachers in understanding student behavior and in making decisions about how to teach. The articles in this section reflect a recent emphasis on applied research conducted in schools, research on the brain, and research on constructivist theories.

Researchers have recently made significant advances in understanding the way our brain works. Information processing refers to the way that the mind receives sensory information, stores it as memory, and recalls it for later use. This procedure is basic to all learning, no matter what teaching approach is taken, and we know that the method used in processing information determines to some extent how much and what we remember. The essays in the first subsection present some of the fundamental principles of brain functioning, information processing and cognition, and human intelligences.

In the past, behaviorism was the best-known approach to learning. Most practicing and prospective teachers are familiar with concepts such as classical conditioning, reinforcement, and punishment, and there is no question that behaviorism has made significant contributions to understanding learning. But behaviorism has also been subject to much misinterpretation, in part because it seems so simple. In fact, the effective use of behavioristic principles is complex and demanding, as the article on praise points out.

Constructivist learning theory is currently the predominant approach to learning that is recognized by educational psychologists. According to constructivists, it is important for students to actively create and reorganize knowledge. There is a need for students to interpret within meaningful contexts so that what is learned is connected to existing knowledge. One article is included that is devoted to constructivist learning. It reviews the essence of a constructivist culture.

Social psychological learning emphasizes the affective, social, moral, and personal development of students. Social psychology is the study of the nature of interpersonal relationships in social situations. In education, this approach looks at teacher-pupil relationships and group processes to derive principles of interaction that affect learning. One article in this section examines the application of social psychological principles by stress-

ing how healthy self-esteem is developed not by focusing on oneself but by being involved in externally oriented, meaningful activities.

Instructional strategies are the teacher behaviors and methods of conveying information that affect learning. Teaching methods or techniques can vary greatly, depending on objectives, group size, types of students, and personality of the teacher. For example, discussion classes are generally more effective for enhancing thinking skills than are individualized sessions or lectures. For the final subsection, four articles have been selected that show how teachers can use principles of cognitive psychology and intelligence in their teaching within the current standards-based environment. The first article emphasizes the importance of concept mapping to encourage and support students' thinking. Differentiated instruction is quickly becoming a major teaching technique, as discussed in the next article by national expert Carol Tomlinson. In the third article, Tominson considers differentiation in light of another recent trend in instruction—standards-based teaching. Technology is also becoming a pervasive opportunity for teaching and learning, and the last article summarizes effective applications of technology in the classroom.

In Search of...
Brain-Based Education

The "In Search of..." television series is no way to present history,
Mr. Bruer points out, and the brain-based education literature is not the way
to present the science of learning.

By John T. Bruer

WE HAVE almost survived the Decade of the Brain. During the 1990s, government agencies, foundations, and advocacy groups engaged in a highly successful effort to raise public awareness about advances in brain research. Brain science became material for cover stories in our national newsmagazines. Increased public awareness raised educators' always simmering interest in the brain to the boiling point. Over the past five years, there have been numerous books, conferences, and entire issues of education journals devoted to what has come to be called "brain-based education."

Brain-based educators tend to support progressive education reforms. They decry the "factory model of education," in which experts create knowledge, teachers disseminate it, and students are graded on how much of it they can absorb and retain. Like many other educators, brain-based educators favor a constructivist, active learning model. Students should be actively engaged in learning and in guiding their own instruction. Brain enthusiasts see neuroscience as perhaps the best weapon with which to destroy our outdated factory model.[1] They argue that teachers should teach for meaning and understanding. To do so, they claim, teachers should create learning environments that are low in threat and high in challenge, and students should be actively engaged and immersed in complex experiences. No reasonable parent or informed educator would take is-

sue with these ideas. Indeed, if more schools taught for understanding and if more teachers had the resources to do so, our schools would be better learning environments.

However, there is nothing new in this critique of traditional education. It is based on a cognitive and constructivist model of learning that is firmly rooted in more than 30 years of psychological research. Whatever scientific evidence we have for or against the efficacy of such educational approaches can be found in any current textbook on educational psychology.[2] None of the evidence comes from brain research. It comes from cognitive and developmental psychology; from the behavioral, not the biological, sciences; from our scientific understanding of the mind, not from our scientific understanding of the brain.

To the extent that brain-based educators' recipe for school and classroom change is well grounded in this behavioral research, their message is valuable. Teachers should know about short- and long-term memory; about primacy/recency effects; about how procedural, declarative, and episodic memory differ; and about how prior knowledge affects our current ability to learn. But to claim that these are "brain-based" findings is misleading.

While we know a considerable amount from psychological research that is pertinent to teaching and learning, we know much less about how the brain functions and learns.[3] For nearly a century, the sci-

ence of the mind (psychology) developed independently from the science of the brain (neuroscience). Psychologists were interested in our mental functions and capacities—how we learn, remember, and think. Neuroscientists were interested in how the brain develops and functions. It was as if psychologists were interested only in our mental software and neuroscientists only in our neural hardware. Deeply held theoretical assumptions in both fields supported a view that mind and brain could, and indeed should, be studied independently.

It is only in the past 15 years or so that these theoretical barriers have fallen. Now scientists called cognitive neuroscientists are beginning to study how our neural hardware might run our mental software, how brain structures support mental functions, how our neural circuits enable us to think and learn. This is an exciting and new scientific endeavor, but it is also a very young one. As a result we know relatively little about learning, thinking, and remembering at the level of brain areas, neural circuits, or synapses; we know very little about how the brain thinks, remembers, and learns.

Yet brain science has always had a seductive appeal for educators.[4] Brain science appears to give hard biological data and explanations that, for some reason, we find more compelling than the "soft" data that come from psychological science. But seductive appeal and a very limited brain science database are a dangerous combination. They make it relatively easy to formulate bold statements about brain science and education that are speculative at best and often far removed from neuroscientific fact. Nonetheless, the allure of brain science ensures that these ideas will often find a substantial and accepting audience. As Joseph LeDoux, a leading authority on the neuroscience of emotion, cautioned educators at a 1996 brain and education conference, "These ideas are easy to sell to the public, but it is easy to take them beyond their actual basis in science."[5]

The danger with much of the brain-based education literature is that it becomes exceedingly difficult to separate the science from the speculation.

And the ideas are far-ranging indeed. Within the literature on the brain and education one finds, for example, that brain science supports Bloom's Taxonomy, Madeline Hunter's effective teaching, whole-language instruction, Vygotsky's theory of social learning, thematic instruction, portfolio assessment, and cooperative learning.

The difficulty is that the brain-based education literature is very much like a docudrama or an episode of "In Search of... " in which an interesting segment on Egyptology suddenly takes a bizarre turn that links Tutankhamen with the alien landing in Roswell, New Mexico. Just where did the episode turn from archaeological fact to speculation or fantasy? That is the same question one must constantly ask when reading about brain-based education.

Educators, like all professionals, should be interested in knowing how basic research, including brain science, might contribute to improved professional practice. The danger with much of the brain-based education literature, as with an "In Search of... " episode, is that it becomes exceedingly difficult to separate the science from the speculation, to sort what we know from what we would like to be the case. If our interest is enhancing teaching and learning by applying science to education, this is not the way to do it. Would we want our children to learn about the Exodus by

watching "In Search of Ramses' Martian Wife"?

We might think of each of the numerous claims that brain-based educators make as similar to an "In Search of... " episode. For each one, we should ask, Where does the science end and the speculation begin? I cannot do that here. So instead I'll concentrate on two ideas that appear prominently in brain-based education articles: the educational significance of brain laterality (right brain versus left brain) and the claim that neuroscience has established that there is a sensitive period for learning.

Left Brain, Right Brain: One More Time

"Right brain versus left brain" is one of those popular ideas that will not die. Speculations about the educational significance of brain laterality have been circulating in the education literature for 30 years. Although repeatedly criticized and dismissed by psychologists and brain scientists, the speculation continues.[6] David Sousa devotes a chapter of *How the Brain Learns* to explaining brain laterality and presents classroom strategies that teachers might use to ensure that both hemispheres are involved in learning.[7] Following the standard line, the *left hemisphere* is the logical hemisphere, involved in speech, reading, and writing. It is the analytical hemisphere that evaluates factual material in a rational way and that understands the literal interpretation of words. It is a serial processor that tracks time and sequences and that recognizes words, letters, and numbers. The right hemisphere is the intuitive, creative hemisphere. It gathers information more from images than from words. It is a parallel processor well suited for pattern recognition and spatial reasoning. It is the hemisphere that recognizes faces, places, and objects.

According to this traditional view of laterality, left-hemisphere-dominant individuals tend to be more verbal, more analytical, and better problem solvers. Females, we are told, are more likely than males to be left-hemisphere dominant. Right-hemisphere-dominant individuals, more typically males, paint and draw well, are good at math, and deal with the visual world more easily than with the verbal. Schools, Sousa points out, are overwhelmingly left-hemisphere places in which left-hemisphere-dominant individuals, mostly girls, feel more comfortable than right-hemisphere-dominant individuals, mostly

boys. Hemispheric dominance also explains why girls are superior to boys in arithmetic—it is linear and logical, and there is only one correct answer to each problem—while girls suffer math anxiety when it comes to the right-hemisphere activities of algebra and geometry. These latter disciplines, unlike arithmetic, are holistic, relational, and spatial and also allow multiple solutions to problems.

Before we consider how, or whether, brain science supports this traditional view, educators should be wary of claims about the educational significance of gender differences in brain laterality. There are tasks that psychologists have used in their studies that reveal gender-based differences in performance. Often, however, these differences are specific to a task. Although males are superior to females at mentally rotating objects, this seems to be the only spatial task for which psychologists have found such a difference.[8] Moreover, when they do find gender differences, these differences tend to be very small. If they were measured on an I.Q.-like scale with a mean of 100 and a standard deviation of 15, these gender differences amount to around five points. Furthermore, the range of difference within genders is broad. Many males have better language skills than most females; many females have better spatial and mathematical skills than most males. The scientific consensus among psychologists and neuroscientists who conduct these studies is that whatever gender differences exist may have interesting consequences for the scientific study of the brain, but they have no practical or instructional consequences.[9]

Now let's consider the brain sciences and how or whether they offer support for some of the particular teaching strategies Sousa recommends. To involve the right hemisphere in learning, Sousa writes, teachers should encourage students to generate and use mental imagery: "For most people, the left hemisphere specializes in coding information verbally while the right hemisphere codes information visually. Although teachers spend much time talking (and sometimes have their students talk) about the learning objective, little time is given to developing visual cues." To ensure that the left hemisphere gets equal time, teachers should let students "read, write, and compute often."[10]

What brain scientists currently know about spatial reasoning and mental imagery provides counterexamples to such simplistic claims as these. Such claims arise out of a folk theory about brain laterality, not a neuroscientific one.

Here are two simple spatial tasks: 1) determine whether one object is above or below another, and 2) determine whether two objects are more or less than one foot apart. Based on our folk theory of the brain, as spatial tasks both of these should be right-hemisphere tasks. However, if we delve a little deeper, as psychologists and neuroscientists tend to do, we see that the information-processing or computational demands of the two tasks are different.[11] The first task requires that we place objects or parts of objects into broad categories—up/down or left/right—but we do not have to determine how far up or down (or left or right) one object is from the other. Psychologists call this *categorical* spatial reasoning. In contrast, the second task is a spatial *coordinate* task, in which we must compute and retain precise distance relations between the objects.

Research over the last decade has shown that categorical and coordinate spatial reasoning are performed by distinct subsystems in the brain.[12] A subsystem in the brain's *left* hemisphere performs categorical spatial reasoning. A subsystem in the brain's *right* hemisphere processes coordinate spatial relationships. Although the research does point to differences in the information-processing abilities and biases of the brain hemispheres, those differences are found at a finer level of analysis than "spatial reasoning." It makes no sense to claim that spatial reasoning is a right-hemisphere task.

Based on research like this, Christopher Chabris and Stephen Kosslyn, leading researchers in the field of spatial reasoning and visual imagery, claim that any model of brain lateralization that assigns conglomerations of complex mental abilities, such as spatial reasoning, to one hemisphere or the other, as our folk theory does, is simply too crude to be scientifically or practically useful. Our folk theory can neither explain what the brain is doing nor generate useful predictions about where novel tasks might be computed in the brain.[13] Unfortunately, it is just such a crude folk theory that brain-based educators rely on when framing their recommendations.

Visual imagery is another example. From the traditional, folk-theoretic perspective, generating and using visual imagery is a right-hemisphere function. Generating and using visual imagery is a complex operation that involves, even at a crude level of analysis, at least five distinct mental subcomponents: 1) to create a visual image of a dog, you must transfer long-term visual memories into a temporary visual memory store; 2) to determine if your imagined dog has a tail, you must zoom in and identify details of the image; 3) to put a blue collar on the dog requires that you add a new element to your previously generated image; 4) to make the dog look the other way demands that you rotate your image of the dog; and 5) to draw or describe the imagined dog, you must scan the visual image with your mind's eye.

There is an abundance of neuroscientific evidence that this complex task is not confined to the right hemisphere. There are patients with brain damage who can recognize visual objects and draw or describe visible objects normally, yet these patients cannot answer questions that require them to generate a mental image. ("Think of a dog. Does it have a long tail?") These patients have long-term visual memories, but they cannot use those memories to generate mental images. All these patients have damage to the rear portion of the left hemisphere.[14]

Studies on split-brain patients, people who have had their two hemispheres surgically disconnected to treat severe epilepsy, allow scientists to present visual stimuli to one hemisphere but not the other. Michael Gazzaniga and Kosslyn showed split-brain patients a lower-case letter and then asked the patients whether the corresponding capital letter had any curved lines.[15] The task required that the patients generate a mental image of the capital letter based on the lower-case letter they had seen. When the stimuli were presented to the patients' left hemispheres, they performed perfectly on the task. However, the patients made many mistakes when the letter stimuli were presented to the right hemisphere. Likewise, brain-imaging studies of normal adult subjects performing imagery tasks show that both hemispheres are active in these tasks.[16] Based on all these data, brain scientists have concluded that the ability to generate visual imagery depends on the left hemisphere.

One of the most accessible presentations of this research appears in *Images of Mind*, by Michael Posner and Mark Raichle, in which they conclude, "The common belief that creating mental imagery is a function of the right hemisphere is clearly false."[17] Again, different brain areas are specialized for different tasks, but that specialization occurs at a finer level of analysis than "using visual imagery." Using visual imagery may be a useful learning strategy, but if it is useful it is not because it involves an otherwise underutilized right hemisphere in learning.

The same problem also subverts claims that one hemisphere or the other is the site of number recognition or reading skills. Here is a simple number task, expressed in two apparently equivalent ways: What is bigger, two or five? What is bigger, 2 or 5? It involves recognizing number symbols and understanding what those symbols mean. According to our folk theory, this should be a left-hemisphere task. But once again our folk theory is too crude.

Numerical comparison involves at least two mental subskills: identifying the number names and then comparing the numerical magnitudes that they designate. Although we seldom think of it, we are "bilingual" when it comes to numbers. We have number words—e.g., *one, two*—to name numbers, and we also have special written symbols, Arabic numerals—e.g., 1, 2. Our numerical bilingualism means that the two comparison questions above place different computational demands on the mind/brain. Using brain-recording techniques, Stanislaus Dehaene found that we identify number words using a system in the brain's left hemisphere, but we identify Arabic numerals using brain areas in both the right and left hemispheres. Once we identify either the number words or the Arabic digits as symbols for numerical quantities, a distinct neural subsystem in the brain's right hemisphere compares magnitudes named by the two number symbols.[18]

Even for such a simple number task as comparison, both hemispheres are involved. Thus it makes no neuroscientific sense to claim that the left hemisphere recognizes numbers. Brain areas are specialized, but at a much finer level than "recognizing numbers." This simple task is already too complex for our folk theory to handle. Forget about algebra and geometry.

Similar research that analyzes speech and reading skills into their component processes also shows that reading is not simply a left-hemisphere task, as our folk theory suggests. Recognizing speech sounds, decoding written words, finding the meanings of words, constructing the gist of a written text, and making inferences as we read all rely on subsystems in both brain hemispheres.[19]

There is another different, but equally misleading, interpretation of brain laterality that occurs in the literature of brain-based education. In *Making Connections*, Renate Caine and Geoffrey Caine are critical of traditional "brain dichotomizers" and warn that the brain does not lend itself to such simple explanations. In their view, the results of research on split brains and hemispheric specialization are inconclusive—"both hemispheres are involved in all activities"—a conclusion that would seem to be consistent with what we have seen in our brief review of spatial reasoning, visual imagery, number skills, and reading.

However, following the folk theory, they do maintain that the left hemisphere processes parts and the right hemisphere processes wholes. In their interpretation, the educational significance of laterality research is that it shows that, within the brain, parts and wholes always interact. Laterality research thus provides scientific support for one of their principles of brain-based education: the brain processes parts and wholes simultaneously. Rather than number comparison or categorical spatial reasoning, the Caines provide a more global example: "Consider a poem, a play, a great novel, or a great work of philosophy. They all involve a sense of the 'wholeness' of things and a capacity to work with patterns, often in timeless ways. In other words, the 'left brain' processes are enriched and supported by 'right brain' processes."[20]

For educators, the Caines see the two-brain doctrine as a "valuable metaphor that helps educators acknowledge two separate but simultaneous tendencies in the brain for organizing information. One is to reduce information to parts; the other is to perceive and work with it as a whole or a series of wholes."[21] Effective brain-based educational strategies overlook neither parts nor wholes, but constantly attempt to provide opportunities in which students can make connections and integrate parts and wholes. Thus the Caines number among their examples of brain-based approaches whole-language instruction,[22] integrated curricula, thematic teaching, and cooperative learning.[23] Similarly, because we make connections best when new information is embedded in meaningful life events and in socially interactive situations, Lev Vygotsky's theory of social learning should also be highly brain compatible.[24]

To the extent that one would want to view this as a metaphor, all I can say is that some of us find some metaphors more appealing than others. To the extent that this is supposed to be an attempt to ground educational principles in brain science, the aliens have just landed in Egypt.

The fundamental problem with the right-brain versus left-brain claims in the education literature is that they rely on intuitions and folk theories about the brain.

Where did things go awry? Although they claim that laterality research in the sense of hemispheric localization is inconclusive, the Caines do maintain the piece of our folk theory that attributes "whole" processing to the right hemisphere and "part" processing to the left hemisphere. Because the two hemispheres are connected in normal healthy brains, they conclude that the brain processes parts and wholes simultaneously. It certainly does—although it probably is not the case that wholes and parts can be so neatly dichotomized. For example, in visual word decoding, the right hemisphere seems to read words letter by letter—by looking at the parts—while the left hemisphere recognizes entire words—the visual word forms.[25]

But again, the parts and wholes to which the brain is sensitive appear to occur at quite a fine-grained level of analysis—categories versus coordinates, generating versus scanning visual images, identifying number words versus Arabic digits. The Caines' example of part/whole interactions—the left-hemisphere comprehension of a text and the right-hemisphere appreciation of wholeness—relates to such a highly complex task that involves so many parts and wholes at different levels of analysis that it is trivially true that the whole brain is involved. Thus their appeal to brain science suffers from the same problem Kosslyn identified in the attempts to use crude theories to understand the brain. The only brain categories that the Caines appeal to are parts and wholes. Then they attempt to understand learning and exceedingly complex tasks in terms of parts and wholes. This approach bothers neither to analyze the brain nor to analyze behaviors.

The danger here is that one might think that there are brain-based reasons to adopt whole-language instruction, integrated curricula, or Vygotskian social learning. There are none. Whether or not these edu-

cational practices should be adopted must be determined on the basis of the impact they have on student learning. The evidence we now have on whole-language instruction is at best inconclusive, and the efficacy of social learning theory remains an open question. Brain science contributes no evidence, pro or con, for the brain-based strategies that the Caines espouse.

The fundamental problem with the right-brain versus left-brain claims that one finds in the education literature is that they rely on our intuitions and folk theories about the brain, rather than on what brain science is actually able to tell us. Our folk theories are too crude and imprecise to have any scientific, predictive, or instructional value. What modern brain science is telling us—and what brain-based educators fail to appreciate—is that it makes no scientific sense to map gross, unanalyzed behaviors and skills—reading, arithmetic, spatial reasoning—onto one brain hemisphere or another.

Brains Like Sponges: The Sensitive Period

A new and popular, but problematic, idea found in the brain-based literature is that there is a critical or sensitive period in brain development, lasting until a child is around 10 years old, during which children learn faster, easier, and with more meaning than at any other time in their lives. David Sousa presented the claim this way in a recent commentary in *Education Week*, titled "Is the Fuss About Brain Research Justified?"

As the child grows, the brain selectively strengthens and prunes connections based on experience. Although this process continues throughout our lives, it seems to be most pronounced between the ages of 2 and 11, as different development areas emerge and taper off.... These so-called "windows of opportunity" represent critical periods when the brain demands certain types of input to create or consolidate neural networks, especially for acquiring language, emotional control, and learning to play music. Certainly, one can learn new information and skills at any age. But what the child learns during that window period will strongly influence what is learned after the window closes.[26]

In a recent *Educational Leadership* article, Pat Wolfe and Ron Brandt prudently caution educators against any quick marriage between brain science and education. However, among the well-established neuroscientific findings about which educators can be confident, they include, "Some abilities are acquired more easily during certain sensitive periods, or 'windows of opportunity.'" Later they continue, "During these years, [the brain] also has a remarkable ability to adapt and reorganize. It appears to develop some capacities with more ease at this time than in the years after puberty. These stages once called 'critical periods' are more accurately described as 'sensitive periods' or 'windows of opportunity.'"[27] Eric Jensen, in *Teaching with the Brain in Mind*, also writes that "the brain learns fastest and easiest during the school years."[28]

If there were neuroscientific evidence for the existence of such a sensitive period, such evidence might appear to provide a biological argument for the importance of elementary teaching and a scientific rationale for redirecting resources, restructuring curricula, and reforming pedagogy to take advantage of the once-in-a-lifetime learning opportunity nature has given us. If teachers could understand when sensitive periods begin and end, the thinking goes, they could structure curricula to take advantage of these unique windows of opportunity. Sousa tells of an experienced fifth-grade teacher who was upset when a mother asked the teacher what she was doing to take advantage of her daughter's windows of opportunity before they closed. Unfortunately, according to Sousa, the teacher was unaware of the windows-of-opportunity research. He warns, "As the public learns more about brain research through the popular press, scenes like this are destined to be repeated, further eroding confidence in teachers and in schools."[29]

This well-established neuroscientific "finding" about a sensitive period for learning originated in the popular press and in advocacy documents. It is an instance where neuroscientists have speculated about the implications of their work for education and where educators have uncritically embraced that speculation. Presenting speculation as fact poses a greater threat to the public's confidence in teachers and schools than does Sousa's fifth-grade teacher.

During 1993, the *Chicago Tribune* ran Ron Kotulak's series of Pulitzer-Prize-winning articles on the new brain science. Kotulak's articles later appeared as a book titled *Inside the Brain: Revolutionary Discoveries of How the Mind Works*. Kotulak, an esteemed science writer, presented the

first explicit statement that I have been able to find on the existence of a sensitive period between ages 4 and 10, during which children's brains learn fastest and easiest.[30] Variations on the claim appear in the Carnegie Corporation of New York's 1996 publication, *Years of Promise: A Comprehensive Learning Strategy for America's Children*, and in *Building Knowledge for a Nation of Learners*, published by the Office of Educational Research and Improvement of the U.S. Department of Education.[31]

A report released in conjunction with the April 1997 White House Conference on Early Brain Development stated, "[B]y the age of three, the brains of children are two and a half times more active than the brains of adults—and they stay that way throughout the first decade of life.... This suggests that young children—particularly infants and toddlers—are biologically primed for learning and that these early years provide a unique window of opportunity or prime time for learning."[32]

If the sensitive period from age 4 to age 10 is a finding about which educators can be confident and one that justifies the current fuss about brain science, we would expect to find an extensive body of neuroscientific research that supports the claim. Surprisingly, brain-based enthusiasts appeal to a very limited body of evidence.

In Kotulak's initial statement of the sensitive-period claim, he refers to the brain-imaging work of Dr. Harry Chugani, M.D., at Wayne State University: "Chugani, whose imaging studies revealed that children's brains learned fastest and easiest between the ages of 4 and 10, said these years are often wasted because of lack of input."[33]

Years of Promise, the Carnegie Corporation report, cites a speech Kotulak presented at a conference on Brain Development in Young Children, held at the University of Chicago on 13 June 1996. Again referring to Chugani's work, Kotulak said that the years from 4 to about 10 "are the wonder years of learning, when a child can easily pick up a foreign language without an accent and learn a musical instrument with ease."[34] *Years of Promise* also cites a review article published by Dr. Chugani that is based on remarks he made at that Chicago conference.[35] *Rethinking the Brain*, a report based on the Chicago conference, also cites the same sources, as does the U.S. Department of Education document. What's more, Wolfe, Brandt, and Jensen

also cite Chugani's work in their discussions of the sensitive period for learning.

A 1996 article on education and the brain that appeared in *Education Week* reported, "By age 4, Chugani found, a child's brain uses more than twice the glucose that an adult brain uses. Between the ages of 4 and 10, the amount of glucose a child's brain uses remains relatively stable. But by age 10, glucose utilization begins to drop off until it reaches adult levels at age 16 or 17. Chugani's findings suggest that a child's peak learning years occur just as all those synapses are forming."[36]

To be fair, these educators are not misrepresenting Chugani's views. He has often been quoted on the existence and educational importance of the sensitive period from age 4 until age 10.[37] In a review of his own work, published in *Preventive Medicine*, Chugani wrote:

The notion of an extended period during childhood when activity-dependent [synapse] stabilization occurs has recently received considerable attention by those individuals and organizations dealing with early intervention to provide "environmental enrichment" and with the optimal design of educational curricula. Thus, it is now believed by many (including this author) that the biological "window of opportunity" when learning is efficient and easily retained is perhaps not fully exploited by our educational system.[38]

Oddly, none of these articles and reports cites the single research article that provides the experimental evidence that originally motivated the claim: a 1987 *Annals of Neurology* article.[39] In that 1987 article, Chugani and his colleagues, M. E. Phelps and J. C. Mazziota, report results of PET (positron emission tomography) scans on 29 epileptic children, ranging in age from five days to 15 years. Because PET scans require the injection of radioactive substances, physicians can scan children only for diagnostic and therapeutic purposes; they cannot scan "normal, healthy" children just out of scientific curiosity. Thus the 1987 study is an extremely important one because it was the first, if not the only, imaging study that attempted to trace brain development from infancy through adolescence.

The scientists administered radioactively labeled glucose to the children and used PET scans to measure the rate at which specific brain areas took up the glucose. The assumption is that areas of the brain that are more active require more energy and so will take up more of the glucose. While the scans were being acquired, the scientists made every effort to eliminate, or at least minimize, all sensory stimulation for the subjects. Thus they measured the rate of glucose uptake when the brain was (presumably) not engaged in any sensory or cognitive processing. That is, they measured resting brain-glucose metabolism.

One of their major findings was that, in all the brain areas they examined, metabolic levels reached adult values when children were approximately 2 years old and continued to increase, reaching rates twice the adult level by age 3 or 4. Resting glucose uptake remained at this elevated level until the children were around 9 years old. At age 9, the rates of brain glucose metabolism started to decline and stabilized at adult values by the end of the teenage years. What the researchers found, then, was a "high plateau" period for metabolic activity in the brain that lasted from roughly age 3 to age 9.

Neither Chugani, his co-authors, nor other neuroscientists have studied how quickly or easily 5-year-olds learn as opposed to 15-year-olds.

What is the significance of this high plateau period? To interpret their findings, Chugani and his colleagues relied on earlier research in which brain scientists had counted synapses in samples of human brain tissue to determine how the number and density of synaptic connections change in the human brain over our life spans. In the late 1970s, Peter Huttenlocher of the University of Chicago found that, starting a few months after birth and continuing until age 3, various parts of the brain formed synapses very rapidly.[40] This early, exuberant synapse growth resulted in synaptic densities in young children's brains that were 50% higher than the densities in mature adult brains. In humans, synaptic densities appear to remain at these elevated levels until around puberty, when some mechanism that is apparently under genetic control causes synapses to be eliminated or pruned back to the lower adult levels.

With this background, Chugani and his colleagues reasoned as follows. There is other evidence suggesting that maintaining synapses and their associated neural structures accounts for most of the glucose that the brain consumes. Their PET study measured changes in the brain's glucose consumption over the life span. Therefore, they reasoned, as the density and number of synapses wax and wane, so too does the rate of brain-glucose metabolism. This 1987 PET study provides important indirect evidence about brain development, based on the study of living brains, that corroborates the direct evidence based on counting synapses in samples of brain tissue taken from patients at autopsy. In the original paper, the scientists stated an important conclusion: "Our findings support the commonly accepted view that brain maturation in humans proceeds at least into the second decade of life."[41]

However, if you read the 1987 paper by Chugani, Phelps, and Mazziota, you will not find a section titled "The Relationship of Elevated Brain Metabolism and Synaptic Densities to Learning." Neither Chugani nor any of his co-authors have studied how quickly or easily 5-year-olds learn as opposed to 15-year-olds. Nor have other neuroscientists studied what high synaptic densities or high brain energy consumption means for the ease, rapidity, and depth of learning.

To connect high brain metabolism or excessive synaptic density with a critical period for learning requires some fancy footwork—or maybe more accurately, sleight of hand. We know that from early childhood until around age 10, children have extra or redundant synaptic connections in their brains. So, the reasoning goes, during this high plateau period of excess brain connectivity, "the individual is given the opportunity to retain and increase the efficiency of connections that, through repeated use during a critical period, are deemed to be important, whereas connections that are used to a lesser extent are more susceptible to being eliminated."[42] This, of course, is simply to assume that the high plateau period is a critical period.

Linking the critical period with learning requires an implicit appeal to another folk belief that appears throughout the history of the brain in education literature. This common assumption is that periods of rapid brain growth or high activity are optimal times, sensitive periods, or windows of opportunity for learning.[43] We get from Chugani's important brain-imaging results

to a critical period for learning via two assumptions, neither of which is supported by neuroscientific data, and neither of which has even been the object of neuroscientific research. The claim that the period of high brain connectivity is a critical period for learning, far from being a neuroscientific finding about which educators can be confident, is at best neuroscientific speculation.

Chugani accurately described the scientific state of affairs in his *Preventive Medicine* review. He *believes*, along with some educators and early childhood advocates, that there is a biological window of opportunity when learning is easy, efficient, and easily retained. But there is no neuroscientific evidence to support this belief. And where there is no scientific evidence, there is no scientific fact.

Furthermore, it would appear that we have a considerable amount of research ahead of us if we are to amass the evidence for or against this belief. Neuroscientists have little idea of how experience before puberty affects either the timing or the extent of synaptic elimination. While they have documented that the pruning of synapses does occur, no reliable studies have compared differences in final adult synaptic connectivity with differences in the experiences of individuals before puberty. Nor do they know whether the animals or individuals with greater synaptic densities in adulthood are necessarily more intelligent and developed. Neuroscientists do not know if prior training and education affect either loss or retention of synapses at puberty.[44]

Nor do neuroscientists know how learning is related to changes in brain metabolism and synaptic connectivity over our lifetimes. As the developmental neurobiologist Patricia Goldman-Rakic told educators, "While children's brains acquire a tremendous amount of information during the early years, most learning takes place after synaptic formation stabilizes."[45] That is, a great deal, if not most, learning takes place after age 10 and after pruning has occurred. If so, we may turn into efficient general learning machines only after puberty, only after synaptic formation stabilizes and our brains are less active.

Finally, the entire discussion of this purported critical period takes place under an implicit assumption that children actually do learn faster, more easily, and more deeply between the ages of 4 and 10. There are certainly critical periods for the development of species-wide skills, such as seeing, hearing, and acquiring a first language, but critical periods are interesting to psychologists because they seem to be the exception rather than the rule in human development. As Jacqueline Johnson and Elissa Newport remind us in their article on critical periods in language learning, "In most domains of learning, skill increases over development."[46]

When we ask whether children actually do learn more easily and meaningfully than adults, the answers we get are usually anecdotes about athletes, musicians, and students of second languages. We have not begun to look at the rate, efficiency, and depth of learning across various age groups in a representative sample of learning domains. We are making an assumption about learning behavior and then relying on highly speculative brain science to explain our assumption. We have a lot more research to do.

So, despite what you read in the papers and in the brain-based education literature, neuroscience has *not* established that there is a sensitive period between the ages of 4 and 10 during which children learn more quickly, easily, and meaningfully. Brain-based educators have uncritically embraced neuroscientific speculation.

The pyramids were built by aliens—to house Elvis.

A February 1996 article in *Newsweek* on the brain and education quoted Linda Darling-Hammond: "Our school system was invented in the late 1800s, and little has changed. Can you imagine if the medical profession ran this way?"[47] Darling-Hammond is right. Our school system must change to reflect what we now know about teaching, learning, mind, and brain. To the extent that we want education to be a research-based enterprise, the medical profession provides a reasonable model. We can only be thankful that members of the medical profession are more careful in applying biological research to their professional practice than some educators are in applying brain research to theirs.

We should not shrug off this problem. It is symptomatic of some deeper problems about how research is presented to educators, about what educators find compelling, about how educators evaluate research, and about how professional development time and dollars are spent. The "In Search of… " series is a television program that provides an entertaining mix of fact, fiction, and fantasy. That can be an amusing exercise, but it is not always instructive. The brain-based education literature represents a genre of writing, most often appearing in professional education

publications, that provides a popular mix of fact, misinterpretation, and speculation. That can be intriguing, but it is not always informative. "In Search of… " is no way to present history, and the brain-based education literature is not the way to present the science of learning.

Notes

1. Renate Nummela Caine and Geoffrey Caine, *Making Connections: Teaching and the Human Brain* (New York: Addison-Wesley, 1994); idem, "Building a Bridge Between the Neurosciences and Education: Cautions and Possibilities," *NASSP Bulletin*, vol. 82, 1998, pp. 1–8; Eric Jensen, *Teaching with the Brain in Mind* (Alexandria, Va.: Association for Supervision and Curriculum Development, 1998); and Robert Sylvester, *A Celebration of Neurons* (Alexandria, Va.: Association for Supervision and Curriculum Development, 1995).

2. See, for example, Michael Pressley and C. B. McCormick, *Advanced Educational Psychology for Educators, Researchers, and Policymakers* (New York: HarperCollins, 1995).

3. John T. Bruer, *Schools for Thought: A Science of Learning in the Classroom* (Cambridge, Mass.: MIT Press, 1993); and idem, "Education and the Brain: A Bridge Too Far," *Educational Researcher*, November 1997, pp. 4–16.

4. Susan F. Chipman, "Integrating Three Perspectives on Learning," in Sarah L. Friedman, Kenneth A. Klivington, and R. W. Peterson, eds., *The Brain, Cognition, and Education* (Orlando, Fla.: Academic Press, 1986), pp. 203–32.

5. *Bridging the Gap Between Neuroscience and Education: Summary of a Workshop Cosponsored by the Education Commission of the States and the Charles A. Dana Foundation* (Denver: Education Commission of the States, 1996), p. 5.

6. Chipman, op. cit.; Howard Gardner, *Art, Mind, and Brain: A Cognitive Approach to Creativity* (New York: Basic Books, 1982); Mike Rose, "Narrowing the Mind and Page: Remedial Writers and Cognitive Reductionism," *College Composition and Communication*, vol. 39, 1988, pp. 267–302; and Jerre Levy, "Right Brain, Left Brain: Fact and Fiction," *Psychology Today*, May 1985, p. 38.

7. David A. Sousa, *How the Brain Learns: A Classroom Teacher's Guide*

(Reston, Va.: National Association of Secondary School Principals, 1995).

8. M. C. Linn and A. C. Petersen, "Emergence and Characterization of Sex Differences in Spatial Ability: A Meta-Analysis," *Child Development*, vol. 56, 1985, pp. 1470–98.

9. Sally Springer and Georg Deutsch, *Left Brain, Right Brain* (New York: W. H. Freeman, 1993).

10. Sousa, pp. 95, 99.

11. Christopher F. Chabris and Stephen M. Kosslyn, "How Do the Cerebral Hemispheres Contribute to Encoding Spatial Relations?," *Current Directions in Psychology*, vol. 7, 1998, pp. 8–14.

12. Ibid.

13. Ibid.

14. Martha Farah, *Visual Agnosias* (Cambridge, Mass.: MIT Press, 1991).

15. Stephen M. Kosslyn et al., "A Computational Analysis of Mental Image Generation: Evidence from Functional Dissociations in Split-Brain Patients," *Journal of Experimental Psychology: General*, vol. 114, 1985, pp. 311–41.

16. Stephen M. Kosslyn et al., "Two Types of Image Generation: Evidence for Left and Right Hemisphere Processes," *Neuropsychologia*, vol. 33, 1995, pp. 1485–1510.

17. Michael I. Posner and Mark E. Raichle, *Images of Mind* (New York: Scientific American Library, 1994), p. 95.

18. Stanislaus Dehaene, "The Organization of Brain Activations in Number Comparison," *Journal of Cognitive Neuroscience*, vol. 8, 1996, pp. 47–68.

19. Mark Jung Beeman and Christine Chiarello, "Complementary Right- and Left-Hemisphere Language Comprehension," *Current Directions in Psychology*, vol. 7, 1998, pp. 2–7.

20. Caine and Caine, p. 37.

21. Ibid., p. 91.

22. Ibid., pp. 9, 48, 91.

23. Ibid., pp. 127–30.

24. Ibid., pp. 47–48.

25. Beeman and Chiarello, op. cit.

26. David A. Sousa, "Is the Fuss About Brain Research Justified?," *Education Week*, 16 December 1998, p. 35.

27. Pat Wolfe and Ron Brandt, "What Do We Know from Brain Research?," *Educational Leadership*, November 1998, p. 12.

28. Jensen, p. 32.

29. Sousa, "Is the Fuss About Brain Research Justified?," p. 35.

30. Ronald Kotulak, *Inside the Brain: Revolutionary Discoveries of How the Mind Works* (Kansas City: Andrews McMeel, 1996), p. 46.

31. *Years of Promise: A Comprehensive Learning Strategy for America's Children* (New York: Carnegie Corporation of New York, 1996), pp. 9–10; and Office of Educational Research and Improvement, *Building Knowledge for a Nation of Learners* (Washington, D.C.: U.S. Department of Education, 1996).

32. Rima Shore, *Rethinking the Brain: New Insights into Early Development* (New York: Families and Work Institute, 1997), pp. 21, 36.

33. Kotulak, p. 46.

34. Ronald Kotulak, "Learning How to Use the Brain," 1996, available on the Web at http://www.newhorizons.org/ofc_21cliusebrain. html.

35. Harry T. Chugani, "Neuroimaging of Developmental Nonlinearity and Developmental Pathologies," in R. W. Thatcher et al., eds., *Developmental Neuroimaging* (San Diego: Academic Press, 1996), pp. 187–95.

36. Debra Viadero, "Brain Trust," *Education Week*, 18 September 1996, pp. 31–33.

37. *Better Beginnings* (Pittsburgh: Office of Child Development, University of Pittsburgh, 1997); A. DiCresce, "Brain Surges," 1997, available on the Web at www.med. wayne.edu/wmp97/brain.htm; and Lynell Hancock, "Why Do Schools Flunk Biology?," *Newsweek,* 19 February 1996, pp. 58–59.

38. Harry Chugani, "A Critical Period of Brain Development: Studies of Cerebral Glucose Utilization with PET," *Preventive Medicine*, vol. 27, 1998, pp. 184–88.

39. Harry T. Chugani, M. E. Phelps, and J. C. Mazziota, "Positron Emission Tomography Study of Human Brain Function Development," *Annals of Neurology*, vol. 22, 1987, pp. 487–97.

40. Peter R. Huttenlocher, "Synaptic Density in Human Frontal Cortex—Developmental Changes of Aging," *Brain Research*, vol. 163, 1979, pp. 195–205; Peter R. Huttenlocher et al., "Synaptogenesis in Human Visual Cortex—Evidence for Synapse Elimination During Normal Development," *Neuroscience Letters*, vol. 33, 1982, pp. 247–52; Peter R. Huttenlocher and Ch. de Courten, "The Development of Synapses in Striate Cortex of Man," *Human Neurobiology*, vol. 6, 1987, pp. 1-9; and Peter R. Huttenlocher and A. S. Dabholkar, "Regional Differences in Synaptogenesis in Human Cerebral Cortex," *Journal of Comparative Neurology*, vol. 387, 1997, pp. 167-78.

41. Chugani, Phelps, and Mazziota, p. 496.

42. Chugani, "Neuroimaging of Developmental Nonlinearity," p. 187.

43. Herman T. Epstein, "Growth Spurts During Brain Development: Implications for Educational Policy and Practice," in S. Chall and A. F. Mirsky, eds., *Education and the Brain* (Chicago: University of Chicago Press, 1978), pp. 343-70; and Chipman, op. cit.

44. Patricia S. Goldman-Rakic, Jean-Pierre Bourgeois, and Pasko Rakic, "Synaptic Substrate of Cognitive Development: Synaptogenesis in the Prefrontal Cortex of the Nonhuman Primate," in N. A. Krasnegor, G. R. Lyon, and P. S. Goldman-Rakic, *Development of the Prefrontal Cortex: Evolution, Neurobiology, and Behavior* (Baltimore: Paul H. Brooks, 1997), pp. 27-47.

45. *Bridging the Gap*, p. 11.

46. Jacqueline S. Johnson and Elissa L. Newport, "Critical Period Effects on Universal Properties," *Cognition*, vol. 39, 1991, p. 215.

47. Hancock, p. 59.

JOHN T. BRUER is president of the James S. McDonnell Foundation, St. Louis.

From *Phi Delta Kappan*, May 1999, pp. 649-657. © 1999 by John T. Bruer. Reprinted by permission.

Educators Need to Know About the Human Brain

Illustration by Jim Hummel

In this response to John Bruer's article in the May 1999 **Kappan,** *Mr. Brandt argues that, used in conjunction with knowledge from other sources, findings from neuroscience are yielding additional insights into the learning process—and that educators would be foolish to ignore this growing body of knowledge. Mr. Bruer was offered an opportunity to provide a rejoinder, but he chose instead to refer readers back to his May article.*

BY RON BRANDT

IN THE MAY 1999 *Kappan,* John Bruer condemns irresponsible claims regarding the use of brain research in education.[1] A well-informed scientist, Bruer is right to critique what he considers misinterpretations, but I think he is mistaken when he discourages educators from trying to understand and apply what is known. Used in conjunction with knowledge from other sources, including cognitive science, educa-tional research, and professional experience, findings from neuroscience are yielding additional insights into the learning process.

In earlier articles Bruer stated flatly, "Right now, brain science has little to offer educational practice or policy" and urged attention instead to cognitive science.[2] But there is no need to erect a Berlin Wall between cognitive science and neuroscience; they are two sides of the same coin. In his *Kappan* article, Bruer recognizes this, noting that, in the past 15 years or so, "theoretical barriers have fallen."

Neuroscientists complain that, historically, cognitivists have shown little interest in the neurological substrate of the cognition they study. If true, such an attitude would be understandable, because until the last decade, few means were available for scientists to investigate the brain directly. Under the circumstances, according to Francis Crick, co-discoverer of the structure of DNA, cognitive psychologists adopted a "functionalist" perspective:

> Just as it is not necessary to know about the actual wiring of a computer when writing programs for it, so a functionalist investigates the information processed by the brain, and the computational processes the brain performs on this information, without considering the neurological implementation of these processes. He usually regards such considerations as totally irrelevant or, at best, premature.[3]

This may be unfair. As evidenced by the lucid explanations of brain research in his new book, *The Myth of the First Three Years*,[4] Bruer is very knowledgeable about neuroscience. But as Crick and some other neuroscientists say, the field of cognitive science must now be broadened to incorporate the flood of new knowledge emerging from brain research. Neuroscientist Joseph LeDoux—contending that cognitive science has ignored emotions, the subject of his research—argues the need for a new, more inclusive field he calls "mind science."[5]

Scholarly Quarrels Serve a Purpose

Educators are used to scholarly quarrels; positions advanced by some researchers are almost invariably contradicted by others. One result is that practitioners seldom look to research for guidance. With so many inconsistencies, how are they to know whose claims are right? But such disagreements are part of how science works. Leslie Brothers, a psychiatrist who writes about the relationships between neuroscience and other fields, notes that among brain researchers, "Unexpected findings strain existing paradigms. Back and forth struggles regarding the proper context and significance of the findings ensue. Ultimately sometimes after many years of discussion old frameworks for understanding are replaced by new ones."[6] In the meantime, those unwilling to wait must decide for themselves—after weighing contrasting views—what seems to make the most sense.

In my reading of the books scientists have been writing about the brain, I have come across several debates that are important to educators. I will briefly highlight two such disagreements and explain possible reasons for them. Then I will cite a few examples of why I think findings from neuroscience—when combined with other knowledge—can be enlightening.

Enrichment in Early Childhood

One of the brain-related issues especially interesting to educators is the place of "enrichment" in early education. Science writer Janet Hopson and anatomist Marian Diamond have written about research conducted since the 1960s establishing that rats allowed to play with toys and other rats have thicker, heavier brains than rats kept in isolation. The extra weight and thickness is mostly because their brains have formed more connections among neurons. Researchers have also found that the growth of rats' brains in response to experience (and apparent shrinkage from lack of it) occurs not just in the weeks following birth, but at all ages. Even more interesting, the same is true for humans. Bruer, who

downplays the concept of "enrichment," nevertheless calls "the ability of the mature brain to change and reorganize... a new, exciting finding of brain science."[7]

So what is in dispute? Whether the findings justify calls for improving the care and education of children. Diamond and Hopson recommend a set of experiences at each age level from birth to adolescence that they believe constitute "enrichment" for humans.[8] Bruer cautions that enriched conditions for rats, which he prefers to call "complex," are really just approximations of rats' natural environment in the wild. Most human children are not kept in cages, so we have no way of knowing what would be the equivalent of an enriched environment for humans. Bruer wants educators to understand the possibility of cultural bias in a loaded word like "enrichment." Experiences like those suggested by Diamond and Hopson may be valuable, he implies, but they do not necessarily affect children's brains in the same way complex environments affect the brains of rats.

Michael Gazzaniga, a prolific author who worked with Roger Sperry on the well-publicized research on split-brain patients, also objects to the idea that certain experiences automatically improve children's brains. "[Following a] White House conference on babies and brains," Gazzaniga writes, "the *New York Times* published an editorial saying neuroscience had informed us that the brain needs crafting during development, and reading is the way to do it.... This kind of casual reasoning drives serious scientists to distraction."[9] Offering what he considers a more accurate position, Gazzaniga declares that "the brain is not primarily an experience-storing device that constantly changes its structure to accommodate new experience. From the evolutionary perspective it is a dynamic computing device that is largely rule driven; it stores information by manipulating the value of simple arithmetic variables."[10]

Educators concerned about the quality of child care in our society must decide which interpretation of the enrichment research seems most reasonable. The issue, they should remember, is not whether children's lives will be better if they have access to books, music, and interesting games—they will, of course—but whether these things are necessary for brain development.

Constructivism Wrong?

Closely related to the enrichment issue (because it also involves the brain's plasticity) and having many implications for education is a controversy between researchers whose work builds on discoveries that many capabilities are "built in" and other scientists who are equally impressed with the brain's ability to change with experience. Diamond and Hopson say, "When you look at the way a child's brain develops, one thing becomes absolutely obvious... *input from the environment helps shape the human brain.*"[11] Gazzaniga, however, rejects the idea of "so-called plasticity." He claims that when "clever neuroscientists... intervene and stimulate neurons in abnormal and bizarre ways,... the brain simply responds differently, and hence the resulting networks are different. This response hardly suggests that the brain is plastic in the sense that it has rewired itself."[12]

Gazzaniga and other neuroscientists who emphasize the evolutionary perspective are so convinced that "brains accrue specialized systems (adaptations) through natural selection" that they ridicule the idea, much cherished by educators, of constructivism.[13] Gazzaniga attacks neuroscientist Terry Sejnowski, who he says

> marries the questionable neurobiology he reviews to the work of Jean Piaget, then suggests children learn domains of knowledge by interacting with the environment.... The constructivist view of the brain is that it has a common mechanism that solves the structure of all problems.... This sort of assertion leaves us breathless because if we know anything, it is

that any old part of the brain can't learn any old thing.[14]

Another evolutionary scientist, Steven Pinker, blames educators for trying to teach mathematics and reading with a constructivist philosophy, which he describes as "a mixture of Piaget's psychology with counterculture and postmodern ideology." American students, he charges, perform poorly because they are taught in accord with this "wrong" idea. "The problem," Pinker writes, "is that the educational establishment is ignorant of evolution."[15]

Educators who understand what cognitive scientists mean when they describe learning as construction[16] have cause to resent Pinker's charges and to wonder who is ignorant of what. Beyond being offended, however, we need to understand the reason he takes such a position.

The Evolved Modular Brain

Richard Restak, a Washington neurologist who has written numerous books about the brain, provides a piece of the puzzle by describing the brain as "modular." Researchers now understand, he writes, that brains are "arranged according to a distributed system composed of large numbers of modular elements linked together.... [N]o... area holds sway over all the others, nor do all areas of the brain 'report' to an overall supervisory center."[17] This decentralized organization, which is presumably the result of millions of years of evolution, incorporates numerous systems for performing particular tasks, such as recognizing faces, throwing objects, and counting. Each ability probably developed in response to a particular environmental challenge.

It may be helpful for educators to understand that human brains are apparently "pre-wired" for capabilities such as oral language and rudimentary mathematics (in the sense that particular neurons seem dedicated to these purposes from birth). In other words, these capabilities are not created entirely through experi-

ence; children's brains are not blank slates.

Knowing that this is really their message, perhaps we can be tolerant of scientists who, as they seek to establish the concept of the evolved modular brain, think it necessary to wage verbal warfare on the equally valid idea that brains also learn from experience. Francis Crick summarizes the interrelationship succinctly: "The brain at birth, we now know, is not a tabula rasa but an elaborate structure with many of its parts already in place. Experience then tunes this rough-and-ready apparatus until it can do a precision job."[18]

You Can't Derive Pedagogy From Biology, But...

With the conflicts over enrichment, plasticity, and evolved capabilities as background, I now return to the original question about the usefulness of brain research to education. My position is simply this: if we had no other knowledge about human behavior and learning, we could certainly not derive much pedagogy from findings about the physical brain. But that is not the case. We do have a great deal of knowledge about learning, which we have acquired in several different ways. As Bruer argues, psychology, especially cognitive psychology, is a key source of that knowledge. We can also draw on other social sciences, such as anthropology, along with educational research and professional experience. When brain research is combined with knowledge from these other sources, it can further illuminate our understanding.

A practical example is Fast ForWord, a research-based program for students with a particular kind of learning disability. Neuroscientists Paula Tallal and Michael Merzenich developed the program based on research documenting brain plasticity in monkeys and on findings that some children have difficulty hearing phonemes, especially consonants, because their brains do not process spoken language quickly enough.[19] If they do not hear the difference between "*b*" and "*p*," for example, they cannot develop phonemic awareness, which reading experts now agree is an essential prerequisite for learning to read.

Fast ForWord consists of computer games that first teach students to distinguish between similar sounds, using artificially slowed speech, and then challenge them gradually to increase their recognition speed. Using the program several hours a day, many children are said to make as much progress in four to six weeks as they would in two years of intensive work with a therapist.

Fast ForWord is a good illustration because it builds on what was already known about reading instruction and the problems of learning-disabled students. For example, in a comprehensive review of the voluminous research on reading, Marilyn Adams had already identified the critical necessity of phonemic awareness.[20] Without that kind of information, and without other knowledge, including that accrued in recent decades about the design of computer games, Fast ForWord might not have been as effective.

Understanding Ourselves And Our Students

Most of us, though, are not in a position to devise new programs or approaches. An important benefit for us of knowledge about the brain may be increased understanding of what we commonly observe about human behavior. I have begun keeping a list of questions that I think neuroscience is helping to answer. Here are three: Why do people often not use in one situation what they have learned someplace else? Why do people sometimes do things such as buying a particular kind of car or picking a fight in school for reasons they are not completely aware of? Why do students often not remember what they have been taught?

Information from brain research cannot provide definitive answers to questions such as these, but, combined with what we already know, it can add to our understanding. For example, the problem of "transfer of training" has plagued educators for at least a century. School curricula were changed when researchers could find no evidence that Latin and other classical studies improved students' general academic abilities. Advocates of character education and thinking skills have found, to their chagrin, that students who have been taught a strategy often fail to use it when circumstances are different. Researchers even have labels to describe knowledge that is not transferred: it is called "inert" or "situational."

The transfer problem becomes clearer when we know about the brain's modular structure explained above. As mentioned, many scientists now believe this structure is the result of evolution. "Evolutionary theory has generated the notion that we are a collection of adaptations —brain devices that allow us to do specific things.... Many systems throughout the brain contribute to a single cognitive function."[21] While these systems are certainly in communication with one another, they are also somewhat independent. Knowing this, educators must take steps to strengthen connections among cognitive functions that might otherwise remain relatively separate. Stanislaus Dehaene, a French mathematician turned neuroscientist, says a priority for mathematics teachers must be integration of the brain's various mathematics systems:

> If my hypothesis is correct, innumeracy is with us for a long time, because it reflects one of the fundamental properties of our brain: its modularity, the compartmentalization of mathematical knowledge within multiple partially autonomous circuits. In order to become proficient in mathematics, one must go beyond these compartmentalized modules and establish a series of flexible links among them.... A good teacher is an alchemist who gives a funda-

mentally modular human brain the semblance of an interactive network.[22]

Another commonly observed characteristic of people, including children in schools, is our tendency to do things without always knowing why. A contributing factor is probably our emotions, which, though still poorly understood, are now being studied by neuroscientists. They have identified connections among the amygdala, the hippocampus, and the frontal lobes, revealing that fear and probably other emotions are processed in the same approximate location (the frontal lobes) where personal and social decisions are made.[23] When we understand that emotions, which probably are the effects of various chemical neurotransmitters,[24] help determine what we remember but that they are usually unconscious (when they become conscious we call them feelings), we can begin to see how emotions may influence our decisions without our knowing it.

A third question that brain research helps answer is why we remember some things but forget others. Every teacher has been exasperated by students who insist they were never taught something when they obviously were. Knowing how memory works not only helps us understand this familiar problem but gives us some clues for what to do about it. The most fundamental thing scientists have learned about memory is that we do not store memories whole and therefore do not retrieve them that way either. When we remember something, we actually reconstruct it by combining elements of the original experience. Neuroscientist Antonio Damasio explains that a memory "is recalled in the form of images at many brain sites rather than at a single site. Although we have the illusion that everything comes together in a single anatomical theater, recent evidence suggests that it does not. Probably the relative simultaneity of activity at different sites binds the separate parts of the mind together."[25]

Our ability to re-create the memory to recombine all or most of the elements (which are stored in millions of neurons) depends on the strength of the original experience, including the emotional load. Daniel Schacter, an expert on memory and the brain, says it concisely: "For better or worse, our recollections are largely at the mercy of our elaborations; only those aspects of experience that are targets of elaborative encoding processes have a high likelihood of being remembered subsequently."[26] Why, then, do students forget what they have been taught? Because the information served no useful purpose in their lives, was thus devoid of emotional impact, and was not "elaborately encoded."

Thinking, Learning, and Feeling All Have a 'Neural Substrate'

My purpose here is not to insist on the correctness of these interpretations or to argue that brain research alone tells us how to run schools. I wish only to show that knowledge about brain functioning is relevant, especially when used to supplement what we know from other sources. Today's educators are fortunate to be living at a time when we are finally beginning to really understand the learning process, including its neural substrate. We are coming to recognize, as Francis Crick says in *The Astonishing Hypothesis*, that all our thoughts, behaviors, and feelings are the result of chemical and electrical activity in the brain and related neural structures. Never again should we talk about psychological

phenomena without recognizing that all of them are "brain-based."

Much remains unclear, and we surely will misinterpret some findings as we try to make sense of the partial information currently available. If so, we must be open to clarification, some of which will come with newer findings. But with today's challenges, educators would be foolish to ignore the growing body of knowledge about our brains.

Notes

1. John T. Bruer, "In Search of… Brain-Based Education," *Phi Delta Kappan*, May 1999, pp. 649–57.
2. John T. Bruer, "Brain Science, Brain Fiction," *Educational Leadership*, November 1998, p. 14. See also John T. Bruer, "Education and the Brain: A Bridge Too Far," *Educational Researcher*, November 1997, pp. 4–16.
3. Francis Crick, *The Astonishing Hypothesis: The Scientific Search for the Soul* (New York: Scribner, 1994), p. 18.
4. John T. Bruer, *The Myth of the First Three Years* (New York: Free Press, 1999).
5. Joseph LeDoux, *The Emotional Brain* (New York: Simon & Schuster, 1996), p. 68.
6. Leslie Brothers, *Friday's Footprint: How Society Shapes the Human Mind* (New York: Oxford University Press, 1997), p. 48.
7. Bruer, "Brain Science, Brain Fiction," p. 18.
8. Marian Diamond and Janet Hopson, *Magic Trees of the Mind: How to Nurture Your Child's Intelligence, Creativity, and Healthy Emotions from Birth Through Adolescence* (New York: Dutton, 1998).
9. Michael S. Gazzaniga, *The Mind's Past* (Berkeley: University of California Press, 1998), p. 29.
10. Ibid., p. 35.

11. Diamond and Hopson, p. 63 (emphasis in the original).
12. Gazzaniga, p. 48.
13. Ibid., p. 9.
14. Ibid., pp. 13–15.
15. Steven Pinker, *How the Mind Works* (New York: Norton, 1997), pp. 341–42. When I complained to Pinker about these comments, he replied in a personal message sent in May 1999 that "ultimately we do not disagree on much" and that in his future writings he would take my observations into account.
16. *Learner-Centered Psychological Principles: A Framework for School Reform and Redesign* (Washington, D.C.: American Psychological Association, 1997).
17. Richard Restak, *The Modular Brain* (New York: Scribner, 1994), pp. 35, xvi–xvii.
18. Crick, p. 10.
19. Beverly A. Wright et al., "Deficits in Auditory Temporal and Spectral Resolution in Language-Impaired Children," *Nature*, 8 May 1997, pp. 176–78.
20. Marilyn J. Adams, *Beginning to Read: Thinking and Learning About Print* (Urbana: Center for the Study of Reading, University of Illinois, 1990).
21. Gazzaniga, p. 10.
22. Stanislaus Dehaene, *The Number Sense: How the Mind Creates Mathematics* (New York: Oxford University Press, 1997), p. 139.
23. LeDoux, op. cit.
24. Candace Pert, *Molecules of Emotion* (New York: Scribner, 1997).
25. Antonio R. Damasio, *Descartes' Error* (New York: Grosset/Putnam, 1994), p. 84.
26. Daniel L. Schacter, *Searching for Memory* (New York: Basic Books, 1996), p. 56.

RON BRANDT is an independent writer and consultant living in Arlington, Va. He was executive editor of Educational Leadership *from 1978 to 1995.*

From *Phi Delta Kappan*, November 1999, pp. 235-238. © 1999 by Phi Delta Kappan International, Inc. Reprinted by permission.

ABILITY AND EXPERTISE

It's Time to Replace the Current Model of Intelligence

BY ROBERT J. STERNBERG

BILLY HAS an IQ of 121 on a standardized individual intelligence test, and Jimmy has an IQ of 94 on the same test. What do these scores, and the difference between them, mean? The conventional answer to this question is that they represent a kind of intellectual predestination: The two children possess inborn gifts that are relatively fixed and will, to a large extent, predict their future achievement. So no one will be surprised if Billy goes on to do well in high school and gets into a good college—or if Jimmy barely gets through school and ends up with a minimum-wage job—because that's what this familiar and widely accepted model of human intelligence would lead us to expect.

But a scientific model is just a way of fitting together pieces of information and things we have observed into a pattern that makes sense. It does not represent the certain or only way of arranging the pieces, and models can be and often are modified or even discarded when we make new discoveries or look at what we know in new ways. This happened, for example, in the early seventeenth century, when the Ptolemaic model of the solar system, in which all the heavenly bodies were said to revolve around the earth, was replaced by the Copernican, sun-centered, model of the solar system.

Many psychologists now question the simple identification of IQ with ability, which the old model of human intelligence posits. They believe that abilities are too broad and too complex to be measured by the kind of IQ test that Billy and Jimmy took. They also believe that environment and genetics play a part and, furthermore, that abilities are not a fixed quantity: They can be modified by education and experience. I'd like to propose a further, and important, building block for this new model of human intelligence—namely that the difference in Billy's

and Jimmy's IQ scores simply means that the two children are at a different stage in developing the expertise measured by the IQ test. Furthermore, I suggest that people who study abilities and those who study expertise are really talking about the same thing. What we are measuring when we administer a Wechsler Intelligence Scale for Children (WISC) or an Iowa Test of Basic Skills (ITBS) or an SAT are the same. They are not different in kind but only in the point at which we are measuring them.

In the Eye of the Beholder

When we give an achievement test, we accept the idea that we are testing a form of expertise, but this is equally true when we administer an IQ test. What differs is the level of expertise we measure and, probably more important, the way we perceive what we are measuring. The familiar IQ/ability model creates a certain expectation: that one kind of accomplishment (IQ test scores) will predict—and, in fact, lead to—another kind of accomplishment (grades or scores on achievement tests). And of course we also use different words to describe the two kinds of accomplishment.

But this way of looking at the two kinds of test scores is a familiar convenience rather than a psychological reality. Solving problems on a verbal-analogies test or a test of mathematical problem solving, which are supposed to test a child's abilities, calls for expertise just the way so-called achievement tests do: You can't do well on these so-called tests of ability without knowing the vocabulary or having some familiarity with problem-solving techniques. The chief difference between ability and achievement tests is not what they measure but the point at which they measure it. IQ and other tests of ability are, typically, administered early in a child's school career, whereas various indications about school performance, such as grades or achievement test scores, are collected later. However, all of the various kinds of assessments are of the same kind, psychologically. They all test—to some extent—what you know and how well you can use it. What distinguishes ability tests from the other kinds of assessments is how the ability tests are used (usually, predictively), rather than what they measure. There is no qualitative distinction.

But if the distinction between what these tests measure does not exist, how do we come to make it? The answer is a complicated story, but the principal reason is historical accident. Briefly, the two kinds of testing were developed separately and used on different groups of people. IQ/ability testing, which originated in Alfred Binet's testing of young children, focused on exceptionally low levels of performance and came to be viewed primarily as predictive. Early studies of expertise were done with adults. They focused on exceptionally high levels of performance and came to be viewed as measures of achievement.

The Traditional Model

According to the traditional model of fixed individual differences, the capabilities that a child inherits interact with the child's environment to produce, at an early age, a relatively fixed potential for achievement. Children fulfill this potential to a greater or lesser degree. Thus, if a child who scores well on ability tests does well in school, we say he is living up to his potential. If, as sometimes happens, his achievement does not match his test scores, we call him an *underachiever*—or if the kid confounds expectations by working hard and doing well, he gets the label of *overachiever*. Ironically, ability test scores are considered a better indicator of what a child can achieve (or should achieve) than what the child actually does. A test of verbal analogies, in this view, might actually tell us more about a person's verbal abilities than the person's comprehension of the reading he or she does in everyday life; or a test of mathematical problem-solving skills might be viewed as more informative than the mathematical problem solving the person does on the job.

According to this model, the more intelligent students (that is, the ones with higher IQs) do better in school. As a result, they are likely to attend selective colleges, go on to professional schools, and eventually get well-paying jobs and enjoy other forms of success. The less intelligent do worse in school and may drop out. At best, they probably have to be satisfied with low-status credentials that reflect hard work rather than ability, and their role in the labor market is to fill the jobs that the more intelligent people don't want to do.

This is the view Richard Herrnstein and Charles Murray present in *The Bell Curve* (1994), and as people who have read the book will remember, it assigns African Americans as a group to the status of an underclass, based on the average "potential" of group members displayed in IQ and other ability tests. Herrnstein and Murray's use of the traditional model has occasioned a great deal of controversy. However, the view of IQ as fixed and determinant is, unfortunately, consistent with many current educational practices and common views about intellectual competence.

Developing Expertise

The idea that abilities are a form of developing expertise offers a more flexible and optimistic view of human capabilities, and one that is more in line with what we are discovering about human intelligence. Children become experts in the skills needed for success on ability tests in much the same ways that they become experts in doing anything else—through a combination of genetic endowment and experience (Ericsson, 1996). To do well on a test, a child needs to acquire, store, and learn how to use at least two kinds of knowledge: explicit knowledge of a domain and implicit or tacit knowledge of a field. Knowledge of a domain is subject-matter knowledge: In American history, for example, it would be the facts, trends, and major ideas about the political, economic, and social development of our country. Implicit knowledge is the kind of knowledge one needs to be successful in a field but which is not part of the subject matter and often is not even talked about. For example, in American history, the role of the Federalist Papers in the shaping of the U.S. Constitution would be explicit knowledge; how to use the library or Internet to research an essay about the Federalist Papers and how to take and organize notes and carry the paper through successive drafts to completion would be implicit knowledge.

Tests measure both explicit and implicit knowledge: knowledge of the subject matter and knowledge about how to take a test. This is as true of ability tests as it is of achievement tests. A verbal-analogies test, for example, measures explicit knowledge of vocabulary and a student's ability to reason with this knowledge, but the test also measures implicit knowledge of how to take a test. Thus, the student has to work within certain time limits and choose the best answer from a list of answers no one of which is exactly right.

To translate the gaining of expertise on test-taking into procedural terms, students need

- direct instruction in how to solve test-like problems—usually this takes place in school;
- practice in solving such problems, again usually in academic contexts;
- an opportunity to watch others, such as teachers or other students, solve test-like problems;

- practice thinking about such problems, sometimes mentally simulating what to do when confronting them;

- rewards for successful solutions (good grades, praise from teachers, other kinds of recognition), thereby reinforcing such behavior.

The difference between Billy's score of 121 and Jimmy's 94 also reflects a number of personal and cultural factors, and they do not all pertain to what we usually consider expertise. For example, the two boys may possess different degrees of "test-wiseness," that is, understanding the tricks of taking tests (Millman, Bishop, and Ebel, 1965; Bond and Harman, 1994). They may feel differing levels of anxiety and/or alertness on the day they are tested, and this would probably show itself in their scores. Cultural differences between them may lead to different attitudes about the importance of doing well on a test, particularly one that clearly does not "count." Most important of all, the boys may be at different levels of developing expertise in the skills that the test measures.

Individual Differences

But saying that IQ tests and other assessments of ability are testing the same thing as achievement tests and that the expertise revealed is not fixed should not be taken to mean that everybody has the same intellectual capacity. The difference in expertise that Billy and Jimmy reveal on their IQ tests may indicate an underlying difference in their capacities. However, IQ tests do not directly measure these differences and neither do any of the other ways in which we currently seek to measure ability (see, for example, Vygotsky, 1978). Individual differences in developing expertise result in much the same way as in most kinds of learning: from (a) the rate of learning (which can be caused by the amount of direct instruction received, the amount of problem solving done, the amount of time and effort spent in thinking about problems, and so on); and from (b) the asymptote of learning—that is, the limit set by ability to what a student can ultimately achieve, given unlimited training. This limit, or asymptote, can be caused by differences in numbers of schemas—the networks of information on various subjects stored in our memories—the organization of schemas, efficiency in using schemas, and so on (see Atkinson, Bower, and Crothers, 1965). For example, children can learn how to solve the various kinds of mathematical problems found in tests of mathematical abilities, whether through regular schooling, a special course, or through assimilation of everyday experience. When they learn, they will learn at different rates, and reach different asymptotes. Ultimately the differences represent genetic and environmental factors that are interacting in ways that we cannot now measure.

Various Kinds of Expertise

As I've already noted, the so-called ability tests typically come earlier in a student's school career than the various types of achievement tests, but what IQ tests measure is not psychologically prior. Achievement tests might just as well be used to predict scores on ability tests—and sometimes they are, as for instance, when school officials try to predict a student's college admissions test scores on the basis of the student's grades. When we look at the test of abilities as though they are psychologically prior, we are confusing the order in which students usually take these tests with some kind of psychological ordering. But in fact, our temporal ordering implies no psychological ordering at all. The recent change in the meaning of the acronym *SAT* (from Scholastic Aptitude Test to Scholastic Assessment Test) reflects the recognition that what was called an aptitude test measures more than just "aptitude"—indeed, it hints at the interchangeability of the two kinds of tests. Nevertheless, the SAT is still widely used as an ability test, and the SAT-II, which more directly measures subject-matter knowledge, as a set of achievement tests.

Tests that claim to measure ability through questions employing vocabulary, reading comprehension, verbal analogies, arithmetic problem solving, and the like are all, in part, tests of achievement. Even abstract-reasoning tests measure achievement in dealing with geometric symbols, which is a skill taught in Western schools (Laboratory of Comparative Human Cognition, 1982). Indeed, if we examine the content of ability tests, it is clear that they measure achievement that the students taking the test should have accomplished several years back. We could just as well use academic performance to predict ability-test scores. The problem with the traditional model is not that it proposes a correlation between ability tests and other forms of achievement. That undoubtedly exists. It is rather the traditional model's proposing that the capacities measured by the tests *cause* later success—or failure—instead of merely preceding it.

An Illusion of Causality

The notion that success on ability tests predicts success in many other areas gains credibility from the fact that some of the skills or qualities that make people more expert at taking tests are also likely to make them successful in other aspects of life in our culture. Taking a test, say, of verbal or figural analogies, or of mathematical problem solving, typically requires skills such as (a) puzzling out what someone else wants (here, the person who wrote the test), (b) command of English vocabulary, (c) reading comprehension, (d) allocation of limited time, (e) sustained concentration, (f) abstract reasoning, (g) quick thinking, (h) symbol manipulation, and (i) suppression of anxiety and other emotions that can interfere with test performance. These skills are also part of what is required for successful performance in school and in many kinds of job performance. Thus, an expert test-taker is likely also to have skills that will be involved in other kinds of expertise as well, such as expertise in getting high grades in school.

To the extent that the expertise required for one kind of performance overlaps with the expertise required for another kind of performance, there will be a correlation between performances. However, the expertise that ability tests measure is not the cause of school or job expertise; it is itself an expertise that overlaps with school or job expertise. Differences in test scores, academic performance, and job performance are all effects of different levels of expertise.

The New Model

The notion of *developing* expertise means that people are constantly in the process of developing expertise when they work within a given domain. Individuals can differ in rate and asymptote of development. However, the main constraint in achieving expertise is not some fixed prior level of capacity, of the kind measured by IQ tests. It is the degree to which students are purposefully engaged in working and teachers in helping them. This involves direct instruction, active participation, role modeling, and reward.

The model of developing expertise has five key elements: metacognitive skills, learning skills, thinking skills, knowledge, and motivation. The elements all influence one another, both directly and indirectly. For example, learning leads to knowledge, but knowledge facilitates further learning.

1. Metacognitive skills. Metacognitive skills refer to students' understanding and control of their own learning. These skills would include what a student knows about writing papers or solving arithmetic word problems, both in regard to the steps that are involved and how these steps can be executed effectively (Sternberg 1985, 1986, 1988; Sternberg and Swerling, 1996).

2. Learning skills. Learning skills are sometimes divided into explicit learning, which occurs when we make an effort to learn, and implicit learning, which occurs when we simply pick up information without any particular effort. Examples of learning skills are distinguishing relevant from irrelevant information; putting together the relevant information; and relating new information to information already stored in memory (Sternberg, 1985, 1986).

3. Thinking skills. There are three main sets of thinking skills. Critical (analytical) thinking skills include analyzing, critiquing, judging, evaluating, comparing and contrasting, and assessing. Creative thinking skills include creating, discovering, inventing, imagining, supposing, and hypothesizing. Practical thinking skills include applying, using, and practicing (Sternberg, 1985, 1986, 1994, 1997). They are the first step in translating thought into real-world action.

4. Knowledge. There are two main kinds of knowledge that are relevant in academic learning. Declarative knowledge is of facts, concepts, principles, laws, and the like. It is "knowing that." Procedure knowledge is of procedures and strategies. It is "knowing how." Of particular importance is procedural tacit knowledge, which involves knowing how the system in which one is operating functions (Sternberg, Wagner, Williams & Horvath, 1995).

5. Motivation. There are a number of different kinds of motivation, and in one or another of its forms, motivation is probably indispensable for school success. Without it, the student never even tries to learn (McClelland, 1985; McClelland, Atkinson, Clark, and Lowell, 1976; Bandura, 1977, 1996; Amabile, 1996; Sternberg and Lubart, 1996).

6. Context. All of the elements discussed above are characteristics of the learner. However, it is a mistake to assume, as conventional tests usually do, that factors external to the student's mastery of the material play no part in how well the student does on a test. Such contextual factors include whether the student is taking the test in his or her native language, whether the test emphasizes speedy performance, the importance to the student of success on the test, and the student's familiarity with the kinds of material on the test.

Novices—beginning learners—work toward expertise through deliberate practice. But this practice requires an interaction of all five of the key elements in the model. At the center, driving the elements, is motivation. Without it, nothing happens. Motivation drives metacognitive skills, which in turn activate learning and thinking skills, which then provide feedback to the metacognitive skills, enabling the student's level of expertise to increase (see also Sternberg, 1985). The declarative and procedural knowledge acquired through the extension of the thinking and learning skills also results in these skills being used more effectively in the future.

All of these processes are affected by, and can in turn affect, the context in which they operate. For example, if a learning experience is in English but the learner has only limited English proficiency, his or her learning will be inferior to that of someone with more advanced English language skills. Or if material is presented orally to someone who is a better visual learner, that individual's performance will be reduced.

Eventually, as the five elements influence one another, the student reaches a kind of expertise at which he or she becomes a reflective practitioner who is able to consciously use a certain set of skills. But expertise occurs at many levels. The expert first-year graduate or law student, for example, is still a far cry from the expert professional. People thus cycle through many times, on the way to successively higher levels of expertise.

Implications for the Classroom

The model of abilities as a form of developing expertise has a number of immediate implications for education, in general, and classroom practice, in particular.

First, teachers and all who use ability and achievement tests should stop distinguishing between what the two kinds of tests assess. The measurements are not different in kind but only in the point at which they are being made.

Second, tests measure *achieved* levels of developing expertise. No test—of abilities or anything else—can specify the highest level a student can achieve.

Third, different kinds of assessments—multiple-choice, short answer, performance-based, portfolio—complement one another in assessing multiple aspects of developing expertise. There is no one "right" kind of assessment.

Fourth, instruction should be geared not just toward imparting a knowledge base, but toward developing reflective analytical, creative, and practical thinking with a knowledge base. Students learn better when they think to learn, even when their learning is assessed with straightforward multiple-choice memory assessments (Sternberg, Torff, and Grigorenko, 1998).

The model I've proposed here views students as novices who are capable of becoming experts in a variety of areas. The traditional model, which posits fixed individual differences—and typically bases the kind of instruction a student gets on these differences—holds many students back from attaining the expertise they are capable of. It is true that for various reasons (including, perhaps, genetic as well as environmentally based differences), not all individuals will reach the same ultimate level of expertise. But they should all be given the opportunity to reach new levels of competence well beyond what they, and in some cases, others may think possible. The fact that Billy and Jimmy have different IQs tells us something about differences in what they now do. It does not tell us anything about what ultimately they will be able to achieve.

References

Amabile, T. M. (1996). *Creativity in context*. Boulder, CO: Westview.

Atkinson, R. C., Bower, G. H., & Crothers, E. J. (1965). *An introduction to mathematical learning theory*. New York: John Wiley & Sons.

Bandura, A. (1977). Self-efficacy: Toward a unifying theory of behavioral change. *Psychological Review, 84*, 181–215.

Bandura, A. (1996). *Self-efficacy: The exercise of control*. New York: Freeman.

Bond, L., & Harman, A. E. (1994). Test-taking strategies. In R. J. Sternberg (Ed.), *Encyclopedia of human intelligence* (Vol. 2, pp. 1073–1077). New York: Macmillan.

Ericsson, A. (Ed.) (1996). *The road to excellence*. Mahwah, NJ: Erlbaum.

Herrnstein, R. J., & Murray, C. (1994). *The bell curve*. New York: Free Press.

Laboratory of Comparative Human Cognition (1982). Culture and intelligence. In R. J. Sternberg (Ed.), *Handbook of human intelligence* (pp. 642–719). New York: Cambridge University Press.

McClelland, D. C. (1985). *Human motivation*. New York: Scott Foresman.

McClelland, D. C., Atkinson, J. W., Clark, R. A., & Lowell, E. L. (1976). *The achievement motive*. New York: Irvington.

Millman, J., Bishop, H., & Ebel, R. (1965). An analysis of test-wiseness. *Educational and Psychological Measurement, 25*, 707–726.

Sternberg, R. J. (1985). *Beyond IQ: A triarchic theory of human intelligence*. New York: Cambridge University Press.

Sternberg, R. J. (1986). *Intelligence applied*. Orlando, FL: Harcourt Brace College Publishers.

Sternberg, R. J. (1988). *The triarchic mind: A new theory of human intelligence*. New York: Viking-Penguin.

Sternberg, R. J. (1994). Diversifying instruction and assessment. *The Educational Forum, 59*(1), 47–53.

Sternberg, R. J. (1997). *Successful intelligence*. New York: Plume.

Sternberg, R. J., & Lubart, T. I. (1995). *Defying the crowd: Cultivating creativity in a culture of conformity*. New York: Free Press.

Sternberg, R. J., & Lubart, T. I. (1996). Investing in creativity. *American Psychologist, 51*, 677–688.

Sternberg, R. J., & Spear-Swerling, L. (1996). *Teaching for thinking*. Washington, DC: APA Books.

Sternberg, R. J., Torff, B., & Grigorenko, E. L. (1998). Teaching triarchically improves school achievement. *Journal of Educational Psychology, 90*, 374–384.

Sternberg, R. J., Wagner, R. K., Williams, W. M., & Horvath, J. (1995). Testing common sense. *American Psychologist, 50*, 912–927.

Vygotsky, L. S. (1978). *Mind in society: The development of higher psychological processes*. Cambridge, MA: Harvard University Press.

This work was supported by the U.S. Office of Educational Research and Improvement (Grant R206R50001), but this support does not imply endorsement of positions taken or conclusions reached.

Robert J. Sternberg *is IBM Professor of Psychology in the Department of Psychology at Yale University. His areas of specialization are human abilities and cognition. A long version of this article appeared in* **Educational Researcher**, *April 1998.*

From the Spring 1999 issue of the *American Educator*, pp. 10-13, 50-51. Reprinted by permission of the *American Educator*, the quarterly journal of the American Federation of Teachers, and Robert J. Sternberg.

CAUTION— PRAISE CAN BE DANGEROUS

By Carol S. Dweck

THE SELF-ESTEEM movement, which was flourishing just a few years ago, is in a state of decline. Although many educators believed that boosting students' self-esteem would boost their academic achievement, this did not happen. But the failure of the self-esteem movement does not mean that we should stop being concerned with what students think of themselves and just concentrate on improving their achievement. Every time teachers give feedback to students, they convey messages that affect students' opinion of themselves, their motivation, and their achievement. And I believe that teachers can and should help students become high achievers who also feel good about themselves. But how, exactly, should teachers go about doing this?

In fact, the self-esteem people were on to something extremely important. Praise, the chief weapon in their armory, is a powerful tool. Used correctly it can help students become adults who delight in intellectual challenge, understand the value of effort, and are able to deal with setbacks. Praise can help students make the most of the gifts they have. But if praise is not handled properly, it can become a negative force, a kind of drug that, rather than strengthening students, makes them passive and dependent on the opinion of others. What teachers—and parents—need is a framework that enables them to use praise wisely and well.

Where Did Things Go Wrong?

I believe the self-esteem movement faltered because of the way in which educators tried to instill self-esteem. Many people held an intuitively appealing theory of self-esteem, which went something like this: Giving students many opportunities to experience success and then praising them for their successes will indicate to them that they are intelligent. If they feel good about their intelligence, they will achieve. They will love learning and be confident and successful learners.

Much research now shows that this idea is wrong. Giving students easy tasks and praising their success tells students that you think they're dumb.[1] It's not hard to see why. Imagine being lavishly praised for something you think is pretty Mickey Mouse. Wouldn't you feel that the person thought you weren't capable of more and was trying to make you feel good about your limited ability?

But what about praising students' ability when they perform well on challenging tasks? In such cases, there would be no question of students' thinking you were just trying to make them feel good. Melissa Kamins, Claudia Mueller, and I decided to put this idea to the test.

Mueller and I had already found, in a study of the relationship between parents' beliefs and their children's expectations, that 85 percent of parents thought they needed to praise their children's intelligence in order to assure them that they were smart.[2] We also knew that many educators and psychologists thought that praising children for being intelligent was of great benefit. Yet in almost 30 years of research, I had seen over and over that children who had maladaptive achievement patterns were already obsessed with their intelligence—and with proving it to others. The children worried about how smart they looked and feared that failing at some task—even a relatively unimportant one—meant they were dumb. They also worried that having to work hard in order to succeed at a task showed they were dumb. Intelligence seemed to be a label to these kids, a feather in their caps, rather than a tool that, with effort, they could become more skillful in using.

In contrast, the more adaptive students focused on the process of learning and achieving. They weren't worried about their intelligence and didn't consider every task a measure of it. Instead, these students were more likely to concern themselves with the effort and strategies they needed in order to master the task. We wondered if praising children for being intelligent, though it seemed like a positive thing to do, could hook them into becoming dependent on praise.

Praise for Intelligence

Claudia Mueller and I conducted six studies, with more than 400 fifth-grade students, to examine the effects of praising children for being intelligent.[3] The students were from different parts of the country (a Midwestern town and a large Eastern city) and came from varied ethnic, racial, and socioeconomic backgrounds. Each of the studies involved several tasks, and all began with the students working, one at a time, on a puzzle task that was challenging but easy enough for all of them to do quite well. After this first set, we praised one-third of the children for their *intelligence*. They were told: "Wow, you got x number correct. That's a really good score. You must be smart at this." One-third of the children were also told that they got a very good score, but they were praised for their *effort*: "You must have worked really hard." The final third were simply praised for their *performance*, with no comment on why they were successful. Then, we looked to see the effects of these different types of praise across all six studies.

We found that after the first trial (in which all of the students were successful) the three groups responded similarly to questions we asked them. They enjoyed the task equally, were equally eager to take the problems home to practice, and were equally confident about their future performance.

In several of the studies, as a followup to the first trial, we gave students a choice of different tasks to work on next. We asked whether they wanted to try a challenging task from which they could learn a lot (but at which they might not succeed) or an easier task (on which they were sure to do well and look smart).

The majority of the students who had received praise for being intelligent the first time around went for the task that would allow them to keep on looking smart. Most of the students who had received praise for their effort (in some studies, as many as 90 percent) wanted the challenging learning task. (The third group, the students who had not been praised for intelligence or effort, were right in the middle and I will not focus on them.)

These findings suggest that when we praise children for their intelligence, we are telling them that this is the name of the game: Look smart; don't risk making mistakes. On the other hand, when we praise children for the effort and hard work that leads to achievement, they want to keep engaging in that process. They are not di-verted from the task of learning by a concern with how smart they might—or might not—look.

The Impact of Difficulty

Next, we gave students a set of problems that were harder and on which they didn't do as well. Afterwards, we repeated the questions we had asked after the first task: How much had they enjoyed the task? Did they want to take the problems home to practice? And how smart did they feel? We found that the students who had been praised for being intelligent did not like this second task and were no longer interested in taking the problems home to practice. What's more, their difficulties led them to question their intelligence. In other words, the same students who had been told they were smart when they succeeded now felt dumb because they had encountered a setback. They had learned to measure themselves from what people said about their performance, and they were dependent on continuing praise in order to maintain their confidence.

In contrast, the students who had received praise for their effort on the easier task liked the more difficult task just as much even though they missed some of the problems. In fact, many of them said they liked the harder problems even more than the easier ones, and they were even more eager to take them home to practice. It was wonderful to see.

Moreover, these youngsters did not think that the difficulty of the task (and their relative lack of success) reflected on their intelligence. They thought, simply, that they had to make a greater effort in order to succeed. Their interest in taking problems home with them to practice on presumably reflected one way they planned to do this.

Thus, the students praised for effort were able to keep their intellectual self-esteem in the face of setbacks. They still thought they were smart; they still enjoyed the challenge; and they planned to work toward future success. The students who had been praised for their intelligence received an initial boost to their egos, but their view of themselves was quickly shaken when the going got rough. As a final test, we gave students a third set of problems that were equal in difficulty to the first set—the one on which all the students had been successful. The results were striking. Although all three groups had performed equally well on the first trial, the students who had received praise for their intelligence (and who had been discouraged by their poor showing on the second trial) now registered the worst performance of the three groups. Indeed, they did significantly worse than they had on the first trial. In contrast, students who were praised for working hard performed the best of the three groups and significantly better than they had originally. So the different kinds of praise apparently affected not just what students thought and felt, but also how well they were able to perform.

Given what we had already seen, we reasoned that when students see their performance as a measure of their intelligence, they are likely to feel stigmatized when they perform poorly and may even try to hide the fact. If, however, students consider a poor performance a temporary setback, which merely reflects how much effort they have put in or their current level of skill, then it will not be a stigma. To test this idea, we gave students the opportunity to tell a student at another school about the task they had just completed by writing a brief description on a prepared form. The form also asked them to report their score on the second, more difficult trial.

More than 40 percent of the students who had been praised for their intelligence lied about their score (to improve it, of course). They did this even though they were reporting their performance to an anonymous peer whom they would never meet. Very few of the students in the other groups exaggerated their performance. This suggests that when we praise students for their intelligence, failure becomes more personal and therefore more of a disgrace. As a result, students become less able to face and therefore deal with their setbacks.

The Messages We Send

Finally, we found that following their experiences with the different kinds of praise, the students believed different things about their intelligence. Students who had received praise for being intelligent told us they thought of intelligence as something innate—a capacity that you just had or didn't have. Students who had been praised for effort told us they thought of intelligence more in terms of their skills, knowledge, and motivation—things over which they had some control and might be able to enhance.

And these negative effects of praising for intelligence were just as strong (and sometimes stronger) for the high-achieving students as for their less successful peers. Perhaps it is even easier to get these youngsters invested in looking smart to others. Maybe they are even more attuned to messages from us that tell them we value them for their intellects.

How can one sentence of praise have such powerful and pervasive effects? In my research, I have been amazed over and over again at how quickly students of all ages pick up on messages about themselves—at how sensitive they are to suggestions about their personal qualities or about the meaning of their actions and experiences. The kinds of praise (and criticism) students receive from their teachers and parents tell them how to think about what they do—and what they are.

This is why we cannot simply forget about students' feelings, their ideas about themselves and their motivation, and just teach them the "facts." No matter how objective we try to be, our feedback conveys messages about what we think is important, what we think of them, and how they should think of themselves. These messages, as

we have seen, can have powerful effects on many things including performance. And it should surprise no one that this susceptibility starts very early.

Melissa Kamins and I found it in kindergarten children.[4] Praise or criticism that focused on children's personal traits (like being smart or good) created a real vulnerability when children hit setbacks. They saw setbacks as showing that they were bad or incompetent—and they were unable to respond constructively. In contrast, praise or criticism that focused on children's strategies or the efforts they made to succeed left them hardy, confident, and in control when they confronted setbacks. A setback did not mean anything bad about them or their personal qualities. It simply meant that something needed to be done, and they set about doing it. Again, a focus on process allowed these young children to maintain their self-esteem and to respond constructively when things went wrong.

Ways of Praising

There are many groups whose achievement is of particular interest to us: minorities, females, the gifted, the underachieving, to name a few. The findings of these studies will tell you why I am so concerned that we not try to encourage the achievement of our students by praising their intelligence. When we worry about low-achieving or vulnerable students, we may want to reassure them they're smart. When we want to motivate high-achieving students, we may want to spur them on by telling them they're gifted. Our research says: Don't do that. Don't get students so invested in these labels that they care more about keeping the label than about learning. Instead of empowering students, praise is likely to render students passive and dependent on something they believe they can't control. And it can hook them into a system in which setbacks signify incompetence and effort is recognized as a sign of weakness rather than a key to success.

This is not to say that we shouldn't praise students. We can praise as much as we please when they learn or do well, but should wax enthusiastic about their strategies, not about how their performance reveals an attribute they are likely to view as innate and beyond their control. We can rave about their effort, their concentration, the effectiveness of their study strategies, the interesting ideas they came up with, the way they followed through. We can ask them questions that show an intelligent appreciation of their work and what they put into it. We can enthusiastically discuss with them what they learned. This, of course, requires more from us than simply telling them that they are smart, but it is much more appreciative of their work, much more constructive, and it does not carry with it the dangers I've been describing.

What about the times a student really impresses us by doing something quickly, easily—and perfectly? Isn't it appropriate to show our admiration for the child's ability? My honest opinion is that we should not. We should not be giving students the impression that we place a high value on their doing perfect work on tasks that are easy for them. A better approach would be to apologize for wasting their time with something that was too easy, and move them to something that is more challenging. When students make progress in or master that more challenging work, that's when our admiration—for their efforts—should come through.

A Challenging Academic Transition

The studies I have been talking about were carried out in a research setting. Two other studies[5] tracked students with these different viewpoints in a real-life situation, as they were making the transition to junior high school and during their first two years of junior high. This is a point at which academic work generally becomes more demanding than it was in elementary school, and many students stumble. The studies compared the attitudes and achievement of students who believed that intelligence is a fixed quantity with students who believed that they could develop their intellectual potential. We were especially interested in any changes in the degree of success students experienced in junior high school and how they dealt with these changes. For the sake of simplicity, I will combine the results from the two studies, for they showed basically the same thing.

First, the students who believed that intelligence is fixed did indeed feel that poor performance meant they were dumb. Furthermore, they reported, in significantly greater numbers than their peers, that if they did badly on a test, they would seriously consider cheating the next time. This was true even for students who were highly skilled and who had a past record of high achievement.

Perhaps even worse, these students believed that having to make an effort meant they were dumb—hardly an attitude to foster good work habits. In fact, these students reported that even though school achievement was very important to them, one of their prime goals in school was to exert as little effort as possible.

In contrast to the hopelessly counterproductive attitude of the first group, the second group of students, those who believed that intellectual potential can be developed, felt that poor performance was often due to a lack of effort, and it called for more studying. They saw effort as worthwhile and important—something necessary even for geniuses if they are to realize their potential.

So once again, for those who are focused on their fixed intelligence and its adequacy, setbacks and even effort bring a loss of face and self-esteem. But challenges, setbacks, and effort are not threatening to the self-esteem of those who are concerned with developing their potential; they represent opportunities to learn. In fact, many of these students told us that they felt smartest when things were difficult; they gained self-esteem when they applied themselves to meeting challenges.

What about the academic achievement of the two groups making the transition to junior high school? In

both studies, we saw that students who believed that intelligence was fixed and was manifest in their performance did more poorly than they had in elementary school. Even many who had been high achievers did much less well. Included among them were many students who entered junior high with high intellectual self-esteem. On the other hand, the students who believed that intellectual potential could be developed showed, as a group, clear gains in their class standing, and many blossomed intellectually. The demands of their new environment, instead of causing them to wilt because they doubted themselves, encouraged them to roll up their sleeves and get to work.

These patterns seem to continue with students entering college. Research with students at highly selective universities found that, although they may enter a situation with equal self-esteem, optimism, and past achievement, students respond to the challenge of college differently: Students in one group by measuring themselves and losing confidence; the others by figuring out what it takes and doing it.[6]

Believing and Achieving

Some of the research my colleagues and I have carried out suggests that it is relatively easy to modify the views of young children in regard to intelligence and effort in a research setting. But is it possible to influence student attitudes in a real-life setting? And do students become set in their beliefs as they grow older? Some exciting new research shows that even college students' views about intelligence and effort can be modified—and that these changes will affect their level of academic achievement.[7] In their study, Aronson and Fried taught minority students at a prestigious university to view their intelligence as a potentiality that could be developed through hard work. For example, they created and showed a film that explained the neural changes that took place in the brain every time students confronted difficulty by exerting effort. The students who were instructed about the relationship between intelligence and effort went on to earn significantly higher grades than their peers who were not. This study, like our intelligence praise studies, shows that (1) students' ideas about their intelligence can be influenced by the messages they receive, and (2) when these ideas change, changes in performance can follow.

But simply getting back to basics and enforcing rigorous standards—which some students will meet and some will not—won't eliminate the pitfalls I have been describing. This approach may convey, even more forcefully, the idea that intelligence is a gift only certain students possess. And it will not, in itself, teach students to value learning and focus on the *process* of achievement or how to deal with obstacles. These students may, more than ever, fear failure because it takes the measure of their intelligence.

A Different Framework

Our research suggests another approach. Instead of trying to convince our students that they are smart or simply enforcing rigorous standards in the hopes that doing so will create high motivation and achievement, teachers should take the following steps: first, get students to focus on their potential to learn; second, teach them to value challenge and learning over looking smart; and third, teach them to concentrate on effort and learning processes in the face of obstacles.

This can be done while holding students to rigorous standards. Within the framework I have outlined, tasks are challenging and effort is highly valued, required, and rewarded. Moreover, we can (and must) give students frank evaluations of their work and their level of skill, but we must make clear that these are evaluations of their current level of performance and skill, not an assessment of their intelligence or their innate ability. In this framework, we do not arrange easy work or constant successes, thinking that we are doing students a favor. We do not lie to students who are doing poorly so they will feel smart: That would rob them of the information they need to work harder and improve. Nor do we just give students hard work that many can't do, thus making them into casualties of the system.

I am not encouraging high-effort situations in which students stay up studying until all hours every night, fearing they will displease their parents or disgrace themselves if they don't get the top test scores. Pushing students to do that is not about valuing learning or about orienting students toward developing their potential. It is about pressuring students to prove their worth through their test scores.

It is also not sufficient to give students piles of homework and say we are teaching them about the importance of effort. We are not talking about quantity here but about teaching students to seek challenging tasks and to engage in an active learning process.

However, we as educators must then be prepared to do our share. We must help students acquire the skills they need for learning, and we must be available as constant resources for learning. It is not enough to keep harping on and praising effort, for this may soon wear thin. And it will not be effective if students don't know *how* to apply their effort appropriately. It is necessary that we as educators understand and teach students how to engage in processes that foster learning, things like task analysis and study skills.[8]

When we focus students on their potential to learn and give them the message that effort is the key to learning, we give them responsibility for and control over their achievement—and over their self-esteem. We acknowledge that learning is not something that someone gives students; nor can they expect to feel good about themselves because teachers tell them they are smart. Both learning and self-esteem are things that students achieve as they tackle challenges and work to master new material.

Students who value learning and effort know how to make and sustain a commitment to valued goals. Unlike some of their peers, they are not afraid to work hard; they know that meaningful tasks involve setbacks; and they know how to bounce back from failure. These are lessons that cannot help but serve them well in life as well as in school.

These are lessons I have learned from my research on students' motivation and achievement, and they are things I wish I had known as a student. There is no reason that every student can't know them now.

Endnotes

1. Meyer, W. U. (1982). Indirect communications about perceived ability estimates. *Journal of Educational Psychology, 74*, 888–897.
2. Mueller, C. M., & Dweck, C. S. (1996). Implicit theories of intelligence: Relation of parental beliefs to children's expectations. Paper presented at the Third National Research Convention of Head Start, Washington, D.C.
3. Mueller, C. M., & Dweck, C. S. (1998). Intelligence praise can undermine motivation and performance. *Journal of Personality and Social Psychology; 75*, 33–52.
4. Kamins, M., & Dweck, C. S. (1999). Person vs. process praise and criticism: Implications for contingent self-worth and coping. *Developmental Psychology*.
5. Henderson, V., & Dweck, C. S. (1990). Achievement and motivation in adolescence: A new model and data. In S. Feldman and G. Elliott (Eds.), *At the threshold: The developing adolescent*. Cambridge, MA: Harvard University Press; and Dweck, C. S., & Sorich, L. (1999). Mastery-oriented thinking. In C. R. Snyder (Ed.). *Coping*. New York: Oxford University Press.
6. Robins, R. W. & Pals, J. (1998). Implicit self-theories of ability in the academic domain: A test of Dweck's model. Unpublished manuscript, University of California at Davis; and Zhao, W., Dweck, C. S., & Mueller, C. (1998). Implicit theories and depression-like responses to failure. Unpublished manuscript, Columbia University.
7. Aronson, J., & Fried, C. (1998). Reducing stereotype threat and boosting academic achievement of African Americans: The role of conceptions of intelligence. Unpublished manuscript, University of Texas.
8. Brown, A. L. (1997). Transforming schools into communities of thinking and learning about serious matters. *American Psychologist, 52*, 399–413.

Carol S. Dweck is a professor of psychology at Columbia University, who has carried out research on self-esteem, motivation, and academic achievement for thirty years. Her new book, Self-Theories: Their Role in Motivation, Personality, and Development, *was just published by The Psychology Press.*

The Challenges of Sustaining a Constructivist Classroom Culture

Mr. Windschitl sees articulating these challenges as a significant step in helping educators create and sustain a classroom culture that values diversity in learning and offers a new vision of the roles of teachers and learners—the culture of constructivism.

By Mark Windschitl

Ms. HUGHES' sixth-grade classroom is a noisy place, and if you come to visit you may have a hard time finding her. Today, students are clustered in small groups, bent over note cards and diagrams they have assembled in order to determine whether they can design a habitat that can support Australian dingoes and marmosets.

The students have just participated in three days of discussion and reading about interrelationships among mammals. They are divided into four groups, each of which has negotiated with Ms. Hughes to devise a complex problem to work on that reflects their interests and abilities. One group chose a design problem: creating a habitat for a local zoo that will support at least three kinds of mammals naturally found in the same geographic area.

The students are now engaged for the next two weeks on this project. They find and share dozens of resources, many of which are spread out on tables and on the floor around the room. Allen brings to class a video he shot at the zoo last week so that everyone can see what different habitats look like. Michelle loads a CD-ROM on mammals that she brought from home, and James donates one of his mother's landscape architecture books for ideas on how to diagram spaces and buildings.

ILLUSTRATION BY JOHN BERRY

During the next two weeks, these students will develop an understanding of how mammal species interact with one another, cope with the environment, and follow the natural cycles of reproduction. Concepts such as "competition for resources" and "reproductive capacity"—whose definitions in other classes might have been memorized—arise instead from a meaningful and multifaceted context. These concepts are built on the experiences of the students and are essential, interconnected considerations in the success of the habitat design. This is one of the many faces of the constructivist classroom.

A growing number of teachers are embracing the fundamental ideas of constructivist learning—that their students' background knowledge profoundly affects how they interpret subject matter and that students learn best when they apply their knowledge to solve authentic problems, engage in "sense-making" dialogue with peers, and strive for deep understanding of core ideas rather than recall of a laundry list of facts. Unfortunately, much of the public conversation about constructivism has been stalled on its philosophical contrasts with more traditional approaches to instruction. Constructivists have offered varying descriptions of how classrooms can be transformed, usually framed in terms of these contrasts. And although these descriptions have prompted educators to reexamine the roles of teachers, the ways in which students learn best, and even what it means to learn, the image of what is possible in constructivist classrooms remains too idealized.

To all the talk about theory, educators must add layers of dialogue about real classroom experiences and concerns about those experiences. An essential part of this dialogue is the articulation of the pedagogical, logistical, and political challenges that face educators who are willing to integrate constructivism into their classroom practice. The new discourse shifts the emphasis from comparisons between constructivism and traditional instruction to the refinement of constructivist practices in real classrooms. This frank conversation about challenges is equally valuable for sympathetic administrators—being informed and reflective about these issues is a necessary prerequisite to offering support for the classroom teacher.

In this article, I characterize and categorize these challenges and describe the kinds of administrative support necessary to create and sustain a culture of constructivist teaching in schools. First, however, it is necessary to examine constructivism as a philosophy on which a systemic classroom culture can be based rather than to view it as a set of discrete instructional practices that may be inserted into the learning environment whenever necessary. The challenges I describe here are challenges precisely because they cause us to reconsider and dare us to change the comfortable (and often unstated) norms, beliefs, and practices of the classroom culture we are so familiar with. Constructivism is more than a set of teaching techniques; it is a coherent pattern of expectations that underlie new relationships between students, teachers, and the world of ideas.

Constructivism as Culture

Constructivism is premised on the belief that learners actively create, interpret, and reorganize knowledge in individual ways. These fluid intellectual transformations occur when students reconcile formal instructional experiences with their existing knowledge, with the cultural and social contexts in which ideas occur, and with a host of other influences that serve to mediate understanding. With respect to instruction, this belief suggests that students should participate in experiences that accommodate these ways of learning. Such experiences include problem-based learning, inquiry activities, dialogues with peers and teachers that encourage making sense of the subject matter, exposure to multiple sources of information, and opportunities for students to demonstrate their understanding in diverse ways.

> ## Constructivism is a culture—not a fragmented collection of practices.

However, before teachers and administrators adopt such practices, they should understand that constructivism cannot make its appearance in the classroom as a set of isolated instructional methods grafted on to otherwise traditional teaching techniques. Rather, it is a culture—a set of beliefs, norms, and practices that constitute the fabric of school life. This culture, like all other cultures, affects the way learners can interact with peers, relate to the teacher, and experience the subject matter. The children's relationships with teachers, their patterns of communication, how they are assessed, and even their notion of "what learning is good for" must all be connected, or the culture risks becoming a fragmented collection of practices that fail to reinforce one another. For example, the constructivist belief that learners are capable of intellectual autonomy must coincide with the belief that students possess a large knowledge base of life experiences and have made sense out of much of what they have experienced. These beliefs are linked with the practice of problem-based learning within relevant and authentic contexts and with the norm of showing mutual respect for one another's ideas in the classroom.

Portraying the constructivist classroom as a culture is important because many challenges for the teacher emerge when new rituals take root or when familiar norms of behavior are transformed into new patterns of teacher/student interaction.[1] By contrast, if discrete practices that have been associated with constructivism (cooperative learning, performance assessments, hands-on experiences) are simply inserted as special activities into the regular school day, then it remains business as usual for the students. Teachers and students do not question their vision of learning, no one takes risks, and hardly a ripple is felt.

Throughout this article then, challenges become apparent when we question the fundamental norms of the classroom—the images and beliefs we hold of teachers and students, the kinds of discourse encouraged in the classroom, the way authority and decision making are controlled, and even what "counts" as learning. I begin with a subtle but powerful influence on classroom instruction.

Images of Teaching: The Chains That Bind Us

Most of us are products of traditional instruction; as learners, we were exposed to teacher-centered instruction, fact-based subject matter, and a steady diet of drill and practice.[2] Our personal histories furnish us with mental models of teaching, and these models of how we were taught shape our behavior in powerful ways. Teachers use these models to imagine lessons in their classrooms, develop innovations, and plan for learning.[3] These images serve to organize sets of beliefs and guide curricular actions.[4] Teachers are more likely to be guided not by instructional theories but by the familiar images of what is "proper and possible" in classroom settings.[5]

Unfortunately, the signs and symbols of teacher-centered education and learning by transmission, which are likely to be a part of teachers' personal histories, persist in classrooms today.[6] In this environment, it is assumed that the more quiet and orderly the classrooms are, the more likely it is that learning is taking place. Individual desks face the front of the room, where the teacher occupies a privileged space of knowing authority; students work individually on identical, skill-based assignments to ensure uniformity of learning. Value statements are embedded everywhere in this environment.

Constructivist teachers envision themselves emerging boldly from the confines of this traditional classroom culture, but the vision first requires critical reflection. Teachers must ask themselves, "Is my role to dispense knowledge or to nurture independent thinkers? How do I show respect for the ideas of the students? Am I here to learn from the students?" Teachers must struggle to develop a new, well-articulated rationale for instructional decisions and cannot depend on their previous teaching or learning experiences for much help in shaping their choice of methods; shifting the centers of authority and activity in accordance with this rationale requires persistence. For example, teachers can be uncomfortable with their apparent lack of control as students engage with their peers during learning activities and may be unwill-

ing to allow supervisors who visit the classroom to observe this kind of environment. Teachers may reconsider their ideas of student-centered learning in favor of conforming to the more traditional images of the teacher as the hub of classroom discourse and attention.[7]

New Demands on the Teacher

Constructivist instruction, especially that which is based on design tasks or problem solving, places high demands on the teacher's subject-matter understanding. The teacher must not only be familiar with the principles underlying a topic of study but must also be prepared for the variety of ways these principles can be explored.

For example, if students are studying density in science class, the teacher must support the understanding of one group of students who want to approach the concept from a purely abstract, mathematical perspective as they construct tables, equations, and graphs to develop their knowledge. In this case, the teacher must understand these different representations of information and how they are interrelated. Another group of students may plan to recount the story of the Titanic, emphasizing the role that density played in the visibility of the iceberg, the ballast of the ship, and the sinking itself. Here, the teacher must be intellectually agile, able to apply his or her mathematical understanding of density to a real-life, inevitably more complex situation.

> # Crafting instruction based on constructivism is not as straightforward as it seems.

Teachers in different subject areas may allow students varying degrees of latitude in exploring content and will differ in how they accept student "constructions" of core curricular ideas. Mathematics is characterized by rule-based propositions and skills that may be open to discovery via many experiential pathways. Most forms of mathematics problems, however, have only one right answer. And if students are allowed to explore problems by their own methods, teachers may find it difficult to see exactly how the students are making sense of the problem-solving process—not all constructions are created equal. Science and social studies present the same challenges, although science is less axiomatic than mathematics, and the issues explored in social studies are open to wider interpretation. Dealing with the "correctness" of student constructions is an ongoing concern, and the arguments have barely been introduced here, but reflection on these issues helps teachers develop a critical awareness of disciplinary "truths" and the viability of various ways of knowing the world.

In addition to the necessity for flexible subject-matter knowledge, constructivism places greater demands on teachers' pedagogical skill. Crafting instruction based on constructivism is not as straightforward as it seems. Educators struggle with how specific instructional techniques (e.g., lecture, discussion, cooperative learning, problem-based learning, inquiry learning) fit into the constructivist model of instruction. Regardless of the particular techniques used in instruction, students will always construct and reorganize knowledge rather than simply assimilate information from teachers or textbooks. The question is not whether to use lecture or discussion, but how to use these techniques to complement rather than dominate student thinking. For example, constructivist principles suggest that students should experience the ideas, phenomena, and artifacts of a discipline before being exposed to formal explanations of them. Students might begin units of instruction in science class by manipulating a pendulum, in math class by constructing polygons, or in social studies by reading letters from Civil War battlefields. Only after these experiences do teachers and students together suggest terminology, explanations, and conceptual organization.

Even though designing instruction is important, constructivist teaching is less about the sequencing of events and more about responding to the needs of a situation.[8] Teachers must employ a sophisticated range of strategies to support individual students' understandings as they engage in the problem-based activities that characterize constructivist classrooms. These strategies include scaffolding, in which the task required of the learner is strategically reduced in complexity; modeling, in which the teacher either thinks aloud about or acts out how she would approach a problem; and coaching, guiding, and advising, which are loosely defined as providing learners with suggestions of varying degrees of explicitness.[9] The teacher is challenged to select the proper strategy and implement it with skill.

Problem-based activities exemplify another core value of the constructivist culture—collaboration. Students are witness to and participate in one another's thinking. Learners are exposed to the clear, cogent thinking of some peers as well as to the inevitable meandering, unreflective thought of others. Students do require training to function effectively in these groups.[10] However, even with training, many capable students are simply not interested in helping their peers, and negative consequences of group work—such as bickering, exclusion, and academic freeloading—are common.[11] These consequences can be minimized if the teacher is familiar with the principles of cooperative learning. And so, having students work together requires that the teacher have additional competencies in cooperative learning strategies and management skills particular to decentralized learning environments.

A final pedagogical challenge involves independent student projects. Depending on the degree of structure the teacher imposes in a classroom, students will have some latitude in choosing problems or design projects that relate to the theme under study. Often, students determine with the teacher suitable criteria for problems and for evidence of learning. Negotiation about criteria prompts questions such as: Is the problem meaningful? Important to the discipline? Complex enough? Does it relate to the theme under study? Does it require original thinking and interpretation, or is it simply fact finding? Will the resolution of this problem help us acquire the concepts and principles fundamental to the theme under study? Because curricular materials are often filled with prepared questions and tasks, teachers seldom have occasion to introduce their students to this idea of "problems about problems." Clearly, teachers must develop their own ability to analyze problems by reflecting on the nature of the discipline and refining their ideas through extended dialogue with colleagues and experiences with students.

Logistical and Political Challenges

Effective forms of constructivist instruction call for major changes in the curriculum, in scheduling, and in assessment.[12] When students are engaged in problem solving and are allowed to help guide their own learning, teachers quickly find that this approach outgrows the 50-minute class period. This situation often means that the teacher will have to negotiate with administrators and other teachers about the possibilities of block scheduling and integrating curricula. If teachers can team with partners from other subject areas, they can extend the length of their class periods and develop more comprehensive themes for study that bridge the worlds of science, social studies, math, and the arts.

The purpose of integrated curricula and extended class periods is to allow students to engage in learning activities that will help them develop deep and elaborate understandings of subject matter. These understandings may be quite different in nature from student to student. Thus there is a need for forms of assessment that allow students to demonstrate what they know and that connect with rigorous criteria of excellence. These are not the paper-and-pencil, objective tests in which learners recognize rather than generate answers or create brief responses to questions in which they have little personal investment. Rather, students are required to produce journals, research reports, physical models, or performances in the forms of plays, debates, dances, or other artistic representations. Assessing these products and performances requires well-designed, flexible rubrics to maintain a link between course objectives and student learning. Designing these rubrics (through negotiation with students) builds consensus about what "purpose" means in a learning activity, about the nature of meaningful criteria, and about how assessments reflect the efficacy of the teacher as a promoter of understanding.

The final and perhaps most politically sensitive issue confronting teachers is that the diversity of understandings emerging from constructivist instruction does not always seem compatible with state and local standards. For example, student groups engaged in science projects on photosynthesis may have radically different approaches to developing their understanding of this phenomenon. One group may choose to focus on chemical reactions at the molecular level while another group may examine how oxygen and carbon dioxide are exchanged between animals and plants on a global scale. These two groups will take disconcertingly divergent paths to understanding photosynthesis.

This kind of project-based learning must be skillfully orchestrated so that, however students choose to investigate and seek resolutions to problems, they will acquire an understanding of key principles and concepts as well as the critical thinking skills that are assessed on standardized tests. Proponents of project-based learning have demonstrated that these kinds of learning outcomes are entirely possible.[13] Artful guidance by the teacher notwithstanding, it can be unsettling for teachers to reconcile the language of "objectives, standards, and benchmarks" with the diversity of understandings that emerge in a constructivist classroom.

Conclusions and Recommendations

How does a school community support the instructional expertise, academic freedom, and professional collaboration necessary to sustain a constructivist culture? First, a core group of committed teachers must systematically investigate constructivism in order to understand its principles and its limitations. The ideas behind constructivism seem intuitive and sensible, but teachers and administrators must go beyond the hyperbole and the one-shot-workshop acquaintance with constructivism. Interested faculty members should conduct a thorough reading campaign, and at least one or two teachers should extend their experience by participating in advanced workshops, attending classes, and witnessing how constructivist cultures operate in other schools. Stipends and released time can be provided for a cadre of lead teachers to attend classes, do extra reading, adapt curriculum, and offer their own workshops to fellow teachers. Workshop topics could include the constructivist implementation of cooperative learning, scaffolding techniques, problem-based learning, or multifaceted assessment strategies.

The faculty members must openly discuss their beliefs about learners and about their roles as teachers. If these beliefs are left unexamined or unchallenged, then individuals have feeble grounding for their personal philosophies. Just as problematically then, everyone operates on different, untested assumptions. And all decisions about curriculum, instruction, and assessment are built on such assumptions.

Personal philosophies of education are particularly important when constructivism is used to furnish underlying principles—important because constructivism means risk taking and a divergence from business as usual. Sooner or later, teachers will be asked, "Why do you teach that way?" Whatever form that question takes, teachers must be able to justify the choices they make. This task will not be as intimidating if the teacher has mindfully linked the aspects of his or her constructivist philosophy to the various dimensions of classroom experience and to the larger goals of education.

The process of making these beliefs explicit can also strengthen teachers' resolve to move beyond the traditional images of what is proper and possible in the classroom. It can make clear to them the characteristics and limitations of the system that encouraged images of teachers as dispensers of information and students as passive recipients of knowledge. Accordingly, teachers must try to arrive at a new vision of their role. This vision must include serving as a facilitator of learning who responds to students' needs with a flexible understanding of subject matter and a sensitivity to how the student is making sense of the world.

Teachers and their principals must be prepared to go on record with these beliefs in discussions with parent groups and the school board. Educators should always have a rationale for what and how they teach; however, because constructivism is so contrary to historical norms, it is even more important in this case that the rationale be well founded, coherent, and applicable to the current school context. Community members will undoubtedly be suspicious of teaching methods that are so different from the ones they remember as students and that sound too much like a laissez-faire approach to learning.

Administrators must also take the lead in supporting a "less is more" approach. The compulsion to cover material is antithetical to the aim of constructivist instruction—the deep and elaborate understanding of selected core ideas. Textbooks, which are often the de facto curriculum, have become encyclopedic, and administrators should make teachers feel secure about using a variety of other resources. They should also provide funds to purchase alternative classroom materials. Furthermore, administrators must be open to suggestions for block scheduling and for integrating curricula, perhaps even arranging for interested teachers to be placed together in team-teaching situations that are premised on the constructivist approach.

To strengthen the school's position on accountability, assessment specialists who understand constructivism can be brought in to connect local standards with instruction and with evidence that learning is taking place. Teachers will undoubtedly appreciate assistance in investigating and evaluating a variety of assessment strategies.

The list of challenges I have described here is not exhaustive. There are certainly others, and the challenges outnumber the solutions at the moment. But articulating these challenges is a significant step in helping educators create and sustain a classroom culture that values diversity in learning and offers a new vision of the roles of teachers and learners—the culture of constructivism.

Notes

1. Pam Bolotin-Joseph, "Understanding Curriculum as Culture," in Pam Bolotin-Joseph, Stevie Bravman, Mark Windschitl, Edward Mikel, and Nancy Green, eds., *Cultures of Curriculum* (Mahwah, N.J.: Erlbaum, forthcoming).

2. Thomas Russell, "Learning to Teach Science: Constructivism, Reflection, and Learning from Experience," in Kenneth Tobin, ed., *The Practice of Constructivism in Science Education* (Hillsdale, N.J.: Erlbaum, 1993), pp. 247–58.

3. Corby Kennison, "Enhancing Teachers' Professional Learning: Relationships Between School Culture and Elementary School Teachers' Beliefs, Images, and Ways of Knowing" (Specialist's thesis, Florida State University, 1990).

4. Kenneth Tobin, "Constructivist Perspectives on Teacher Learning," in idem, ed., pp. 215–26; and Kenneth Tobin and Sarah Ulerick, "An Interpretation of High School Science Teaching Based on Metaphors and Beliefs for Specific Roles," paper presented at the annual meeting of the American Educational Research Association, San Francisco, 1989.

5. Kenneth Zeichner and Robert Tabachnick, "Are the Effects of University Teacher Education Washed Out by School Experience?," *Journal of Teacher Education*, vol. 32, 1981, pp. 7–11.

6. Adriana Groisman, Bonnie Shapiro, and John Willinsky, "The Potential of Semiotics to Inform Understanding of Events in Science Education," *International Journal of Science Education*, vol. 13, 1991, pp. 217–26.

7. James H. Mosenthal and Deborah Ball, "Constructing New Forms of Teaching: Subject Matter Knowledge in In-service Teacher Education," *Journal of Teacher Education*, vol. 43, 1992, pp. 347–56.

8. David Lebow, "Constructivist Values for Instructional Systems Design: Five Principles Toward a New Mindset," *Educational Technology, Research, and Development*, vol. 41, no. 3, 1993, pp. 4–16.

9. Jeong-Im Choi and Michael Hannafin, "Situated Cognition and Learning Environments: Roles, Structures, and Implications for Design," *Educational Technology, Research, and Development*, vol. 43, no. 2, 1995, pp. 53–69.

10. David W. Johnson, Roger T. Johnson, and Karl A. Smith, *Active Learning: Cooperation in the College Classroom* (Edina, Minn.: Interaction Book Company, 1991).

11. Robert E. Slavin, *Cooperative Learning* (Boston: Allyn and Bacon, 1995).

12. Phyllis Blumenfeld et al., "Motivating Project-Based Learning: Sustaining the Doing, Supporting the Learning," *Educational Psychologist*, vol. 26, 1991, pp. 369–98.

13. Ibid. 9.

MARK WINDSCHITL is an assistant professor of curriculum and instruction in the College of Education, University of Washington, Seattle.

From *Phi Delta Kappan*, June 1999, pp. 751-755. © 1999 by Phi Delta Kappa International, Inc. Reprinted by permission.

The Tyranny of Self-Oriented Self-Esteem

by James H. McMillan, Judy Singh, and Leo G. Simonetta

In Ryann's second-grade classroom there was a poster on one wall to celebrate each individual student. For one week during the year each student was the "special child" of the class, and the space on the poster indicated unique and valued things about the child, such as a favorite color, hobbies, or family. Students put up pictures and other items to announce publicly what they thought was good about themselves. (Ryann, daughter of one of the authors, liked being a "special child" for a week, but the parent was not as enthusiastic.)

Activities for this type are common in elementary schools, all seeking to boost the self-esteem of the students. They assume that self-esteem is the key to achievement, and in fact much evidence, both anecdotal and research-based, shows that students achieve more with self-esteem. Teachers also seem to accept self-esteem as critical for intellectual development and necessary for students to excel or even achieve needed competence in academic tasks. According to Barbara Lerner, "Teachers generally seem to accept the modern dogma that self-esteem is the critical variable for intellectual development—the master key to learning. Children… cannot achieve excellence, or even competence, until their self-esteem is raised."[1]

Linking self-esteem to success and overall well-being is so well accepted that there are many institutes, foundations, task forces, and centers dedicated to promoting self-esteem programs. For example, there is the California Task Force to Promote Self-Esteem and Personal and Social Responsibility, the Center for Self-Esteem, the National Council for Self-Esteem.[2] In addition, an increasing number of books, monographs, audiocassettes, and videocassettes stress developing self-esteem, as well as "how to" programs for teachers at all levels. The fundamental idea is that once educators focus on improving students' self-esteem, not only will behavior and achievement improve, but students also will be more satisfied, better adjusted, and happier. The assumption is that concentrating on enhancing self-esteem will produce these positive outcomes.

But is it possible, with the best of intentions, to overemphasize self-esteem with self-oriented activities?

What are we teaching our children by encouraging and reinforcing a self-focus, and what are its long-term consequences? Since the mid-'60s, psychology has transformed our way of thinking about explanations for people's behaviors, shifting from outside the self (behaviorism) to within the self. The psychologist Martin Seligman terms our current culture one of "maximal selfs," in which the individual should be gratified, fulfilled, self-actualized, and in control.[3] Seligman argues that this revolutionary change has caused increased depression, hopelessness, and other personal difficulties because of the dual burden of high expectations and self-control. Since the focus is on ourselves as being responsible, and on an expectation that we will be most content and happy if we concentrate on what is best for us, coping with failure to reach our expectations becomes difficult. If Seligman is correct, many facets of current self-esteem programs may be based on fundamentally flawed and misdirected theory. In this article the theory of self-oriented self-esteem programs will be reviewed, with illustrations of suggested practices based on this theory and the results that can be expected from this approach. An alternative theory will be recommended, with suggested practices.

Self-Oriented Self-Esteem

Many self-esteem programs fundamentally encourage students to think more about themselves, to be more introspective and self-oriented. The idea is that the self can be enhanced by focusing on it positively. Barbara Lerner refers to this as "feel-good-now self-esteem."[4] Jack Canfield, a well-known advocate of self-esteem enhancement, has suggested several strategies for the classroom that emphasize introspection: 1) assume an attitude of 100 percent responsibility by getting students to think about what they are saying to themselves; 2) focus on the positive—"I spend a lot of my time having students recall, write about, draw, and share their past experiences"; 3) learn to monitor your self-talk by replacing negative thoughts with positive—"I can learn to do anything I want, I am smart, I love and accept myself the way I am"; and 4) identify your strengths and weaknesses.[5]

A popular self-esteem book for educators suggests enhancing self-esteem with one or more of the following: improving self-evaluation skills; developing a sense of personal worth; reflecting on self-esteem; thinking of oneself in positive terms; discovering reasons the individual is unhappy; or examining sources of and influences on self-esteem. Their emphasis is on enhancing students' positive self-perceptions.[6] Such ideas are often implemented in classroom activities that teach students introspective thinking: for example, keeping a journal about themselves and indicating "what I like best about myself",[7] teaching a unit entitled "I Am Great" that emphasizes their individuality through self-portraits, silhouettes of themselves, "who am I," and "coat of arms" exercises,[8] and programs such as Developing Understanding of Self and Others (DUSO), Toward Affective Development, and Dimensions of Personality. Some less-complex programs simply encourage student self-talk with phrases such as "I'm terrific" or "I'm great." All these activities or programs are designed to promote self-acceptance and self-awareness, to help students become aware of their unique characteristics, and to "put children in touch with themselves."[9]

> ## Accomplishment means that self-esteem is enhanced as children work hard to meet externally set, reasonable standards of achievement.

Although these are well-intentional programs, their encouragement of self-introspection may distort a normal, healthy perspective about oneself into self-importance, self-gratification, and ultimately selfishness. If the message is that "me" is most important, will selfishness be viewed as normal and expected? Are we making a virtue of self-preoccupation? If so, such "selfism" may have negative consequences. As William Damon points out, "A young mind might too readily interpret a blanket incantation toward self-esteem as a lure toward self-centeredness."[10] Damon believes that placing the child at the center of the universe is psychologically dangerous because "… it draws the child's attention away from the social realities to which the child must adapt for proper character development."[11] Children taught to place themselves first care most for their own personal experiences, and in doing so they do not learn how to develop respect for others. According to Lerner, the feel-good-now variety of self-esteem eventually leads to unhappiness, restlessness, and dissatisfaction.[12] Finally, Seligman argues that our obsession with self is responsible for an alarming increase in depression and other mental difficulties.[13] It is well-documented that such problems result from rumination and obsessive thinking about oneself.[14]

There are other negative consequences of overemphasizing self-oriented self-esteem. For most students, and surely young children, the idea of self-esteem is abstract and hard to understand. Generalized statements such as "you're valued," or "you're great," or "you're special" have no objective reality. They are simply holistic messages that, untied to something tangible and real, have little meaning.[15] Teachers making such statements will lose credibility because children are adept at discerning valid feedback from such vague generalizations. Students may develop a skepticism toward and distrust of adults, or even worse may learn to tune them out entirely, as the teacher "shades the truth [with] empty rhetoric, transparent flattery, bland distortions of reality."[16] By trying to bolster self-esteem with messages that are not "entirely" true, teachers inadvertently undermine the trust of the child. For students who already have low self-esteem, such statements reinforce a noncaring attitude from adults. From the perspective of children, caring adults

"tell it like it is" and don't hide the truth—they don't cover up or make things up that aren't true.

In contrast, there is ample evidence that our mental health improves as we forget ourselves and focus on activities that are not self-oriented. Often we are most happy when we are so involved in outside pursuits that we don't think about ourselves. This leads us to an alternative theoretical foundation for self-esteem: the notion that healthy self-esteem results not from self-preoccupation and analysis but just the opposite—from not being self-oriented but being occupied by interests and pursuits external to self. Indeed, many self-esteem enhancement programs appear to be based on this idea.

Accomplishment and External-to-Self-Oriented Self-Esteem

As an alternative to the self-orientation approach, we suggest that a healthy esteem results not from self-preoccupation and analysis but from activities that result in meaningful accomplishment or have an external-to-self orientation. Accomplishment means that self-esteem is enhanced as children work hard to meet externally set, reasonable standards of achievement. Lerner calls this "earned" self-esteem: "Earned self-esteem is based on success in meeting the tests of reality—measuring up to standards—at home and in school. It is necessarily hard-won, and develops slowly, but is stable and long-lasting, and provides a secure foundation for further growth and development. It is not a precondition for learning but a product of it."[17]

Achieving meaningful success in schoolwork enhances self-esteem after many years of meeting standards and demands. A foundation for self-esteem based on tangible evidence is internalized by students because it makes sense to them in their social environment. Internally meaningful performance and accomplishment can be attributed to ability and effort. Such internal attributions underlie a sense of self-efficacy so that the child becomes confident in being a capable learner. Striving for achievement also directs children's thinking off themselves and on something external to themselves. This change in thinking orientation determines self-esteem programs that theoretically are diametrically opposed to self-oriented programs.

Recently there have been signs that psychologists may be changing their views about the emphasis on selfism to enhance self-esteem. Seligman maintains that many have lost a sense of commitment to larger entities outside themselves—country, church, community, family, God, or a purpose that transcends themselves. Without these connections people are left to find meaning and fulfillment in themselves.[18] The negative consequences of de-emphasizing other people, groups, community, and the larger society include vandalism, violence, racial tensions, high divorce rates, and drug abuse. Some psychologists attribute the growth of the "me" generation and selfish behavior to the emphasis on individuality and related themes.[19] Others argue that schools should promote selflessness by emphasizing group welfare over individuals, involvement rather than isolation, and self-denial rather than self-centeredness.[20]

These authors suggest that student well-being is best enhanced by pursuits that take attention away from self, in which one gets "lost." Such pursuits could include a hobby; a concern for helping others; having a purpose or cause bigger than oneself; submitting to duty or to a role in community; or academic success following meaningful effort. The hypothesis is that self-esteem is a byproduct of successful external-to-self experiences. The more success a student has in such activities, the stronger his or her own self-esteem will be.

From a social-psychological perspective, participating constructively with others is necessary for positive self-esteem. As stated by Damon:

> Growing up in large part means learning to participate constructively in the social world. This in turn means developing real skills, getting along with others, acquiring respect for social rules and legitimate authority, caring about those in need, and assuming social responsibility in a host of ways. All of these efforts necessarily bring children out of themselves. They require children to orient themselves toward other people and other people's standards.[21]

By focusing outside themselves children learn respect for others and an objective reference for acquiring a stable and meaningful sense of themselves.

It is the outward focus that forms the foundation for self-esteem.

Some examples of self-esteem programs appear to be based on this external-to-self hypothesis. One is a successful program in which students are involved in an art project structured to enhance a feeling of belonging and accomplishment. Self-esteem is improved by involving students in meaningful group activity; not by self-introspection.[22] Another program reports that children acquire self-esteem from successful experiences and appropriate feedback in motor skill development.[23] Several other programs also stress successful achievement in affecting self-esteem.[24] In each case the program involves students in some meaningful activity, rather than focusing on themselves.

Conclusion

Clearly, educators need to concentrate their efforts on improving students' self-esteem. The important question is: how should this be done? We have suggested that approaches emphasizing meaningful achievement and external-to-self pursuits will result in more healthy self-esteem than programs that are self-oriented.

Teachers and administrators need to design programs directing student attention away from the self, not toward it. Paradoxically, positive self-esteem develops as students forget about self-esteem, focus on external pursuits, and obtain positive feedback following meaningful involvement and effort.

Notes

1. Barbara Lerner, "Self-esteem and Excellence: The Choice and the Paradox," *American Educator* 9 (1985): 10–16.
2. Jack Canfield, "Improving Students' Self-esteem," *Educational Leadership* 48 (1990): 48–50.
3. Martin E. P. Seligman, "Boomer Blues: With Too Great Expectations, the Baby-Boomers Are Sliding into Individualistic Melancholy," *Psychology Today* 22 (1988): 50–55.
4. Lerner, "Self-esteem and Excellence."
5. Canfield, "Improving Students' Self-esteem."
6. James A. Beane and Richard P. Lipka, *Self-concept, Self-esteem, and the Curriculum* (Boston: Allyn and Bacon, 1984).
7. Anne E. Gottsdanker-Willenkens and Patricia Y. Leonard, "All about Me: Language Arts Strategies to Enhance Self-Concept," *Reading Teacher* 37 (1984): 801–802.
8. Richard L. Papenfuss, John D. Curtis, Barbara J. Beier, and Joseph D. Menze, "Teaching Positive Self-concepts in the Classroom," *Journal of School Health* 53 (1983): 618–620.
9. Frederic J. Medway and Robert C. Smith, Jr., "An Examination of Contemporary Elementary School Affective Education Programs," *Psychology in the Schools* 15 (1978): 266.
10. William Damon, "Putting Substance into Self-Esteem: A Focus on Academic and Moral Values," *Educational Horizons* (Fall 1991): 13.
11. Ibid., 17.
12. Lerner, "Self-esteem and Excellence."
13. Seligman, "Boomer Blues."
14. Thomas J. Lasley and John Bregenzer, "Toward Selflessness," *Journal of Human Behavior and Learning* 3 (1986): 20–27.
15. Damon, "Putting Substance into Self-esteem."
16. Ibid., 15.
17. Lerner, "Self-esteem and Excellence," 13.
18. Martin E. P. Seligman, *Learned Optimism: The Skill to Conquer Life's Obstacles, Large and Small* (New York: Random House, 1990).
19. Sami I. Boulos, "The Anatomy of the 'Me' Generation," *Education* 102 (1982): 238–242.
20. Lasley and Bregenzer, "Toward Selflessness."
21. William Damon, "Putting Substance into Self-esteem," 16–17.
22. Marilee M. Cowan and Faith M. Clover, "Enhancement of Self-concept through Discipline-based Art Education," *Art Education* 44 (1991): 38–45.
23. Linda K. Bunker, "The Role of Play and Motor Skill Development in Building Children's Self-confidence and Self-esteem," *Elementary School Journal* 91 (1991): 467–471.
24. David L. Silvernail, *Developing Positive Student Self-concept* (Washington, D.C.: National Education Association, 1987).

From *Educational Horizons*, Winter 2001, pp. 92-95. © 2001 by Educational Horizons. Reprinted with permission of the author.

Concept Mapping as a Mindtool for Critical Thinking

ABSTRACT Concept mapping is a mindtool (cognitive tool) that can enhance the interdependence of declarative and procedural knowledge to produce yet another form of knowledge representation known as structural knowledge (Jonassen, 1996). Structural knowledge is best described as knowing *why* something is the case. It helps learners integrate and interrelate declarative and procedural knowledge by activating the perceived static nature of declarative knowledge and by increasing the awareness of why one knows how to do something. By using computer-based concept mapping tools as a cognitive or learning strategy, learners can sharpen inference-making and critical thinking skills and can avoid the acquisition and accumulation of inert (unusable) knowledge. This article discusses the use and application of two computer-based concept mapping tools, Inspiration® and Semnet®, in educational contexts to foster meaningful learning and understanding. Inspiration® and Semnet® are visual thinking environments that allow users to create concept maps, semantic networks, outlines, graphic organizers and other comprehension monitoring activities. The article addresses the use of computer-based concept mapping as a learning strategy, an instructional strategy, and as a collaborative thinking tool, offering guidelines for educators on how to implement these uses in the classroom.

NADA DABBAGH

Introduction

Knowledge representation refers to how we represent information in long-term and working memory (Gagne, Yekovich, & Yekovich, 1993). Knowledge representation can take many forms (mental representations) depending on the type of knowledge learned and the cognitive strategy used in acquiring that knowledge. For example, declarative knowledge—which is best described as knowing *that* something is the case—is represented in the form of propositions. Propositions are knowledge units often referred to as schema (Jonassen, 1988). These knowledge units form a *propositional network* and are comprised of arguments (topics and attributes) and relations that constrain those arguments (Gagne, Yekovich & Yekovich, 19934). Our schema for "school" for example is comprised of arguments such as teachers, students, classes, grades, classrooms, and books, and relations that

constrain those arguments such as "teachers teach students," "students learn from teachers," and "grades measure students' performance" (Figure 1).

Procedural knowledge, on the other hand, is knowing *how* to do something and is represented in the form of productions or if-then contingency statements (Figure 2). Productions are condition–action rules that enable people to solve problems, make decisions, and develop plans (Gagne et al., 1993; Jonassen, 1988). In other words, they "produce" an action or a mental or physical behavior.

Productions can be interrelated to form a production system which can lead to a complex behavior. Developing production systems for different types of knowledge enhances inference-making and critical-thinking skills.

Declarative knowledge and procedural knowledge are interdependent (Jonassen, 1996). Although one might think that acquiring propositional knowledge is a prerequisite for forming productions, in some cases forming

For example....our schema of school

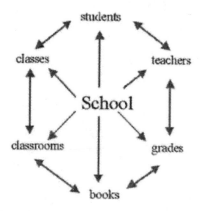

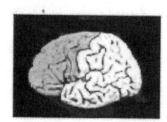

THIRD INTERNATIONAL CONFERENCE ON FUNCTIONAL MAPPING OF THE HUMAN BRAIN
Copenhagen, Denmark. May 19-23, 1997

Figure 1: A propositional network of a school schema

procedural knowledge can lead to the acquisition of declarative knowledge, and *applying* declarative knowledge can lead to the acquisition of production systems. The interdependence of these two types of knowledge is largely dependent on the cognitive (or metacognitive) strategy that the learner is using while acquiring the knowledge. At the lower end of the spectrum, rehearsal strategies involving oral repetition of content, copying, and underlining will most likely result in a learner's ability to recall and state facts as is, and elaboration strategies such as paraphrasing and summarizing content will most likely result in concept learning. On the higher end of the spectrum, comprehension monitoring strategies involving self-questioning (a form of reflection) and using advance organizers to guide one's learning will most likely result in analysis, synthesis, and evaluation processes that are higher-order learning outcomes (Bloom, 1956). The above discussion indicates that learning strategies can affect the encoding process and hence the learning outcome and associated performance (Weinstein & Mayer, 1986).

Concept mapping is a mindtool (a cognitive tool) that can enhance the interdependence of declarative and procedural knowledge to produce yet another form of knowledge representation known as *structural knowledge* (Jonassen, 1996). Structural knowledge is best described as knowing *why* something is the case. It helps learners integrate and interrelate declarative and procedural knowledge by activating the perceived static nature of declarative knowledge and by increasing the awareness of *why* one knows *how* to do something. It is reflected in richer propositional networks known as semantic networks that communicate more knowledge about the interrelatedness of concepts articulated by the learner, revealing a deeper form of knowledge representation known as mental models (Jonassen & Tessmer, 1997). Concept mapping can lead to the development of rich mental models in learners requiring them to think about a knowledge domain in meaningful ways. By using this mindtool as a cognitive or learning strategy, learners can sharpen inference-making and critical-thinking skills and can avoid the acquisition and accumulation of inert (unusable) knowledge (Hannafin, 1992).

Studies about the effectiveness of concept mapping as a cognitive tool date back to the early 1980s, when a group of researchers at Cornell University became interested in studying changes in students' understandings of science concepts over a 12-year span of schooling (Novak, 1990). A need for developing a tool to represent students' understanding of concepts and more importantly *changes* in students' understanding over time, led to the creation of a cognitive map (later known as a concept map) as a graphical organizing structure for concepts. Several stud-

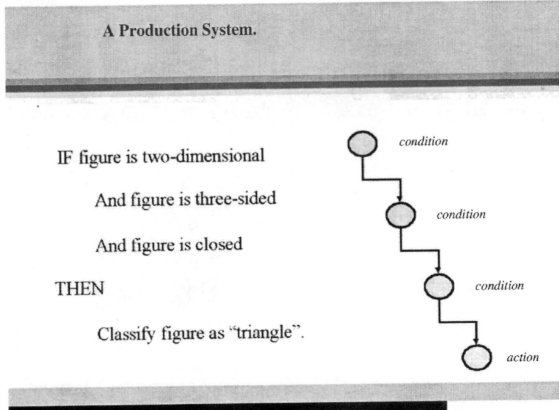

A Production System.

IF figure is two-dimensional

And figure is three-sided

And figure is closed

THEN

Classify figure as "triangle".

condition

condition

condition

action

Figure 2: A production sequence based on contingency statements

ies later emerged employing the use of this new visual tool or spatial representation of knowledge, some challenging Piaget's developmental theory in asserting that primary-grade children are capable of understanding abstract concepts by developing very thoughtful concept maps which they can explain intelligently to others (Symington & Novak, 1982). Other studies by Novak et al. demonstrated that graduate students found that concept maps helped them *learn how to learn* and were useful as a tool to represent changes in their knowledge structures over time. These same graduate students also indicated that concept maps were useful for representing knowledge in any discipline and that concept maps were helpful in organizing and understanding new subject matter (Novak, 1990). Another study conducted by Dagher and Cossman (1990) aimed at analyzing science teaching in schools found that verbal explanations of science concepts are not well-suited for helping students construct concept maps. The study suggested that some categories of propositions that are analogical, functional, and mechanical in nature would be more appropriate for developing concept maps. Such categories would enable more *conceptually transparent* concept maps (Wandersee, 1990) making it possible to better evaluate students' understandings, changes in understandings and misconceptions in understandings of science concepts. Concept mapping techniques began as paper-based and evolved to computer-based tools with the innovation of visual de-

sign software. This article discusses the use of two computer-based concept mapping tools, Inspiration® and Semnet®, in an educational setting to foster meaningful learning and understanding.

Computer-Based Concept Mapping Tools

Inspiration® and Semnet® are computer-based visual thinking environments that allow users to create concept maps (also known as semantic networks or nets), webs, outlines, and graphic organizers. They are easy-to-use, multiplatform, and Web-enabled (can be ported to the Web). The basic elements of concept mapping software are *nodes* and *links*. Learners use nodes to represent ideas and links to represent relationships that connect ideas. Applying these elements to our earlier example of the schema for the concept "school," *students* and *teachers* would each be a node in the concept map and *students learn from teachers* would be a link. As the nodes and links become interrelated, a structural knowledge representation emerges paving the way for a meaningful understanding of the knowledge domain depicted. In order to build a concept map, the learner must "transform the knowledge to be mapped from its current linear form to a context-dependent form" (Wandersee, 1990, p. 927). This process forces the learner to interact with the knowledge domain, identify the key concepts, and relate them to

LEARNING STRATEGY	CATEGORY	EDUCATIONAL EXAMPLE
Planning	Organization strategy for basic learning tasks	Preparing advance organizers for learning
Organizing	Organizational strategy for basic learning tasks	Grouping or ordering to-be-learned items from a list or a section of prose
Outlining	Organizational strategy for complextasks	Outlining a passage or creating a hierarchy
Webbing	Organizational strategy for complex tasks	Creating a diagram to show the relationship among facts and concepts
Writing	Elaboration strategies for complex tasks	Paraphrasing, summarizing, or describing how new information relates to existing knowledge
Knowledge mapping Brainstorming Concept mapping	Elaboration strategies for complex tasks	Creating analogies, metaphors, and other structures that describe how new or more complex information relates to existing information
Reflection Exploration	Comprehension monitoring strategies	Checking for comprehension failures using self-questioning and other methods that help students find the main ideas and elaborate on important information

Table 1

each other in a meaningful way. Prior knowledge and personal experience play an important role in this learning task ultimately creating a reorganization of existing schemata into a new knowledge structure that is useful and pertinent.

The main advantage to the utilization of computer-based concept mapping tools such as Inspiration® and Semnet® is that they remove the drudgery and mess of revising paper-based concept maps (Anderson-Inman & Zeitz, 1993). Computer-based concept maps can be modified dynamically making it possible for learners to reflect their improved understanding of a content domain over time by revising their concept maps quickly and easily. Revisions can also be initiated or guided by teachers, which makes concept mapping effective as a means of assessing student learning (McClure, Sonak, & Suen, 1999). Computer-based concept maps can also be used as planning tools to organize a project or a learning activity. In essence, concept mapping can be used as a learning strategy, an instructional strategy, a strategy for planning a curriculum, and a means of assessing students' understanding of abstract concepts (Novak, 1990). Although the focus of this article is primarily on the use of computer-based concept mapping as a learning strategy, other uses will be briefly explored.

Concept Mapping as a Learning Strategy

Inspiration® supports the following learning strategies that according to Weinstein and Mayer (1986) fall under four categories: organizational strategies for basic learning tasks, organizational strategies for complex learning tasks, elaboration strategies for complex learning tasks, and comprehension monitoring skills. Table 1 displays the strategies, the associated category, and an educational context.

It is evident from the above associations that Inspiration® can have extensive classroom uses that support students in *learning how to learn*. Students can use this mindtool as an organizational strategy to identify important concepts of a content domain and the interrelationships between them. This process serves the same purpose as outlining a chapter but requires a more thorough analysis of the content (Jonassen, 1996). Students are engaged in generating a semantic network that mirrors their understanding of the content under study. This spatial representation of ideas and relationships becomes a scaffold for acquiring new knowledge (Spoehr, 1994). As students progress in the learning process, they can revisit their concept maps and modify the content by adding new ideas, formalizing undeveloped ideas and reorganizing relationships between ideas based on new understandings. This exploratory and reflective process serves as a comprehension monitoring strategy that helps students move through the three stages of knowledge acquisition proposed by schema theorists (e.g., accretion, restructuring, and tuning) proposed by Norman (1978). The following is an example to illustrate the above.

In EDIT 704, a graduate course at George Mason University that addresses learning theory and instructional

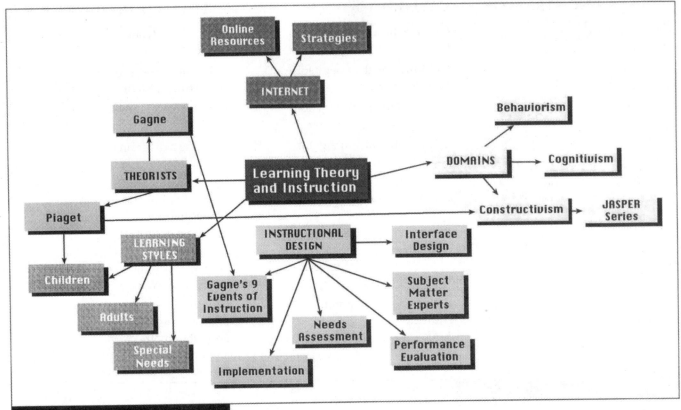

Figure 3: First iteration of a concept map

technology, students used Inspiration® to construct concept maps to represent their understanding of the various learning theories and their relationship to instruction in preparation for a research paper on learning theory. Beginning with propositional networks that largely depicted the acquisition of declarative knowledge, students revised their concept maps every couple of weeks ending with elaborate semantic networks that reflected a deeper and more meaningful understanding of the content (structural knowledge), based on new readings and instructional activities conducted throughout the course. The semantic network provided a rich information base guiding students in their end semester writing task. In this example, students used concept mapping both as an organizing tool and a comprehension monitoring tool. [Shown] is an example of a student's propositional network (first iteration) and its evolution into a semantic network (fourth iteration). The first iteration (Figure 3) supports the organizational strategy for basic learning tasks and the knowledge acquisition phase of accretion. The learner is organizing concepts in clusters based on the readings and prior knowledge. The structure is incomplete; however, it acts as a prototype module for the construction of a new knowledge module (Norman, 1978). The concept map relates the following five concepts to the main concept of learning theory and instructional design: theorists, the Internet, domains, instructional design, and learning styles. The learner has provided further groupings for each of these concepts

however no relationships or elaborations have yet been identified.

The fourth iteration (Figure 4) supports the organizational strategy for complex learning tasks (webbing) and the knowledge-acquisition phase of restructuring. The learner has achieved new insight into the structure of the topic and is making elaborations by creating relationships between the concepts in the diagram. The concept map shows evidence in "jumps in understanding" specifically as it relates to the concept of "theorists."

The learner is recognizing deficiencies in previous concept maps and restructuring the knowledge base by making inferences and adding analogies (Norman, 1978). A noticeable inference in this concept map is the finding of similarities between Ausubel's meaningful reception learning and schema theory.

Inspiration® also supports nonvisual thinkers by allowing users to toggle between the diagram view (the visual representation of the concept map) and an outline view. At any time during the creation of a concept map, a user can toggle to the outline view to view the concept map in an outline form. The outline view provides a hierarchical structure of the concept map based on the links between nodes. Users can use this view to add new topics, insert subtopics, and rearrange the organizational structure of the concept map. Users can also type notes in outline view under each topic or subtopic to help convert the concept map into a document in preparation of a writing assignment. All changes performed in the *outline view*

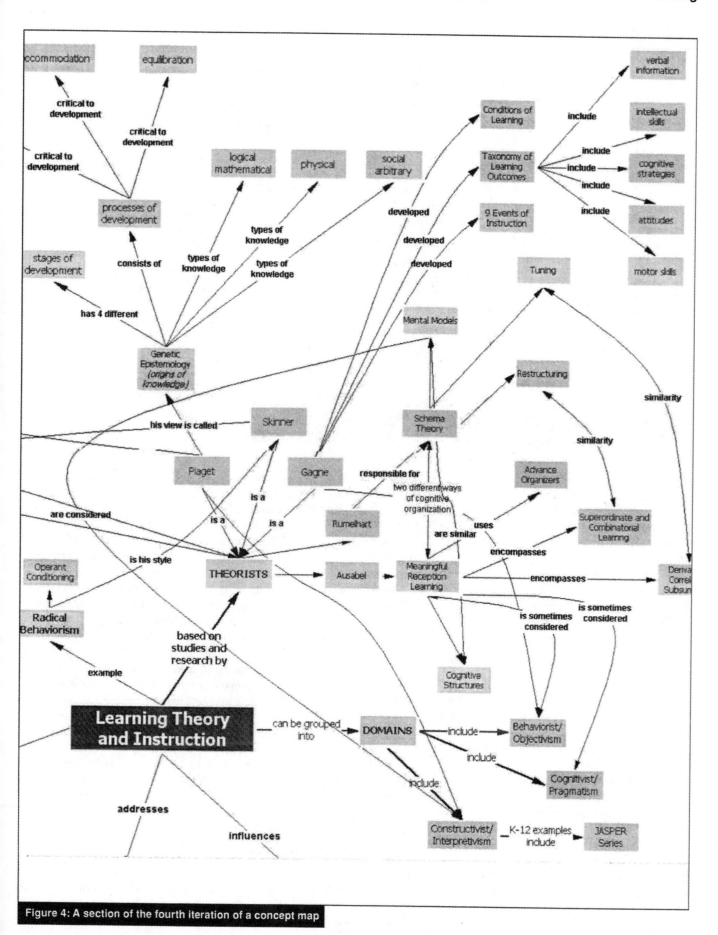

Figure 4: A section of the fourth iteration of a concept map

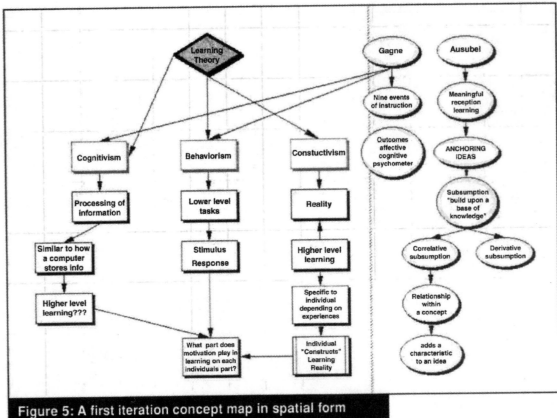

Figure 5: A first iteration concept map in spatial form

are reflected in the *diagram view* and vice versa. Figure 5 shows a diagram view of a concept map on learning theory created in Inspiration® in EDIT 704, and Figure 6 shows the corresponding outline view. The intuitiveness of the software in converting the concepts and links to an outline view (and vice versa) makes it easier for the linear thinker (or the visual thinker) to fine tune the structure when viewing it in a more familiar form.

Concept Mapping as an Instructional Strategy

Inspiration® also has a *rapid fire* feature that allows users to get down their ideas as fast as they can think of them without having to create new symbols each time. This feature can support brainstorming as a learning strategy and can be used by teachers as a tool to generate an organized structure for new or complex content, based on student input. For example, teachers can pose questions during class that encourage students to generate analogies and metaphors to help them relate new content to existing knowledge, and they can capture student responses by entering them instantaneously into Inspiration® using the rapid fire feature. At the end of such a brainstorming session, a student-generated concept map emerges that can serve as an advance organizer for future class discussions. This example can also be perceived as a preinstruc-

tion or assessment exercise, allowing teachers to inspect students' existing knowledge structures to identify misconceptions and adapt instruction to facilitate new learning (McClure, Sonak, & Suen, 1999). Other features of Inspiration® include a library of symbols that range from pictures of animals to geometric shapes allowing users to contextualize their concept maps. Users can also create their own symbols to illustrate concepts and use colors and other drawing tools to highlight and accentuate the main ideas and interrelationships.

It is not difficult from the above discussion to visualize the effectiveness of this computer-based concept mapping tool in facilitating student learning. Students can use it as a study aid to organize thoughts, create outlines, plan research papers, and examine content domains by extracting main concepts and ideas and realizing the interconnectedness of those ideas. Teachers can use this tool as a planning aid to actively generate graphic organizers for content, create lesson plans, and adapt instruction to students' needs by monitoring students' use of concept mapping to develop key concepts of a content domain.

Concept Mapping as a Collaborative Thinking Tool

The other visual learning tool discussed in this paper is Semnet®. SemNet® software can be used to represent knowledge domains much in the same way Inspiration®

```
+ Learning Theory
    I. + Constructivism
        A. = Reality
    II. + Behaviorism
        A. + Lower level tasks
            1. + Stimulus
            Response
                a) - What part does motivation play in learning on each individuals
                    part?
    III. + Cognitivism
        A. + Processing of information
            1. + Similar to how a computer stores info
                a) - Higher level learning???
    IV. + Miscellaneous Thoughts
        A. + Specific to individual depending on experiences
            1. - Individual "Constructs" Learning Reality
        B. - Higher level learning
        C. + Gagne
            1. - Name events of instruction
        D. - Outcomes
            affective
            cognitive
            psychomotor
        E. Ausubel
            1. + Meaningful reception learning
                a) + ANCHORING IDEAS
                    (1) - Subsumption
                    "build upon a base of knowledge"
                    (a) - Correlative subsumption
                        1) + Relationship within a concept
                        (1) - adds a characteristic to an idea
                    (b) Derivative subsumtion
```

Figure 6: The same concept map in outline form

does. It allows users to organize ideas about any topic in the form of a semantic network linked by named relations. However, the main difference between Semnet® and Inspiration® is that Semnet® creates a hypertext environment that allows the user to navigate between concepts through the named relations by emphasizing the concept-relation-concept in the construction of the knowledge map. This is based on the principle that concepts are ideas that can usually be described by a word or a phrase and that concepts can be understood through their relations to other concepts. Thus Semnet® "preserves the subject-verb-object relationship between two concepts to show the core concept, relationship, and related concepts as a 'web' or knowledge to which other illustrative material may be linked and attached" (Semnet Research Group, 1991). For example, the concept music can be understood through the word "music" and also through its relations to other concepts (Figure 7).

Those relations are elaborated using the subject-verb-object, which is the basis for normal sentence construction, as can be seen in Figure 7. A concept-relation-concept is known as an instance. In Figure 7, there are seven instances. By providing this structure, Semnet® forces

students to elaborate on the linkages between nodes (concepts) in a concept map promoting the interdependence between declarative and procedural knowledge right from the start and eliminating the propositional stage. While students are constructing semantic networks or knowledge maps, they are actively seeking information to describe concepts by naming them and naming relationships that link two or more concepts together. In the process, they are creating an information map of their knowledge structure and this is much more useful than rote memorization. According to Weinstein and Mayer (1986), this supports elaboration strategies of complex tasks. The dots appearing next to the related concepts—emotion, balance, life, style, form, rhythm, melody, harmony, and so on—imply that the user has created an individual net or knowledge structure for each of those concepts. By clicking on a related concept, Semnet® will show the user the individual net in which the related concept becomes the central or core concept.

This cascading metaphor of connecting *instances* through active links to other instances is a unique feature of Semnet® software that makes it ideal for use as a collaborative thinking tool. Different users can create individual concept maps (or nets) that can be merged together to create a larger and more encompassing net through a social knowledge construction process that involves collaboration. Collaboration in this context implies the clarification of ideas through the use of concept maps. According to the Semnet® Research Group (1991), Semnet® software "can support collaborative endeavors such as curriculum development by teams of professionals." Curriculum developers can form a community of practice and communicate their expertise by constructing individual concept maps to represent a model curriculum and then use these maps as a shared resource to initiate a discussion aimed at synthesizing ideas. Novak (1990) emphasized how this process can facilitate building a science curriculum, for example, around the *major conceptual schemes* of science (reflecting the psychological structure of knowledge) instead of the traditional topical (logical) arrangement of the science curriculum currently in place. He further elaborates (referencing Wandersee, 1990) by stating that "concept maps can be used to present both a global view of a K–12 science curriculum built around basic science concepts, and varying degrees of magnification to the level of a specific science lesson with each map showing key concepts and concept relationships necessary to understand the larger or the more explicit domain of science" (p. 944). Semnet® software provides the technological potential of dynamically linking individual maps to construct a larger map, making it possible to "telescope from a macro to a microscopic concept map for the domain to be studied" (Novak, 1990, p. 944). Using Semnet® software as a tool to engage in curriculum building supports the process of social negotiation that is a fundamental principle of communities of practice and what

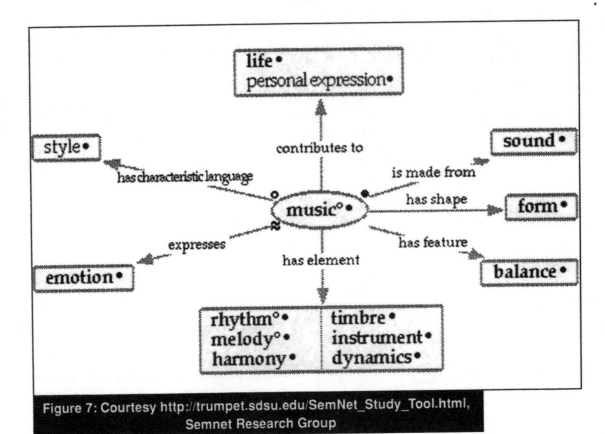

Figure 7: Courtesy http://trumpet.sdsu.edu/SemNet_Study_Tool.html, Semnet Research Group

makes this exercise truly collaborative. This process can have major implications for classroom use. Teachers can engage students in collaborative activities that require the construction of individual computer-based concept maps to be used as blueprints for the realization of a larger task (project) that requires the integration of these maps into a single comprehensive structure.

To summarize, Table 2 outlines the three concept mapping strategies discussed above (concept mapping as a learning strategy, concept mapping as an instructional strategy, and concept mapping as a collaborative thinking tool) and their implications for instruction and classroom use.

Conclusion

Concept mapping is a powerful and effective cognitive tool that encourages students to organize their knowledge about a content domain and to be explicit about the nature of relationships between ideas (Spoehr, 1994). Concept mapping forces students to think meaningfully about the content domain in order to identify and verify important concepts, classify concepts, describe the relationship between concepts and assess its meaning, analyze the nature of the relationship, and form the link or connection which engages the most critical thinking (Jonassen, 1996). Depending on how concept mapping is utilized in an instructional context, it can alter the en-

coding process that in turn affects the learning outcome and performance of students. As a learning strategy, concept mapping can support organizational strategies, elaboration strategies, and comprehension monitoring strategies in varying degrees of complexity. Computer-based concept mapping tools such as Inspiration® and Semnet® can facilitate these learning strategies by helping students create propositional and semantic networks to articulate and communicate their meaningful understanding and hence structural representation of a knowledge domain and by providing rich information structures that can synthesis, and evaluation of knowledge.

As an instructional strategy, teachers can use computer-based concept mapping to engage students in a generative, preinstructional dialogue about concepts and principles of a knowledge domain and subsequently capture this dialogue in a concept map to create an advance organizer of the content to be studied based on students' input. Teachers can also use this advance organizer as a diagnostic tool to create appropriate lesson plans aimed at clarifying misconceptions that students may have about the knowledge domain under study. Finally, computer-based concept mapping can be used as a collaborative tool to foster teamwork and facilitate project-based activities by encouraging the sharing, discussion, and integration of spatial representations of content in order to construct a more cohesive and comprehensive knowledge structure.

CONCEPT MAPPING CAN BE USED AS A:	SPECIFIC ACTIVITIES INCLUDE:	THESE ACTIVITIES CAN FACILITATE THE FOLLOWING CLASSROOM APPLICATION:
Learning strategy or a study tool	Planning, organizing, outlining, webbing, knowledge mapping, reflection, exploration	Writing a paper Conducting research Designing a science experiment Outlining a chapter Creating story Webs
Instructional strategy or a teaching tool	Planning, organizing, brainstorming, preinstruction assessment exercise	Preparing an advance organizer Preparing a lesson plan Organizing assessment Supporting generative learning activities
Collaborative thinking tool	Curriculum planning, project planning, collaboration, exploration, reflection, knowledge building	Creating communities of practice Facilitating interdisciplinary projects Collecting and organizing information and resources

Table 2

REFERENCES

Anderson-Inman, L., & Zeitz, L. (1993). Computer-based concept mapping: Active studying for active learners. *The Computer Teacher, 21*(1), 6–8, 10–11.

Dagher, Z., & Crossman, G. W. (1990, April). *The nature of verbal explanations given by science teachers.* Paper presented at the annual meeting of the National Association for Research in Science Teaching, Atlanta, GA.

Gagne, E. D., Yekovich, C. W., & Yekovich, F. R. (1993). *The cognitive psychology of school learning.* New York: HarperCollins College Publishers.

Hannafin, M. J. (1992). Emerging technologies, ISD, and learning environments: Critical perspectives. *Educational Technology Research & Development, 40*(1), 49–63.

Inspiration® Software, Inc. www.inspiration.com.

Jonassen, D. H., & Tessmer, M. (1997). An outcomes-based taxonomy for instructional systems design, evaluation, and research. *Training Research Journal, 2,* 11–46.

Jonassen, D. H. (1996). *Computers in the Classroom: Mindtools for Critical Thinking.* Englewood Cliffs, NJ: Prentice Hall Inc.

Jonassen, D. H. (1988). Designing structured hypertext and structuring access to hypertext. *Educational Technology, 28*(11), 13–16.

Norman, D. (1978) Notes toward a theory of complex learning. In A. M. Lesgold, J. W. Pelligrino, S. D. Fokkema, & R. Glaser (Eds.), *Cognitive psychology and education.* Norwell, MA: Plenum Publishers.

Novak, J. D. (1990). Concept mapping: A useful tool for science education. *Journal of Research in Science Teaching, 27*(10), 937–949.

Parsons, J. J., & Oja, D. (1996). *Computer concepts.* CTI, Cambridge, MA.

Semnet Research Group, Inc. (1991). *Semnet study tool.* http://trumpet.sdsu.edu/semnet.html

McClure J., Sonak, B., & Suen, H. (1995). Concept map assessment of classroom learning: Reliability, validity, and logistical practicality. *Journal of Research in Science Teaching, 36*(4), 475–492.

Spoehr, K. T. (1994). Enhancing the acquisition of conceptual structures through hypermedia. In K. McGilly (Ed.), *Classroom lessons: Integrating cognitive theory and classroom practice.* Cambridge, MA: MIT Press.

Symington, D. & Novak, J. D. (1982). Teaching children how to learn. *Educational magazine, 39*(5), 13–16.

Wandersee, J. H. (1990). Concept Mapping and the Cartography of Cognition. *Journal of Research in Science Teaching, 27*(10), 923–936.

Weinstein, C. E., & Mayer, R. E. (1986). The Teaching of Learning Strategies. In Wittrock (Ed.), *Handbook of research on teaching.* New York: Macmillan Publishing.

Nada Dabbagh is an assistant professor in the instructional technology program at George Mason University. She teaches graduate courses in instructional design, Web-based instruction, and learning theory. She is currently working on a book that examines the pedagogical implications of the use of Web-based course management tools in designing and developing online learning environments.

Dr. Nada Dabbagh Assistant Professor Instructional Design and Development MS-5D6, Commerce II Building Graduate School of Education George Mason University Fairfax, VA 22030 ndabbagh@gmu.edu

Mapping a Route Toward Differentiated Instruction

Even though students may learn in many ways, the essential skills and content they learn can remain steady. That is, students can take different roads to the same destination.

Carol Ann Tomlinson

Developing academically responsive classrooms is important for a country built on the twin values of equity and excellence. Our schools can achieve both of these competing values only to the degree that they can establish heterogeneous communities of learning (attending to issues of equity) built solidly on high-quality curriculum and instruction that strive to maximize the capacity of each learner (attending to issues of excellence).

A serious pursuit of differentiation, or personalized instruction, causes us to grapple with many of our traditional—if questionable—ways of "doing school." Is it reasonable to expect all 2nd graders to learn the same thing, in the same ways, over the same time span? Do single-textbook adoptions send inaccurate messages about the sameness of all learners? Can students learn to take more responsibility for their own learning? Do report cards drive our instruction? Should the classroom teacher be a solitary specialist on all learner needs, or could we support genuinely effective generalist-specialist teams? Can we reconcile learning standards with learner variance?

The questions resist comfortable answers—and are powerfully important. En route to answering them, we try various roads to differentiation. The concreteness of having something ready to do Monday morning is satisfying and inescapable. After all, the students will arrive and the day must be planned. So we talk about using reading buddies in varied ways to support a range of readers or perhaps developing a learning contract with several options for practicing math skills. Maybe we could try a tiered lesson or interest centers. Three students who clearly understand the chapter need an independent study project. Perhaps we should begin with a differentiated project assignment, allowing students to choose a project about the Middle Ages. That's often how our journey toward differentiation begins.

We have to know where we want to end up before we start out—and plan to get there.

The nature of teaching requires doing. There's not much time to sit and ponder the imponderables. To a point, that's fine—and, in any case, inevitable. A reflective teacher can test many principles from everyday interactions in the classroom. In other words, philosophy can derive from action.

We can't skip one step, however. The first step in making differentiation work is the hardest. In fact, the same first step is required to make all teaching and learning effective: We have to know where we want to end up before we start out and plan to get there. That is, we must have solid curriculum and instruction in place before we differentiate them. That's harder than it seems.

Looking Inside Two Classrooms

Mr. Appleton is teaching about ancient Rome. His students are reading the textbook in class today. He suggests that they take notes of important details as they read. When they finish, they answer the questions at the end of the chapter. Students who don't finish must do so at home. Tomorrow, they will answer the questions together in class. Mr. Appleton likes to lecture and works hard to prepare his lectures. He expects students to take notes. Later, he will give a quiz on both the notes and the text. He will give students a study sheet before the test, clearly spelling out what will be on the test.

Mrs. Baker is also teaching about ancient Rome. She gives her students graphic organizers to use as they read the textbook chapter and goes over the organizers with the class so that anyone who missed details can fill them in. She brings in pictures of the art and the architecture of the period and tells how important the Romans were in shaping our architecture, language, and laws. When she invites some students to dress in togas for a future class, someone suggests bringing in food so that they can have a Roman banquet— and they do. One day, students do a word-search puzzle of vocabulary words about Rome. On another day, they watch a movie clip that shows gladiators and the Colosseum and talk about the favored "entertainment" of the period. Later, Mrs. Baker reads aloud several myths, and students talk about the myths that they remember from 6th grade. When it's time to study for the test,

the teacher lets students go over the chapter together, which they like much better than working at home alone, she says.

She also wants students to like studying about Rome, so she offers a choice of 10 projects. Among the options are creating a poster listing important Roman gods and goddesses, their roles, and their symbols; developing a travel brochure for ancient Rome that a Roman of the day might have used; writing a poem about life in Rome; dressing dolls like citizens of Rome or drawing the fashions of the time; building a model of an important ancient Roman building or a Roman villa; and making a map of the Holy Roman Empire. Students can also propose their own topic.

Thinking About the Two Classrooms

Mr. Appleton's class is not differentiated. He does not appear to notice or respond to student differences. Mrs. Baker's is differentiated—at least by some definitions. Each class has serious flaws in its foundations, however, and for that reason, Mrs. Baker's class may not be any more successful than Mr. Appleton's— and perhaps less so.

Successful teaching requires two elements: student understanding and student engagement. In other words, students must really understand, or make sense of, what they have studied. They should also feel engaged in or "hooked by" the ways that they have learned. The latter can greatly enhance the former and can help young people realize that learning is satisfying.

Mr. Appleton's class appears to lack engagement. There's nothing much to make learning appealing. He may be satisfied by his lecture, but it's doubtful that many of the students are impressed. It is also doubtful that much real student understanding will come from the teaching-learning scenario. Rather, the goal seems to be memorizing data for a test.

Memorizing and understanding are very different. The first has a short life span and little potential to transfer into a broader world. However, at least Mr. Appleton appears clear about what the students should memorize for the test. Mrs. Baker's class lacks even that clarity.

Students in Mrs. Baker's classroom are likely engaged. It is a lively, learner–friendly place with opportunity for student movement, student choice, and peer work. Further, Mrs. Baker's list of project options draws on different student interests or talents—and she is even open to their suggestions.

Although Mrs. Baker succeeds to some degree with engagement, a clear sense of what students should understand as a result of their study is almost totally missing. Thus her careful work to provide choice and to build a comfortable environment for her learners may not net meaningful, long-term learning. Her students are studying "something about ancient Rome." Nothing focuses or ties together the ideas and information that they encounter. Activities are more about being happy than about making meaning. No set of common information, ideas, or skills will stem from completing the various projects. In essence, she has accomplished little for the long haul. Her "differentiation" provides varied avenues to "mush"—multiple versions of fog. Her students work with different tasks, not differentiated ones.

Mr. Appleton's class provides little engagement, little understanding, and scant opportunity for attending to student differences. Mrs. Baker's class provides some engagement, little understanding, and no meaningful differentiation.

An Alternative Approach

To make differentiation work—in fact, to make teaching and learning work—teachers must develop an alternative approach to instructional planning beyond "covering the text" or "creating activities that students will like."

Ms. Cassell has planned her year around a few key concepts that will help students relate to, organize, and retain what they study in history. She has also developed principles or generalizations that govern or uncover how the concepts work. Further, for each unit, she has established a defined set of facts and terms that are essential for students to know to be literate and informed about the topic. She has listed skills for which she and the students are responsible as the year progresses. Finally, she has developed essential questions to intrigue her students and to cause them to engage with her in a quest for understanding.

Ms. Cassell's master list of facts, terms, concepts, principles, and skills stems from her understanding of the discipline of history as well as from the district's learning standards. As the year evolves, Ms. Cassell continually assesses the readiness, interests, and learning profiles of her students and involves them in goal setting and decision making about their learning. As she comes to understand her students and their needs more fully, she modifies her instructional framework and her instruction.

Ms. Cassell is also teaching about ancient Rome. Among the key concepts in this unit, as in many others throughout the year, are culture, change, and interdependence. Students will be responsible for important terms, such as *republic, patrician, plebeian, veto, villa,* and *Romance language;* names of key individuals, for example, Julius Caesar, Cicero, and Virgil; and names of important places, for instance, the Pantheon and the Colosseum.

For this unit, students explore key generalizations or principles: Varied cultures share common elements. Cultures are shaped by beliefs and values, customs, geography, and resources. People are shaped by and shape their cultures. Societies and cultures change for both internal and external reasons. Elements

of a society and its cultures are interdependent.

Among important skills that students apply are using resources on history effectively, interpreting information from resources, blending data from several resources, and organizing effective paragraphs. The essential question that Ms. Cassell often poses to her students is, How would your life and culture be different if you lived in a different time and place?

Looking Inside the Third Classroom

Early in the unit, Ms. Cassell's students begin work, both at home and in class, on two sequential tasks that will extend throughout the unit as part of their larger study of ancient Rome. Both tasks are differentiated.

For the first task, students assume the role of someone from ancient Rome, such as a soldier, a teacher, a healer, a farmer, a slave, or a farmer's wife. Students base their choice solely on their own interests. They work both alone and with others who select the same topic and use a wide variety of print, video, computer, and human resources to understand what their life in ancient Rome would have been like.

Ultimately, students create a first-person data sheet that their classmates can use as a resource for their second task. The data sheet calls for the person in the role to provide accurate, interesting, and detailed information about what his or her daily schedule would be like, what he or she would eat and wear, where he or she would live, how he or she would be treated by the law, what sorts of problems or challenges he or she would face, the current events of the time, and so on.

Ms. Cassell works with both the whole class and small groups on evaluating the availability and appropriate use of data sources, writing effective paragraphs, and blending information from several sources into a coherent whole. Students use these skills as they develop

the first-person data sheets. The teacher's goal is for each student to increase his or her skill level in each area.

The second task calls on students to compare and contrast their own lives with the lives of children of similar age in ancient Rome. Unlike the first task, which was based on student interest, this one is differentiated primarily on the basis of student readiness. The teacher assigns each student a scenario establishing his or her family context for the task: "You are the eldest son of a lawmaker living during the later years of the period known as Pax Romana," for example. Ms. Cassell bases the complexity of the scenario on the student's skill with researching and thinking about history. Most students work with families unlike those in their first task. Students who need continuity between the tasks, however, can continue in a role familiar from their first investigation.

All students use the previously developed first-person data sheets as well as a range of other resources to gather background information. They must address a common set of specified questions: How is what you eat shaped by the economics of your family and by your location? What is your level of education and how is that affected by your status in society? How is your life interdependent with the lives of others in ancient Rome? How will Rome change during your lifetime? How will those changes affect your life? All students must also meet certain research and writing criteria.

Despite the common elements, the task is differentiated in several ways. It is differentiated by interest because each student adds questions that are directed by personal interests: What games did children play? What was the practice of science like then? What was the purpose and style of art?

Readiness differentiation occurs because each student adds personal research and writing goals, often with the teacher's help, to his or her criteria for success. A wide range of research resources is available, including books with varied readability levels, video and audio tapes, models, and access to informed people. The teacher also addresses readiness through small-group sessions in which she provides different sorts of teacher and peer support, different kinds of modeling, and different kinds of coaching for success, depending on the readiness levels of students.

Finally, the teacher adds to each student's investigation one specific question whose degree of difficulty is based on her most recent assessments of student knowledge, facility with research, and thinking about history. An example of a more complex question is, How will your life differ from that of the previous generation in your family, and how will your grandchildren's lives compare with yours? A less complex, but still challenging question is, How will language change from the generation before you to two generations after you, and why will those changes take place?

Learning-profile differentiation is reflected in the different media that students use to express their findings: journal entries, an oral monologue, or a videotape presentation. Guidelines for each type of product ensure quality and focus on essential understandings and skills established for the unit. Students may work alone or with a "parallel partner" who is working with the same role, although each student must ultimately produce his or her own product.

At other points in the study of ancient Rome, Ms. Cassell differentiates instruction. Sometimes she varies the sorts of graphic organizers that students use when they read, do research, or take notes in class. She may use review groups of mixed readiness and then conduct review games with students of like readiness working together. She works hard to ask a range of questions that move from concrete and familiar to abstract and unfamiliar in all class discussions. She sometimes provides

homework options in which students select the tasks that they believe will help them understand important ideas or use important skills best. Of course, the class also plans, works, reviews, and debates as a whole group.

Students find Ms. Cassell's class engaging—and not just because it's fun. It's engaging because it shows the connection between their own lives and life long ago. It helps them see the interconnectedness among times in history and make links with other subjects. It tickles their curiosity. And it provides a challenge that pushes each learner a bit further than is comfortable—and then supports success. Sometimes those things are fun. Often they are knotty and hard. Always they dignify the learner and the subject.

Successful differentiation is squarely rooted in student engagement plus student understanding.

Ms. Cassell's class is highly likely to be effective for her varied learners, in part because she continually attempts to reach her students where they are and move them on— she differentiates instruction. The success of the differentiation, however, is not a stand-alone matter. It is successful because it is squarely rooted in student engagement plus student understanding.

This teacher knows where she wants her students to arrive at the end of their shared learning journey and where her students are along that journey at a given time. Because she is clear about the destination and the path of the travelers, she can effectively guide them, and she varies or differentiates her instruction to accomplish this goal. Further, her destination is not merely the amassing of data but rather the constructing of understanding. Her class provides a good example of the close and necessary relationship between

effective curriculum and instruction and effective differentiation.

The First Step Is the Compass

Mr. Appleton may have a sense of what he wants his students to know at the end of the road, but not about what his students should understand and be able to do. He teaches facts, but no key concepts, guiding principles, or essential questions. With a fact-based curriculum, differentiating instruction is difficult. Perhaps some students could learn more facts and some, fewer. Perhaps some students could have more time to drill the facts, and some, less. It's difficult to envision a defensible way to differentiate a fact-driven curriculum, probably because the curriculum itself is difficult to defend.

Mrs. Baker also appears to lack a clear vision of the meaning of her subject, of the nature of her discipline and what it adds to human understanding, and of why it should matter to a young learner to study old times. There is little clarity about facts—let alone concepts, guiding principles, or essential questions. Further, she confuses folly with engagement. She thinks that she is differentiating instruction, but without instructional clarity, her activities and projects are merely different— not differentiated. Because there is no instructional clarity, there is no basis for defensible differentiation.

Differentiation is not so much the "stuff" as the "how." If the "stuff" is ill conceived, the "how" is doomed.

Ms. Cassell plans for what students should know, understand, and be able to do at the end of a sequence of learning. She dignifies each learner by planning tasks that are interesting, relevant, and powerful. She invites each student to wonder. She determines where each student is in knowledge, skill, and understanding and where he or she needs to move. She differentiates instruction to facilitate that goal. For her, differentiation is one piece of the mosaic of professional expertise. It is not a strategy to be plugged in occasionally or often, but is a way of thinking about the classroom. In her class, there is a platform for differentiation.

Ms. Cassell helps us see that differentiated instruction must dignify each learner with learning that is "whole," important, and meaning making. The core of *what* the students learn remains relatively steady. *How* the student learns—including degree of difficulty, working arrangements, modes of expression, and sorts of scaffolding—may vary considerably. Differentiation is not so much the "stuff" as the "how." If the "stuff" is ill conceived, the "how" is doomed.

The old saw is correct: Every journey *does* begin with a single step. The journey to successfully differentiated or personalized classrooms will succeed only if we carefully take the first step—ensuring a foundation of best-practice curriculum and instruction.

Carol Ann Tomlinson is Associate Professor of Educational Leadership, Foundations and Policy at the Curry School of Education, University of Virginia, Charlottesville, VA 22903 (e-mail: cat3y@virginia.edu). She is the author of *The Differentiated Classroom: Responding to the Needs of All Learners* (ASCD, 1999).

From *Educational Leadership,* September 1999, pp. 12-16. © 1999 by the Association for Supervision and Curriculum Development. All rights reserved. Reprinted by permission.

Reconcilable Differences? Standards-Based Teaching and Differentiation

Standards-based instruction and differentiated learning can be compatible approaches in today's classrooms.

Carol Ann Tomlinson

Recent demands for more standards-based teaching can feel like a huge impediment to encouraging differentiated instruction, especially for teachers and principals who recognize student variance and want to address it appropriately. A relatively new phenomenon (at least in its current form), standards-based instruction dominates the educational terrain in a time of great academic diversity in contemporary classrooms. In fact, standards-based instruction and the high-stakes testing that drives it can often feel like a locomotive rolling over everything in its path, including individualized learning.

Students learn best when learning opportunities are natural.

When any phenomenon in education suggests that we may have to jettison common sense and good pedagogy, we must first examine it in light of what we know about high-quality instruction. In other words, if we understand how standards-based teaching does or does not align with sound teaching and learning practices, we can then approach what look like barriers to differentiation. In truth, the conflict between focusing on standards and focusing on individual learners' needs exists only if we use standards in ways that cause us to abandon what we know about effective curriculum and instruction.

Differentiation: A Way of Thinking About the Classroom

What we call *differentiation* is not a recipe for teaching. It is not an instructional strategy. It is not what a teacher

does when he or she has time. It is a way of thinking about teaching and learning. It is a philosophy. As such, it is based on a set of beliefs:

Students learn best when they can make a connection between the curriculum and their interests and life experiences.

- Students who are the same age differ in their readiness to learn, their interests, their styles of learning, their experiences, and their life circumstances.
- The differences in students are significant enough to make a major impact on what students need to learn, the pace at which they need to learn it, and the support they need from teachers and others to learn it well.
- Students will learn best when supportive adults push them slightly beyond where they can work without assistance.
- Students will learn best when they can make a connection between the curriculum and their interests and life experiences.
- Students will learn best when learning opportunities are natural.
- Students are more effective learners when classrooms and schools create a sense of community in which students feel significant and respected.
- The central job of schools is to maximize the capacity of each student.

By definition, differentiation is wary of approaches to teaching and learning that standardize. Standard-issue students are rare, and educational approaches that ignore academic diversity in favor of standardization are likely to be counterproductive in reaching the full range of learners.

Differentiation must be a refinement of, not a substitute for, high-quality curriculum and instruction. Expert or distinguished teaching focuses on the understandings and skills of a discipline, causes students to wrestle with profound ideas, calls on students to use what they learn in important ways, helps students organize and make sense of ideas and information, and aids students in connecting the classroom with a wider world (Brandt, 1998; Danielson, 1996; Schlechty, 1997; Wiggins & McTighe, 1998).

Differentiation—one facet of expert teaching—reminds us that these things are unlikely to happen for the full range of students unless curriculum and instruction fit each individual, unless students have choices about what to learn and how, unless students take part in setting learning goals, and unless the classroom connects with the experiences and interest of the individual (Tomlinson, 1995, 1999). Differentiation says, "Building on core teaching and learning practices that are solid, here's what you do to refine them for maximum individual growth."

We first need to ask, Is a given teaching or learning approach likely to have a positive impact on the core of effective teaching and learning? When we are content with the answer, we can ask further, What is the effect of the practice on individuals in an academically diverse population? The latter question always helps us refine the effectiveness of the former but cannot substitute for it.

Standards-Based Teaching

For many teachers, curriculum has become a prescribed set of academic standards, instructional pacing has become a race against a clock to cover the standards, and the sole goal of teaching has been reduced to raising student test scores on a single test, the value of which has scarcely been questioned in the public forum. Teachers feel as though they are torn in opposing directions: They are admonished to attend to student differences, but they must ensure that every student becomes competent in the same subject matter and can demonstrate the competencies on an assessment that is differentiated neither in form nor in time constraints.

To examine the dichotomy between standards-based teaching and differentiation, we must ask questions about how standards influence the quality of teaching and learning. What is the impact of standards-based teaching on the quality of education in general? Then we can assess ways in which standards-based approaches make an impact on gifted or academically challenged students whose abilities are outside the usual norms of achievement.

- Do the standards reflect the knowledge, understandings, and skills valued most by experts in the disciplines that they represent?
- Are we using standards as a curriculum, or are they reflected in the curriculum?
- Are we slavishly covering standards at breakneck pace, or have we found ways to organize the standards within our curriculum so that students have time to make sense of ideas and skills?
- Does our current focus on standards enliven classrooms, or does it eliminate joy, creativity, and inquiry?
- Do standards make learning more or less relevant and alluring to students?
- Does our use of standards remind us that we are teaching human beings, or does it cause us to forget that fact?

If we are satisfied that our standards-based practices yield positive answers, we can look fruitfully at how to make adaptations to address the needs of academically diverse learners. If our answers are less than satisfactory, we should address the problems. Such problems inevitably point to cracks in the foundation of quality teaching and learning, and we diminish our profession by failing to attend to them. Differentiating curriculum and instruction cannot make up for ill-conceived curriculum and instruction.

Negative Cases

The following examples are recent and real. Sadly, they are not rare. They also show how good intentions can go awry.

- In one standards-driven district, primary grade teachers attended a staff-development session that they had requested and in which they had high interest. The staff developer asked them to list some concepts that they taught so that the session would be linked to what went on in their classrooms. When—even with coaching and examples—no one was able to name the concepts they taught, the staff developer asked for the topics they taught. More awkward silence followed. A few teachers said that they sometimes took a day or two to talk about holidays, such as Halloween, Christmas, or Kwanza, because young students were excited about special occasions. Other teachers explained that they no longer taught units or topics (and certainly not concepts). Their entire curriculum had become a list of skills that students learned out of context of any meaning or utility—except that the test was coming, and all 6- through 8-year-olds were expected to perform.

- A highly successful elementary school was started two decades ago to serve a student population that speaks more than 25 languages and whose homes are often marked by economic stress. The librarian in the school recently remarked,

> This has always been the best place in the world to teach. The students have loved it. Their parents have trusted it. Our students have done well. The teachers have always been excited to come to work. It has been a place of energy and inspired teaching. In the last two years [since the inception of a standards-based program and high-stakes testing], I've watched us become what we were created to avoid. We are telling instead of teaching. We fight to find time to reach out to the kids. Joy in classrooms has been replaced by fear that is first felt by the teachers and then by the students. We're trying hard to keep alive what we believe in, but I'm not sure we can.

• In another standards-driven district, middle school teachers listed student names in one of there columns: *Definitely, Maybe,* and *No Hope.* The designations showed who would surely pass the standards tests, who might pass, and who had no chance of passing. The teachers separated the students into columns because, they said, there was no point in worrying about students who already knew enough to pass the test, and there was no point in wasting time on students who could not be raised to the standard. "It's the only way to go," said one teacher. "It's what we have to do to get the points on this year's test."

"I no longer see my curriculum as a list to be covered, and I no longer see my students as duplicates of one another."

In all these places, teachers feel torn between an external impetus to cover the standards and a desire to address the diverse academic needs. In truth, the problem is not a contradiction between standards and appropriately responsive instruction. The problem lies in an ill-conceived interpretation and use of standards that erode the underpinnings of effective teaching and learning. The problem is not that we can't attend to the needs of individual learners, but rather that we've lost the essential frameworks of the disciplines in addition to the coherence, understanding, purpose, and joy in learning. Our first obligation is to ensure that standards-based teaching practice does not conflict with best teaching practice. Once those are aligned, differentiation—or attention to the diverse needs of learners—follows naturally.

Standards and Differentiation

There is no contradiction between effective standards-based instruction and differentiation. Curriculum tells us *what* to teach: Differentiation tells us *how.* Thus, if we elect to teach a standards-based curriculum, differentiation simply suggests ways in which we can make that curriculum work best for varied learners. In other words, differentiation can show us how to teach the same standard to a range of learners by employing a variety of teaching and learning modes.

Choose any standard. Differentiation suggests that you can challenge all learners by providing materials and tasks on the standard at varied levels of difficulty, with varying degrees of scaffolding, through multiple instructional groups, and with time variations. Further, differentiation suggests that teachers can craft lessons in ways that tap into multiple student interests to promote heightened learner interest in the standard. Teachers can encourage student success by varying ways in which students work: alone or collaboratively, in auditory or visual modes, or through practical or creative means.

Positive Cases

• Science teachers in one small district delineated the key facts, concepts, principles, and skills of their discipline for K–12. Having laid out the framework, they examined the state-prescribed standards for science and mapped them for K–12. They found that the standards in their state did a pretty good job of reflecting the facts and skills of science but did a poor job of making explicit the concepts and principles of science. With the two frameworks in front of them, the teachers could fill in gaps—and more important, could organize their curriculum in ways that were coherent and manageable. Their work helped their colleagues see the big picture of science instruction for K–12 over time, organize instruction conceptually, and teach with the essential principles of science in mind. The result was a districtwide science curriculum that made better sense to teachers and students alike, helped students think like scientists, reduced the teachers' sense of racing to cover disjointed information, and still attended to prescribed standards.

• In a high school Algebra II class, the teacher acknowledged that some of her students lacked prerequisite skills, whereas others learned as rapidly as she could teach or even without her help. At the outset of each chapter, the teacher delineated for students the specific skills, concepts, and understandings that they needed to master for that segment of the curriculum—both to have a solid grasp of mathematics and to pass the upcoming standards exam. She helped students make connections to past concepts, understandings, and skills. She divided each week into segments of teacher-led instruction, whole-class instruction, and small-group work.

For group-work sessions, she sometimes met with students who were advanced in a particular topic to urge on their thinking, to help them solve problems in multiple ways, and to apply their understandings and skills to complex, real-life problems. Sometimes she met with students who needed additional instruction or guided assistance in applying what they were learning. Sometimes she created mixed-readiness teams of students whose goal was solving a problem in the most effective way possible. The teacher randomly called on students to present and defend their team's approach, thus maximizing the likelihood that every student had a model for solving an important problem and was able to explain the reasoning behind the solution. These problem-solving groups often evolved into teacher-created study groups that worked together to ensure that everyone had his or her questions answered. Not only did the teacher provide some class time for the study groups, but she also encouraged regular after-school meetings in her room, where she was able to monitor group progress and assist if needed. She recalls,

> The hardest thing for me was learning to teach a class where I wasn't always working with the class as a whole, but that has been rewarding, too. I know my students better. They know Algebra II better—and I think I probably understand it better, too. I haven't made a math prodigy out of everyone, of course, but I can honestly say the students like algebra better and are more confident in their capacity to learn. Their scores on the standards test improved, even though I targeted some ideas and skills more than others. I think what that fact tells me is that if I help students organize their mathematical knowledge and thinking, they can fare better in unfamiliar territory.

• In an elementary classroom, a teacher organized many of her standards around three key concepts—connections, environments, and change—and their related principles; for example, living things are changed by and change their environments. She used them to study history, science, language arts, and sometimes mathematics. Although she generally taught each of the three subjects separately, she helped students make links among them; she created activities for the students that called for reading skills in social studies, for example, and social studies skills in science. That approach, she said, allowed everyone to work with the same big ideas and skills in a lesson while she could adjust materials, activities, and projects for varied readiness levels, diverse interests, and multiple modes of learning. Bringing the students together for class discussions was no problem, she reflected, because everyone's work focused on the essentials—even though students might get to those essentials in different ways. "It took me some time to rethink the standards and how I taught them," she recalled.

> But I feel as if I'm a better teacher. I understand what I'm teaching better, and I certainly have

come to understand the students I teach more fully. I no longer see my curriculum as a list to be covered, and I no longer see my students as duplicates of one another.

In these settings, teachers have retained—or, in some cases, have discovered for the first time—the essential frameworks of the disciplines and the coherence, understanding, purpose, and joy in learning. The teachers have struggled to meet their first obligation—to ensure that standards-based teaching practice is not in conflict with best teaching practice. Once the teachers aligned standards with high-quality instruction, differentiation followed naturally.

Grading Practices

The following questions help ensure that grading practices are productive for all students.

- How do learners benefit from a grading system that reminds everyone that students with disabilities or who speak English as a second language do not perform as well as students without disabilities or for whom English is their native tongue?

- What do we gain by telling our most able learners that they are "excellent" on the basis of a standard that requires modest effort, calls for no intellectual risk, necessitates no persistence, and demands that they develop few academic coping skills?

- In what ways do our current grading practices motivate struggling or advanced learners to persist in the face of difficulty?

- Is there an opportunity for struggling learners to encounter excellence in our current grading practices?

- Is there an opportunity for advanced learners to encounter struggle in our current grading practices?

—Carol Ann Tomlinson

Quality and Personalization

Overwhelmed by the task, a teacher recently pleaded, "I have all these students with all these different needs; how can anyone expect me to differentiate in my classroom?" Odd as the comment sounds, she spoke for many of us. The more complex the task, the more inviting it is to retreat to the familiar—to find a standardized approach and cling to it.

Thus, we find ourselves saying, "I know I'm missing lots of my students, but if I don't hurry to cover all the standards, how will they succeed on the test?" Or, "I know it would be good to involve students in thinking and problem solving, but there's just no time." The deeper issue is about what happens when we use any approach that allows us to lose sight of the soul of teaching and learning. A secondary factor is that such approaches make it difficult to attend to individual differences.

Do standardizing practices fail academically diverse learners? Of course they do. Whatever practices invite us to be paint-by-number teachers will largely fail students who do not fit the template. Paint-by-number approaches will fall short for all of us—teachers and students alike—because they abandon quality. Paint-by-number approaches will fail teachers because they confuse technical expedience with artistry. They will fail students because they confuse compliance with thoughtful engagement. Any educational approach that does not invite us to teach individuals is deeply flawed.

Teaching is hard. Teaching well is fiercely so. Confronted by too many students, a schedule with breaks, a pile of papers that regenerates daily, and incessant de-

mands from every educational stakeholder, no wonder we become habitual and standardized in our practices. Not only do we have no time to question why we do what we do, but we also experience the discomfort of change when we do ask the knotty questions. Nonetheless, our profession cannot progress and our increasingly diverse students cannot succeed if we do less.

References

Brandt, R. (1998). *Powerful teaching*. Alexandria, VA: ASCD.

Danielson, C. (1996). *Enhancing professional practice: A framework for teaching*. Alexandria, VA: ASCD.

Schlechty, P. (1997). *Inventing better schools: An action plan for educational reform*. San Francisco: Jossey-Bass.

Tomlinson, C. (1995). *How to differentiate instruction in mixed-ability classrooms*. Alexandria, VA: ASCD.

Tomlinson, C. (1999). *The differentiated classroom: Responding to the needs of all learners*. Alexandria, VA: ASCD.

Wiggins, G., & McTighe, J. (1998). *Understanding by design*. Alexandria, VA: ASCD.

Carol Ann Tomlinson is Associate Professor of Educational Leadership, Foundations, and Policy. She may be reached at the Curry School of Education, the University of Virginia, Room 287, 405 Emmet St., Charlottesville, VA 22903.

Educating the Net Generation

As technology becomes an integral part of our classrooms and schools, educators can look to the students—the Net Generation—to help make the shift to more student-centered learning.

Don Tapscott

Every time I enter a discussion about efforts to get computers into schools, someone insists that computers aren't the answer. "It won't help to just throw computers at the wall, hoping something will stick. I've seen lots of computers sitting unused in classrooms."

I have become convinced that the most potent force for change is the students themselves.

Agreed. Computers alone won't do the trick. They are a necessary but insufficient condition for moving our schools to new heights of effectiveness. We've still got to learn how best to use this technology. And I have become convinced that the most potent force for change is the students themselves.

Why look to the kids? Because they are different from any generation before them. They are the first to grow up surrounded by digital media. Computers are everywhere—in the home, school, factory, and office—as are digital technologies—cameras, video games, and CD-ROMs. Today's kids are so bathed in bits that they think technology is part of the natural landscape. To them, digital technology is no more intimidating than a VCR or a toaster. And these new media are increasingly connected by the Internet, that expanding web of networks that is attracting one million new users a month.

The Net Generation

The Net affects us all—the way we create wealth, the nature of commerce and marketing, the delivery system for entertain-

ment, the role and dynamics of learning, and the nature of government. It should not surprise us that those first to grow up with this new medium are defined by their relationship to it. I call them the Net Generation—the N-Geners.

According to Teenage Research Unlimited (1997), teens feel that being online is as "in" as dating and partying! And this exploding popularity is occurring while the Net is still in its infancy and, as such, is painfully slow; primitive; limited in capabilities; lacking complete security, reliability, and ubiquity; and subject to both hyperbole and ridicule. Nevertheless, children love it and keep coming back after each frustrating experience. They know its potential.

What do students do on the Net? They manage their personal finances; organize protest movements; check facts; discuss zits; check the scores of their favorite team and chat online with its superstars; organize groups to save the rain forest; cast votes; learn more about the illness of their little sister; go to a virtual birthday party; or get video clips from a soon-to-be-released movie.

Chat groups and computer conferences are populated by young people hungry for expression and self-discovery. Younger kids love to meet people and talk about anything. As they mature, their communications center on topics and themes. For all ages, "E-mail me" has become the parting expression of a generation.

Digital Anxiety

For many adults, all this digital activity is a source of high anxiety. Are kids really benefitting from the digital media? Can technology truly improve the process of learning, or is it dumbing down and misguiding educational efforts? What about

Net addiction? Is it useful for children to spend time in online chat rooms, and what are they doing there? Are some becoming glued to the screen? What about cyberdating and cybersex? Aren't video games leading to a violent generation? Is technology stressing kids out—as it seems to be doing to adults? Has the Net become a virtual world—drawing children away from parental authority and responsible adult influence—where untold new problems and dangers lie? What is the real risk of online predators, and can children be effectively protected? How can we shield kids from sleaze and porn? As these children come of age, will they lack the social skills for effective participation in the work force?

These questions are just a sampling of the widespread concern raised not just by cynics, moralists, and technophobes, but also by reasonable and well-meaning educators, parents, and members of the community.

Everybody, relax. The kids are all right. They are learning, developing, and thriving in the digital world. They need better tools, better access, better services—*more* freedom to explore, not less. Rather than convey hostility and mistrust, we need to change *our* way of thinking and behaving. This means all of us—parents, educators, lawmakers, and business leaders alike.

Digital kids are learning precisely the social skills required for effective interaction in the digital economy.

Digital kids are learning precisely the social skills required for effective interaction in the digital economy. They are learning about peer relationships, teamwork, critical thinking, fun, friendships across geographies, self-expression, and self-confidence.

Conventional wisdom says that because children are multitasking—jumping from one computer-based activity to another—their attention span is reduced. Research does not support this view. Ironically, the same people who charge that today's kids are becoming "glued to the screen" also say that kids' attention spans are declining.

At root is the fear that children will not be able to focus and therefore will not learn. This concern is consistent with the view that the primary challenge of learning is to absorb specific information. However, many argue—and I agree—that the content of a particular lesson is less important than learning how to learn. As John Dewey wrote,

Perhaps the greatest of all pedagogical fallacies is the notion that a person learns only the particular thing he is studying at the time. Collateral learning... may be and often is more important than the spelling lesson or

lesson in geography or history that is learned. (1963, p. 48)

The Challenge of Schooling

The new technologies have helped create a culture for learning (Papert, 1996) in which the learner enjoys enhanced interactivity and connections with others. Rather than listen to a professor regurgitate facts and theories, students discuss ideas and learn from one another, with the teacher acting as a participant in the learning. Students construct narratives that make sense out of their own experiences.

The ultimate interactive learning environment is the Internet itself.

Initial research strongly supports the benefits of this kind of learning. For example, in 1996, 33 students in a social studies course at California State University in Northridge were randomly divided into two groups, one taught in a traditional classroom and the other taught virtually on the Web. The teaching model wasn't fundamentally changed—both groups received the same texts, lectures, and exams. Despite this, the Web-based class scored, on average, 20 percent higher than the traditional class. The Web class had more contact with one another and were more interested in the class work. The students also felt that they understood the material better and had greater flexibility to determine how they learned (Schutte, n.d.).

The ultimate interactive learning environment is the Internet itself. Increasingly, this technology includes the vast repository of human knowledge, the tools to manage this knowledge, access to people, and a growing galaxy of services ranging from sandbox environments for preschoolers to virtual laboratories for medical students studying neural psychiatry. Today's baby will tomorrow learn about Michelangelo by walking through the Sistine Chapel, watching Michelangelo paint, and perhaps stopping for a conversation. Students will stroll on the moon. Petroleum engineers will penetrate the earth with the drill bit. Doctors will navigate the cardiovascular system. Researchers will browse through a library. Auto designers will sit in the back seat of the car they are designing to see how it feels and to examine the external view.

Eight Shifts of Interactive Learning

The digital media is causing educators and students alike to shift to new ways of thinking about teaching and learning.

1. From linear to hypermedia learning. Traditional approaches to learning are linear and date back to using books as a learning tool. Stories, novels, and other narratives are generally linear. Most textbooks are written to be tackled from the beginning to the end. TV shows and instructional videos are also designed to be watched from beginning to end.

Students need better tools, better access, better services—more freedom to explore, not less.

But N-Gen access to information is more interactive and nonsequential. Notice how a child channel surfs when watching television. I've found that my kids go back and forth among various TV shows and video games when they're in the family room. No doubt that as TV becomes a Net appliance, children will increasingly depend on this nonlinear way of processing information.

2. From instruction to construction and discovery. Seymour Papert says,

> The scandal of education is that every time you teach something, you deprive a child of the pleasure and benefit of discovery. (de Pommereau, 1996, p. 68)

With new technologies, we will experience a shift away from traditional types of pedagogy to the creation of learning partnerships and learning cultures. This is not to say that teachers should not plan activities or design curriculums. They might, however, design the curriculum in partnership with learners or even help learners design the curriculum themselves.

This constructivist approach to teaching and learning means that rather than assimilate knowledge that is broadcast by an instructor, the learner constructs knowledge anew. Constructivists argue that people learn best by *doing* rather than simply by *listening*. The evidence supporting constructivism is persuasive, but that shouldn't be too surprising. When youngsters are enthusiastic about a fact or a concept that they themselves discovered, they will better retain the information and use it in creative, meaningful ways.

3. From teacher-centered to learner-centered education. The new media focus the learning experience on the individual rather than on the transmitter. Clearly, learner-centered education improves the child's motivation to learn.

The shift from teacher-centered to learner-centered education does not suggest that the teacher is suddenly playing a less important role. A teacher is equally crucial and valuable in the learner-centered context, for he or she creates and structures what happens in the classroom.

Learner-centered education begins with an evaluation of abilities, learning styles, social contexts, and other important factors that affect the student. Evaluation software programs can tailor the learning experience for each individual child. Learner-centered education is also more active, with students discussing, debating, researching, and collaborating on projects with one another and with the teacher.

4. From absorbing material to learning how to navigate and how to learn. This means learning how to synthesize, not just analyze. N-Geners can assess and analyze facts—a formidable challenge in a data galaxy of easily accessible information sources. But more important, they can synthesize. They are engaged in information sources and people on the Net, and then they construct higher-level structures and mental images.

5. From school to lifelong learning. For young baby boomers looking forward to the world of work, life often felt divided—between the period when you *learned* and the period when you *did*. You went to school and maybe to university and learned a trade or profession. For the rest of your life, your challenge was simply to keep up with developments in your field. But things have changed. Today, many boomers reinvent their knowledge base constantly. Learning has become a continuous, lifelong process. The N-Gen is entering a world of lifelong learning from day one, and unlike the schools of the boomers, today's educational system can anticipate how to prepare students for lifelong learning.

6. From one-size-fits-all to customized learning. The digital media enables students to be treated as individuals—to have highly customized learning experiences based on their backgrounds, individual talents, age levels, cognitive styles, and interpersonal preferences.

As Papert puts it,

> What I see as the real contribution of digital media to education is a flexibility that could allow every individual to find personal paths to learning. This will make it possible for the dream of every progressive educator to come true: In the learning environment of the future, every learner will be "special." (1996, p. 16)

In fact, Papert believes in a "community of learning" shared by students and teachers:

> Socialization is not best done by segregating children into classrooms with kids of the same age. The computer is a medium in which what you make lends itself to be modified and shared. When kids get together on a project, there is abundant discussion; they show it to other kids, other kids want to see it, kids learn to share knowledge with other people—much more than in the classroom. (1997, p. 11)

7. From learning as torture to learning as fun. Maybe torture is an exaggeration, but for many kids, class is not exactly the highlight of their day. Some educators have decried the fact that a generation schooled on *Sesame Street* expects to be entertained at school—and to enjoy the learning experience. They argue that learning and entertainment should be clearly separated.

Why shouldn't learning be entertaining? In *Merriam-Webster's Collegiate Dictionary,* the third definition of the verb *to entertain* is "to keep, hold, or maintain in the mind" and "to receive and take into consideration." In other words, entertainment has always been a profound part of the learning process, and teachers throughout history have been asked to convince their students to entertain ideas. From this perspective, the best teachers were the entertainers. Using the new media, the learner also becomes the entertainer and, in doing so, enjoys, is motivated toward, and feels responsible for learning.

8. From the teacher as transmitter to the teacher as facilitator. Learning is becoming a social activity, facilitated by a new generation of educators.

The topic is saltwater fish. The 6th grade teacher divides the class into teams, asking each team to prepare a presentation on a fish of its choice. Students have access to the Web and are allowed to use any resources. They must cover the topics of history, breathing, propulsion, reproduction, diet, predators, and "cool facts." They must also address questions to others in their team or to others in the class, not to the teacher.

Two weeks later, Melissa's group is first. The students have created a shark project home page with hot links for each topic. As the students talk, they project their presentation onto a screen at the front of the class. They have video clips of different types of sharks and also a clip from Jacques Cousteau discussing the shark as an endangered species. They then use the Web to go live to Aquarius, an underwater site located off the Florida Keys. The class can ask questions of the Aquarius staff, although most inquiries are directed to the project team. One such discussion focuses on which is greater: the dangers posed by sharks to humans or the dangers posed by humans to sharks.

The class decides to hold an online forum on this topic and invites kids from classes in other countries to participate. The team asks students to browse through its project at any time, from any location, because the forum will be up for the rest of the school year. In fact, the team decides to maintain the site by adding new links and fresh information throughout the year. The assignment becomes a living project. Learners from around the world find the shark home page helpful and build links to it.

In this example, the teacher acts as consultant to the teams, facilitates the learning process, and participates as a technical consultant on the new media. The teacher doesn't have to compete with Jacques Cousteau's expertise on underwater life; her teaching is supported by his expertise.

Turning to the Net Generation

Needless to say, a whole generation of teachers needs to learn new tools, new approaches, and new skills. This will be a challenge, not just because of resistance to change by some teachers, but also because of the current atmosphere of financial cutbacks, low teacher morale, increased workloads, and reduced retraining budgets.

But as we make this inevitable transition, we may best turn to the generation raised on and immersed in new technologies. Give students the tools, and they will be the single most important source of guidance on how to make their schools relevant and effective places to learn.

References

de Pommereau, I. (1997, April 21). Computers give children the key to learning. *Christian Science Monitor,* p. 68.

Dewey, J. (1963). *Experience and education.* London: Collier Books.

Papert, S. (1996). *The connected family: Bridging the digital generation gap.* Marietta, GA: Longstreet Press.

Schutte, J. G. (n.d.). *Virtual teaching in higher education* [On-line]. Available: http://www.csun. edu/sociology/virtexp.htm.

Teenage Research Unlimited, Inc. (1996, January). Press release. Northbrook, IL: Author.

Teenage Research Unlimited, Inc. (1997, Spring). Teenage marketing and lifestyle update. Northbrook, IL: Author.

Don Tapscott is President of New Paradigm Learning Corporation and Chairman of Alliance for Converging Technologies, 133 King St. E., Ste. 300, Toronto, ON M5C 1G6, Canada (Website:http://nplc.com; e-mail: nplc@nplc.com).

UNIT 5
Motivation and Classroom Management

Unit Selections

Key Points to Consider

- Discuss several ways to motivate both at-risk and typical students. What difference is there?

- Why should motivational style be consistent with instructional techniques?

- How are motivation and classroom management related?

- Discuss several ways to discipline both typical students and those with exceptionalities.

- How are classroom management and discipline different? Discuss whether discipline can be developed within students, or whether it must be imposed by teachers, supporting your argument with data derived from your reading.

 **Links: www.dushkin.com/online/**
These sites are annotated in the World Wide Web pages.

Canada's Schoolnet Staff Room
  http://www.schoolnet.ca/home/e/
National Institute on the Education of At-Risk Students
  http://www.ed.gov/offices/OERI/At-Risk/

The term *motivation* is used by educators to describe the processes of initiating, directing, and sustaining goal-oriented behavior. Motivation is a complex phenomenon, involving many factors that affect an individual's choice of action and perseverance in completing tasks. Furthermore, the reasons why people engage in particular behaviors can only be inferred; motivation cannot be directly measured.

Several theories of motivation, each highlighting different reasons for sustained goal-oriented behavior, have been proposed. We will discuss three of them: behavioral, humanistic, and cognitive. The behavioral theory of motivation suggests that an important reason for engaging in behavior is that reinforcement follows the action. If the reinforcement is controlled by someone else and is arbitrarily related to the behavior (such as money, a token, or a smile), then the motivation is extrinsic. In contrast, behavior may also be initiated and sustained for intrinsic reasons such as curiosity or mastery.

Humanistic approaches to motivation are concerned with the social and psychological needs of individuals. Humans are motivated to engage in behavior to meet these needs. Abraham Maslow, a founder of humanistic psychology, proposes that there is a hierarchy of needs that directs behavior, beginning with physiological and safety needs and progressing to self-actualization. Some other important needs that influence motivation are affiliation and belonging with others, love, self-esteem, influence with others, recognition, status, competence, achievement, and autonomy.

The dominant view of motivation in the educational psychology literature is the cognitive approach. This set of theories proposes that our beliefs about our successes and failures affect our expectations and goals concerning future performance. Students who believe that their success is due to their abilities and efforts are motivated toward mastery of skills. Students who blame their failures on inadequate abilities have low self-efficacy and tend to set ability and performance goals that protect their self-image.

Richard Ryan and Edward Deci, in the unit's first selection, review new research on the classic concepts of intrinsic and extrinsic motivation. They discuss the merits of each for helping students become self-regulating learners. Intrinsic forms of motivation are clearly self-regulating. Yet the authors recognize that educators cannot always rely on intrinsic motivation to promote learning. They also discuss two forms of extrinsic motivation that can also promote self-regulation. One is promoting identification with the personal importance of a behavior and the second is integrated regulation where the person internalizes the instrumental value of the action. In the next selection, Martin Covington also attempts to reconcile intrinsic and extrinsic motivation by discussing ways in which student interest, criterion-referenced grading, and recognition for learning can lessen the negative effects of extrinsic reinforcers. Next, Barry Zimmerman discusses the role of self-efficacy in students' motivation and learning. He argues that self-efficacy predicts student effort as well as the use of self-regulating strategies such as goal setting, self-evaluation, and strategy use.

No matter how effectively students are motivated, teachers always need to exercise management of behavior in the classroom. Classroom management is more than controlling the behavior of students or disciplining them following misbehavior. Instead, teachers need to initiate and maintain a classroom environment that supports successful teaching and learning. The skills that effective teachers use include preplanning, deliberate introduction of rules and procedures, immediate assertiveness, continual monitoring, consistent feedback to students, and specific consequences.

The first three articles in this subsection present different perspectives on classroom management that should help teachers deal with the common situation of having to manage a group that includes typical and special needs students. The first selection, "Teaching Students to Regulate Their Own Behavior," gives advice to teachers with inclusive classrooms about how to help students with special needs learn to regulate their own behavior and, at the same time, take some of the time demands away from the teacher. The next two articles offer contrasting views of the role of reinforcement for managing student behavior in developmentally appropriate classrooms. Next, David Bicard offers a framework for introducing rules in a positive matter. Finally, Suzanne Adams and Donna Sasse Wittmer describe a social problem-solving model for helping children resolve their own conflicts. This model is also offered as an approach to working with students with disabilities.

Intrinsic and Extrinsic Motivations: Classic Definitions and New Directions

Intrinsic and extrinsic types of motivation have been widely studied, and the distinction between them has shed important light on both developmental and educational practices. In this review we revisit the classic definitions of intrinsic and extrinsic motivation in light of contemporary research and theory. Intrinsic motivation remains an important construct, reflecting the natural human propensity to learn and assimilate. However, extrinsic motivation is argued to vary considerably in its relative autonomy and thus can either reflect external control or true self-regulation. The relations of both classes of motives to basic human needs for autonomy, competence and relatedness are discussed.

Richard M. Ryan and Edward L. Deci

To be motivated means *to be moved* to do something. A person who feels no impetus or inspiration to act is thus characterized as unmotivated, whereas someone who is energized or activated toward an end is considered motivated. Most everyone who works or plays with others is, accordingly, concerned with motivation, facing the question of how much motivation those others, or oneself, has for a task, and practitioners of all types face the perennial task of fostering more versus less motivation in those around them. Most theories of motivation reflect these concerns by viewing motivation as an unitary phenomenon, one that varies from very little motivation to act to a great deal of it.

Yet, even brief reflection suggests that motivation is hardly a unitary phenomenon. People have not only different amounts, but also different kinds of motivation. That is, they vary not only in *level* of motivation (i.e., how much motivation), but also in the *orientation* of that motivation (i.e., what type of motivation). Orientation of motivation concerns the underlying attitudes and goals that give rise to action—that is, it concerns the why of actions. As an example, a student can be highly motivated to do homework out of curiosity and interest or, alternatively, because he or she wants to procure the approval of a teacher or parent. A student could be motivated to learn a new set of skills because he or she understands their potential utility or value or because learning the skills will yield a good grade and the privileges a good grade affords. In these examples the amount of motivation does not necessarily vary, but the nature and focus of the motivation being evidenced certainly does.

In Self-Determination Theory (SDT; Deci & Ryan, 1985) we distinguish between different types of motivation based on the different reasons or goals that give rise to an action. The most basic distinction is between *intrinsic motivation*, which refers to doing something because it is inherently interesting or enjoyable, and *extrinsic motivation*, which refers to doing something because it leads to a separable outcome. Over three decades of research has shown that the quality of experience and performance can be very different when one is behaving for intrinsic versus extrinsic reasons. One purpose of this review is to revisit this classic distinction between intrinsic and extrinsic motivation and to summarize the functional differences of these two general types of motivation.

Intrinsic motivation has emerged as an important phenomenon for educators—a natural wellspring of learning and achievement that can be systematically catalyzed or undermined by parent and teacher practices (Ryan & Stiller, 1991). Because intrinsic motivation results in high-quality learning and creativity, it is especially important to detail the factors and forces that engender versus undermine it.

However, equally important in the current review is the explication of the very different types of motivation that fall into the category of extrinsic motivation. In the classic literature, extrinsic motivation has typically been characterized as a pale and impoverished (even if powerful) form of motivation that contrasts with intrinsic motivation (e.g., deCharms, 1968). However, SDT proposes that there are varied types of extrinsic motivation, some of which do, indeed, represent impoverished forms of motivation and some of which represent active, agentic states.

Students can perform extrinsically motivated actions with resentment, resistance, and disinterest or, alternatively, with an attitude of willingness that reflects an inner acceptance of the value or utility of a task. In the former case—the classic case of extrinsic motivation—one feels externally propelled into action; in the later case, the extrinsic goal is self-endorsed and thus adopted with a sense of volition. Understanding these different types of extrinsic motivation, and what fosters each of them, is an important issue for educators who cannot always rely on intrinsic motivation to foster learning. Frankly speaking, because many of the tasks that educators want their students to perform are not inherently interesting or enjoyable, knowing how to promote more active and volitional (versus passive and controlling) forms of extrinsic motivation becomes an essential strategy for successful teaching. We detail in this article not only the different types of motivational orientation that exist within the global extrinsic category, but moreover, their differential antecedents and consequences.

In sum, our aim in this article is to revisit the classic distinction between intrinsic and extrinsic motivation and detail the conditions that foster each. Second, we describe a model of differing types of extrinsic motivation. Our concern here is with how teachers, parents and other socializers can lead students to internalize the responsibility and sense of value for extrinsic goals or, alternatively, how they can foster the more typically depicted "alienated" type of extrinsic motivation that is associated with low student persistence, interest, and involvement.

INTRINSIC MOTIVATION

Intrinsic motivation is defined as the doing of an activity for its inherent satisfactions rather than for some separable consequence. When intrinsically motivated a person is moved to act for the fun or challenge entailed rather than because of external prods, pressures, or rewards. The phenomenon of intrinsic motivation was first acknowledged within experimental studies of animal behavior, where it was discovered that many organisms engage in exploratory, playful, and curiosity-driven behaviors even in the absence of reinforcement or reward (White, 1959). These spontaneous behaviors, although clearly bestowing adaptive benefits on the organism, appear not to be done for any such instrumental reason, but rather for the positive experiences associated with exercising and extending one's capacities.

In humans, intrinsic motivation is not the only form of motivation, or even of volitional activity, but it is a pervasive and important one. From birth onward, humans, in their healthiest states, are active, inquisitive, curious, and playful creatures, displaying a ubiquitous readiness to learn and explore, and they do not require extraneous incentives to do so. This natural motivational tendency is a critical element in cognitive, social, and physical development because it is through acting on one's inherent interests that one grows in knowledge and skills. The inclinations to take interest in novelty, to actively assimilate, and to creatively apply our skills is not limited to childhood, but is a significant feature of human nature that affects performance, persistence, and well-being across life's epochs (Ryan & LaGuardia, in press).

Although, in one sense, intrinsic motivation exists within individuals, in another sense intrinsic motivation exists in the relation between individuals and activities. People are intrinsically motivated for some activities and not others, and not everyone is intrinsically motivated for any particular task.

Because intrinsic motivation exists in the nexus between a person and a task, some authors have defined intrinsic motivation in terms of the task being interesting while others have defined it in terms of the satisfactions a person gains from intrinsically motivated task engagement. In part, these different definitions derive from the fact that the concept of intrinsic motivation was proposed as a critical reaction to the two behavioral theories that were dominant in empirical psychology from the 1940s to the 1960s.

Specifically, because operant theory (Skinner, 1953) maintained that all behaviors are motivated by rewards (i.e., by separable consequence such as food or money), intrinsically motivated activities were said to be ones for which the reward was in the activity itself. Thus, researchers investigated what task characteristics make an activity interesting. In contrast, because learning theory (Hull, 1943) asserted that all behaviors are motivated by physiological drives (and their derivatives), intrinsically motivated activities were said to be ones that provided satisfaction of innate psychological needs. Thus, researchers explored what basic needs are satisfied by intrinsically motivated behaviors.

Our own approach focuses primarily on psychological needs—namely, the innate needs for competence, autonomy, and relatedness—but we of course recognize that basic need satisfaction accrues in part from engaging in interesting activities. Thus, we do sometimes speak of intrinsically interesting activities, but when we do so we are really only talking about tasks that, on average, many people find to be intrinsically interesting. There is considerable practical utility in focusing on task properties and their potential intrinsic interest, as it leads toward improved task design or selection to enhance motivation.

Operational Definitions

Intrinsic motivation has been operationally defined in various ways, although there have been two measures that have been most often used. Basic experimental research (e.g., Deci, 1971) has rested primarily on a behavioral measure of intrinsic motivation called the "free choice" measure. In experiments using this measure participants are exposed to a task under varying conditions (e.g., getting a reward or not). Following this period, the experimenter tells participants they will not be asked to work with the target task any further, and they are then left alone in the experimental room with the target task as well as various distractor activities. They thus have a period of "free choice" about whether to return to the activity, and it is assumed that, if there is no extrinsic reason to do the task (e.g., no reward and no approval), then the more time they spend with the target task, the more intrinsically motivated they are for that task. This measure has been the mainstay through which the dynamics of intrinsic motivation have been experimentally studied.

The other common approach to the measurement of intrinsic motivation is the use of self-reports of interest and enjoyment of the activity per se. Experimental studies typically rely on task-specific measures (e.g., Ryan, 1982; Harackiewicz, 1979). Most field studies have instead used more general, "domain" focused measures, such as one's intrinsic motivation for school (e.g., Harter, 1981).

Facilitating versus Undermining Intrinsic Motivation

Despite the observable evidence that humans are liberally endowed with intrinsic motivational tendencies, this propensity appears to be expressed only under specifiable conditions. Research into intrinsic motivation has thus placed much emphasis on those conditions that elicit, sustain, and enhance this special type of motivation versus those that subdue or diminish it. Self-Determination Theory is specifically framed in terms of social and environmental factors that *facilitate* versus *undermine* intrinsic motivation. This language reflects the assumption that intrinsic motivation, being an inherent organismic propensity, is catalyzed (rather than *caused)* when individuals are in conditions that conduce toward its expression.

Cognitive Evaluation Theory (CET) was presented by Deci and Ryan (1985) to specify the factors in social contexts that produce variability in intrinsic motivation. CET, which is considered a subtheory of self-determination theory, argues that interpersonal events and structures (e.g., rewards, communications, feedback) that conduce toward *feelings of competence* during action can enhance intrinsic motivation for that action because they allow satisfaction of the basic psychological need for competence. Accordingly, for example, optimal challenges, effectance promoting feedback, and freedom from demeaning evaluations are all predicted to facilitate intrinsic motivation.

CET further specifies that feelings of competence will *not* enhance intrinsic motivation unless they are accompanied by *a sense of autonomy* or, in attributional terms, by an *internal perceived locus of causality* (IPLOC; deCharms, 1968). Thus, people must not only experience perceived competence (or self-efficacy), they must also experience their behavior to be self-determined if intrinsic motivation is to be maintained or enhanced. Stated differently, for a high level of intrinsic motivation people must experience satisfaction of the needs both for competence and autonomy. Much of the research has focused on the effects of immediate contextual conditions that either support or thwart the needs for competence and autonomy, but some has recognized that the supports can, to some extent, come from individuals' abiding inner resources that support their ongoing feelings of competence and autonomy.

The tenets of CET, with their primary focus on the needs for competence and autonomy, were formulated to integrate a set of results from initial studies of the effects of rewards, feedback, and other external events on intrinsic motivation. Subsequently, they have been confirmed in both laboratory experiments and applied field studies, many of which have been done in classrooms.

Several early studies showed that positive performance feedback enhanced intrinsic motivation (e.g., Deci, 1971; Harack-iewicz, 1979), whereas negative performance feedback diminished it (e.g., Deci & Cascio, 1972). Others (e.g., Vallerand & Reid, 1984) showed that perceived competence mediated these effects, and still others supported the hypothesis that increases in perceived competence must be accompanied by a sense of autonomy in order for the enhanced feelings of competence to result in increased intrinsic motivation (Ryan, 1982).

In fact, the majority of the research on the effects of environmental events on intrinsic motivation has focused on the issue of autonomy versus control rather than that of competence. And this issue has been considerably more controversial. The research began with the demonstration that extrinsic rewards can undermine intrinsic motivation (Deci, 1971; Lepper, Greene, & Nisbett, 1973), which we interpret in terms of the reward shifting people from a more internal to external perceived locus of causality. Although the issue of rewards has been hotly debated, a recent meta-analysis (Deci, Koestner, & Ryan, in press) confirms that virtually every type of expected tangible reward made contingent on task performance does, in fact, undermine intrinsic motivation. Furthermore, not only tangible rewards, but also threats (Deci & Cascio, 1972), deadlines (Amabile, De-Jong, & Lepper, 1976), directives (Koestner, Ryan, Bernieri, & Holt, 1984), and competition pressure (Reeve & Deci, 1996) diminish intrinsic motivation because, according to CET, people experience them as controllers of their behavior. On the other hand, choice and the opportunity for self-direction (e.g., Zuckerman, Porac, Lathin, Smith, & Deci, 1978) appear to enhance intrinsic motivation, as they afford a greater sense of autonomy.

The significance of autonomy versus control for the maintenance of intrinsic motivation has been clearly observed in studies of classroom learning. For example, several studies have shown that autonomy-supportive (in contrast to controlling) teachers catalyze in their students greater intrinsic motivation, curiosity, and the desire for challenge (e.g., Deci, Nezlek, & Sheinman, 1981; Ryan & Grolnick, 1986). Students who are overly controlled not only lose initiative but also learn less well, especially when learning is complex or requires conceptual, creative processing (Benware & Deci, 1984; Grolnick & Ryan, 1987). Similarly, studies show children of parents who are more autonomy supportive to be more mastery oriented—more likely to spontaneously explore and extend themselves—than children of parents who are more controlling (Grolnick, Deci, & Ryan, 1997).

To summarize, the CET aspect of SDT suggests that classroom and home environments can facilitate or forestall intrinsic motivation by supporting versus thwarting the needs for autonomy and competence. However, it is critical to remember that intrinsic motivation will occur only for activities that hold intrinsic interest for an individual—those that have the appeal of novelty, challenge, or aesthetic value for that individual. For activities that do not hold such appeal, the principles of CET do not apply. To understand the motivation for activities that are not experienced as inherently interesting, we need to look more deeply into the nature and dynamics of extrinsic motivation.

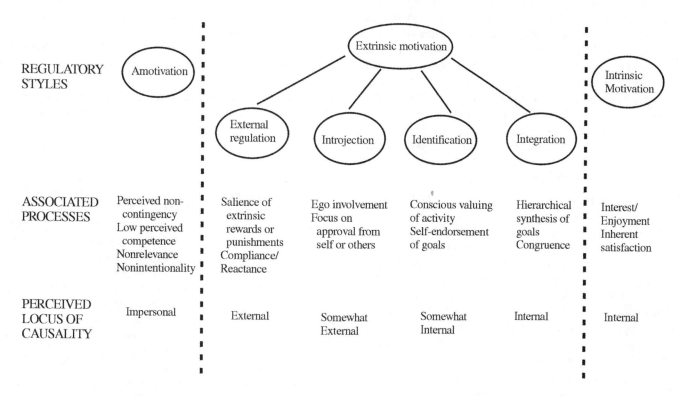

FIG. 1. A taxonomy of human motivation.

EXTRINSIC MOTIVATION

Although intrinsic motivation is clearly an important type of motivation, most of the activities people do are not, strictly speaking, intrinsically motivated. This is especially the case after early childhood, as the freedom to be intrinsically motivated becomes increasingly curtailed by social demands and roles that require individuals to assume responsibility for non-intrinsically interesting tasks. In schools, for example, it appears that intrinsic motivation becomes weaker with each advancing grade.

Extrinsic motivation is a construct that pertains whenever an activity is done in order to attain some separable outcome. Extrinsic motivation thus contrasts with intrinsic motivation, which refers to doing an activity simply for the enjoyment of the activity itself, rather than its instrumental value. However, unlike some perspectives that view extrinsically motivated behavior as invariantly nonautonomous, SDT proposes that extrinsic motivation can vary greatly in the degree to which it is autonomous. For example, a student who does his homework only because he fears parental sanctions for not doing it is extrinsically motivated because he is doing the work in order to attain the separable outcome of avoiding sanctions. Similarly, a student who does the work because she personally believes it is valuable for her chosen career is also extrinsically motivated because she too is doing it for its instrumental value rather than because she finds it interesting. Both examples involve instrumentalities, yet the latter case entails personal endorsement and a feeling of choice, whereas the former involves mere compli-

ance with an external control. Both represent intentional behavior, but the two types of extrinsic motivation vary in their relative autonomy.

Given that many of the educational activities prescribed in schools are not designed to be intrinsically interesting, a central question concerns how to motivate students to value and self-regulate such activities, and without external pressure, to carry them out on their own. This problem is described within SDT in terms of fostering the *internalization and integration* of values and behavioral regulations (Deci & Ryan, 1985). Internalization is the process of taking in a value or regulation, and integration is the process by which individuals more fully transform the regulation into their own so that it will emanate from their sense of self. Thought of as a continuum, the concept of internalization describes how one's motivation for behavior can range from amotivation or unwillingness, to passive compliance, to active personal commitment. With increasing internalization (and its associated sense of personal commitment) come greater persistence, more positive self-perceptions, and better quality of engagement.

Within SDT a second subtheory, referred to as *Organismic Integration Theory* (OIT), was introduced to detail the different forms of extrinsic motivation and the contextual factors that either promote or hinder internalization and integration of the regulation for these behaviors (Deci & Ryan, 1985). Figure 1 illustrates the OIT taxonomy of types of motivation, arranged from left to right in terms of the extent to which the motivation for one's behavior emanates from one's self.

At the far left is *amotivation*, which is the state of lacking an intention to act. When amotivated, a person's behavior lacks intentionality and a sense of personal causation. Amotivation results from not valuing an activity (Ryan, 1995), not feeling competent to do it (Deci, 1975), or not believing it will yield a desired outcome (Seligman, 1975). Theorists who have treated motivation as a unitary concept (e.g., Bandura, 1986) have been concerned only with the distinction between what we call amotivation and motivation. However, one can see from Fig. 1 that to the right of amotivation are various types of motivation that we have organized to reflect their differing degrees of autonomy or self-determination.

Just to the right of amotivation, is a category that represents the least autonomous forms of extrinsic motivation, a category we label *external regulation*. Such behaviors are performed to satisfy an external demand or obtain an externally imposed reward contingency. Individuals typically experience externally regulated behavior as controlled or alienated, and their actions have an *external perceived locus of causality* (EPLOC; deCharms, 1968). External regulation is the only kind of motivation recognized by operant theorists (e.g., Skinner, 1953), and it is this type of extrinsic motivation that was typically contrasted with intrinsic motivation in early lab studies and discussions.

A second type of extrinsic motivation is *introjected regulation*. Introjection describes a type of internal regulation that is still quite controlling because people perform such actions with the feeling of pressure in order to avoid guilt or anxiety or to attain ego-enhancements or pride. Put differently, introjection represents regulation by contingent self-esteem. A classic form of introjection is *ego involvement* (Nicholls, 1984; Ryan, 1982), in which a person performs an act in order to enhance or maintain self-esteem and the feeling of worth. Although the regulation is internal to the person, introjected behaviors are not experienced as fully part of the self and thus still have an EPLOC.

A more autonomous, or self-determined, form of extrinsic motivation is regulation through *identification*. Here, the person has identified with the personal importance of a behavior and has thus accepted its regulation as his or her own. A boy who memorizes spelling lists because he sees it as relevant to writing, which he values as a life goal, has identified with the value of this learning activity.

Finally, the most autonomous form of extrinsic motivation is *integrated regulation*. Integration occurs when identified regulations have been fully assimilated to the self. This occurs through self-examination and bringing new regulations into congruence with one's other values and needs. The more one internalizes the reasons for an action and assimilates them to the self, the more one's extrinsically motivated actions become self-determined. Integrated forms of motivation share many qualities with intrinsic motivation, being both autonomous and unconflicted. However, they are still extrinsic because behavior motivated by integrated regulation is done for its presumed instrumental value with respect to some outcome that is separate from the behavior, even though it is volitional and valued by the self.

At the far right hand end of the figure is intrinsic motivation. This placement emphasizes that intrinsic motivation is a prototype of self-determined activity. Yet, as implied above, this does not mean that as extrinsic regulations become more internalized they are transformed into intrinsic motivation.

The process of internalization is developmentally important, as social values and regulations are continually being internalized over the life span. Still, we do not suggest that the continuum underlying types of extrinsic motivation is a *developmental* continuum, per se. One does not have to progress through each stage of internalization with respect to a particular regulation; indeed, one can initially adopt a new behavioral regulation at any point along this continuum depending upon prior experiences and situational factors (Ryan, 1995). Some behaviors could begin as introjects, others as identifications. A person might originally get exposed to an activity because of an external regulation (e.g., a reward), and (if the reward is not perceived as too controlling) such exposure might allow the person to experience the activity's intrinsically interesting properties, resulting in an orientation shift. Or a person who has identified with the value of an activity might lose that sense of value under a controlling mentor and move "backward" into an external regulatory mode. Thus, while there are predictable reasons for movement between orientations, there is no necessary "sequence." Developmental issues are, however, evident in two ways: (1) the types of behaviors and values that can be assimilated to the self increase with growing cognitive and ego capacities and (2) it appears that people's general regulatory style does, on average, tend to become more "internal" over time (e.g., Chandler & Connell, 1987), in accord with the general organismic tendencies toward autonomy and self-regulation (Ryan, 1995).

Ryan and Connell (1989) tested the formulation that these different types of motivation do indeed lie along a continuum of relative autonomy. They investigated achievement behaviors (e.g., doing homework) among elementary school children, assessing external, introjected, identified, and intrinsic reasons for engaging in these behaviors. They found that the four types of regulation were intercorrelated according to a quasi-simplex (ordered correlation) pattern, thus providing evidence for an underlying continuum of autonomy. Differences in attitudes and adjustment were also associated with the different types of extrinsic motivation. For example, the more students were externally regulated the less they showed interest, value, or effort, and the more they indicated a tendency to blame others, such as the teacher, for negative outcomes. Introjected regulation was positively related to expending effort, but was also related to more anxiety and to poorer coping with failures. Identified regulation was associated with greater enjoyment of school and more positive coping styles. And intrinsic motivation was correlated with interest, enjoyment, felt competence, and positive coping.

Subsequent studies have extended these findings concerning types of extrinsic motivation, showing for example that more autonomous extrinsic motivation is associated with greater engagement (Connell & Wellborn, 1990), better performance (Miserandino, 1996), less dropping out (Vallerand & Bissonnette, 1992), higher quality learning (Grolnick & Ryan, 1987), and greater psychological well-being (Sheldon & Kasser, 1995), among other outcomes. Additionally, there appears to be cross-cultural generalizability to the model as presented in Fig. 1 (e.g., Hayamizu, 1997).

Greater internalization appears, then, to yield manifold adaptive advantages (Ryan, Kuhl, & Deci, 1997), including more behavioral effectiveness (due to lessened conflict and greater access to personal resources) and greater experienced well-being. Given the clear significance of internalization for both personal experience and behavioral and performance outcomes, the critical applied issue concerns how to promote the autonomous regulation of extrinsically motivated behaviors.

Because extrinsically motivated behaviors are not inherently interesting and thus must initially be externally prompted, the primary reason people are likely to be willing to do the behaviors is that they are valued by significant others to whom they feel (or would like to feel) connected, whether that be a family, a peer group, or a society. This suggests that the groundwork for facilitating internalization is providing a sense of belongingness and connectedness to the persons, group, or culture disseminating a goal, or what in SDT we call a sense of *relatedness*. In classrooms this means that students' feeling respected and cared for by the teacher is essential for their willingness to accept the proffered classroom values. In support of this, Ryan, Stiller, and Lynch (1994) found that relatedness to teachers (and parents) was associated with greater internalization of school-related behavioral regulations.

A second issue concerns perceived *competence*. Adopting as one's own an extrinsic goal requires that one feel efficacious with respect to it. Students will more likely adopt and internalize a goal if they understand it and have the relevant skills to succeed at it. Thus, we theorize that supports for competence (e.g., offering optimal challenges and effectance-relevant feedback) facilitate internalization.

According to the SDT approach, a regulation that has been internalized may be only introjected, and that type of regulation could well leave people feeling satisfaction of their needs for competence and relatedness. However, to only introject a regulation and thus to be controlled by it will not leave the people feeling self-determined. We therefore suggest that autonomy support also facilitates internalization; in fact, it is the critical element for a regulation being integrated rather than just introjected. Controlling contexts may yield introjected regulation if they support competence and relatedness, but only autonomy supportive contexts will yield integrated self-regulation. To fully internalize a regulation, and thus to become autonomous with respect to it, people must inwardly grasp its meaning and worth. It is these meanings that become internalized and integrated in environments that provide supports for the needs for competence, relatedness, and autonomy.

Again, research has supported this reasoning. Deci, Eghrari, Patrick, and Leone (1994) experimentally demonstrated that providing a meaningful rationale for an uninteresting behavior, along with supports for autonomy and relatedness, promoted internalization and integration. Controlling contexts yielded less overall internalization, but even more interesting, the internal-

ization that did occur in controlling contexts tended to be only introjected. In a study involving parent interviews, Grolnick and Ryan (1989) found higher levels of internalization and integration of school-related values among children whose parents were more supportive of autonomy and relatedness. Williams and Deci (1996) used a longitudinal design to show greater internalization among medical students whose instructors were more autonomy and competence supportive. These are a few of the findings in this area that suggest how supports for relatedness and competence facilitate internalization and how support for autonomy additionally facilitates the integration of behavioral regulations. When that occurs, people not only feel competent and related, but also self-determined, as they carry out extrinsically valued activities.

CONCLUSIONS

We have briefly presented self-determination theory in order to make the critical distinction between behaviors that are volitional and accompanied by the experience of freedom and autonomy—those that emanate from one's sense of self—and those that are accompanied by the experience of pressure and control and are not representative of one's self. Intrinsically motivated behaviors, which are performed out of interest and satisfy the innate psychological needs for competence and autonomy are the prototype of self-determined behavior. Extrinsically motivated behaviors—those that are executed because they are instrumental to some separable consequence—can vary in the extent to which they represent self-determination. Internalization and integration are the processes through which extrinsically motivated behaviors become more self-determined.

We reviewed studies that have specified the social contextual conditions that support intrinsic motivation and facilitate internalization and integration of extrinsically motivated tasks. The studies have been interpreted in terms of the basic psychological needs. That is, we saw that social contextual conditions that support one's feelings of competence, autonomy, and relatedness are the basis for one maintaining intrinsic motivation and becoming more self-determined with respect to extrinsic motivation. We pointed out that in schools, the facilitation of more self-determined learning requires classroom conditions that allow satisfaction of these three basic human needs—that is that support the innate needs to feel connected, effective, and agentic as one is exposed to new ideas and exercises new skills.

REFERENCES

Amabile, T. M., DeJong, W., & Lepper, M. R. (1976). Effects of externally imposed deadlines on subsequent intrinsic motivation. *Journal of Personality and Social Psychology*, **34**, 92–98.

Bandura, A. (1986). *Social foundations of thought and action: A social cognitive theory.* Englewood Cliffs, NJ: Prentice–Hall.

Benware, C., & Deci, E. L. (1984). Quality of learning with an active versus passive motivational set. *American Educational Research Journal*, **21**, 755–765.

Chandler, C. L., & Connell, J. P. (1987). Children's intrinsic, extrinsic and internalized motivation: A developmental study of children's reasons for liked and disliked behaviours. *British Journal of Developmental Psychology*, **5**, 357–365.

Connell, J. P., & Wellborn, J. G. (1990). Competence, autonomy and relatedness: A motivational analysis of self-system processes. In M. R. Gunnar & L. A. Sroufe Eds.), *The Minnesota symposium on child psychology* (Vol. 22, pp. 43–77). Hillsdale, NJ: Erlbaum.

deCharms, R. (1968). *Personal causation*. New York: Academic Press.

Deci, E. L. (1971). Effects of externally mediated rewards on intrinsic motivation. *Journal of Personality and Social Psychology*, **18**, 105–115.

Deci, E. L. (1975). *Intrinsic motivation*. New York: Plenum.

Deci, E. L., & Cascio, W. F. (1972, April). *Changes in intrinsic motivation as a function of negative feedback and threats*. Presented at the meeting of the Eastern Psychological Association, Boston.

Deci, E. L., Eghrari, H., Patrick, B. C., & Leone, D. R. (1994). Facilitating internalization: The self-determination theory perspective. *Journal of Personality*, **62**, 119–142.

Deci, E. L., Koestner, R., & Ryan, R. M. (1998). *Extrinsic rewards and intrinsic motivation: Clear and reliable effects*. Unpublished manuscript, University of Rochester.

Deci, E. L., Nezlek, J., & Scheinman, L. (1981). Characteristics of the rewarder and intrinsic motivation of the rewardee. *Journal of Personality and Social Psychology*, **40**, 1–10.

Deci, E. L., & Ryan, R. M. (1985). *Intrinsic motivation and self-determination in human behavior*. New York: Plenum.

Grolnick, W. S., Deci, E. L., & Ryan, R. M. (1997). Internalization within the family: The self-determination perspective. In J. E. Grusec & L. Kuczynski (Eds.), *Parenting and children's internalization of values: A handbook of contemporary theory* (pp. 135–161). New York: Wiley.

Grolnick, W. S., & Ryan, R. M. (1987). Autonomy in children's learning: An experimental and individual difference investigation. *Journal of Personality and Social Psychology*, **52**, 890–898.

Harackiewicz, J. (1979). The effects of reward contingency and performance feedback on intrinsic motivation. *Journal of Personality and Social Psychology*, **37**, 1352–1363.

Harter, S. (1981). A new self-report scale of intrinsic versus extrinsic orientation in the classroom: Motivational and informational components. *Developmental Psychology*, **17**, 300–312.

Hayamizu, T. (1997). Between intrinsic and extrinsic motivation: Examination of reasons for academic study based on the theory of internalization. *Japanese Psychological Research*, **39**, 98–108.

Hull, C. L. (1943). *Principles of behavior*. New York: Appleton–Century–Crofts.

Koestner, R., Ryan, R. M., Bernieri, F., & Holt, K. (1984). Setting limits on children's behavior: The differential effects of controlling versus informational styles on intrinsic motivation and creativity. *Journal of Personality*, **52**, 233–248.

Lepper, M. R., Greene, D., & Nisbett, R. E. (1973). Undermining children's intrinsic interest with extrinsic rewards: A test of the "overjustification" hypothesis. *Journal of Personality and Social Psychology*, **28**, 129–137.

Miserandino, M. (1996). Children who do well in school: Individual differences in perceived competence and autonomy in above-average children. *Journal of Educational Psychology*, **88**, 203–214.

Nicholls, J. G. (1984). Achievement motivation: Conceptions of ability, subjective experience, task choice, and performance. *Psychological Review*, **91**, 328–346.

Reeve, J., & Deci, E. L. (1996). Elements of the competitive situation that affect intrinsic motivation. *Personality and Social Psychology Bulletin*, **22**, 24–33.

Ryan, R. M. (1982). Control and information in the intrapersonal sphere: An extension of cognitive evaluation theory. *Journal of Personality and Social Psychology*, **43**, 450–461.

Ryan, R. M. (1995). Psychological needs and the facilitation of integrative processes. *Journal of Personality*, **63**, 397–427.

Ryan, R. M., & Connell, J. P. (1989). Perceived locus of causality and internalization: Examining reasons for acting in two domains. *Journal of Personality and Social Psychology*, **57**, 749–761.

Ryan, R. M., & Grolnick, W. S. (1986). Origins and pawns in the classroom: Self-report and projective assessments of individual differences in children's perceptions. *Journal of Personality and Social Psychology*, **50**, 550–558.

Ryan, R. M., Kuhl, J., & Deci, E. L. (1997). Nature and autonomy: Organizational view of social and neurobiological aspects of self-regulation in behavior and development. *Development and Psychopathology*, **9**, 701–728.

Ryan, R. M., & Stiller, J. (1991). The social contexts of internalization: Parent and teacher influences on autonomy, motivation and learning. In P. R. Pintrich & M. L. Maehr (Eds.), *Advances in motivation and achievement* (Vol. 7, pp. 115–149). Greenwich, CT: JAI Press.

Ryan, R. M., Stiller, J., & Lynch, J. H. (1994). Representations of relationships to teachers, parents, and friends as predictors of academic motivation and self-esteem. *Journal of Early Adolescence*, **14**, 226–249.

Seligman, M. (1975). *Helplessness: On depression, development, and death*. San Francisco: W. H. Freeman.

Sheldon, K. M., & Kasser, T. (1995). Coherence and congruence: Two aspects of personality integration. *Journal of Personality and Social Psychology*, **68**, 531–543.

Skinner, B. F. (1953). *Science and human behavior*. New York: Macmillan.

Vallerand, R. J., & Bissonnette, R. (1992). Intrinsic, extrinsic, and amotivational styles as predictors of behavior: A prospective study. *Journal of Personality*, **60**, 599–620.

Vallerand, R. J., & Reid, G. (1984). On the causal effects of perceived competence on intrinsic motivation: A test of cognitive evaluation theory. *Journal of Sport Psychology*, **6**, 94–102.

White, R. W. (1959). Motivation reconsidered. *Psychological Review*, **66**, 297–333.

Williams, G. C., & Deci, E. L. (1996). Internalization of biopsychosocial values by medical students: A test of self-determination theory. *Journal of Personality and Social Psychology*, **70**, 767–779.

Zuckerman, M., Porac, J., Lathin, D., Smith, R., & Deci, E. L. (1978). On the importance of self-determination for intrinsically motivated behavior. *Personality and Social Psychology Bulletin*, **4**, 443–446.

Address correspondence and reprint requests to Richard Ryan, University of Rochester, Meliora 492, Rochester, NY 14627.

Intrinsic Versus Extrinsic Motivation in Schools: A Reconciliation

Abstract

This article explores the nature of the relationships between intrinsic and extrinsic motivation in schools, and in particular examines critically the assertion that these processes are necessarily antagonistic. The weight of evidence suggests that rewards in the form of school grades and the focus of many students on doing well, gradewise, need not necessarily interfere with learning for its own sake. Educational implications of these findings are considered. One such implication is that focusing on students' interests can be a valuable motivational strategy.

Keywords:
   motivation; achievement; appreciation

Martin V. Covington[1]

Department of Psychology, University of California at Berkeley, Berkeley, California

When psychologists speak of motivation, they typically refer to the reasons that individuals are aroused to action. Over the past 50 years, two quite different kinds of reasons have emerged in the thinking of psychologists: intrinsic and extrinsic reasons. Individuals are said to be driven to act for extrinsic reasons when they anticipate some kind of tangible payoff, such as good grades, recognition, or gold stars. These rewards are said to be extrinsic because they are unrelated to the action. In effect, the activity becomes a means to an end. By contrast, individuals are said to be intrinsically motivated when they engage in activities for their own sake. In this instance, the rewards reside in the actions themselves; that is, the actions are their own reinforcement. Put differently, in the case of intrinsic motivation, the repetition of an action does not depend as much on some external inducement as on the satisfaction derived from overcoming a personal challenge, learning something new, or discovering things of personal interest.

For generations, observers have extolled the virtues of learning for its own sake, not only because of the benefits of personal growth or enhanced well-being, but also because intrinsically based learning is the handmaiden to better, more efficient learning. For example, intrinsically engaged students are more likely than extrinsically driven students to employ deep-level, sophisticated study strategies in their work (Ames & Archer, 1988). Perhaps most noteworthy for establishing causal, not merely correlational, relationships are studies (e.g., Schunk, 1996) in which students were randomly assigned to varying achievement conditions. Those students who were directed to work for the goals of mastery, exploration, and appreciation demonstrated greater task involvement and used more effective learning strategies than children who were directed to focus on their performance alone.

At the same time, experts also lament the prospects of encouraging intrinsic engagement in a world controlled by extrinsic rewards (e.g., Kohn, 1993). My purpose here is to explore briefly the nature of the relationship between intrinsic and extrinsic motivation in schools, and in particular to examine critically the assertion that these processes are necessarily antagonistic, such that the will to learn for its own sake is inhibited or even destroyed by the offering of extrinsic rewards and incentives like school grades.

It is important to be clear about what the issue is. The issue is not that offering tangible rewards will necessarily interfere with learning. To the contrary, offering students tangible rewards sometimes actually increases learning, especially if the assignment is seen as a chore or boring. Rather, the issue is whether offering rewards focuses undue attention on the tangible payoffs, thereby decreasing students' appreciation of what they are learning.

OBSTACLES TO INTRINSIC ENGAGEMENT

The potentially destructive impact of tangible rewards on the will to learn for its own sake has been documented in several ways. First, there is the prospect that once these rewards are no longer available, students will show little or no inclination to continue in their studies (Covington, 1998). Second, there is the possibility that offering rewards to students for doing what already interests them may also undercut personal task involvement. For example, if a teacher tries to encourage intrinsic values directly, say, by praising students for pursuing a hobby, then, paradoxically, these interests may actually be discouraged. This phenomenon is the so-called overjustification effect (Lepper, Greene, & Nisbett, 1973). According to one interpretation, such discouragement occurs because the value of an already justifiable activity becomes suspect by the promise of additional rewards—hence the term overjustification—so that the individual reasons, "If someone has to pay me to do this, then it must not be worth doing for its own sake."

The goal of fostering a love of learning is complicated not only by offering or withholding tangible rewards, but also by the scarcity of these rewards. In many classrooms, an inadequate supply of rewards (e.g., good grades) is distributed by teachers unequally, with the greatest number of rewards going to the best performers or to the fastest learners. This arrangement is based on the false assumption that achievement is maximized when students compete for a limited number of rewards. Although this may maximize motivation, students are aroused for the wrong reasons—to win over others and to avoid losing—and these reasons eventually lead to failure and resentment (Covington, 1998). In this competitive context, grades stand as a mark of worthiness, because it is widely assumed in our society that one is only as worthy as one's ability to achieve competitively.

If high grades not only are important for the tangible future benefits they bestow—being the gateway to prestigious occupations—but also serve as an indication of one's personal worth, then what becomes of the valuing of learning in the scramble for grades? Is not the valuing and appreciation of learning marginalized? No, apparently not. There can be little doubt that students also value learning, irrespective of the grades they receive (see Covington, 1999).

A RECONCILIATION

How can we resolve this apparent contradiction? The observations of students themselves provide some answers (Covington, 1999; Covington & Wiedenhaupt, 1997).

First, students readily acknowledge that they strive for the highest grades possible, but—and this is the important point—different students have different reasons for a grade focus. It is these reasons that in turn determine the degree to which students become intrinsically engaged. For instance, when students strive for high grades as a mark of approval, to impress other people, or to avoid failure, they will value learning only to the extent that it serves to aggrandize their ability status, not for any inherent attraction of the material itself. If, by contrast, students have a task-oriented purpose in striving for high grades (e.g., if they use grades as feedback for how they can improve and learn more), then they will appreciate their accomplishments for their positive proper-ties. In effect, it is not necessarily the presence of grades per se, or even a dominant grade focus, that influences the degree to which learning is appreciated. Rather, students' valuing of what they learn depends on their initial reasons for learning and the meaning they attach to their grades. This implies that striving for good grades and caring for learning are not necessarily incompatible goals. The degree of compatibility of these goals is influenced by the reasons for learning.

Second, the degree to which students become intrinsically engaged in their schoolwork depends in part on whether they are achieving their grade goals, that is, whether they feel successful. On the one hand, being successful in one's studies promotes an appreciation for what one is learning. On the other hand, falling short of one's grade goals may intensify one's concentration on doing better (to the point that appreciation of the subject matter is excluded), divert attention to protecting one's sense of worth, or cause feelings of hopelessness about ever succeeding, feelings that bode ill for both the goal of appreciation and the goal of achievement. Thus, the degree of goal compatibility is also influenced by experiences of success and failure.

Third, students also indicate that they often manipulate academic circumstances to create a tolerable balance between grades and caring. The most frequent strategies involve making school more interesting by deliberately seeking out what is of interest to them, even in the case of boring assignments, or arranging a course of study, or even a college major, around personal interests. Thus, the compatibility of grades and caring is also influenced by personal interests.

From these observations, we can conclude that students are more likely to value what they are learning, and to enjoy the process, (a) when they are achieving their grade goals; (b) when the dominant reasons for learning are task-oriented reasons, not self-aggrandizing or failure-avoiding reasons; and (c) when what they are studying is of personal interest.

The role of personal interest in this equation is especially noteworthy. Although it is not surprising that people enjoy learning more about what already interests them, what is intriguing is the extent to which pursuing one's own interests offsets the potentially negative effects of receiving a disappointing grade. In fact, the evidence suggests that a student's appreciation for what he or she is learning is far greater when the student is failing but interested in the task than when the same student is succeeding, gradewise, but has little interest in the subject-matter content.

A related point concerning this equation also deserves comment. Receiving a good grade, especially for interesting work, increases, not decreases, intrinsic engagement. This finding seems to contradict the previously mentioned expectation that providing people with tangible payoffs for pursuing what already interests them will dampen their enthusiasm. Students themselves offer several plausible explanations for why these worries may be exaggerated, if not groundless. Based on their experiences, some students report anecdotally that doing well causes positive feelings like pride, which in turn increases their enthusiasm for learning. Other anecdotal observations suggest that doing well reduces worry about failing, so that students are freer to explore what is most interesting. And, according to yet other students, being successful stimulates them to study more, and the more they learn, the more interesting the material is likely to become. Whatever the explanation, it seems that the effects of tangible payoffs on intrinsic processes are far from simple.

EDUCATIONAL IMPLICATIONS

What practical steps do these findings suggest for how schools can

serve both the goal of disseminating knowledge and the goal of promoting an appreciation of what is learned in the face of an ever-present grade focus?

First, the most obvious implication is that a major instructional goal should be to arrange schooling around the personal interests of students. Second, obviously learning cannot always be arranged around personal preferences, nor can students always succeed. Nonetheless, instructional practices can alter the meaning of failure when it occurs. Basically, this step involves eliminating the climate of scarcity of rewards by defining success not in the relative sense of outperforming others, but rather absolutely, that is, in terms of whether students measure up to a given standard of performance, irrespective of how many other students do well or poorly (Covington & Teel, 1996). When well-defined standards of performance are provided, the failure to achieve them tends to motivate students to try harder because failure implies falling short of a goal, not falling short as a person.

Third, in addition to creating grading systems that encourage intrinsic reasons for learning, teachers should provide payoffs that actively strengthen and reward these positive reasons. Although students focus primarily on the prospects of getting a good grade, they are also more likely to invest greater time and energy (beyond what is necessary for the grade) in those tasks for which there are additional tangible, yet intrinsically oriented payoffs. These payoffs include the opportunity to share the results of their work with others, or the chance to explain more deeply and personally why what they learned was important to them. This suggestion implies that, far from being incompatible, intrinsic and extrinsic reasons for learning are both encouraged by tangible rewards, but by different kinds of tangible rewards. This proposition sheds an entirely new light on the concerns raised by many experts re-

garding the overjustification effect. It is not the offering of tangible rewards that undercuts personal task engagement so much as it is the absence of those kinds of payoffs that encourage and recognize the importance of being involved in and caring about what one is learning.

Finally, students are the first to acknowledge a conflict between the goals of striving for high grades and enjoying learning. However, the conflict arises, they say, not out of any incompatibility of goals. Rather, the demands of school leave little room to pursue either goal fully, let alone to pursue the two goals together. As a result, students must prioritize these objectives, a process that typically favors the goal of striving for grades, and they lament what they forfeit. But prioritizing is not the same as incompatibility. The recommendations made in this review can act to balance these priorities more in favor of intrinsic engagement and a love of learning.

Recommended Reading

Cameron, J., & Pierce, W. D. (1994). Reinforcement, reward and intrinsic motivation: A meta-analysis. *Review of Educational Research, 64*, 363–423.

Condry, J., & Koslowski, B. (1979). Can education be made "intrinsically interesting" to children? In D. Katz (Ed.), *Current topics in early childhood education* (Vol. II, pp. 227–260). Norwood, NJ: Ablex.

Cordova, D. I., & Lepper, M. R. (1996). Intrinsic motivation and the process of learning: Beneficial effects of contextualization, personalization and choice. *Journal of Educational Psychology, 88*, 715–730.

Covington, M. V. (1992). *Making the grade: A self-worth perspective on motivation and school reform*. New York: Cambridge University Press.

Elliot, A. J., & Harackiewicz, J. M. (1996). Approach and avoidance achievement goals and intrinsic motivation: A mediational analysis. *Journal of Personality and Social Psychology, 70*, 461–475.

Note

1. Address correspondence to Martin V. Covington, Department of Psychology, 3210 Tolman Hall, University of California at Berkeley, Berkeley, CA 94720-1650.

References

Ames, C., & Archer, J. (1988). Achievement goals in the classroom: Student learning strategies and motivation processes. *Journal of Educational Psychology, 80,* 260–267.

Covington, M. V. (1998). *The will to learn: A guide for motivating young people.* New York: Cambridge University Press.

Covington, M. V. (1999). Caring about learning: The nature and nurturing of subject-matter appreciation. *Educational Researchers, 34,* 127–136.

Covington, M. V., & Teel, K. M. (1996). *Overcoming student failure: Changing motives and incentives for learning.* Washington, DC: American Psychological Association.

Covington, M. V., & Wiedenhaupt, S. (1997). Turning work into play: The nature and nurturing of intrinsic task engagement. In R. Perry & J. C. Smart (Eds.), *Effective teaching in higher education: Research and practice, special edition* (pp. 101–114). New York: Agathon Press.

Kohn, A. (1993). *Punished by rewards.* New York: Houghton Mifflin.

Lepper, M. R., Greene, D., & Nisbett, R. E. (1973). Undermining children's intrinsic interest with extrinsic rewards: A test of the "overjustification" hypothesis. *Journal of Personality and Social Psychology, 28,* 129–137.

Schunk, D. H. (1996). Goal and self-evaluative influences during children's cognitive skill learning. *American Educational Research Journal, 33,* 359–382.

Self-Efficacy: An Essential Motive to Learn

During the past two decades, self-efficacy has emerged as a highly effective predictor of students' motivation and learning. As a performance-based measure of perceived capability, self-efficacy differs conceptually and psychometrically from related motivational constructs, such as outcome expectations, self-concept, or locus of control. Researchers have succeeded in verifying its discriminant validity as well as convergent validity in predicting common motivational outcomes, such as students' activity choices, effort, persistence, and emotional reactions. Self-efficacy beliefs have been found to be sensitive to subtle changes in students' performance context, to interact with self-regulated learning processes, and to mediate students' academic achievement. © 2000 Academic Press

Barry J. Zimmerman

Graduate School and University Center of City University of New York

Educators have long recognized that students' beliefs about their academic capabilities play an essential role in their motivation to achieve, but self-conceptions regarding academic performance initially proved difficult to measure in a scientifically valid way. Initial efforts to study students' self-beliefs gave little attention to the role of environmental influences, such as specific features of performance contexts or domains of academic functioning. In the late 1970s, a number of researchers began to assess self-beliefs in a more task-specific way, and one of the most important of these efforts focused on self-efficacy. In 1977(a) Bandura proposed a theory of the origins, mediating mechanisms, and diverse effects of beliefs of personal efficacy, and he provided guidelines for measurement of self-efficacy beliefs for different domains of functioning. In the present article, I define self-efficacy and distinguish it from related conceptions in the literature, describe its role in academic motivation and learning (with special attention to students' capabilities to regulate their own learning activities), and discuss its susceptibility to instruction and other social-cultural influences. Because of space limitations, I cite only key studies and do not consider other issues such as theoretical controversies or gender differences in self-efficacy. For comprehensive reviews of research on academic

self-efficacy, I recommend Bandura (1997), Pajares (1996b, 1997), Schunk (1989), and Zimmerman (1995).

SELF-EFFICACY AND ITS DIMENSIONS

Before Bandura (1977a) introduced self-efficacy as a key component in social cognitive theory, he discussed human motivation primarily in terms of outcome expectations. However, during the treatment of phobic individuals with mastery modeling techniques, individual differences in generalization were found regardless of the fact that all subjects could successfully interact with the target of their fear (e.g., touch a snake or dog) without adverse consequences at the end of therapy. Although the subjects developed a strong outcome expectancy that proper techniques (e.g., for handling a snake or dog) would protect them from adverse consequences (such as biting), they still differed in their perceived capabilities to use the techniques outside the therapeutic setting. Bandura labeled this individual difference *self-efficacy* and sought to measure it using task-specific scales. Although self-efficacy and outcome expectations were both hypothesized to affect motivation, he suggested that self-efficacy would play a larger role because "the types of outcomes people anticipate depend largely on their judgments of how well they will be able to perform in given situations" (Bandura, 1986, p. 392).

The effect of prior math experiences on math problem solving was mediated primarily by self-efficacy beliefs, but self-concept played a small but significant role.

Bandura (1977a, 1997) formally defined perceived self-efficacy as personal judgments of one's capabilities to organize and execute courses of action to attain designated goals, and he sought to assess its level, generality, and strength across activities and contexts. The *level* of self-efficacy refers to its dependence on the difficulty of a particular task, such as spelling words of increasing difficulty; *generality* pertains to the transferability of self-efficacy beliefs across activities, such as from algebra to statistics; *strength* of perceived efficacy is measured by the amount of one's certainty about performing a given task. These properties of self-efficacy judgments are measured using questionnaire items that are task specific, vary in difficulty, and capture degrees of confidence (e.g., from 0 to 100%).

With regard to their content, self-efficacy measures focus on *performance capabilities* rather than on personal qualities, such as one's physical or psychological characteristics. Respondents judge their capabilities to fulfill given task demands, such as solving fraction problems in arithmetic, not who they are personally or how they feel about themselves in general. Self-efficacy beliefs are not a single disposition but rather are *multidimensional* in form and differ on the basis of the domain of functioning. For example, efficacy beliefs about performing on a history test may differ from beliefs about a biology examination. Self-efficacy measures are also designed to be sensitive to variations in performance *context*, such as learning in a noisy lounge compared to the quietude of the library. In addition, perceptions of efficacy depend on a *mastery criterion* of performance rather than on normative or other criteria. For example, students rate their certainty about solving a crossword puzzle of a particular difficulty level, not how well they expect to do on the puzzle in comparison to other students. Finally, self-efficacy judgments specifically refer to *future* functioning and are assessed before students perform the relevant activities. This antecedent property positions self-efficacy judgments to play a causal role in academic motivation.

SELF-EFFICACY AND RELATED BELIEFS

Self-efficacy beliefs differ conceptually and psychometrically from closely related constructs, such as outcome expectations, self-concept, and perceived control. The conceptual distinction that Bandura (1986) drew between academic self-efficacy and *outcome expectancies* was studied psychometrically in research on reading and writing achievement. Shell, Murphy, and Bruning (1989) measured self-efficacy in terms of perceived capability to perform various reading and writing activities, and they assessed outcome expectancies regarding the value of these activities in attaining various outcomes in employment, social pursuits, family life, education, and citizenship. Efficacy beliefs and outcome expectancies jointly predicted 32% of the variance in reading achievement, with perceived efficacy accounting for virtually all the variance. Only perceived self-efficacy was a significant predictor of writing achievement. These results not only show the discriminant validity of self-efficacy measures, they support Bandura's contention that self-efficacy plays a larger role than outcome expectancies in motivation.

One of the closest constructs to self-efficacy is *self-concept*. The latter belief is a more general self-descriptive construct that incorporates many forms of self-knowledge and self-evaluative feelings (Marsh & Shavelson, 1985). Historically, self-concept was defined by phenomenologists (e.g., Rogers, 1951) as a global perception of oneself and one's self-esteem reactions to that self-perception, but this global measure of self-belief was not found to be related consistently to students' academic performance (Hattie, 1992; Wylie, 1968). Perhaps as a result, a number of theorists (e.g., Harter, 1978; Marsh & Shavelson, 1985) reconceptualized self-concept as a hierarchical construct, with a global self-concept at the apex of a self-hierarchy but added subcategories such as academic self-concept in the middle of the hierarchy and academic domain-specific self-concepts at the bottom. The latter self-concept measures emphasize *self-esteem reactions* by posing self-evaluative questions, such as "How good are you in English?" By contrast, self-efficacy items focus exclusively on task-specific *performance expectations,* such as "How certain are you that you can diagram this sentence?" Although prior task reactions and future performance expectations are often correlated, Bandura (1997) notes it is possible conceptually to have high self-efficacy about a capability that one does not particularly esteem as well as the reverse.

...there is evidence that the more capable students judge themselves to be, the more challenging the goals they embrace.

There is growing evidence that, although self-efficacy beliefs are correlated with domain-specific self-concepts, self-efficacy measures offer predictive advantages when a task is familiar and can be specified precisely. For example, Pajares and Miller (1994) used path analysis procedures to examine the predictive and mediational roles of these two constructs in mathematical problem solving by college students. Math self-efficacy was more predictive of problem solving than was math self-concept or, for that matter, perceived usefulness of mathematics, prior experience with mathematics, or gender. The effect of prior math experiences on math problem solving was mediated primarily by self-efficacy beliefs, but self-concept played a small but significant role. Thus, when self-concept and self-efficacy beliefs are both included in regression equations, self-efficacy beliefs display discriminant validity by independently predicting future academic achievement. Although self-efficacy questionnaire items should be adapted to specific tasks, the scope of these tasks can vary on the basis of the user's intended purpose, ranging from proficiency in an academic domain (e.g., writing or mathematics) to proficiency in a subskill (e.g., grammar or fractions). This second criterion for developing self-efficacy measures involves their *correspondence* to the performance capability in question. Pajares (1996a) demonstrated that the predictiveness of self-efficacy measures increases as a function of both their specificity and correspondence to a skill. Thus, self-efficacy differs from self-concept in both its specificity and correspondence to varying performance tasks and contexts.

Another closely associated construct to self-efficacy is *perceived control,* which emerged from research on locus of control (Rotter, 1966). Perceived control refers to general expectancies about whether outcomes are controlled by one's behavior or by external forces, and it is theorized that an internal locus of control should support self-directed courses of action, whereas an external locus of control should discourage them. Locus-of-control scales are neither task nor domain specific in their item content but rather refer to general beliefs about the internality or externality of causality. Bandura (1986) has questioned the value of general control beliefs because students may feel anxious about controlling one type of subject matter or performance setting (e.g., solving mathematical problems in a limited time period) but not others. In support of this contention, Smith (1989) found that locus of control measures did not predict improvements in academic performance or reductions in anxiety in highly self-anxious students who underwent an intensive coping skills training program, but self-efficacy scales did predict such improvements.

In summary, measures of self-efficacy are not only conceptually distinctive from closely associated constructs such as outcome expectancies, self-concept, and perceived control, they have discriminant validity in predicting a variety of academic outcomes.

ROLE OF SELF-EFFICACY IN ACADEMIC MOTIVATION

Self-efficacy beliefs have also shown convergent validity in influencing such key indices of academic motivation as choice of activities, level of effort, persistence, and emotional reactions. There is evidence (Bandura, 1997) that self-efficacious students participate more readily, work harder, persist longer, and have fewer adverse emotional reactions when they encounter difficulties than do those who doubt their capabilities.

In terms of *choice of activities,* self-efficacious students undertake difficult and challenging tasks more readily than do in-

efficacious students. Bandura and Schunk (1981) found that students' mathematical self-efficacy beliefs were predictive of their choice of engaging in subtraction problems rather than in a different type of task: The higher the children's sense of efficacy, the greater their choice of the arithmetic activity. Zimmerman and Kitsantas (1997; 1999) also found self-efficacy to be highly correlated with students' rated intrinsic interest in a motoric learning task as well as in a writing revision task. Furthermore, measures of self-efficacy correlate significantly with students' choice of majors in college, success in course work, and perseverance (Hackett & Betz, 1989; Lent, Brown, & Larkin, 1984).

Two decades of research have clearly established the validity of self-efficacy as a predictor of students' motivation and learning.

Self-efficacy beliefs are predictive of two measures of students' *effort:* rate of performance and expenditure of energy. For example, Schunk and colleagues found that perceived self-efficacy for learning correlates positively with students' rate of solution of arithmetic problems (Schunk & Hanson, 1985; Schunk, Hanson, & Cox, 1987). Salomon (1984) has found that self-efficacy is positively related to self-rated mental effort and achievement during students' learning from text material that was perceived as difficult. Regarding the effects of perceived self-efficacy on *persistence,* path analyses have shown that it influences students' skill acquisition both directly and indirectly by increasing their persistence (Schunk, 1981). The direct effect indicates that perceived self-efficacy influences students' methods of learning as well as their motivational processes. These results validate the mediational role that self-efficacy plays in motivating persistence and academic achievement. In a meta-analytic review of nearly 70 studies of persistence and rate measures of motivation, Multon, Brown, and Lent (1991) found a significant positive effect size of students' self-efficacy beliefs.

Student's beliefs about their efficacy to manage academic task demands can also influence them *emotionally* by decreasing their stress, anxiety, and depression (Bandura, 1997). For example, Pajares and Kranzler (1995) have studied the relationship between self-efficacy and students' anxiety reactions regarding mathematics. Although the two measures were negatively correlated, only self-efficacy was predictive of mathematics performance when compared in a joint path analysis. There is also evidence that students' performance in academically threatening situations depends more on efficacy beliefs than on anxiety arousal. Siegel, Galassi, and Ware (1985) found that self-efficacy beliefs are more predictive of math performance than is math anxiety. The strength of efficacy beliefs accounted for more than 13% of the variance in their final math grades, whereas math anxiety did not prove to be a significant predictor. These studies provide clear evidence of the discriminant and predictive validity of self-efficacy measures, and they suggest particular benefit if educators focus on fostering a positive sense of personal efficacy rather than merely diminishing scholastic anxiety.

SELF-EFFICACY AND SELF-REGULATION OF LEARNING

Self-efficacy beliefs also provide students with a sense of agency to motivate their learning through use of such self-regulatory processes as goal setting, self-monitoring, self-evaluation, and strategy use. For example, there is evidence (Zimmerman, Bandura, & Martinez-Pons, 1992) that the more capable students judge themselves to be, the more challenging the *goals* they embrace. When self-efficacy and personal goal setting from the beginning of a school term were used jointly to predict final course grades in high school social studies, they increased prediction by 31% over a measure of prior grades in social studies. Similarly, when self-efficacy and personal goal setting were compared with the verbal subscale of the Scholastic Aptitude Test, there was an increase of 35% in predicting college students' final grades in a writing course (Zimmerman & Bandura, 1994). Although prior course grades and general measures of ability are considered exemplary predictors of achievement, these studies demonstrated that self-efficacy beliefs and goal setting add significantly to the predictiveness of these measures.

The effects of efficacy beliefs on students' *self-monitoring* was studied during concept learning (Bouffard-Bouchard, Parent, & Larivee, 1991). Efficacious students were better at monitoring their working time, more persistent, less likely to reject correct hypotheses prematurely, and better at solving conceptual problems than inefficacious students of equal ability. Self-efficacy beliefs also affect the *self-evaluation* standards students use to judge the outcomes of their self-monitoring. In a path analytic study (Zimmerman & Bandura, 1994), self-efficacy for writing beliefs significantly predicted college students' personal standards for the quality of writing considered self-satisfying as well as their goal setting and writing proficiency. Self-efficacy beliefs also motivate students' use of *learning strategies*. With fifth, eighth, and eleventh grade students, there were developmental increases in perceived verbal and mathematical efficacy as well as strategy use, and there was a substantial relation (16 to 18% shared variance) between efficacy beliefs and strategy use across the three grade levels of schooling (Zimmerman & Martinez-Pons, 1990).

The greater motivation and self-regulation of learning of self-efficacious students produces higher *academic achievement* according to a range of measures. Multon, Brown, and Lent (1991) found an overall effect size of .38, indicating that self-efficacy accounted for approximately 14% of the variance in students' academic performance across a variety of student samples, experimental designs, and criterion measures. This represents further evidence of the convergent validity of self-efficacy beliefs.

INSTRUCTIONAL AND SOCIAL INFLUENCES ON SELF-EFFICACY BELIEFS

In contrast to trait measures of self-perceptions, self-efficacy indices focus on cognitive beliefs that are readily influenced by four types of experience: enactive attainment, vicarious experience, verbal persuasion, and physiological states. *Enactive* experiences are the most influential source of efficacy belief because they are predicated on the outcomes of personal experiences, whereas *vicarious* influences depend on an observer's self-comparison with as well as outcomes attained by a model. If a model is viewed as more able or talented, observers will discount the relevance of the model's performance outcomes for themselves. *Verbal persuasion* has an even more limited impact on students' self-efficacy because outcomes are described, not directly witnessed, and thus depend on the credibility of the persuader. Finally, students base their self-efficacy judgments on their perceived *physiological reactions,* such as fatigue, stress, and other emotions that are often interpreted as indicators of physical incapability. Unlike self-beliefs assumed to have trait-like stability across time and setting, self-efficacy is assumed to be responsive to changes in personal context and outcomes, whether experienced directly, vicariously, verbally, or physiologically. As a result of this sensitivity, self-efficacy beliefs are studied as indicators of change during instructional interventions as well as indicators of initial individual differences.

To facilitate improvements in perceived efficacy, researchers have trained students with learning and motivational deficiencies by modeling specific self-regulatory techniques, describing their form, and providing enactive feedback regarding their impact. For example, youngsters who observed an adult model the use [of] a cognitive strategy had significantly higher levels of perceived efficacy and academic skills than youngsters who received didactic instruction (Schunk, 1981). Asking students to set proximal goals enhanced self-efficacy and skill development more effectively than asking them to set distal goals because the proximal attainments provide evidence of growing capability (Bandura & Schunk, 1981). Verbally encouraging students to set their own goals improved not only their efficacy beliefs and achievement but also their commitment to attaining the goals (Schunk, 1985). The frequency and immediacy of enactive feedback also created higher perceptions of personal efficacy (Schunk, 1983). When students were taught to attribute their enactive feedback to effort, they perceived greater progress, maintained higher motivation, and reported greater efficacy for further learning (Schunk, 1987). In these investigations, Schunk and his colleagues not only demonstrated the sensitivity of efficacy beliefs to instructional interventions, but also the mediational role of these beliefs in explaining changes in learners' self-regulation and achievement outcomes (Berry, 1987; Schunk, 1981). Self-efficacy beliefs increased prediction of academic outcomes as much as 25% of the variance above instructional influences. Clearly, students' self-efficacy beliefs are responsive to changes in instructional experience and play a causal role in students' development and use of academic competencies.

CONCLUSION

Students' self-perceptions of efficacy are distinctive from related motivational constructs because of their specificity and close correspondence to performance tasks. These cognitive beliefs differ conceptually and psychometrically from trait self-belief measures due to their sensitivity to variations in experience and task and situational context. Two decades of research have clearly established the validity of self-efficacy as a predictor of students' motivation and learning. Although self-efficacy correlates with other related constructs, it has also shown discriminant validity by its unique predictiveness of these outcomes when included in multiple regression analyses. It has shown convergent validity in predicting diverse forms of motivation, such as students' activity choices, effort, persistence, and emotional reactions. Finally, when studied as a mediating variable in training studies, self-efficacy has proven to be responsive to improvements in students' methods of learning (especially those involving greater self-regulation) and predictive of achievement outcomes. This empirical evidence of its role as a potent mediator of students' learning and motivation confirms the historic wisdom of educators that students' self-beliefs about academic capabilities do play an essential role in their motivation to achieve.

I express my gratitude to Frank Pajares and Manuel Martinez-Pons for their helpful comments on an earlier draft of this article.

Address correspondence and reprint requests to Barry J. Zimmerman, Educational Psychology Program, CUNY Graduate School, 365 Fifth Ave., New York, NY 10016–4309.

From *Contemporary Educational Psychology*, Volume 25, January 2000, pp. 82-91. © 2000 by Academic Press. Reprinted by permission of the publisher.

Teaching Students to Regulate Their Own Behavior

Lewis R. Johnson

Christine E. Johnson

During the 1994–95 school year, 43% of all students with disabilities were served in general education classrooms (18th Annual Report, 1997).	Children and Adults with Attention Deficit Disorders (CHADD) estimates that there are 3.5 million children with ADHD (CHADD, 1993).	Of the 5.4 million children nationwide with disabilities, 8.7% are identified as emotionally disturbed/behavior disordered, and 80% of these children are co-diagnosed with ADHD (Mathes & Bender, 1997).

Before general education teachers refer a child to special education services, the teachers must implement program modifications and strategies and document that the modifications were insufficient to remedy the student's problem. For these reasons, general educators and special education teachers/consultants need methods to successfully include students with disabilities in general education programs.

A Question of Generalization

Sometimes, consultants and classroom teachers collaboratively develop prereferral interventions or behavior management plans that require the teacher to monitor, record, and issue contingent reinforcers. This type of behavior management program is time-consuming; and if more than one student in the class is "on a plan," it can be overwhelming.

In 1973 Glynn, Thomas, and Shee described an effective procedure for general education teachers to employ so students can self-monitor and improve their on-task behavior. Although recent research has focused on the use of self-regulation techniques for students with disabilities in special education settings, it is peculiar that the technique is not used more in general education classrooms as prereferral interventions and to facilitate inclusion of students with disabilities. Self-regulation techniques can be used with students from preschool age through postsecondary age when educators adapt the level of sophistication to the age group. One limitation of self-regulation training conducted by special education teachers in the special education setting is the lack of generalization of the behavior change in the general education setting.

Self-regulation requires students to stop, think about what they are doing, compare their behavior to a criterion, record the results of their comparison, and receive reinforcement for their behavior if it meets the criterion.

One way to facilitate generalization of skills is to provide the training in the setting in which you want the generalization to occur (Guevremont, Osnes, & Stokes, 1988). In this article we present a description of self-regulation and the specific procedures for teaching students to employ self-regulation of classroom work-study behavior.

Components of Self-Regulation

Self-regulation requires students to stop, think about what they are doing, compare their behavior to a criterion, record the results of their comparison, and receive reinforcement for their behavior if it meets the criterion (Webber, Scheuermann, McCall, & Coleman, 1993). Self-monitoring involves all the steps in self-regulation, except the issuing of reinforcement.

When you begin the program, first teach students to ask the monitoring question aloud. Then, as the program becomes more routine, students ask the monitoring question in a whisper. In the initial stages of self-regulation, use a tone sounded in the classroom at random intervals to cue the students to ask the question. Cued monitoring is much more effective than uncued monitoring. When you must conduct a training session outside the general classroom, the use of the same tone aids in maintaining the skills across settings.

Self-regulation techniques can be used with students from preschool age through postsecondary age. Self-regulation is most widely used during independent seatwork.

The Steps of Self-Regulation

Students use the following sequence of steps to use self-regulation:

1. Self-observation—looking at one's own behavior given a predetermined criterion.

2. Self-assessment—deciding if the behavior has occurred, through some self-questioning activity.

3. Self-recording—recording the decision made during self-assessment on a private recording form.

4. Self-determination of reinforcement—setting a criterion for success, and selecting a reinforcer from a menu of reinforcers.

5. Self-administration of reinforcement—administering a reinforcer to oneself (Glynn et al., 1973).

According to Barkley (1990), 3%–5% of all school-age children may have attention deficit hyperactivity disorder (ADHD).

Target Behavior

Self-regulation is most widely used during independent seatwork; however, you may apply the technique to a variety of classroom activities. Here are kinds of behavior commonly targeted by self-regulation:

- Staying on task.
- Assignment completion (productivity).

- Appropriate classroom behavior (such as staying in one's seat).
- Accuracy of completed work (percent correct).

The student should focus on positive behavior. The choice of a target behavior for self-regulation is important and may be individually selected, depending on student needs.

Initially, you may want to select a single target behavior for the entire class group. Then, after the students learn the technique, you may want to select different kinds of behavior to target to meet the needs of individual students. Although teachers most frequently select on-task behavior, improvement in on-task behavior may not promote improved academic outcomes. Researchers have found that a *combination* of types of target behavior, including both work-study and accuracy of assignment completion, seems to work best (Rooney, Polloway, & Hallahan, 1985). Young students respond to task completion as a criterion, whereas older students respond best to completion of tasks with an accuracy criterion (Maag, Reid, & DiGanni, 1993).

Procedure

Before you begin a self-regulatory program, collect program data to determine the students' current level of performance regarding the behavior problem. The special education teacher/consultant or a classroom assistant can collect preintervention "on-task" data using an interval observation method on several students over several visits.

For interval observation, the observer records "+" or "–" every 10 seconds to indicate if the student was on/off task during that interval. The observer then divides the number of intervals marked "+" by the total number of intervals in the observation to get a percentage of time on task (see Figure 1). Then the teacher begins the procedure for teaching the students to self-regulate their behavior, as follows:

1. Model the procedure, using a suitable behavior. Model being cued to engage in self-observation/recording by a tone provided by an audiotape (available from ADD Warehouse; see box, "Internet Sites").

2. Students observe you modeling the procedure.

Internet Sites for ADHD

Children and Adults with Attention Deficit Disorders

http://www.chadd.org

Teaching Children with ADHD

http://www.kidsource.com/kidsource/content2/add.html

A.D.D. Warehouse (catalog)

http://www.addwarehouse.com

ADD Treatment Information

http://www.mediconsult.com/add/shareware/ decad_brain/cope.html

The Five Steps of Self-Regulation

1. Self-observation.
2. Self-assessment.
3. Self-recording.
4. Self-determination of reinforcement.
5. Self-administration of reinforcement.

3. The students practice self-observation/recording on a single behavior.

4. Students employ the procedure daily.

5. The students graph their own observation data, in a manner appropriate to the age and ability of students.

6. Introduce self-reinforcement, such as "I did a good job staying on task," to the students. Better grades and teacher praise are effective reinforcers of accurate and honest self-recording.

7. Collect posttraining data over several observation sessions.

8. Suggest that some students self-observe and record a different behavior, based on individual student need.

9. With each student, review the weekly self-recording data. Introduce the concept of self-determination of a goal and self-reinforcement.

To teach students to use the self-regulation procedure, use the following direct instruction approaches—modeling and guided practice.

Figure 1. Classroom Observation of "On-Task" Student Behavior

Student	1	2	3	4	5	6	7	8	9	10	11	12	13	14	15	16	17	18	19	20	%

Format for Training Grade 2 Students: Modeling

1. "Class, I am concerned that when a student correctly responds to a question, I have not been providing praise as regularly as I should have. I need to find a way to improve how I respond to students who answer my questions."

2. *Thinking aloud*, say: "I will use this tape, which makes a sound every so often to remind me to ask myself, 'Did I offer praise for correct student answers?' If I did offer praise since the last tone, I will put a mark in the *yes* column on my record sheet if I said something like 'thank you' or 'that's correct.'" (See Figure 2 for the recording sheet.)

3. "Class, what am I going to ask myself?" Group response—

4. "Class, if I said something like 'thank you' or 'that's correct' to a student, what will I mark?" Group response—

You should then begin the tape, which has several tones at intervals of 2–4 minutes, and then begin a short group lesson that lends itself to individual student responding. At the sound of each tone, the teacher will ask in a volume so all students can hear, "Did I offer praise?" Each time, record on the chalkboard or on an overhead a mark in the "Yes" or "No" column.

After the short lesson is done, "think aloud," making comments about the number of marks in each column and how the students responded to the lesson. This think-aloud action is necessary to demonstrate to the students the relationship between the data collection and an evaluation of the outcome—the lesson.

After you have fully modeled the self-regulation procedure with the "think alouds," begin training the class using the single target behavior, such as on-task behavior.

Format for Training Group 2 Students: Guided Practice

1. Distribute a "Check Yourself" recording form to each student, and make a "Yes/No" box on the chalkboard. Say, "Class, when you hear the tone, ask yourself, 'Am I working?'" Provide examples of what is considered working and not working. This aspect of training is important so students will be able to make a quick decision and record it without asking you about a common task-related behavior. (Figures 3 and 4 show variations on the "Check Yourself" student form.)

Researchers have found that a *combination* of types of target behavior, including both work-study and accuracy of assignment completion, seems to work best

---

2. Begin the tape of the tones and continue talking: "When you hear the tone, ask yourself in your quiet voice, 'Am I working?' Put a check mark in the 'Yes' box or the 'No' box. Are you always going to be working or listening to the lessons? No, sometimes you won't. That's OK. This strategy will help you become a better student. It is not possible to always be working on an assignment."

3. Continue teaching the group lesson started during the modeling phase and the tape of the recorded tones. When the class hears the first tone, the students (with your assistance) ask out loud, "Am I working?" You answer "Yes" and record a check in the "Yes" box on the chalkboard. Each student will record the response on his or her record sheet. The procedure continues with tones at random intervals, which are frequent enough to allow four or five recordings within a 10–15-minute time period.

4. At the conclusion of the lesson, say, "You did a good job asking the 'Am I working?' question and recording your answer. We will practice this again later."

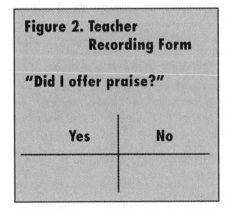

Figure 2. Teacher Recording Form

"Did I offer praise?"

| Yes | No |

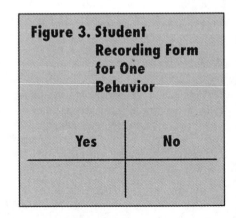

Figure 3. Student Recording Form for One Behavior

| Yes | No |

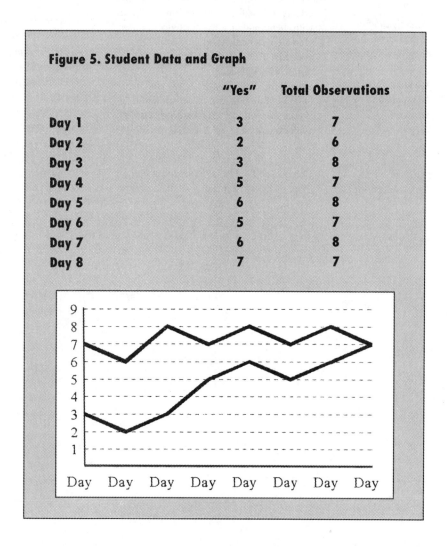

Figure 4. Student Recording Form for Several Types of Behavior

	Yes	No
"Am I working?"		
"Did I stay in my seat?"		
"Did I do my work?"		

Figure 5. Student Data and Graph

	"Yes"	Total Observations
Day 1	3	7
Day 2	2	6
Day 3	3	8
Day 4	5	7
Day 5	6	8
Day 6	5	7
Day 7	6	8
Day 8	7	7

Graphing and Record Keeping

Graphing the self-recording data can be an excellent activity for upper elementary age students to help them keep a long-term record of their performance and begin to set behavior goals. Older students can compute and record the percentage of "Yes" responses. Younger students may need to count total number of checks, "Yes" and "No," and record that total on a graph. Then they will count just the "Yes" checks and record that total on the graph. The goal is to make the distance between the total number of checks and number of "Yes" checks as small as possible. (See Figure 5 for an example of student data and a sample graph.)

Benefits and Potential

The strengths of the self-regulatory program include the following:

- Reduced teacher time for monitoring and responding to student behavior.
- The ability to vary the target behavior from simple on-task behavior to the complex self-monitoring of strategy usage.

- The ability to individualize target behavior to accommodate a variety of student ability levels.

The teaching of self-regulation has the potential of providing students with a skill that will have an ongoing benefit as students become self-directed, lifelong learners.

References

18th Annual Report affirms CEC's policy on inclusive settings. (1997). *CEC Today, 3*(7), 1.

Barkley, R. A. (1990). *Attention-deficit hyperactivity disorder: A handbook for the diagnosis and treatment.* New York: Guilford.*

Children and Adults with Attention Deficit Disorders. (1993). *CHADD facts 8: The national organization working for children and adults with attention deficit disorders.* Washington, DC: Author.*

Glynn, E. L., Thomas, J. D., & Shee, S. M. (1973). Behavioral self-control of on-task behavior in an elementary classroom. *Journal of Applied Behavior Analysis, 6*(1), 105–113.

Guevremont, D. C., Osnes, P. G., & Stokes, T. P. (1988). The functional role of preschoolers' verbalizations in the generalization of self-instructional training. *Journal of Applied Behavior Analysis, 21*(1), 45–55.

Maag, J. W., Reid, R., & DiGanni, S. A., (1993). Differential effects of self-monitoring attention, accuracy, and productivity. *Journal of Applied Behavior Analysis, 26*(3), 329–344.

Mathes, M. Y., & Bender, W. N. (1997). The effects of self-monitoring on children with attention-deficit/hyperactivity disorder who are receiving pharmacological interventions. *Remedial and Special Education, 18*(2), 121–128.

Rooney, K. J., Polloway, E. A., & Hallahan, D. P. (1985). The use of self-monitoring procedures with low IQ learning disabled students. *Journal of Learning Disabilities, 18,* 384–389.

Webber, J., Scheuermann, B., McCall, C., & Coleman, M. (1993). Research on self-monitoring as a behavior management technique in special education classrooms: A descriptive review. *Remedial and Special Education, 14*(2), 38–56.

BooksNow

Lewis R. Johnson *(CEC Chapter #345), Assistant Professor, Department of Special Education;* **Christine E. Johnson**, *Graduate Student, Department of Speech Pathology, Arkansas State University, State University.*

Address correspondence to Lewis R. Johnson, P.O. Box 1450, Arkansas State University, State University, AR 72467 (e-mail: Ljohnson@kiowa.astate.edu).

From *Teaching Exceptional Children,* March/April 1999, pp. 6-10. © 1999 by The Council for Exceptional Children. Reprinted by permission.

Reinforcement in Developmentally Appropriate Early Childhood Classrooms

As greater numbers of children with disabilities participate in early childhood programs, teachers are faced with the challenge of expanding their repertoire of teaching and guidance practices to accommodate the needs of children with diverse abilities and needs.

Tashawna K. Duncan, Kristen M. Kemple, and Tina M. Smith

Each day from 10:30 to 11:00, the children in Mrs. Kitchens's 1st-grade classroom are expected to sit silently in their desks and copy words from the chalkboard into their notebooks. Children who finish early are required to remain silently in their seats. After five minutes has passed, Mrs. Kitchens assesses whether every child in the class has been behaving according to the rules. If they have been, she makes a check mark on the chalkboard and announces, "Good! There's a check." If even one child has violated the rules, she announces "no check." At the end of the week, if 20 or more checks have accrued on the board, the whole group is awarded an extra-long Friday recess period. This longed-for reward is rarely achieved, however.

Five-year-old Rodney has recently joined Mr. Romero's kindergarten class. On his first day in his new class, Rodney punched a classmate and usurped the tricycle the other boy was riding. On Rodney's second day in the class, he shoved a child off a swing and dumped another out of her chair at the snack table. In an effort to deal with Rodney's problematic behavior, Mr. Romero is taking a number of steps, including making sure that Rodney knows the classroom rules and routines, helping Rodney learn language and skills to resolve conflicts, exploring ways to make Rodney feel welcome and a special part of the class, and arranging for a consultation with a special education specialist to see if support services would

be appropriate. Mr. Romero is concerned for the emotional and physical safety of the other children, and he believes that Rodney will have a hard time making friends if his reputation as an aggressor is allowed to solidify. He feels the need to act fast. Deciding that a system of reinforcement, along with other strategies, may help Rodney control his aggressive behavior, Mr. Romero implements a token reinforcement system. Rodney earns a ticket, accompanied by praise, for each 30-minute period during which he does not behave aggressively. At the end of the day, Rodney can trade a specified number of earned tickets for his choice of small toys.

The above examples illustrate two teachers' efforts to use the behavioral strategy of reinforcement—with varying degrees of appropriateness. In Mrs. Kitchens's class, reinforcement is being used as a means to get children to sit still and be quiet in the context of a developmentally inappropriate lesson. In an effort to keep children "on task," Mrs. Kitchens substitutes a control tactic for a meaningful and engaging curriculum. Mr. Romero, on the other hand, is making efforts to identify and address the reasons for Rodney's behavior. Furthermore, he believes that Rodney's behavior is so detrimental to himself and to the other children that additional measures must be used to achieve quick results and restore a sense of psychological safety in the classroom community. Mr. Romero utilizes a variety of strategies in the hopes of creating lasting change in Rodney's behavior.

Inclusion of Children With Special Needs

The trend toward including children with disabilities in early childhood education settings is growing (Wolery & Wilbers, 1994). As greater numbers of children with disabilities participate in early childhood programs, teachers are faced with the challenge of expanding their repertoire of teaching and guidance practices to accommodate the needs of children with diverse abilities and needs. To this end, teachers responsible for the care and education of diverse groups of young children are encouraged to examine their beliefs about their role in promoting children's development and learning, and to explore their understanding of developmentally appropriate practices as outlined by the National Association for the Education of Young Children (NAEYC) (Bredekamp & Copple, 1997).

Historically, early childhood special education has had stronger roots in behavioral psychology and applied behavior analysis than has early childhood education.

Recent federal legislation requires that children be educated in the "least restrictive environment." This means that, to the maximum extent possible, the setting in which children with special needs are educated should be the same as that in which typically developing children are educated, and that specialized services should be provided within the regular classroom (Thomas & Russo, 1995).

Early Childhood Education and Early Childhood Special Education

Most early childhood teachers have little or no training in early childhood special education. Historically, differences have existed between teachers who work with young children with disabilities and teachers who work with typically developing children, including different educational preparation, separate professional organiza-

tions, and reliance on different bodies of research (Wolery & Wilbers, 1994). As both groups of children are increasingly cared for and educated in the same programs, early childhood educators and early childhood special educators are called upon to work in collaboration to ensure that children receive individually appropriate education. This collaborative effort requires that all teachers have familiarity with and respect for the philosophy and practices of both disciplines.

Historically, early childhood special education has had stronger roots in behavioral psychology and applied behavior analysis than has early childhood education. As Wolery and Bredekamp (1994) noted, developmentally appropriate practices (DAP) (as outlined by NAEYC) have their roots primarily in maturational and constructivist perspectives. While current early childhood special education practices also tend to be rooted in constructivist perspectives, the additional influence of cultural transmission perspectives (including behaviorist models of learning) is evident. Given their diverse origins, it should not be surprising that the two disciplines would advocate, on occasion, different practices (Wolery & Bredekamp, 1994). This potential tension is exemplified in an editor's note found in the recent NAEYC publication *Including Children With Special Needs in Early Childhood Programs* (Wolery & Wilbers, 1994). Carol Copple (the series' editor) stated,

> Certainly early childhood educators are well aware of the limits of behaviorism as the sole approach to children's learning and are wary of overreliance on rewards as a motivational technique. From this vantage point, some readers may have a negative first response to some of the techniques described in this chapter. Although we must be aware of the limitations and pitfalls of such methods, I urge readers to keep an open mind about them.... They are not for every situation, but when used appropriately, they often succeed where other methods fail. (Wolery & Wilbers, 1994, p. 119)

The current authors hope that readers will be open to considering the judicious use of methods of reinforcement described in this article. When included as part of a total developmentally appropriate program and used after careful assessment of individual needs, these methods can be important tools for implementing *individually* appropriate practice.

Developmentally Appropriate Practice

In 1987, NAEYC published *Developmentally Appropriate Practice in Early Childhood Programs Serving Children From Birth to Age 8* (Bredekamp, 1987), which was revised and published in 1997 as *Developmentally Appropriate Practice in*

Figure 1

DAP Guidelines:
Developmentally Appropriate Practice for
3- Through 5-Year-Olds: Motivation and Guidance*

Appropriate Practices

Teachers draw on children's curiosity and desire to make sense of their world to motivate them to become involved in interesting learning activities. Teachers use verbal encouragement in ways that are genuine and related to an actual task or behavior, and acknowledge children's work with specific comments like, "I see you drew your older sister bigger than your brother."

In cases of children with special needs, such as those identified on an Individualized Education Plan, those resulting from environmental stress, such as violence, or when a child's aggressive behavior continually threatens others, teachers may develop an individualized behavioral plan based on observation of possible environmental "triggers" and/or other factors associated with the behavior. *This plan includes motivation and intervention strategies that assist and support the child to develop self-control and appropriate social behaviors.* (italics added)

Inappropriate Practices

A preponderance of experiences are either uninteresting and unchallenging, or so difficult and frustrating so as to diminish children's intrinsic motivation to learn. *To obtain children's participation, teachers typically rely on extrinsic rewards (stickers, privileges, etc.) or threats of punishment.* (italics added) Children with special needs or behavioral problems are isolated or punished for failure to meet group expectations rather than being provided with learning experiences at a reasonable level of difficulty.

Teachers constantly and indiscriminately use praise ("What a pretty picture"; "That's nice") so that it becomes meaningless and useless in motivating children. (italics added)

*Guidelines for 6-to 8-year-olds are virtually identical. See Bredekamp & Copple, 1997.

Early Childhood Programs (Bredekamp & Copple, 1997). Many have argued that DAP (see Figure 1) provides an appropriate educational context for the inclusion of young children with disabilities, assuming that the interpretations of DAP guidelines leave room for adaptations and extensions to meet the child's specific needs (Bredekamp, 1993; Carta, 1995; Carta, Atwater, Schwartz, & McConnell, 1993; Carta, Schwartz, Atwater, & McConnell, 1991; Wolery & Bredekamp, 1994; Wolery, Strain, & Bailey, 1992; Wolery, Werts, & Holcombe-Ligon, 1994). For some young children, this may mean the use of behavioral strategies, such as planned programs of systematic reinforcement. In fact, the current DAP guidelines do not identify reinforcement systems as inappropriate practice. Some early childhood educators, however, view many forms of reinforcement as completely unacceptable. If inclusion is to succeed, it may be necessary for teachers to consider using such strategies for particular children in particular circumstances.

While reinforcement through use of stickers, privileges, and praise is *not* identified as developmentally *inappropriate* practice, it does become inappropriate when used in exclusion of other means of promoting children's engagement and motivation, and when used indiscriminately (for the wrong children, and/or in the wrong situations). Children's active engagement is a guiding principle in both DAP and early childhood special education (Carta et al., 1993). As Carta et al. (1993) have pointed out, however, many young children with disabilities are less likely to engage spontaneously with materials in their environments (Peck, 1985; Weiner & Weiner, 1974). The teacher's active encouragement is needed to help such children become actively involved in learning opportunities. A principal goal of early intervention is to facilitate young children's active engagement with materials, activities, and the social environment through systematic instruction (Wolery et al., 1992). Such instruction may include use of reinforcement as incentives.

Behavioral Strategies in Early Childhood Education

Table 1		
Examples of Social, Activity, and Tangible Reinforcers in the Early Childhood Setting		
Social	**Activity**	**Tangible**
Praise	Extra playground time	Stickers
Smile	A special recording or tape	Prizes
Hugs	A party	Trinkets
Pat on back	Tablewasher or other desirable privilege	Tokens
Light squeeze on shoulder	Playing with an intriguing new toy	
Intangible- -Tangible		

Behavioral theory holds that behaviors acquired and displayed by young children can be attributed almost exclusively to their environment. Several behavioral strategies are employed by early childhood teachers to facilitate children's learning, including the use of praise and external rewards. However, practitioners often fail to identify these strategies in their repertoire and dismiss, out of hand, their use in the classroom. Misunderstandings may exist concerning the appropriate use and potential effectiveness of these strategies for young children. As a result, they are not always well accepted in the early childhood community (Henderick, 1998; Rodd, 1996; see also Strain et al., 1992).

A review of contemporary literature suggests that behavioral strategies are appropriate for creating and maintaining an environment conducive to growth and development (e.g., Peters, Neisworth, & Yawkey, 1985; Schloss & Smith, 1998). Research has demonstrated that behavioral strategies are successful in school settings with various diverse populations, including those with young children (Kazdin, 1994). Furthermore, while many such "best practices" are unrecognized by early childhood professionals, they are grounded in behavioral theory (Strain et al., 1992).

The Use of Positive Reinforcement

Positive reinforcement is perhaps the strategy most palatable to educators who are concerned about the misuse of behavioral strategies. A particular behavior is said to be positively reinforced when the behavior is followed by the presentation of a reward (e.g., praise, stickers) that results in increased frequency of the particular behavior (Schloss & Smith, 1998). For example, Stella has been reluctant to wash her hands before lunch. Mrs. Johnson begins consistently praising Stella when she washes her hands by saying, "Now your hands are nice and clean and ready for lunch!" Stella becomes more likely to wash her hands without protest. In this case, we can say that Stella's handwashing behavior has been positively reinforced.

Most frequently, positive reinforcement strategies are used to teach, maintain, or strengthen a variety of behaviors (Zirpoli, 1995). Although some early childhood teachers may be reluctant to endorse the use of reinforcement, they often unknowingly employ reinforcement strategies every day in their classroom (Henderick, 1998; Wolery, 1994).

Types of Reinforcers

Reinforcers frequently used by teachers generally fall within one of three categories: social, activity, or tangible (see Table 1). These three categories can be viewed along a continuum ranging from least to most intrusive. Social reinforcers are the least intrusive, in that they mimic the natural consequences of positive, prosocial behavior. At the other end of the continuum are tangible reinforcers. Tangible reinforcers involve the introduction of rewards that ordinarily may not be part of the routine. In selecting a reinforcer, the goal is to select the least intrusive reinforcer that is likely to be effective. If reinforcers other than social ones are necessary, teachers should develop a plan to move gradually toward social reinforcers. The following sections describe each category of reinforcers and how they can be used effectively within the context of developmentally appropriate practice.

Social reinforcers. Teachers employ social reinforcers when they use interpersonal interactions to reinforce behaviors (Schloss & Smith, 1998). Some commonly used social reinforcers include positive nonverbal behaviors (e.g., smiling) and praise (Alberto & Troutman, 1990; Sulzer-Azaroff & Mayer, 1991). Because they are convenient, practical, and can be highly effective, social reinforcers are the most widely accepted and frequently used type of reinforcer in the early childhood classroom (Sulzer-Azaroff & Mayer, 1991). One means of effectively reinforcing a child's behavior via social reinforcement is by using a "positive personal message" (Gordon, 1974; Kostelnik, Stein, Whiren, & Soderman, 1998). For example, Ms. Tarrant says, "Sally, you put the caps back on the markers. I'm pleased. Now the markers won't get dried up. They'll be fresh and ready when someone else wants to use them." This positive personal message reminds Sally of the rule (put the caps on the markers) at a time when Sally has clear and immediate proof that she is able to follow the rule. The personal message pinpoints a specific desirable behavior, and lets the child know why the behavior is appropriate. When used appropriately, social reinforcers have been shown to enhance children's self-esteem (Sulzer-Azaroff & Mayer, 1991). When used in tandem with less natural (e.g., tangible) reinforcers, social reinforcers have been shown to enhance the power of those less natural reinforcers (Sulzer-Azaroff & Mayer, 1991).

Many early childhood teachers have concerns about the use of tangible reinforcers and believe that they cannot be used appropriately in the early childhood classroom.

Of the various types of social reinforcers, praise is used most frequently and deliberately by teachers (Alberto & Troutman, 1990). In recent years, several articles have been published on the topic of praise (Hitz & Driscoll, 1988; Marshall, 1995; Van der Wilt, 1996). While praise has the potential to enhance children's self-esteem, research has demonstrated that certain kinds of praise may actually lower children's self-confidence, inhibit achievement, and make children reliant on external (as opposed to internal) controls (Kamii, 1984; Stringer & Hurt, 1981, as cited in Hitz & Driscoll, 1988). These authors have drawn distinctions between "effective praise" (sometimes called "encouragement") and "ineffective praise."

Effective praise is consistent with commonly held goals of early childhood education: promoting children's positive self-concept, autonomy, self-reliance, and motivation for learning (Hitz & Driscoll, 1988).

Effective praise is specific. Instead of saying, "Justin, what a lovely job you did cleaning up the blocks," Mrs. Constanz says, "Justin, you put each block in its place on the shelf." In this case, Mrs. Constanz leaves judgment about the *quality* of the effort to the child. By pinpointing specific aspects of the child's behavior or product (rather than using vague, general praise), Mrs. Constanz communicates that she has paid attention to, and is genuinely interested in, what the child has done (Hitz & Driscoll, 1988).

Effective praise generally is delivered privately. Public uses of praise, such as, "I like the way Carlos is sitting so quietly," have a variety of disadvantages. Such statements are typically intended to manipulate children into following another child's example. In the example, the message was, "Carlos is doing a better job of sitting than are the rest of you." With time, young children may come to resent this management, and resent a child who is the frequent recipient of such public praise (Chandler, 1981; Gordon, 1974). As an alternative, the teacher could whisper the statement quietly to Carlos, and/or say to the other children, "Think about what you need to do to be ready to listen." As individual children comply, the teacher may quickly acknowledge each child, "Caitlin is ready, Tyler is ready; thank you, Nicholas, Lakeesha, and Ali…" (Marshall, 1995).

Another characteristic of effective praise is that it emphasizes improvement of process, rather than the finished product. As Daryl passes out individual placemats to his classmates, he states their names. Mrs. Thompson says, "Daryl, you are learning more names. You remembered Tom and Peg today." She could have said, "Daryl, you are a great rememberer," but she chose not to, because Daryl knows that he did not remember everyone's name, and tomorrow he may forget some that he knew today. In this example, Mrs. Thompson's praise is specific and is focused on the individual child's improvement.

Activity reinforcers. Teachers employ activity reinforcers when they use access to a pleasurable activity as a reinforcer (Sulzer-Azaroff & Mayer, 1991). Some commonly used and effective activity reinforcers include doing a special project, being a classroom helper, and having extra free-choice time (Sulzer-Azaroff & Mayer, 1991). When using activity reinforcers, teachers create a schedule in which an enjoyable activity follows the behavior they are trying to change or modify (Sulzer-Azaroff & Mayer, 1991). Teachers often use such activity reinforcers unknowingly. Following social reinforcers, activity reinforcers are the most frequently used (Alberto & Troutman, 1990), probably because teachers view them as more convenient and less intrusive than tangible reinforcers (Sulzer-Azaroff & Mayer, 1991). When used appropri-

Figure 2

Guidelines for Using Reinforcers

Reinforcers are unique to an individual. There are no universal reinforcers. What one child finds reinforcing another child may not. Therefore, teachers must consider each child's interests when selecting appropriate reinforcers.

Reinforcers must be perceived by children as being worth the time and energy it takes to achieve them. In other words, the reinforcer must be more desirable to the child than the behavior the teacher is attempting to modify.

Teacher expectations must be clear to the children. Children must clearly understand what specific behaviors are expected of them and know what is required of them to earn the reinforcer.

Reinforcers must be awarded immediately after the desired behavior. If reinforcers are not awarded immediately, they will not be effective.

Use more natural reinforcers whenever possible. Teachers should first consider the least intrusive reinforcer to modify children's behavior. For example, consider social reinforcers before tangible reinforcers.

Use reinforcers less frequently when children begin to exhibit the desired behavior. Later, after the targeted behavior is modified, teachers can phase out the use of reinforcement.

ately, activity reinforcers can modify a wide variety of behaviors. The following examples illustrate the appropriate use of activity reinforcers.

In Miss Annie's class, a brief playground period is scheduled to follow center clean-up time. Miss Annie reminds the children that the sooner they have the centers cleaned up, the sooner they will be able to enjoy the playground. It appears that the playground time is reinforcing children's quick clean-up behavior: They consistently get the job done with little dawdling.

As part of a total plan to reduce Christopher's habit of using his cupped hands to toss water out of the water table, Mrs. Jackson has told Christopher that each day he plays without throwing water out of the table, he may be table washer after snack time (which Christopher delights in doing). This strategy was implemented following efforts to help Christopher develop appropriate behavior through demonstrations and by redirecting him with water toys chosen specifically to match his interests.

Tangible reinforcers. Teachers sometimes employ tangible reinforcers, such as stickers and prizes, to strengthen and modify behavior in the early childhood classroom. Tangible reinforcers are most often used to modify and maintain the behavior of children with severe behavior problems (Vaughn, Bos, & Schumm, 1997).

Stacey, who has mild mental retardation, is a member of Miss Hamrick's preschool class. She rarely participates during free-choice activities. Miss Hamrick has tried a variety of strategies to increase Stacey's engagement, in-

cluding using effective praise, making sure a range of activity options are developmentally appropriate for Stacey, modeling appropriate behaviors, and implementing prompting strategies. None of these strategies appear to work. Aware of Stacey's love of the TV show "Barney," Miss Hamrick decides to award Barney stickers to Stacey when she actively participates. Stacey begins to participate more often in classroom activities.

One major advantage of tangible reinforcers is that they almost always guarantee quick behavioral change (Alberto & Troutman, 1990), even when other strategies (including other types of reinforcers) fail. Although the use of tangible reinforcers can be very effective, their use in early childhood classrooms has been highly controversial. Many early childhood teachers have concerns about the use of tangible reinforcers and believe that they cannot be used appropriately in the early childhood classroom. Such reinforcers often are intrusive, and their effective use requires large amounts of teacher time and commitment.

Given these disadvantages, when using tangible reinforcers teachers should gradually move toward using more intangible, less intrusive reinforcers (Henderick, 1998). Teachers can accomplish this goal by accompanying all tangible reinforcers with social reinforcers (e.g., praise). Later, as children begin to exhibit the desired behavior consistently, the teacher may begin to taper off the use of tangible reinforcers while maintaining the use of social reinforcers. Eventually, the teacher will no longer need to award tangible reinforcers after the desired behavior occurs. In time, the teacher also should be able to fade out the use of social reinforcers, and the children will begin to assume control over their own behaviors.

Questions Frequently Asked About Reinforcement Strategies

The following is a discussion of some of the most common concerns about reinforcement strategies, particularly tangible ones.

Are reinforcers bribes? Some have described reinforcement strategies as bribery (Kohn, 1993). Kazdin (1975) argues that such characterizations misconstrue the concepts of reinforcement and bribery:

> Bribery refers to the illicit use of rewards, gifts, or favors to pervert judgment or corrupt the conduct of someone. With bribery, reward is used for the purpose of changing behavior, but the behavior is corrupt, illegal or immoral in some way. With reinforcement, as typically employed, events are delivered for behaviors which are generally agreed upon to benefit the client, society, or both. (p. 50)

Kazdin's arguments point to clear distinctions between bribery and giving reinforcement for appropriate behaviors. No one would doubt that receiving pay for work is reinforcing, but few would suggest it is bribery. The difference may lie in the fact that bribes usually are conducted in secret for an improper purpose.

Does the use of reinforcers lower intrinsic motivation? Intrinsic motivation refers to motivation that comes from within the child or from the activity in which the child is involved. Thus, an intrinsically motivated child would engage in an activity for its own sake (Eisenberger & Cameron, 1996). For example, external rewards frequently are used to motivate children extrinsically.

Some researchers have suggested that the use of reinforcers undermines intrinsic motivation (Kohn, 1993; Lepper & Greene, 1975). Lepper & Greene (1975) conducted a series of experiments on the effects of offering a child a tangible reward to engage in an initially interesting task in the absence of any expectation of external rewards. The results of their experiments suggested that extrinsic rewards can lower intrinsic motivation (Lepper & Greene, 1975). Therefore, when reinforcement is withdrawn after increasing a particular behavior, an individual may engage in an activity less often than before the reinforcement was introduced (Eisenberger & Cameron, 1996). Recent research offers alternative conclusions. After conducting a meta-analysis of over 20 years of research, Cameron and Pierce (1994) concluded that a tangible reward system contingent on performance will not have a negative effect on children's intrinsic motivation. In fact, they propose that external rewards, when used appropriately, can play an invaluable role in increas-

ing children's intrinsic motivation (Cameron & Pierce, 1994, 1996; seel also Eisenberger & Cameron, 1996, 1998).

Although the evidence is still inconclusive, the results do suggest that negative effects of rewards occur under limited conditions, such as giving tangible rewards without regard to performance level. For example, if a teacher rewards a child regardless of performance, the child's intrinsic motivation may diminish for the particular activity. When external rewards are contingent on a child's performance, however, they can be used to enhance the child's intrinsic motivation for the particular activity. This is true because the positive or negative experiences surrounding an activity or task are likely to influence whether the activity is perceived as intrinsically enjoyable or unpleasurable (Eisenberger & Cameron, 1996). Therefore, the authors advocate the use of external reinforcement for behaviors that, for a particular child, are not currently intrinsically reinforcing. For example, children who hit other children to obtain desired toys may find getting what they want to be more intrinsically reinforcing than positive social behavior. In this case, the introduction of external reinforcers for prosocial behavior is unlikely to diminish intrinsic motivation.

By using reinforcement, are teachers "paying" children to learn? Some argue that rather than being "paid" to behave a certain way or complete certain tasks, children should do these things simply because they are the right thing to do (Harlen, 1996; Schloss & Smith, 1998; Sulzer-Azaroff & Mayer, 1991). Children's individual differences (e.g., ability levels) often require teachers to use a number of strategies to meet each child's individual needs. An important goal of early childhood education is to move children toward behaving appropriately for moral reasons; in other words, "because it is the right thing to do." Strong evidence exists, however, that the behavior of preschoolers and primary grade children is largely controlled by external factors (Bandura, 1986; Walker, deVries, & Trevarthen, 1989). The move from external control to internalized "self-discipline" is only gradually achieved during this age. Adults can help children learn to behave in appropriate ways for moral reasons by combining developmentally appropriate explanations with carefully chosen consequences (see Kostelnik et al., 1998).

Must teachers use reinforcement "equally"? It is important that early childhood teachers recognize children's unique differences (Bredekamp & Copple, 1997) and structure the early childhood classroom environment so that it meets each child's individual needs. This does not mean, however, that all children will be treated the same or even equally. In fact, the premise that all children should be treated equally is incongruent with developmentally appropriate practices (Zirpoli, 1995; see also Bredekamp & Copple, 1997). Early childhood teachers must recognize that all children are unique and develop

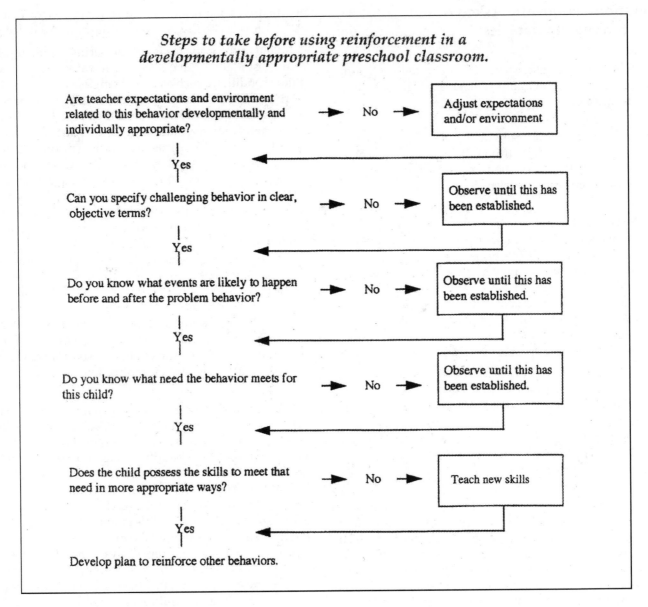

Figure 3

at different rates (Bredekamp & Copple, 1997); therefore, some children may require special accommodations.

Using Reinforcers Effectively

Sometimes, reinforcement strategies fail because they are implemented incorrectly. Early childhood teachers should consider general guidelines when using reinforcers in their classroom (see Figure 2). Furthermore, the teacher must fully understand the behavior and the function it serves for the child before beginning a reinforcement program (see Figure 3).

Once a decision has been made to use reinforcement strategies, teachers must carefully consider implementation to ensure that the strategies are effective and to minimize any potential effects on the child's intrinsic motivation. This process can be viewed as consisting of four states: 1) behavior identification, 2) selection of reinforcers, 3) implementation, 4) and evaluation and fading.

Behavior identification. In identifying the behavior, it is important to be as clear and objective as possible about the exact nature of the behavior, as well as about the times and settings under which the plan will be implemented. For example, while running in the classroom setting is dangerous, it is an important developmental activity outside the classroom. In order for the strategy to be successful, the child must understand not only "what" is being targeted, but also "when" and "where."

Selection of reinforcers. The selection of reinforcers is a crucial step, because a successful reinforcer must be more powerful than the intrinsic reward of engaging in the behavior. However, the reinforcement plan also must be as naturalistic as possible. Tangible reinforcers should be used only as a last resort, either because other classes of reinforcers have been unsuccessful or because it is necessary to eliminate a behavior immediately (e.g., ones that are dangerous to the child or others). Social reinforcers should be considered first, by following the guidelines for effective praise. If praise is unsuccessful, teachers may want to consider using an activity reinforcer. One way to select activity reinforcers is to think about the following question: If given complete free choice in the classroom, what would this child choose to do?

Another very important consideration in the selection of reinforcers involves understanding the function that the challenging behavior is serving. For example, many preschoolers engage in challenging behaviors in order to gain attention. If children are not given more appropriate ways to obtain needed attention, the program is unlikely ot be successful.

Implementation. In the implementation stage, the child receives the reinforcer contingent upon the appropriate behavior. Intitially, the child may need to receive reinforcement very frequently if the challenging behavior occurs frequently. As the child's behavior improves, the time between rewards can be extended. Another strategy is to "shape" the child's behavior, which teachers can do by breaking down the desired behavior into small steps. Each step is then reinforced on each occurrence. Teachers move to the next step only when the previous one is mastered (Schloss & Smith, 1998). Activity or tangible reinforcers should be accompanied by social praise.

Evaluation and fading. Before beginning the intervention, base line observations need to be made so that any improvement can be systematically evaluated. As the program is implemented, the teacher will want to continue keeping records. As the child's behavior improves, the reinforcement should be phased out. This can be done by reducing the frequency of the reinforcer and beginning to rely on social praise more often than on tangible or activity reinforcers. If the child begins to revert to "bad habits," the program can be adjusted.

When Are Reinforcers Appropriate?

Reinforcement strategies, when used appropriately, can have numerous benefits. They are not, however, a cure-all. In the introductory example, Mrs. Kitchens attempted to use reinforcement as a substitute for appropriate practice. Rather than attempting to rely on reinforcement as a primary means of motivation and management, teachers may incorporate such strategies within the context of a developmentally appropriate program. Use of reinforcement certainly cannot substitute for a teacher establishing a warm, nurturing, and enticing classroom with develop-

mentally appropraite materials, activities, and interactions (Wolery, 1994). Within such developmentally appropriate contexts, reinforcement strategies provide teachers with an effective means to help those children who require additional assistance in meeting particular behavioral, cognitive, and social goals. In all cases, the reinforcement strategy must be ethically definible, compliant with all relevant school policies (Wolery & Bredekamp, 1994), and consistent with the program's philosophy.

Decisions about individual appropriateness are not always easy to make. Teachers must take into consideration all relevant factors bearing on the appropriateness of the strategy selected. Teachers are better equipped to make these assessments when they have solid knowledge of typical and atypical child development; are well acquainted with the needs, capabilities, and personalities of the children in their care; and are familiar with a wide continuum of strategies. Furthermore, they also must consider the student's familial and cultural experiences, the expectations and experiences of the student's family, and the mores of the society in which the student interacts (Bredekamp & Copple, 1997). The DAP guidelines (Bredekamp & Copple, 1997) emphasize the importance of children's cultural backgrounds. Developmentally appropriate practices should not discriminate against children from diverse backgrounds; rather, they should level the playing field (see Bredekamp & Copple, 1997). Therefore, when considering the use of various reinforcement strategies, teachers must consider the whole child, including his or her abilities, special needs, personality, and cultural background.

When a teacher works with young children who present a broad range of abilities, challenges, and cultural values, it is particularly improtant that he or she be an adaptive and thoughtful problem-solver, while respecting children's individuality. A widened range of acceptable options from which to choose, coupled with a keen sense of individual and situational needs, can empower teachers to make good decisions for a diversity of young children.

References

Alberto, P. A., & Troutman, A.C. (1990). *Applied behavior analysis for teachers* (3rd ed.). Columbus, OH: Merrill.

Bandura, A. (1986). *Social foundations of thought and action: A social cognitive theory.* Englewood Cliffs, NJ: Prentice-Hall.

Bredekamp, S. (1987). *Developmentally appropriate practice in early childhood programs serving children from birth through age eight.* Washington, DC: National Association for the Education of Young Children.

Bredekamp, S. (1993). The relationship between early childhood education and early childhood special education: Healthy marriage or family feud? *Topics in Early Childhood Special Education, 13*(3), 258–273.

Bredekamp, S., & Copple, C. (1997). *Developmentally appropriate practice in early childhood programs* (Rev. ed.). Washington,

DC: National Association for the Education of Young Children.

Cameron, J., & Pierce, W. D. (1994) Reinforcement, reward, and intrinsic motivation: A meta-analysis. *Review of Educational Research, 64,* 363–423.

Cameron, J., & Pierce, W. D. (1996). The debate about rewards and intrinsic motivation: A meta-analysis. *Review of Educational Research, 66,* 39–51.

Carta, J. (1995). Developmentally appropriate practice: A critical analysis as applied to young children with disabilities. *Focus on Exceptional Children, 27*(8), 1–14.

Carta, J. J., Atwater, J. B., Schwartz, I. S., & McConnell, S. R. (1993). Developmentally appropriate practices and early childhood special education: A reaction to Johnson & McChesney Johnson. *Topics in Special Education, 13,* 243–254.

Carta, J. J., Schwartz, I. S., Atwater, J. B., & McConnell, S. R. (1991). Developmentally appropriate practice: Appraising its usefulness for young children with disabilities. *Topics in Early Childhood Special Education, 11*(1), 1–20.

Chandler, T. A. (1981). What's wrong with success and praise? *Arithmetic Teacher, 29*(4), 10–12.

Eisenberger, R., & Cameron, J. (1996). Detrimental effects of reward: Reality or myth. *American Psychologist, 51*(11), 1153–1166.

Eisenberger, R., & Cameron, J. (1998). Reward, intrinsic interest, and creativity: New findings. *American Psychologist, 53*(6), 676–679.

Gordon, T. (1974). *Teacher effectiveness training.* New York: Wyden.

Harlen, J. C. (1996) *Behavior management strategies for teachers: Achieving instructional effectiveness, student success, and student motivation; every teacher and every student can!* Springfield, IL: C.C. Thomas.

Henderick, J. (1998). *Total learning: Development curriculum for the young child.* Columbus, OH: Merrill.

Hitz, R., & Driscoll, A. (1988). Praise or encouragement? *Young Children, 43*(5), 6–13.

Kamii, C. (1984). The aim of education envisioned by Piaget. *Phi Delta Kappan, 65*(6), 410–415.

Kazdin, A. E. (1975). *Behavior modification in applied settings.* Pacific Grove, CA: Brooks/Cole.

Kazdin, A. E. (1994). *Behavior modification in applied settings* (5th ed.). Pacific Grove, CA: Brooks/Cole.

Kohn, A. (1993). *Punished by rewards: The trouble with gold stars, incentive plans, A's, praise and other bribes.* New York: Houghton Mifflin.

Kostelnik, M. J., Stein, L. C., Whiren, A. P., & Soderman, A. K. (1998). *Guiding children's social development* (2nd ed.). New York: Delmar.

Lepper, M. R., & Greene, D. (1975). When two rewards are worse than one: Effects of extrinsic rewards on intrinsic motivation. *Phi Delta Kappan, 56*(8), 565–566.

Marshall, H. H. (1995). Beyond "I like the way…" *Young Children, 50*(2), 26–28.

Peck, C. (1985). Increasing opportunities for social control by children with autism and severe handicaps: effects on student behavior and percieved classroom climate. *Journal of the Association for Persons With Severe Handicaps, 10*(4), 183–193.

Peters, D., Neisworth, J. T., & Yawkey, T. D. (1985). *Early childhood education: From theory to practice.* Monterey, CA: Brooks/Cole.

Rodd, J. (1996). *Understanding young children's behavior: A guide for early childhood professionals.* New York: Teachers College Press.

Schloss, P. J., & Smith, M. A. (1998). *Applied behavior analyses in the classroom* (Rev. ed.). Boston: Allyn and Bacon.

Strain, P. S., McConnell, S. R., Carta, J. J., Fowler, S. A., Neisworth, J. T., & Wolery, M. (1992). Behaviorism in early intervention. *Topics in Early Childhood Special Education, 12*(1), 121–141.

Sulzer-Azaroff, B., & Mayer, G. R. (1991). *Behavior analysis for lasting change.* New York: Harcourt Brace.

Thomas, S. B., & Russo, C. J. (1995). *Special education law: Issues and implications for the 90's.* Topeka, KS: National Organization on Legal Problems of Education.

Van der Wilt, J. (1996). Beyond stickers and popcorn parties. *Dimensions of Early Childhood, 24*(1), 17–20.

Vaughn, S., Bos, C. S., & Schumm, J. S. (1997). *Teaching mainstreamed, diverse, and at-risk students in the general education classroom.* Boston: Allyn and Bacon.

Walker, L. J., DeVries, B., & Trevarthen, S. D. (1989). Moral stages and moral orientations in real-life and hypothetical dilemmas. *Child Development, 58*(3), 842–858.

Weiner, E. A., & Weiner, B. J. (1974). Differentiation of retarded and normal children through toy-play analysis. *Multivariate Behavioral Research, 9*(2), 245–257.

Wolery, M. (1994). *Including children with special needs in early childhood programs.* Washington, DC: National Association for the Education of Young Children.

Wolery, M., & Bredekamp, S. (1994). Developmentally appropriate practices and young children with disabilities: Contextual issues in the discussion. *Journal of Early Intervention, 18,* 331–341.

Wolery, M., Strain, P. S., & Bailey, D. (1992). Reaching potentials of children with special needs. In S. Bredekamp & T. Rosegrant (Eds.), *Reaching potentials: Appropriate curriculum and assessment for young children. Vol. 1* (pp. 92–111). Washington, DC: National Association for the Education of Young Children.

Wolery, M., Werts, M. G., & Holcombe-Ligon, A. (1994). Current practices with young children who have disabilities: Issues in placement, assessment and instruction. *Focus on Exceptional Children, 26*(6), 1–12.

Wolery, M., & Wilbers, J. S. (1994). Introduction to the inclusion of young children with special needs in early childhood programs. In M. Wolery & J. S. Wilbers (Eds.), *Including children with special needs in early childhood programs* (pp. 1–22). Washington, DC: National Association for the Education of Young Children.

Zirpoli, T. J. (1995). *Understanding and affecting the behavior of young children.* Englewood Cliffs, NJ: Merrill.

Tashawna K. Duncan is a doctoral candidate, Department of Educational Psychology; Kristen M. Kemple is Associate Professor, School of Teaching and Learning; and Tina M. Smith is Assistant Professor, Department of Educational Psychology, University of Florida, Gainesville.

From *Childhood Education,* Summer 2000, pp. 194-199. Reprinted by permission of Tashawna K. Duncan, Kristen M. Kemple, Tina M. Smith, and the Association for Childhood Education International. © 2000 by ACEI.

Another View on "*Reinforcement in Developmentally Appropriate Early Childhood Classrooms*"

Behavior modification through the use of reinforcers is a superficial effort to lead the child down the road of development without using the road map of developmental theory, which views the child's actions with regard to developmental constructs.

Charles H. Wolfgang

In the Summer 2000 issue of *Childhood Education*, the article written by Tashawna Duncan, Kristen Kemple, and Tina Smith supports reinforcement as a developmentally appropriate practice (Bredekamp & Copple, 1997). In the present article, the author contrasts the Duncan-Kemple-Smith position with another view: How to use developmental theory to inform us of appropriate strategies for dealing with young children in the classroom. The use of behavioral techniques such as reinforcers often can produce desired behavior changes. Behavior modification through the use of reinforcers, however, is a superficial effort to lead the child down the road of development without using the road map of developmental theory, which views the child's actions with regard to developmental constructs.

Let's take the Duncan-Kemple-Smith example. *"Five-year-old Rodney has recently joined Mr. Romero's kindergarten class. On his first day in his new class, Rodney punched a classmate and usurped the tricycle the other boy was riding. On Rodney's second day in the class, he shoved a child on a swing and dumped another out of her chair at the snack table"* (Duncan, Kemple, & Smith, 2000, p. 194). In essence, the authors support behavioral theory and advocate addressing Rodney's negative actions through the use of social reinforcers (e.g., praise, and similar teacher attention), *activity reinforcers* (e.g., earning use of a toy such as a tricycle with "good" behavior), and *tangible reinforcers* (e.g., stickers). Unfortunately, applying reinforcers to extinguish Rodney's "aggression" overlooks the context of how children develop.

The developmentalist, by contrast, would attempt to change Rodney's antisocial behaviors by trying to understand his developmental needs—specifically, what may be causing such behaviors in the first place. As this is Rodney's first day in his new class, the first question for the developmentalist, knowing the literature on attachment and separation fears (Mahler, 1970, 1975; Speers, 1970a, 1970b), would be: Did the teacher help Rodney make a gradual transition from home to school, and allow time for him to bond with his new teacher and become comfortable in this strange new world of the kindergarten classroom? The developmentalists may use supportive actions to help the child make a successful transition (Jervis, 1999). In Rodney's case, the teacher could have made home visits, giving Rodney a chance to meet his teacher on his own "turf"; permitted Rodney to bring a "transitional object" (his cuddle toy or his "Linus" blanket) (Wolfgang & Wolfgang, 1999); and encouraged a parent to stay in the class the first day or two so that Rodney could "wean" himself from parental support.

Developmentalists may, in fact, view Rodney's aggressive actions as *heroic* attempts to get his needs met in a strange new world. The developmentalist might ask: Are there enough tricycles (or similar favorite items) that would permit him to play in parallel form as a developmental step into associative and cooperative play? (Parten, 1971). Or is the playground developmentally appropriate? Are back-and-forth swings, because of the preoperational child's inability to understand movement between states, or states vs. transformations (Piaget & Inhelder, 1958), appropriate at the kindergarten level? Is the organization of snacks and the arrangement of chairs done in such a manner that certain chairs (e.g., those that allow children to sit with the teacher) are favored, thus causing competition? In viewing Rodney's aggressive behaviors, a developmentalist also would ask: Are the environment, procedures, rules, and daily activities developmentally appropriate for this child, especially when we have children with special needs in our classroom?

The teacher who is armed with a repertoire of *social reinforcers, activity reinforcers,* and *tangible reinforcers,* and who uses them daily as the general mode of guidance for children, is missing an opportunity to understand how a child's actions may give us insight into his developmental needs. When we have a medical visit, the doctor says, "Where does it hurt?" We show where the pain is, and the doctor then considers each ailment suggested by pain in that location. Similarly, "punching, pushing, and taking others' possessions" should prompt us to learn about this child's developmental needs, to draw on our knowledge to give

meaning to the child's "symptoms," and to use developmentally appropriate practices.

Rather than administering a reinforcer to change the child's behavior, the developmental teacher asks: How does that child separate and bond? Can he cuddle with supportive adults, such as the teacher? How does he eat and handle himself at snack or at rest time? Can he handle demanding activities such as finger painting, water play, or painting? Can he do socio-dramatic play? How do his social skills relate to typical developmental stages? Can he express his needs with words while under pressure in a social situation? (Wolfgang, 1977; Wolfgang & Wolfgang, 1999). These questions can be posed only from within an understanding of certain developmental theories—Mahler's theories of bonding and attachment (1970, 1975), Anna Freud's developmental lines (1968, 1971), play research and theory (Erikson, 1950; Freud, 1968; Peller, 1969; Smilansky, 1969), and Parten's social stages (1971).

Considering Rodney From a Developmentally Appropriate Perspective

Young children who do not feel empowered or do not believe they will get their needs met begin to deal with their world in an automatic, reflexive manner. They may respond through verbal aggression (swearing or using bathroom talk), physical aggression (punching, pushing, and taking others' possessions), or passivity (flat, expressionless behavior accompanied by excessive thumb sucking, masturbation, or even self-abusive activities, such as striking their own head) (Wolfgang, 1977).

Children slowly "learn to be the cause" of events in their world over the first three years of life. The young infant attaches to a significant person, then begins a gradual separation process: first learning causality as a baby by throwing a spoon in order to get others to pick it up, acting upon objects during toddlerhood by

opening all the kitchen cabinet doors and banging on pots and pans, and using language to achieve a goal in late toddlerhood by asking mommy for something. Thus, the child becomes socially adaptive. If development went well during these first three years, children will enter kindergarten expecting the best, with the confidence that they can master what lies before them. If this development has not gone well, they may enter kindergarten as Rodney did— by "punching, pushing, and taking others' possessions."

In behavioral theory, we address children's inappropriate behavior by moving away when the child acts out; otherwise, we would be reinforcing the behavior by attending to them. For example, we may ignore a child when he cries, in an effort to eliminate the crying. Developmentalists take just the opposite approach. The kindergarten teacher's first goal should be to rebond with Rodney, then gradually teach him to channel his energy (aggression is simply misdirected energy) from the body to the toy, from the toy to play, and from play to work (Freud, 1968).

On the third day of school, the developmental teacher would direct Rodney into a host of activities that permit him to divert his aggression (energy) from his body into the toy (pounding at the carpentry table, pounding with clay, or pursuing aggressive play themes in the safe, make-believe world of small animal toys). At the same time, the teacher would attempt to bond with Rodney (even to the point of cuddling him), so that he would begin to realize that he can depend on this caring adult to help get what he needs (Wolfgang, 1977; Wolfgang & Wolfgang, 1999).

Instead of permitting Rodney to have the tricycle after he goes for a period of time without pushing or hitting as a reinforcement (*activity reinforcers*), the developmental teacher might allow Rodney to use a tricycle whenever he wants, because it is an excellent outlet for his energy. Thus, Rodney can transfer his aggression from other children to the toy. The teacher may tape his picture or name to a chair at snack time so that he will know that this seat will always be reserved for him, and thus know that he does not need to fight for one.

Next, after Rodney has aggressively used the carpentry equipment, clay, or the make-believe rubber animal toys (such as lions and tigers), the teacher would help him cross the bridge into "making something" with the clay, or "making a story" with the animals. He then will move from the toy to play. Once he learns isolated play (Parten, 1971), the teacher can encourage others to join him; he will then move from parallel to associative play, and then to cooperative play (Smilansky, 1968; Smilansky & Shefatya, 1990), whereby he becomes a role-player with others and practices the social skills of give-and-take.

Rodney pushes, shoves, and hits because he does not yet have the social skills to work with others and to get his needs met. Reinforcing "good" behavior does not teach him the developmental skills he needs to function. Through role-play (as in socio-dramatic play), the child moves from isolated play into cooperation with others, which requires sophisticated social and language skills. Rodney, through such play, would be empowered and, therefore, would not need the teacher reinforcements, or control. He can develop effective adaptive skills.

As part of their advice for Rodney's teacher, Duncan, Kemple, and Smith write, "*Mr. Romero is concerned for the emotional and physical safety of the other children, and he believes that Rodney will have a hard time making friends if his reputation as an aggressor is allowed to solidify. He feels the need to act fast. Deciding that a system of reinforcement, along with other strategies, may help Rodney control his aggressive behavior, Mr. Romero implements a token reinforcement system. Rodney earns a ticket, accompanied by praise, for each 30-minute period during which he does not behave aggressively. At the end of the day, Rodney can trade a specified*

number of earned tickets for his choice of small toys" (p. 194).

While it is certainly necessary to protect the other children and ensure fairness, the authors' advice fails to incorporate developmentally appropriate practice. At circle time, and possibly even before Rodney has arrived, a teacher using a developmentalist approach would have discussed Rodney's arrival with the other kindergarten children to help them develop empathy for Rodney, who is, after all, getting accustomed to a new place. The teacher could ask the children to think about how Rodney might feel, why he might push and shove and take other children's toys, and why the teacher might need to do special things for this new person. Young children can understand these concepts, and as they watch the developmental teacher guiding the "misbehaving" child they will become secure in the knowledge that the teacher will not punish them for similar actions. Thus, they can learn to master their own aggressive impulses as they watch Rodney strive for self-control and social skills.

When we narrow our view of children's growth to one observable behavior, we lose the holistic view of the child.

The Duncan-Kemple-Smith article includes a short review of studies (e.g., Schloss & Smith, 1998; Zirpoli, 1995) demonstrating that reinforcers are effective in eliminating unwanted behaviors in early childhood settings. It is often true that behavioral techniques are powerful and effective when they are used with the narrow goal of changing a particular behavior. These brief targeted studies, however, do not answer the following questions: Should this behavior be extinguished? What

caused the behavior in the first place? What are the new behaviors that result when this behavior is extinguished? There is no doubt that an experienced behavioral teacher using reinforcers can extinguish Rodney's aggression.

What happens, however, if we return the next month to observe Rodney and find that new problem behaviors have developed? In short, targeting one behavior obscures the perspective on the dynamic aspect of human behavior and the interdependence of social, emotional, and cognitive development. When we narrow our view of children's growth to one observable behavior, we lose the holistic view of the child.

Another Look at Specific Behavioral Techniques

In light of recommended developmentally appropriate practices, behavioral constructs of reinforcement raise some concerns.

Social Reinforcers (e.g., praise and similar teacher attention). The narrow behavioral nature of a social reinforcer, such as teacher praise and attention, boxes the teacher into scripted behavior when used with young children. Teacher attention toward the child should be based on the teacher's insights into, and empathy with, the child's real development needs, as well as on an understanding of the necessary steps for the child to gradually gain autonomy.

Activity Reinforcers (e.g., earning use of a toy with "good" behavior). In a developmental classroom, there are no activities, materials, and toys that are considered "treats." Instead, these items and processes are basic to the educational developmental model itself. One example of activity reinforcers from the Duncan, Kemple, and Smith article shows the teacher reminding the children that they must first clean up before they are permitted to go out to the playground. No one can disagree with the need to teach young children to clean up; with a child like Rodney, however, cleaning up will only come after he has become a co-player and a worker with others. This will take time. He should never be barred from a play activity, especially during his first days of kindergarten. Following the developmental construct of Anna Freud (1968), activities on the playground, with the guidance of an informed developmental teacher, are exactly what Rodney needs to help him gain control of his own behavior and attain true maturity. The developmentally appropriate classroom does not use toys, materials, and activities as "activity treats" or *activity reinforcers*; all toys, materials, and activities are there to contribute to children's development.

Tangible Reinforcers (e.g., stickers). One kindergarten teacher once stated, "My students would kill for a sticker." Because Rodney does not yet have the developmental social skills to function at an age-appropriate level, he will miss out on such tangible reinforcers as stickers and feel resentment and anger toward those who do receive them. In fact, Rodney may push and hit to get a sticker. The use of stickers as a tangible reinforcer may achieve short-term success, but bring about unintended, long-term consequences for the children who do not, as yet, have the social skills to merit the reward.

Conclusion

The behavioral constructs of social reinforcers, activity reinforcers, and tangible reinforcers can be learned quickly by beginning teachers of young children, provide them with feelings of empowerment and control, and may help, in the short term, to curb children's aggressive behavior. It may be helpful, however, to view aggression from a developmental point of view—as children's attempts to adapt to new situations. Behavioral techniques that shape and change children's surface behaviors without placing these behaviors within a developmental context may, in the long run, interfere with the child's developmental needs and cause much harm.

References

Bredekamp, S., & Copple, C. (1997). *Developmentally appropriate practice in early childhood programs* (Rev. ed.). Washington, DC: National Association for the Education of Young Children.

Duncan, T. K., Kemple, K. M., & Smith, T. M. (2000). Reinforcement in developmentally appropriate early childhood classrooms. *Childhood Education, 76*, 194–203.

Erikson, E. (1950). *Childhood and society*. New York: Norton Press.

Freud, A. (1968). *Normality and pathology in childhood: Assessments of development*. New York: International Universities Press.

Freud, A. (1971). *The ego and the mechanisms of defense*. New York: International Universities Press.

Jervis, K. (1999). *Separation: Strategies for helping two- to four-year-olds*. Washington, DC: National Association for the Education of Young Children.

Mahler, M. S. (1970). *On human symbiosis and the vicissitudes of individuation*. New York: International Universities Press.

Mahler, M. S. (1975). *The psychological birth of the human infant*. New York: Basic Books.

Parten, M. B. (1971). Social play among preschool children. In R. E. Herron &

B. Sutton-Smith (Eds.), *Child's play* (pp. 83–95). New York: John Wiley and Sons.

Peller, L. E. (1969). Libidinal phases, ego development and play. In *Psychoanalytic study of the child, no. 9* (pp. 178–197). New York: International Universities Press.

Piaget, J., & Inhelder, B. (1958). *The growth of logical thinking: From childhood to adolescence*. New York: Basic Books.

Smilansky, S. (1969). *The effects of sociodramatic play on disadvantaged preschool children*. New York: John Wiley & Sons.

Smilansky, S. J., & Shefatya, L. (1990). *Facilitating play: Medium for promoting cognitive, social-emotional and academic development in young children*. Gaithersburg, MD: Psychosocial & Educational Publishing.

Speers, R. W. (1970a). Recapitulation of separation-individuation processes when the normal three-year-old enters nursery school. In J. McDevitt (Ed.), *Separation-individuation: Essays in honor of Margaret Mahler* (pp. 38–67). New York: International Universities Press.

Speers, R. W. (1970b). *Variations in Separation — Individuation and implications for play abilities and learning as studied in the three-year-old in nursery school*. Pittsburgh, PA: University of Pittsburgh Press.

Wolfgang, C. H. (1977). *Helping aggressive and passive preschoolers through play*. Columbus, OH: Charles E. Merrill Publishing.

Wolfgang, C. H., & Wolfgang, M. E. (1999). *School for young children: Developmentally appropriate practices*. Boston: Allyn and Bacon.

Charles H. Wolfgang is Professor of Early Childhood Education, Florida State University, Tallahassee.

Using Classroom Rules to Construct Behavior

I've come to a frightening conclusion that I am the decisive element in the classroom. It's my approach that creates the climate. It's my daily mood that makes the weather. As a teacher, I possess a tremendous power to make a child's life miserable or joyous. I can be a tool of torture or an instrument of inspiration. I can humiliate or humor, hurt or heal. In all situations, it is my response that decides whether a crisis will be escalated or de-escalated and a child humanized or dehumanized. (Haim Ginott, *The Teacher*, January 2000)

David F. Bicard

In many middle school classrooms, teachers attempt to influence the behavior of students through the use of rules. However, rules alone exert little effect on student behavior. Teachers may sometimes be unaware of the effects their actions have on the behavior of their students. Two classic studies may help to illustrate the effects of teacher-made rules and teacher behavior on the activity of their students. Madsen, Becker, and Thomas (1968) found that when a teacher provided rules alone to her students, the students' appropriate and inappropriate behavior remained at relatively the same level as when she provided no rules. Major decreases in inappropriate conduct and increases in appropriate conduct occurred when the teacher showed approval for appropriate behavior in combination with ignoring some inappropriate behavior. Similarly, Thomas, Becker, and Armstrong (1968) found that teachers could produce or eliminate appropriate and inappropriate behavior by varying approval and disapproval statements. When the teachers delivered positive statements to their students regarding their classroom behavior, the students maintained appropriate conduct; and when the teachers withdrew positive statements and delivered frequent disapproval statements, inappropriate behavior increased.

While rules by themselves may not be effective, they do provide structure, communicate teacher expectations, provide a foundation for learning, and help maintain a well-run and organized classroom. Positive rules, along with consistent action by the teacher, set the stage for praising student achievement that benefits the teacher as much as the students. Good classrooms where students are highly involved do not just happen. They exist because effective teachers have constructed the types of classroom conditions and student interactions necessary for a positive learning environment (Emmer, Evertson, Clements, & Worsham, 1994). In *Middle School Journal*, Mills (1997) described how one effective teacher named Suzan constructed her classroom to ensure successful learning. Suzan "modeled a way of teaching, learning, and behaving that she shared, both explicitly and implicitly, with her students.... [Her approach] held expectations for student responsibility, for a caring atmosphere, and for student success".... Throughout this article we will return to Suzan's classroom to demonstrate how effective teachers can use words and actions to construct positive rules for their students.

Rules are one of the most cost effective forms of classroom management available to teachers (Catania, 1998). However, not all teachers recognize the benefits of teaching rules. In *Setting Limits in the Classroom*, Mackenzie (1996) noted 10 common misconceptions held by teachers about the use of rules, among them, "teaching rules is the parents' job," "students should know what I expect," "I can't afford to take precious time away from instruction," and "explaining my rules to students should be enough." The reality is that in the classroom, teaching rules is one of the teacher's jobs, with parents' help. In addition, students need time to learn the rules and expectations of their teachers. Rules need to be taught with words as well as actions; the time invested up front will pay huge dividends in the end.

Figure 1

Examples of Positive, Negative, and Vague Rules		
Positive	**Negative**	**Vague**
Raise your hand when you want to talk.	Don't interrupt others.	Respect others.
Keep your eyes on the teacher.	Don't look around the room.	Listen to the teacher.
Bring a pencil to class every day.	Don't come to class without a pencil.	Come to class prepared.
Before you leave make sure your desk is clean.	You are not ready to leave until your desk is clean.	Keep the classroom neat.
Be in your seat when the bell rings.	Don't be out of your seat when the bell rings.	Be on time for class.

Ginott (2000) suggested that teachers are the decisive element in the classroom. In that role, they should take the responsibility for constructing and implementing positive rules as a management system to build academic success. This article describes the characteristics of positive rules, offers suggestions for developing and implementing the rules, and provides guidelines for what to do when students break the rules.

Characteristics of Positive Rules

The first part of this section will describe the differences between some common rules that exist in many middle school classrooms. The second part discusses an often overlooked, yet extremely important, component of effective rules. These small differences in the way teachers construct rules may have a big influence on the way students behave in the classroom.

Positive rules specify appropriate student behavior in observable terms

Rules come in three basic varieties: positive rules that communicate how to behave, negative rules that communicate how not to behave, and vague rules that communicate neither how nor how not to behave (Figure 1). A common rule about completing assigned work can be worded positively ("Answer each problem until you are done"), negatively ("Don't stop unless you are done"), or vaguely ("Stay on task"). Small differences in wording make a substantial difference in the way students will respond and how teachers will focus their attention. The positive version of the rule lets the student know how to

behave so that teachers can provide approval when students follow the rule. Conversely, in the negative and vague examples, nothing has been said on how to respond; the student is left with only how not to respond. More important, in the negative and vague examples, teachers are more likely to recognize students only when they do not follow the rule. When rules state what the student *can do* in specific and observable terms, both teachers and students can easily recognize whether a rule is being followed. Teachers are more likely to notice appropriate behavior and celebrate student success. Positive rules tell students what to do instead of what not to do and are thus more instructive (Paine, Radicchi, Rosellini, Deutchman, & Darch, 1983).

When rules state only what the student *cannot do* or are *vague*, teacher attention will likely be on punishment for inappropriate behavior (Zirpoli & Melloy, 1993). When teacher attention is focused on punishment, the classroom becomes coercive, authoritarian, and punitive. It becomes a teacher's job to investigate violations, determine guilt, and mete out sentences. Less time is left for teaching. Frequent disapproval may also deter student learning in other ways. Greer (1981) found that the use of disapproval statements by teachers resulted in the students avoiding what was taught during free time. For example, if when teaching reading a teacher delivers frequent disapproval statements to his or her students, the students will be less likely to read books when they have leisure time. As Sulzer-Azaroff and Mayer (1986) noted, "One more critical disadvantage to resorting to punishment too frequently is that the practice inadvertently may teach others to use it as well" (p. 146).

A key component of effective rules is that the rules specify observable student behavior. In this respect *observable* means something a teacher can count, for example raising a hand. When a teacher can count behaviors, students become accountable for those behaviors. Vague rules such as "respect others" or "stay on task" may be as difficult for students to follow as they are for teachers to enforce because behaviors are extremely difficult to count. A teacher who can observe specific instances of appropriate student conduct is prepared to celebrate students' successes.

When attention is focused on appropriate behavior through the use of positive rules, teachers promote a sense of personal efficacy in students that communicates the trust, competence, responsibility, affiliation, and awareness so important in middle level curriculum (Stevenson, 1998). In short, teachers should be in the business of constructing behaviors not eliminating them (W. L. Heward, personal communication, February 12, 1998).

Suzan "told her students what she expected and wanted.... She reminded the students of proper lab behavior before each lab activity.... She gave examples of acceptable comments that focused on their learning and encouraged students" (Mills, 1997, pp. 33–34). Yet simply stating positive rules is only the first step of effective classroom management.

Positive rules specify observable consequences

Another important, though often overlooked, component of effective rules is a statement of consequences. Consequences are the *quid pro quo* of rules, letting students know what they get in return. Classroom studies conducted by Braam and Malott (1990) and Mistr and Glenn (1992) have shown that rules specifying only response requirements did not reliably guide student behavior; conversely when rules specified observable behavior *and* consequences, they were effective in maintaining appropriate behavior. Consequences are important because they teach responsibility and accountability to the teacher as well as the student. Providing clear consequences will help to break the cycle of limit-testing so common with middle school students. In the example, "Raise your hand when you want to talk," the students are left to discover what will happen next; they may raise their hands and then begin to talk. If the teacher provides a consequence, for example, "and I will call on you when it's your turn," the students will not have to guess. This is especially significant when we look at negative rules, such as "Don't talk until called upon." When a consequence is provided, "or your name will be written on the board," the focus of attention will necessarily be on elimination of behavior. It is also important that students be aware of the consequences for not following the rules. For example, during science experiments Mills' (1997) expert teacher "reminded the students of the cost of activities and suggested the principal, 'won't give me money for labs if you're not mature enough to handle them well'" (p. 34).

Developing Positive Rules

Three strategies help develop effective rules. The first strategy helps teachers to conceptualize a basic framework for identifying situations in which rules should be specified. The next two strategies are specific processes teachers can use to develop successful classroom rules.

Develop a framework before the school year

All rules must follow the policies and procedures of the school; however, these are typically general guidelines that can easily be incorporated into a set of classroom rules. Once teachers, or a team of teachers, have information about school policy and procedures, they can begin to plan rules for their classrooms and team areas. Paine and associates (1983) maintained that the best time to develop rules is *before* the school year begins. Teachers should decide what kinds of situations to cover and what kinds of rules to write for those situations. For example, a

Figure 2

Keys to Developing and Implementing Positive Rules in Classrooms
Characteristics of Positive Rules
• Positive rules specify appropriate student behavior in observable terms
• Positive rules specify observable consequences
Developing Positive Rules
• Develop a framework before the school year begins
• Include students in the decision-making process
• Get agreement by students, teachers, and parents
Using Positive Rules Effectively
• Teach the rules
• Catch students following the rules
• Monitor your behavior
• Include students as monitors
What to Do When Students Break the Rules
• Use the least intrusive procedures first
• Praise other students for following the rules
• Give verbal redirection
• Remain unemotional yet firm when intervening

science teacher may have one set of rules during experiments and another during whole-class time. This basic framework will help teachers to guide students toward a formalized version of the rules.

Rules are one of the most cost effective forms of classroom management available to teachers.

Include students in the decision-making process

Once the guidelines are in place, the next step is involving students in deciding the specific rules. Student participation in rule setting has been demonstrated to be effective for increased compliance (Dickerson & Creedon, 1981), lower numbers of violations (Felixbrod & O'Leary, 1974), and academic success (Lovitt & Curtis, 1969). Emmer, Evertson, Clements, and Worsham (1994) noted that involving students in rule setting helps to promote student ownership and responsibility. Incorporating students in the process communicates respect and concern, lets students know they are important elements in the classroom, and serves to promote student acceptance.

There are a number of techniques teachers can use. For example, the first day of class can begin with a discussion of the role of rules in society and their application to the classroom. A teacher could ask the students to describe model behavior, then use this as a basis for discussing what types of rules are appropriate in the classroom. Specifying student behaviors in observable terms provides the foundation for the rules, and identifying teacher behavior provides the foundation for the consequences. The teacher may need to guide the students in providing positive examples, as middle school students tend to focus on violations (Emmer et al., 1994). Suzan had students "brainstorm appropriate comments and role-play supportive situations" (Mills, 1997, p. 35). It is important to note that student-made rules are sometimes too stringent, so again, it is a good idea to have a basic framework in mind prior to discussing rules with the students.

Try to keep the rules to a minimum: It is recommended that teachers use no more than three or four rules for each situation. To help students remember the rules and help teachers make praise statements within the wording of the rules, keep the wording as simple as possible. When the rules are established consequences must also be established. A simple method for achieving positive rules and consequences is to ask students to list possible consequences for following classroom rules. These can be favorite classroom activities, free time, or a note to parents. Students should also list consequences for not following the rules—for example, a "three strikes policy," then loss of free time, then a note to parents. An example of a positive rule might be when a student completes assigned work before the end of class, the teacher will give him or her five minutes of free time. Teachers can decide on whole class and individual contingencies based on the list each student completes. This process will allow flexibility in classroom management.

Create a contract for the students, teachers, and parents

Once the rules are in place have each student write the rules on a piece of paper, sign it, take it home for the parents or guardians to sign, and bring it back to school the next day. Jones and Jones (1990) recommended including a statement about classroom philosophy regarding management and instruction: "This lets you present the issues of rules in a positive manner that indicates their relationship to effective instruction and student learning." The contingency contract provides a number of useful advantages: students cannot say they were unaware of the rules; parents know the expectations of the teachers and have agreed, fostering a home-school partnership; and there is a record on file for future reference. (For more in-

formation regarding contingency contracts see Cooper, Heron, & Heward, 1987, pp. 466–485.)

Using Rules Effectively

Now that the rules have been specified and the consequences set forth, teachers are ready to begin using the rules to guide student learning. It is worth mentioning again that, without reliable enforcement by teachers, rules have very little effect on student conduct.

When rules specified observable behavior and consequences, they were effective in maintaining appropriate behavior.

Teach the rules

A crucial component of positive classroom management is how teachers implement the rules. The first step in teaching the rules is to post them prominently in the classroom. Suzan, "at the beginning of the year displayed a life-size female adolescent labeled 'scientist,' a smaller poster of rules near a frog saying 'hop to it'" (Mills, 1997, p. 33). An effective strategy is to designate a student from each class to make a poster listing the rules and consequences, or, if teachers decide on one set of rules for all their classes, a competition can be held and prizes awarded for the three best posters. For the first two or three days after the rules are in place, devote five minutes of class time to teaching the rules through examples. Doing this at the beginning of each class is an excellent way to keep the students engaged while taking attendance or gathering materials. Teachers can guide this discussion or designate a student to lead the class. It is important to have all the students state the rules, then have students role-play acceptable and unacceptable behavior. This is a perfect time to begin to catch students following the rules and praise them. Teachers can continue teaching the rules in this fashion each Monday for the first month of the school year and again the first Monday after long breaks. Whenever students need a "booster shot" during the school year, teachers can go back to this activity. Although this procedure may seem somewhat elementary, it is useful to teach rule following just as one would teach any other subject.

Catch students following the rules

Teaching positive rules does not end in the first five minutes of class or in the first week of school; it continues throughout the school year. Suzan "provided numerous opportunities for students to experience success. Her students experienced frequent success and received teacher praise for their efforts" (Mills, 1997, p. 35). Praise should be immediate, consistent, and contingent upon "catching the students being good." Consistent means a teacher reliably recognizes student behavior as it occurs. Contingent specifies a relationship between praise and the student's behavior. When students are behaving appropriately, follow the "if, then rule"—*if* students have done something appropriate, *then* praise them (Paine et al., 1983). An example from Mills (1997) illustrates this point. "Suzan once shared the compliments that a substitute teacher had made about the students and thanked them for their good behavior…. 'When I saw the work you had done in groups [while I was gone] I knew you had been wonderful'" (p. 35).

When praising always identify the rule, the behavior, and the student or students by name, "I like the way Jennifer put things away when the bell rang because that shows she is ready to learn. Nice job Jennifer." Public praise can occur in several situations: while teaching, when near a student, or in the presence of other teachers. This may be especially helpful for some students who are having difficulty in other classrooms. Sometimes public praise might be a problem with middle school students, so teachers may want to praise some students only when nearby or in private. Teachers can write a note on a student's paper or praise the student during individual seat work. Sometimes a call home to parents or even to a student is a good technique. For Suzan, "quiet, supportive exchanges with individual students took place literally during every occasion" (Mills, 1997, p. 34).

Monitor teacher behavior

An effective way to achieve success using positive rules is for teachers to monitor their own behavior. Initially, teachers can count the number of approval and disapproval statements. It is not as difficult as one would think. Generally, middle level teachers are excellent time managers. Begin counting, and when five minutes have passed, note the number of approval and disapproval statements. This then becomes a measure per unit of time. Teachers may be surprised and somewhat shocked at how little praise has been given. A good rule of thumb is to have a 3:1 ratio of approval to disapproval statements (Englemann & Carnine, 1991).

One technique for helping to pinpoint specific approval statements is a variation of "the timer game" (Lovitt, 1995, p. 322). Identify the behaviors to "catch," for example, students active at work stations making entries in their notebooks. Set a goal such as five praise statements in five minutes. The next and easiest step is for teachers to identify a reward for themselves, maybe a chocolate bar at lunch. Once these are in place, teachers can set a timer for five minutes and begin teaching. During teaching simply make a mark on a spare piece of pa-

per for every praise statement. When the timer goes off, students will probably be very interested in what is going on. This is a good time to let them in on the secret. Take a few minutes to discuss this practice and why it is being used. The students may be willing to assist in counting. It also has the added benefit of notifying students of what behaviors are being monitored and may help to promote appropriate classroom conduct.

Student participation in rule setting has been demonstrated to be effective for increased compliance.

Another useful strategy is to place "reminders" in the classroom such as a sign in the back of the room to prompt the teacher. Mills (1997) reported that in Suzan's classroom, "virtually every week, new student work was displayed…. Before class started, Suzan would call my attention to the students' work, call students over to show me their efforts or explain the concept, and tell me loudly how proud she was of their efforts" (pp. 35–36). Monitoring teacher behavior helps to promote a positive classroom environment. In the classroom it is the teacher who sets the standards. By modeling appropriate behavior teachers communicate with words and actions that they value a supportive, responsible, and respectful classroom.

Include students as monitors

Students play an active role in controlling peer behavior (Lovitt, 1995). Middle school teachers are well aware of the effects of peer attention on student behavior. Unfortunately, this has usually been correlated with inappropriate behavior. The results of a study by Carden-Smith and Fowler (1984) suggested that peers can serve to increase and maintain appropriate classroom behavior, provided they are given proper instruction and feedback from a teacher. Here is how Suzan involved students as monitors, "One particular day, the students had given oral reports and presented visuals on different animals; following each report the students asked for questions and comments. All students received praise from classmates about some aspect of their reports or drawings" (Mills, 1997, p. 35). Suzan "reminded her students during lab activities to 'check with your buddy' or 'help your partner'" (Mills, 1997, p. 34). Encouraging students to praise their peers has many benefits. In the above example, a mutually reinforcing relationship is established that will increase the probability of more praise statements to follow. Another example shows how involving students frees the teacher to take on other responsibilities:

> During the first observation, a group of students who finished their assignments early were designated by Suzan as "wizards." Suzan explained the next assignment to the wizards, and they were to provide and explain the worksheet to other students as they completed their work. All students were to seek help from the wizards before they asked questions of Suzan. (Mills, 1997, p. 35)

A useful and highly effective strategy for involving students as peer monitors is a variation of "the good behavior game" (Barrish, Saunders, & Wolf, 1969). This strategy is appropriate for whole groups or individual students. The technique requires teachers to model appropriate behaviors and then designate a student or group of students to identify instances of appropriate behavior by other students. In this game all students can win if they simply engage in appropriate behavior. Each team or individual can choose rewards the students and teacher have selected prior to the game. Successfully including peers as monitors may take some time and creativity on the part of a teacher, but the benefits of a cohesive, nurturing classroom are well worth the investment.

What to Do When Students Break the Rules

There will be times when students behave in unacceptable ways. This is as true for the best students as it is for the worst. The decisions teachers make during these times can escalate or de-escalate an already unfavorable situation. Heward has noted that teachers can maintain and increase deviant behavioral patterns even though they are trying to help their students. This process

> begins with a teacher request that the student ignores and follows a predictable and escalating sequence of teacher pleas and threats that the student counters with excuses, arguments, and eventually a full-blown tantrum. The aggression and tantrumming is so aversive to the teacher that she withdraws the request (thereby reinforcing and strengthening the student's disruptive behavior) so the student will stop the tormenting (thereby reinforcing the teacher for withdrawing the request). (Heward, 2000)

This increasing escalation of disruptive behavior is called *coercive pain control* (Rhode, Jensen, & Reavis, 1998) because the student learns to use painful behavior to escape or avoid the teacher's requests. It is best to try to anticipate these times by preparing a plan of action before

the situation occurs. The following five proven strategies can be used separately or in combination to assist teachers when students behave unacceptably in the classroom.

Use the least intrusive procedures first

The first technique to use is simply to arrange seating patterns so teachers can reach every part of their classrooms. Second, certain objects may be removed from the classroom if they prove to be distracting. However, keep in mind that having interesting objects in the classroom provides a great teaching opportunity since the student's attention is naturally directed toward the object. Another useful, unobtrusive technique is known as "planned ignoring" (Walker & Shea, 1995). Before attempting to use this technique, first try to determine why the student is engaging in unacceptable behavior. If it is determined he or she is doing this to get attention, then any response (positive or negative) will increase the probability of this behavior re-occurring in the future. With planned ignoring the teacher does not make any contact with the student. This technique works especially well in combination with praising other students. When a teacher uses this technique, at first unacceptable behavior may increase in intensity or duration. This should not be cause for alarm because it is an indication that the technique is working. It is important to resist the temptation to react. Once the student stops the unacceptable behavior the teacher can catch some appropriate behavior and praise it. If the teacher determines the unacceptable behavior is maintained by other students or is dangerous, then planned ignoring will not work and should not be attempted. At this point a teacher may want to intervene directly.

Teaching positive rules does not end in the first five minutes of class or in the first week of school; it continues throughout the school year.

Praise other students for following the rules

Praising other students for following the rules serves as a reminder to a student that he or she is not behaving appropriately. This reminder encourages the student to adjust his or her own behavior (Sulzer-Azaroff & Mayer, 1986). For example, if James is staring out the window when most of the other students are working diligently on math problems, the teacher may call a student by name and praise him—"I like the way DeMarco is working; one bonus point for DeMarco." More often than not, James will then begin to work on his math. After a few seconds, praise James to encourage him to keep working. This strategy is effective and has the benefit of notifying the student who is acting inappropriately without having to single him out. At the same time, it recognizes a student who is behaving appropriately.

Use proximity control and signal interference

Proximity control and signal interference are two less obtrusive techniques that are frequently used in conjunction with one another (Walker & Shea, 1995). When teachers move around the classroom their presence often serves as a cue to students, who stop behaving unacceptably. When a student is misbehaving, casually move in the direction of the student and attempt to make eye contact. Sometimes simply making eye contact is enough, other times nonverbal cues such as facial expressions, toe taps, or body language may be necessary. These nonverbal signals may alert a student that a behavior is disruptive. Walker and Shea noted, "In addition, proximity can have a positive effect on students experiencing anxiety and frustration. The physical presence of a teacher or parent available to assist has a calming effect on troubled children" (p. 228). Often nonverbal signals help the student to "save face" with his peers and promote a sense of respect on the part of the teacher. This technique is also appropriate for reinforcing acceptable behavior. After making eye contact, the teacher can simply smile or give a thumbs-up sign (Walker & Shea, 1995).

Peers can serve to increase and maintain appropriate classroom behavior, provided they are given proper instruction and feedback from a teacher.

Give verbal redirection

Occasionally students engage in minor disruptions during daily classroom routines such as attendance, returning homework, or when listening to daily messages over the intercom. This is a good time to channel their energy toward acceptable behavior. For example Lynn passes a note to Juan through Chuck. Ask Lynn to assist in passing out homework. Ask Juan a question about an upcoming activity and tell Chuck to read today's assignment off the blackboard. Verbal redirection can be an extremely effective technique, but caution should be used if the student is engaging in the behavior to get the teacher's attention.

Remain unemotional yet firm when intervening

It is best to remain unemotional yet firm when dealing with rule violations. As classroom leaders, teachers set the tone when things do not go as planned. The most effective strategy teachers can use is to handle minor disruptions before they become worse. Jones and Jones (1990) noted, "An inappropriately angry teacher's response creates tension and increases disobedience and disruptive behavior. When a teacher reacts calmly and quickly to a student's disruptive behavior, other students respond by improving their own behavior" (p. 295). The first step when intervening is to make contact with the student. Never assume the student is aware he or she is breaking a classroom rule; let the student know what is acceptable: "Carlos, the rule is, raise your hand when you want to speak, and I will call on you as soon as possible." As soon as Carlos raises his hand, the teacher should call on him and praise him for behaving responsibly. Teachers can intervene publicly as a message to the entire class; however, it is best to deliver reprimands in private. When teachers show respect for students, they will be more likely to comply with the teacher's instructions, and the teacher has averted turning a minor disruption into a major catastrophe.

Conclusion

Following this four-part framework for constructing behaviors can result in positive approaches to middle level classroom management. Figure 2 provides an outline of this approach for reference. The goal of setting positive rules and procedures is to maintain a healthy and respectful classroom. As the decisive element, teachers can create a supportive, caring community of learners through the words they choose and the actions they take. Mills (1997) captured this approach this way: "Suzan communicated to her students a pervasive caring by helping them feel a sense of belonging; learn acceptable, supportive behaviors; experience frequent success; and assume they have a promising future" (p. 34).

References

Barrish, H. H., Saunders, M., & Wolf, M. M. (1969). Good behavior game: Effects of individual contingencies for group consequences on disruptive behavior in a classroom. *Journal of Applied Behavior Analysis, 2,* 119–124.

Braam, C., & Malott, R. M. (1990). "I'll do it when the snow melts": The effects of deadlines and delayed outcomes on rule-governed behavior in preschool children. *The Analysis of Verbal Behavior, 8,* 67–76.

Carden-Smith, L. K., & Fowler, S. A. (1984). Positive peer pressure: The effects of peer monitoring on children's disruptive behavior. *Journal of Applied Behavior Analysis, 17,* 213–227.

Catania, A. C. (1998). *Learning* (4th ed.). Upper Saddle River, NJ: Prentice Hall.

Cooper, J. O., Heron, T. E., & Heward, W. L. (1987). *Applied behavior analysis*. Upper Saddle River, NJ: Prentice Hall/Merrill.

Dickerson, E. A., & Creedon, C. F. (1981). Self-selection of standards by children: The relative effectiveness of pupil-selected and teacher-selected standards of performance. *Journal of Applied Behavior Analysis, 14*, 425–433.

Englemann, D., & Carnine, D. (1991). *Theory of instruction* (rev. ed.). Eugene, OR: ADI Press.

Emmer, E. T., Everston, C. M., Clements, B. S., & Worsham, M. E. (1994). *Classroom management for secondary teachers* (3rd ed.). Needham, MA: Allyn and Bacon.

Felixbrod, J., & O'Leary, K. (1974). Self-determination of academic standards by children: Toward freedom from external control. *Journal of Educational Psychology, 66*, 845–850.

Ginott, H. (2000). *The teacher*. Retrieved January 6, 2000 from the World Wide Web: http://www.geocities.com/Heartland/Plains/3565/ haimginott.htm

Greer, R. D. (1981). An operant approach to motivation and affect: Ten years of research in music learning. In Documentary report of the Ann Arbor symposium: *Application of psychology to the teaching and learning of music*. Washington, DC: Music Educators National Conference.

Heward, W. L. (2000). *Exceptional children: An introduction to special education* (6th ed.). Upper Saddle River, NJ: Prentice Hall.

Jones, V. F., & Jones, L. S. (1990). *Comprehensive classroom management*. Needham Heights, MA: Allyn and Bacon.

Lovitt, T. C. (1995). *Tactics for teaching* (2nd ed.). Upper Saddle River, NJ: Prentice Hall.

Lovitt, T. C., & Curtis, K. (1969). Academic response rate as a function of teacher- and self-imposed contingencies. *Journal of Applied Behavior Analysis, 2*, 49–53.

Madsen, C. H., Becker, W. C., & Thomas, D. R. (1968). Rules, praise, and ignoring: Elements of elementary classroom control. *Journal of Applied Behavior Analysis, 1*, 139–150.

Mackenzie, R. J. (1996). *Setting limits in the classroom*. Rocklin, CA: Prima Publishing.

Mills, R. A. (1997). Expert teaching and successful learning at the middle level: One teacher's story. *Middle School Journal, 29*(1), 30–38.

Mistr, K. N., & Glenn, S. S. (1992). Evocative and function-altering effects of contingency-specifying stimuli. *The Analysis of Verbal Behavior, 10*, 11–21.

Paine, S. C., Radicchi, J., Rosellini, L. C., Deutchman, L., & Darch, C. B. (1983). *Structuring your classroom for academic success*. Champaign, IL: Research Press.

Rhode, G., Jensen, W. R., & Reavis, H. K. (1998). *The tough kid book: Practical classroom management strategies*. Longmont, CO: Sopris West.

Stevenson, C. (1998). Finding our priorities for middle level curriculum. *Middle School Journal, 29*(4), 53–57.

Sulzer-Azaroff, B., & Mayer, G. R. (1986). *Achieving educational excellence using behavioral strategies*. New York: CBS College Publishing.

Thomas, D. R., Becker, W. C., & Armstrong, M. (1968). Production and elimination of disruptive classroom behavior by systematically varying teachers' behavior. *Journal of Applied Behavior Analysis, 1*, 35–45.

Walker, J., & Shea, T. M. (1995). *Behavior management: A practical approach for educators*. Englewood Cliffs, NJ: Prentice Hall.

Zirpoli, T. J., & Melloy, K. J. (1993). *Behavior management: Applications for teachers and parents*. Don Mills, Ontario: Macmillan Publishing.

Author's Note: Support for this article was provided by a Leadership Training Grant (#H3253980018) from the Office of Special Education and Rehabilitation Services, U.S. Department of Education. I thank David A. and Barbara Bicard for being the decisive elements in my life. I also thank William L. Heward for his constructive comments.

David F. Bicard is a doctoral student in special education at The Ohio State University, Columbus.

"I Had It First"

Teaching Young Children To Solve Problems Peacefully

The classroom climate improves as incidences of aggression
and victimization decrease and positive social skills are promoted.

Suzanne K. Adams and Donna Sasse Wittmer

*Two 4-year-old girls are arguing over a picture book. The
teacher suggests that they go to the "peace table" to find a solution. A little while later, Erica has her arm around Melissa as
they approach the teacher and announce their solution. They
will share the book, with each of them holding one edge of the
book while they read.*

*A teacher in a preschool classroom of 3- and 4-year-olds is frus-
trated by the number of children who use Tinker Toys, Legos,
and bristle blocks to create some form of weapon and then run
around the room imitating fictional crime fighters. The teacher
raises her concern with the children in a class meeting. After
some creative brainstorming, the children decide that toys from
the table toy area should be "sit down toys"; the children will
sit on the floor or at a table to build, instead of running around
with their creations. This simple rule makes a noticeable difference. The children's creations are more creative and less likely
to be used as weapons.*

These classroom anecdotes demonstrate that very
young children can use a problem-solving process to resolve interpersonal conflicts. These accomplishments are
particularly striking, given that early childhood teachers
report an increase over the last five to 10 years in the number of children coming to school angry, aggressive, or
lacking the social skills to get along with classmates (Adams, 1998).

Teachers of young children recognize the benefits of
helping children learn social problem-solving strategies
that can be generalized across situations and settings. As
the children become more independent at solving problems peacefully, the teachers will need to spend less valuable time arbitrating disputes. The classroom climate
improves as incidences of aggression and victimization
decrease and positive social skills are promoted. A systematic approach to teaching a problem-solving process
can yield such positive outcomes (Carlsson-Paige &
Levin, 1992; DeVries & Zan, 1994; Levin, 1994).

Social Problem-Solving Model

Early childhood settings can offer children opportunities
to learn and practice fundamental problem-solving skills.
Various writers recommend differing processes (Carlsson-Paige & Levin, 1998; Dinwiddie, 1994; Hewitt &
Heidemann, 1998; Janke & Peterson, 1995; Kreidler, 1996;
Levin, 1994; Shure, 1992), but typically include the basic
steps of: 1) defining the problem, 2) generating alternative
solutions, 3) evaluating proposed solutions, 4) agreeing
on a solution, and 5) following through to determine if
the chosen solution is successful.

Many teachers have success with a problem-solving
approach that presents five steps to problem solving,
which includes the children asking themselves questions
and seeking answers in order to arrive at a solution to the
problem at hand (Committee for Children, 1991).

1. What Is the Problem? Identifying the problem incorporates a discussion of each child's point of view—that is,
the feelings and needs of both the victim and the aggressor
(Dinwiddie, 1994). This process helps to define the problem or conflict as a shared one, with two competing and
valid points of view. Children usually phrase the problem
from their own point of view based on concrete actions,
such as "Alex took my truck" or "Craig won't give me the
fire truck," rather than "We both want the truck." It is up
to the teacher to show how both children have legitimate,
albeit incompatible, points of view, and to clarify the feelings of each party in the dispute: "Craig, how did you feel
when Alex grabbed the truck?" and "Alex, look at Craig's
face. How do you think he is feeling?"

The role of the teacher at this step is to help children tune in to each other's needs and feelings, and then redefine the problem as a shared one. "So the problem is, Craig was using the truck and Alex wants the truck, too. You both want to play with the truck."

2. *What Can I Do?* In brainstorming sessions, participants think of many ideas in a short amount of time. At this point, teachers encourage ideas without evaluating or placing judgments on the suggested solutions. It is useful to have children, even 4-year-olds, suggest whatever ideas come to mind, good or bad, so that they have a chance to evaluate the consequences of impulsive and aggressive behavior (see step 3). If a child suggests a less-than-ideal option, the teacher should include it on the list with a comment such as, "Yes, you are right. Sometimes children do grab toys. Let's write that down."

3. *What Might Happen If ...?* In this step, the class evaluates ideas by generating consequences for each solution. "What might happen if Craig decides to push Alex away? Is that safe? How would Alex feel?" At this point, any potential solutions that are unsafe or that hurt another child's feelings are eliminated. For other ideas, the children need to answer the questions "Is it fair? Will it work?" Now is the time to respond to any of the children's inappropriate suggestions from the brainstorming session. For younger children (4-year-olds), the teacher may need to show puppets acting out some of the solutions, so that the children can judge the appropriateness of the ideas.

4. *Choose a Solution and Use It.* Once children decide on a best solution, they need to determine how to implement their plan successfully. Young children often verbalize such solutions as "take turns with the truck." Given the natural egocentricity of young children, however, they each tend to assume they can go first.

Some teachers have developed methods that children use to decide who actually goes first. (One creative teacher placed several Popsicle sticks in a can so that only the tips of the sticks were visible. The bottom of one stick was colored with green marker. The child drawing the green stick would take the first turn.) Once it is decided who goes first, the teacher helps the children determine the length of the turn. It may be necessary for the teacher to watch the clock, or set up a timer, to ensure fair turn-taking.

The teacher's role in this step is to verbalize the chosen solution: "So you've decided to take turns with the truck"; clarify how the solution will be implemented; and monitor the children's progress to ensure the agreement is going according to plan.

5. *Is It Working? If Not, What Can I Do Now?* During this final, evaluative, step of problem solving, children have an opportunity to reflect on how well their plan worked and on their feelings about the outcome. If any child is not satisfied with the outcome, he or she may decide to try another solution instead. They would then need to retrace the five steps to problem solving.

Techniques To Teach the Problem-Solving Steps to Young Children

Teachers can support development of problem-solving skills by directly teaching them to children, demonstrating and modeling their use in a variety of ways, and guiding children to use the problem-solving process in their ongoing interactions with peers. Methods to teach problem solving include the following:

Facilitating Regular Class Meetings. As a venue for modeling the problem-solving process, teachers conduct regular class meetings. In these meetings, small or large groups of children meet with the teacher to solve specific problems. The first goal of class meetings is to generate open discussion among the children. To do this, teachers must accept and validate each child's contribution to the discussion. Children must believe that their ideas and feelings will be respected and protected. The second goal is to develop the children's ability to solve problems by using the social problem-solving approach described above. It is vital that children, not the teacher, propose and choose the solutions they think will work.

Class meetings should be regularly scheduled at a specific time each day, or several days a week. The teacher also can spontaneously call for a class meeting in response to a more immediate problem, such as a playground incident.

Successful class meetings require time, patience, and practice. Teachers need to establish a comfortable and secure atmosphere.

Successful class meetings require time, patience, and practice. Teachers need to establish a comfortable and secure atmosphere (Developmental Studies Center, 1996; DeVries & Zan, 1994). Early class meetings typically focus on getting to know one another, creating a sense of community and belonging, and building positive social and communication skills. Gradually, the teacher introduces the problem-solving process, using the techniques presented below.

Using Puppet Role-Plays. Puppets provide a captivating means of holding children's attention. The author has observed young children relating to and identifying with puppets, almost as if they were fellow classmates. Puppets can be used to role-play problems based on common classroom situations (such as name calling, lack of sharing, or difficulty taking turns), or in response to actual conflicts (such as two children arguing over who gets to use the watering can to water the plants). Playing out the scenario with puppets protects the identities and feelings of the children involved in the specific conflict. Puppet role-plays also allow the teacher to raise his or her concerns ("I've noticed that during clean-up time, some children continue to play and don't help others clean up. What can we do about this problem?"), or to introduce or reinforce specific skills such as taking turns, asking the teacher for help, listening in a group, or asking another child to play.

William Kreidler (1984) suggests that the teacher identify some puppets as "problem puppets." The children name the puppets and may even create a "home" for them, using a small box. These puppets are the ones used during class meetings that focus on problem solving. The teacher operates the puppets, enacting the problem situation up to the point of conflict (i.e., the point where someone is going to hit, yell, cry, or call the teacher). The puppets "freeze" at the point of conflict, and the teacher then involves the children in the problem-solving steps. Once the children choose the solution they like best, the puppets role-play its conclusion.

Using Children's Literature To Teach Conflict Resolution. Children love to listen to stories and often identify strongly with the characters. Books can introduce or extend a conflict resolution skill, provide a nonthreatening way to talk about conflict, and show characters learning to solve problems nonviolently.

William Kreidler (1994) makes the following suggestions for reading books about conflict:

- Read the book up to the point of conflict.
- Ask the children how they think the characters are feeling. "How is Koala Bear feeling now?"
- Have the children identify the conflict. "Children, what's the problem here?"
- Brainstorm ways that the characters could solve the conflict. Discuss which one the children think the characters in the story will use.
- Read the rest of the story. Discuss the characters' solution to their conflict. "Was that a good solution? Why? How do the characters feel now?"

Using Pictures and Posters As a Stimulus. Large photographs or posters can provide a stimulus to discussions of conflict scenarios. Teachers can create a story, based on the picture (as they would with puppets and books), leading up to a conflict. Then, they would talk the children through the steps to problem solving. For example, using a large photograph depicting a crying young girl, the teacher might say, "This is Sarah. Look at her face. Let me tell you what happened to her. One day at preschool, Sarah asked two friends if she could play with them in the playhouse. Her friends said, 'No, we're busy!' How do you think that made Sarah feel? What is the problem? What do you think Sarah could do?" In one classroom presented with this scenario, the children brainstormed the following solutions for Sarah to try: ask the girls again

if she could play with them, find someone else to play with, or ask the teacher for help.

Acting Out Make-Believe Role-Plays. Role-playing is a good technique for practicing solutions to conflict and promoting children's ability to see a situation from another person's perspective. Usually a teacher-directed, small-group activity, teachers describe a conflict situation, define the roles, and have the children act out different ways to resolve the conflict.

One teacher asked the children to set the snack table with four place settings, and then chose five children to role-play how they would handle attempting to sit down for snack. Another teacher asked two children to simulate an argument over who could ride a tricycle: one child sat on the seat as another child held on to the handlebars, blocking her way. The rest of the children, identified the problem, and the two girls acted out scenarios to complete the problem-solving process.

Telling Stories. Because many preschoolers like to create their own stories, teachers can encourage a problem-related story theme. The teacher may initiate this activity by saying, "Tell me a story about a little girl who wanted the toy someone else had and what she did to try and get the toy." For younger children, who may need more structure, the teacher can provide the beginning of a fairy tale-type story and then ask a child to finish. "Once upon a time there was a boy named Kevin (do not use the name of a child in the class) who did not get along with anyone at school because he couldn't share. One day, a little girl started to play with a blue car and Kevin grabbed the car so fast it scared her and made her cry." Children who enjoy make-believe and imaginary play can act out their problem-solving stories as a role-play.

Getting Started in Your Classroom

Introduce the problem-solving process gradually. Start by having children engage in the first two steps. Role-play a short problem with the puppets, then stop and ask the children, "What is the problem here?" Rephrase their answers to establish a shared problem, such as, "They both want to play with the computer." Have the children identify how the puppets are likely feeling. Then have them brainstorm some possible solutions, which you write on a large piece of paper.

Later in the day, remind the children of the problem, and read aloud their earlier answers. Now, do the next two steps with the children. Evaluate each possible solution, asking, "Is it safe?" "Is it fair?" "Will it work?" "How will they feel?" Ask the children to choose one idea that "passes the test," and use the puppets to act out the solution. Repeat this two-part process several times. Eventually, the children can complete the first four steps during a class meeting, then the puppets will role-play the chosen solution, and, finally, the children will decide if the selected idea worked (step 5).

Some teachers introduce a "peace table" or a "peace rug" as a site for conflict resolution. When a conflict erupts, the children involved go to the designated area to complete the problem-solving steps.

Some teachers introduce a "peace table" or a "peace rug" as a site for conflict resolution. When a conflict erupts, the children involved go to the designated area to complete the problem-solving steps. Moving to an area away from the initial conflict may help to defuse the emotions and allow children to concentrate more on the process of solving the problem.

Situations Where a Social Problem-Solving Process Can Be Used

After the children have been exposed to the problem-solving process through the strategies described above, teachers can facilitate their use in real-life classroom situations.

Negotiating Routine Conflicts Over Property, Territory, or Teasing. Such conflicts occur frequently during children's play and interactions in the early childhood setting.

One Head Start classroom has been working on the five steps to problem solving since October. The teacher, Julie, has been paying particular attention to two 3-year-old girls, who she describes as "feisty" (because they are known to pull hair or pinch when frustrated by a conflict). One day in February, Julie brings in a set of new plastic dishes, a dishpan, a dish drying rack, a Handiwipe for washing dishes, and two dish towels. At free-play time, both of these girls head straight for the dramatic play area and grab the Handiwipe. Julie gets ready to intervene, then hears one of the little girls say, "We have a problem here. We both want to wash dishes. What can we do?" The girls, on their own, decide to cut the Handiwipe in half. They proceed to share the dishpan happily, and wash the dishes together.

Negotiating Responses to Behavior Problems With an Individual Child. In this case, the teacher typically initiates a conversation with a child.

A teacher in an early childhood classroom approaches a little boy during a quiet time and invites him to sit and draw a picture with her. They proceed to draw a picture about the book that was read in class that morning. As they draw, the teacher says, "I've noticed that you have trouble sitting next to your friends during story time. Sometimes you get too close to other children or you get up on your knees and children can't see the book. What do you think we can do about this problem?" After giving it some thought, the child decides that he should sit in a cube chair in the back row. (The other children typically sit on the floor in loosely defined rows facing the teacher.) He seems to know that the cube chair will help define his "space" and allow him to sit up high enough to see the book.

When the Teacher Is Willing To Share Power Over a Decision. Such decisions can relate to the schedule, a routine, or an activity that affects the class. In this case, either the teacher or a child may present the problem to the class.

During a class meeting, a preschool teacher introduces a problem by saying, "Children, I need your help with a problem. Every day, several children want to feed the gerbil. If too many children feed the gerbil, he can't eat all the food and so just plays with it. Lots of times, he knocks part of the food out of the cage and it makes a mess on the floor. How can we pick just one child to feed the gerbil every day?" The children decide to make "feed the gerbil" a job on the daily classroom chore chart.

Conclusion

As teachers teach and facilitate a social problem-solving process, both they and the children reap the benefits. Children gain independence as they learn to solve difficult problems and express feelings in acceptable ways. When faced with conflict, they are better able to have their needs met without resorting to aggression. They learn to negotiate fair solutions and assert themselves appropriately to avoid becoming victims of other children's aggression. Children with effective problem-solving skills gain self-esteem as they learn to interact with others in more positive ways.

Social problem-solving skills can be learned by all children. This process is not exclusive to highly verbal, high-achieving, or socially competent children. The learning process may take longer for children with developmental delays or for children already demonstrating social problems. When teaching these skills to children with language delays or auditory processing difficulties, teachers can pair short phrases with pictures, or use sign language. For example, Katlyn, whose ability to speak is virtually nonexistent, learned to make the sign for "stop" when she did not like what another child was doing. Children who exhibit aggressive behavior can discover acceptable ways to have their needs met without impinging on the rights of others. They learn what to *do*, rather than simply what *not* to do (as when they are sent to time-out for behavioral infractions). Children who tend to withdraw can become empowered to express their feelings and assert themselves appropriately, reducing the chances that more powerful children will victimize them.

Teachers who make the initial investment of time, energy, and thoughtful planning to teach social problem solving to children will reap time benefits later, as they spend less time disciplining children and intervening in their conflicts. These teachers then have more time to do more meaningful and productive things in the classroom. Teachers also have the satisfaction of knowing that they have promoted coping skills that enhance children's abilities to live peacefully.

Note: Since 1994, the ECE-CARES Project has trained over 1,100 early childhood teachers and implemented CARES Strategies in classrooms serving over 10,000 children and their families. Data collected from a sample of these classrooms indicate that children demonstrate significant increases in positive social skills and significant decreases in problem behaviors.

Children's Books Related to Problem Solving

DePaola, T. (1980). *The knight and the dragon.* New York: Putnam.

Henkes, K. (1991). *Chrysanthemum.* New York: Greenwillow Books.

Jones, R. (1995). *Matthew and Tilly.* New York: Puffin Books.

Lionni, L. (1996). *It's mine.* New York: Random House.

Polland, B. K. (2000). *We can work it out: Conflict resolution for children.* Berkeley, CA: Tricycle Press.

Naylor, P. R. (1994). *King of the playground.* New York: Aladdin Books.

Zolotow, C. (1969). *The hating book.* New York: HarperCollins Children's Books.

References

Adams, S. (1998). *ECE-CARES Rural Project: Safe and Drug-Free Schools and Communities Grant Program report.* Denver, CO: University of Colorado at Denver.

Carlsson-Paige, N., & Levin, D. E. (1992). Making peace in violent times: A constructivist approach to conflict resolution. *Young Children, 48*(1), 4–13.

Carlsson-Paige, N., & Levin, D. E. (1998). *Before push comes to shove.* St. Paul, MN: Redleaf Press.

Committee for Children. (1991). *Second Step: A violence prevention curriculum for preschoolers and kindergartners.* Seattle, WA: Author.

Developmental Studies Center. (1996). *Ways we want our class to be: Class meetings that build commitment to kindness and learning.* Oakland, CA: Author.

DeVries, R., & Zan, B. (1994). *Moral classrooms, moral children: Creating a constructivist atmosphere in early education.* New York: Teachers College.

Dinwiddie, S. A. (1994). The saga of Sally, Sammy, and the red pen: Facilitating children's social problem solving. *Young Children, 49*(5), 13–19.

Hewitt, D., & Heidemann, S. (1998). *The optimistic classroom: Creative ways to give children hope.* St. Paul, MN: Redleaf Press.

Janke, R. A., & Peterson, J. P. (1995). *Peacemaker's ABCs for young children.* St. Croix, MN: Growing Communities for Peace.

Kreidler, W.J. (1984). *Creative conflict resolution: More than 200 activities for keeping peace in the classroom.* Glencoe, IL: Scott Foresman Company.

Kreidler, W.J. (1994). *Teaching conflict resolution through children's literature.* New York: Scholastic Professional Books.

Kreidler, W.J. (1996). *Adventures in peacemaking: A conflict resolution guide for early childhood providers.* Boston: Educators for Social Responsibility.

Levin, D. E. (1994). *Teaching young children in violent times.* Cambridge, MA: Educators for Social Responsibility.

Shure, M. B. (1992). *I can problem solve: An interpersonal cognitive problem-solving program.* Champaign, IL: Research Press.

Suzanne K. Adams is Assistant Research Professor, Early Childhood Education, University of Colorado, Denver, and the Director of the ECE-CARES Project. Donna Sasse Wittmer is Associate Professor, Early Childhood Education, University of Colorado, Denver.

UNIT 6

Assessment

Unit Selections

Key Points to Consider

- What fundamental concepts from contemporary learning and motivation theories have specific implications for how teachers assess their students? Are such practices consistent with what is promulgated with standardized tests?

- What are some important principles for using standardized test scores to improve instruction? What are some limitations of standardized tests?

- What are some examples of performance assessment? What are the strengths and limitations of these assessments?

- Many educators believe that schools should identify the brightest, most capable students. What are the assessment implications of this philosophy? How would low-achieving students be affected?

- What principles of assessment should teachers adopt for their own classroom testing? Is it necessary or feasible to develop a table of specifications for each test? How do we know if the test scores teachers use are reliable and if valid inferences are drawn from the scores?

- How can teachers grade thinking skills such as analysis, application, and reasoning? How should objectives for student learning and grading be integrated? What are some grading practices to avoid? Why?

 **Links: www.dushkin.com/online/**
These sites are annotated in the World Wide Web pages.

Awesome Library for Teachers
http://www.neat-schoolhouse.org/teacher.html

Phi Delta Kappa International
http://www.pdkintl.org

Washington (State) Center for the Improvement of Student Learning
http://www.K12.wa.us/reform/

In which reading group does Jon belong? How do I construct tests? How do I know when my students have mastered the course objectives? How can I explain test results to Mary's parents? Teachers answer these questions, and many more, by applying principles of assessment. Assessment refers to procedures for measuring and recording student performance and constructing grades that communicate to others levels of proficiency or relative standing. Assessment principles constitute a set of concepts that are integral to the teaching-learning process. Indeed, a significant amount of teacher time is spent in assessment activities, and with more accountability has come a greater emphasis on assessment.

Assessment provides a foundation for making sound evaluative judgments about students' learning and achievement. Teachers need to use fair and unbiased criteria in order to assess student learning objectively and accurately and make appropriate decisions about student placement. For example, in assigning Jon to a reading group, the teacher will use his test scores as an indication of his skill level. Are the inferences from the test results valid for the school's reading program? Are his test scores consistent over several months or years? Are they consistent with his performance in class? The teacher should ask and then answer these questions so that he or she can make intelligent decisions about Jon. On the other hand, will knowledge of the test scores affect the teacher's perception of classroom performance and create a self-fulfilling prophecy? Teachers also evaluate students in order to assign grades, and the challenge is to balance "objective" test scores with more subjective, informally gathered information. Both kinds of evaluative information are necessary, but both can be inaccurate and are frequently misused.

In the first article in this unit, some fundamental assessment concepts are presented as a foundation for valid, reliable, and fair classroom assessment. Performance-based assessment is promoted by Judy Arter in the second article. This form of assessment has great potential to integrate measurement procedures with instructional methods more effectively and to focus student learning on the application of thinking and problem-solving skills in real-life contexts. Arter demonstrates this through a thorough review of all aspects of performance assessment, including scoring criteria, rubrics, and principles of grading. She also shows how performance assessment, in comparison to other kinds of assessment, is based on constructivistic learning theory.

Alfie Kohn presents a provocative perspective on standardized testing that argues that such tests have very detrimental effects on student learning. Notably, he suggests that high-stakes tests encourage low-level learning. In the last article, Thomas Guskey examines grading practices and makes suggestions for how to assign grades so that the results provide accurate and helpful information as well as motivate students in the context of our standards-oriented school environment.

Fundamental assessment principles for teachers and school administrators

James H. McMillan
Virginia Commonwealth University

While several authors have argued that there are a number of "essential" assessment concepts, principles, techniques, and procedures that teachers and administrators need to know about (e.g. Calfee & Masuda,1997; Cizek, 1997; Ebel, 1962; Farr & Griffin, 1973; Fleming & Chambers, 1983; Gullickson, 1985, 1986; Mayo, 1967; McMillan, 2001; Sanders & Vogel, 1993; Schafer, 1991; Stiggins & Conklin, 1992), there continues to be relatively little emphasis on assessment in the preparation of, or professional development of, teachers and administrators (Stiggins, 2000). In addition to the admonitions of many authors, there are established professional standards for assessment skills of teachers (*Standards for Teacher Competence in Educational Assessment of Students* ([1990]), a framework of assessment tasks for administrators (Impara & Plake, 1996), the Code of Professional Responsibilities in Educational Measurement (1995), the Code of Fair Testing Practices (1988), and the new edition of *Standards for Educational and Psychological Testing* (1999). If that isn't enough information, a project directed by Arlen Gullickson at The Evaluation Center of Western Michigan University will publish standards for evaluations of students in the near future.

The purpose of this article is to use suggestions and guidelines from these sources, in light of current assessment demands and contemporary theories of learning and motivation, to present eleven "basic principles" to guide the assessment training and professional development of teachers and administrators. That is, what is it about assessment, whether large-scale or classroom, that is fundamental for effective understanding and application? What are the "big ideas" that, when well understood and applied, will effectively guide good assessment practices, regardless of the grade level, subject matter, developer, or user of the results? As Jerome Bruner stated it many years ago in his classic, *The Process of Education*: "...the curriculum of a subject should be determined by the most fundamental understanding that can be achieved of the underlying principles that give structure to that subject." (Bruner, 1960, p.31). What principles, in other words, provide the most essential, fundamental "structure" of assessment knowledge and skills that result in effective educational practices and improved student learning?

Assessment is inherently a process of professional judgment.

The first principle is that professional judgment is the foundation for assessment and, as such, is needed to properly understand and use all aspects of assessment. The measurement of student performance may seem "objective" with such practices as machine scoring and multiple-choice test items, but even these approaches are based on professional assumptions and values. Whether that judgment occurs in constructing test questions, scoring essays, creating rubrics, grading participation, combining scores, or interpreting standardized test scores, the essence of the process is making professional interpretations and decisions. Understanding this principle helps teachers and administrators realize the importance of their own judgments and those of others in evaluating the quality of assessment and the meaning of the results.

Assessment is based on separate but related principles of measurement evidence and evaluation.

It is important to understand the difference between measurement evidence (differentiating degrees of a trait by description or by assigning scores) and evaluation (interpretation of the description or scores). Essential measurement evidence skills include the ability to understand and interpret the meaning of descriptive statistical procedures, including variability, correlation, percentiles, standard scores, growth-scale scores, norming, and principles of combining scores for grading. A conceptual understanding of these techniques is needed (not necessarily knowing how to compute statistics) for such tasks as interpreting student strengths and weaknesses, reliability and validity evidence, grade determination, and making admissions decisions. Schafer (1991) has indicated that these concepts and techniques comprise part of an essential language for educators. They also provide a common basis for communication about "results," interpretation of evidence, and appropriate use of data. This is increasingly important given the pervasiveness of standards-based, high-stakes, large-scale assessments. Evaluation concerns merit and worth of the data as applied to a specific use or context. It involves what Shepard (2000) has described as the systematic analysis of evidence. Like students, teachers and administrators need analysis skills to effectively interpret evidence and make value judgments about the meaning of the results.

Assessment decision-making is influenced by a series of tensions.

Competing purposes, uses, and pressures result in tension for teachers and administrators as they make assessment-related decisions. For example, good teaching is characterized by assessments that motivate and engage students in ways that are consistent with their philosophies of teaching and learning and with theories of development, learning and motivation. Most teachers want to use constructed-response assessments because they believe this kind of testing is best to ascertain student understanding. On the other hand, factors external to the classroom, such as mandated large-scale testing, promote different assessment strategies, such as using selected-response tests and providing practice in objective test-taking (McMillan & Nash, 2000). Further examples of tensions include the following.

- Learning vs auditing
- Formative (informal and ongoing) vs summative (formal and at the end)
- Criterion-referenced vs norm-referenced
- Value-added vs absolute standards
- Traditional vs alternative
- Authentic vs contrived
- Speeded tests vs power tests
- Standardized tests vs classroom tests

These tensions suggest that decisions about assessment are best made with a full understanding of how different factors influence the nature of the assessment. Once all the alternatives are understood, priorities need to be made; trade-offs are inevitable. With an appreciation of the tensions teachers and administrators will hopefully make better informed, better justified assessment decisions.

Assessment influences student motivation and learning.

Grant Wiggins (1998) has used the term 'educative assessment' to describe techniques and issues that educators should consider when they design and use assessments. His message is that the nature of assessment influences what is learned and the degree of meaningful engagement by students in the learning process. While Wiggins contends that assessments should be authentic, with feedback and opportunities for revision to improve rather than simply audit learning, the more general principle is understanding how different assessments affect students. Will students be more engaged if assessment tasks are problem-based? How do students study when they know the test consists of multiple-choice items? What is the nature of feedback, and when is it given to students? How does assessment affect student effort?

Answers to such questions help teachers and administrators understand that assessment has powerful effects on motivation and learning. For example, recent research summarized by Black & Wiliam (1998) shows that student self-assessment skills, learned and applied as part of formative assessment, enhance student achievement.

Assessment contains error.

Teachers and administrators need to not only know that there is error in all classroom and standardized assessments, but also more specifically how reliability is determined and how much error is likely. With so much emphasis today on high-stakes testing for promotion, graduation, teacher and administrator accountability, and school accreditation, it is critical that all educators understand concepts like standard error of measurement, reliability coefficients, confidence intervals, and standard setting. Two reliability principles deserve special attention. The first is that reliability refers to scores, not instruments. Second, teachers and administrators need to understand that, typically, error is underestimated. A recent paper by Rogosa (1999) effectively illustrates the concept of underestimation of error by showing in terms of percentile rank probable true score hit-rate and test-retest results.

Good assessment enhances instruction.

Just as assessment impacts student learning and motivation, it also influences the nature of instruction in the classroom. There has been considerable recent literature that has promoted assessment as something that is integrated with instruction, and not an activity that merely audits learning (Shepard, 2000). When assessment is integrated with instruction it informs teachers about what activities and assignments will be most useful, what level of teaching is most appropriate, and how summative assessments provide diagnostic information. For instance, during instruction activities informal, formative assessment helps teachers know when to move on, when to ask more questions, when to give more examples, and what responses to student questions are most appropriate. Standardized test scores, when used appropriately, help teachers understand student strengths and weaknesses to target further instruction.

Good assessment is valid.

Validity is a concept that needs to be fully understood. Like reliability, there are technical terms and issues associated with validity that are essential in helping teachers and administrators make reasonable and appropriate inferences from assessment results (e.g., types of validity evidence, validity generalization, construct underrepresentation, construct-irrelevant variance, and discriminant and convergent evidence). Of critical importance is the concept of evidence based on consequences, a new major validity category in the recently revised *Standards*. Both intended and unintended consequences of assessment need to be examined with appropriate evidence that supports particular arguments or points of view. Of equal importance is getting teachers and administrators to understand their role in gathering and interpreting validity evidence.

Good assessment is fair and ethical.

Arguably, the most important change in the recently published *Standards* is an entire new major section entitled "Fairness in Testing." The *Standards* presents four views of fairness: as absence of bias (e.g., offensiveness and unfair penalization), as equitable treatment, as equality in outcomes, and as opportunity to learn. It includes entire chapters on the rights and responsibilities of test takers, testing individuals of diverse linguistic backgrounds, and testing individuals with disabilities or special needs. Three additional areas are also important:

- Student knowledge of learning targets and the nature of the assessments prior to instruction (e.g., knowing what will be tested, how it will be graded, scoring criteria, anchors, exemplars, and examples of performance).
- Student prerequisite knowledge and skills, including test-taking skills.
- Avoiding stereotypes.

Good assessments use multiple methods.

Assessment that is fair, leading to valid inferences with a minimum of error, is a series of measures that show student understanding through multiple methods. A complete picture of what students understand and can do is put together in pieces comprised by different approaches to assessment. While testing experts and testing companies stress that important decisions should not be made on the basis of a single test score, some educators at the local level, and some (many?) politicians at the state and at the national level, seem determined to violate this principle. There is a need to understand the entire range of assessment techniques and methods, with the realization that each has limitations.

Good assessment is efficient and feasible.

Teachers and school administrators have limited time and resources. Consideration must be given to the efficiency of different approaches to assessment, balancing needs to implement methods required to provide a full understanding with the time needed to develop and implement the methods, and score results. Teacher skills and knowledge are important to consider, as well as the level of support and resources.

Good assessment appropriately incorporates technology.

As technology advances and teachers become more proficient in the use of technology, there will be increased opportunities for teachers and administrators to use computer-based techniques (e.g., item banks, electronic grading, computer-adapted testing, computer-based simulations), Internet resources, and more complex, detailed ways of reporting results. There is,

however, a danger that technology will contribute to the mindless use of new resources, such as using items on-line developed by some companies without adequate evidence of reliability, validity, and fairness, and crunching numbers with software programs without sufficient thought about weighting, error, and averaging.

To summarize, what is most essential about assessment is understanding how general, fundamental assessment principles and ideas can be used to enhance student learning and teacher effectiveness. This will be achieved as teachers and administrators learn about conceptual and technical assessment concepts, methods, and procedures, for both large-scale and classroom assessments, and apply these fundamentals to instruction.

Notes:

An earlier version of this paper was presented at the Annual Meeting of the American Educational Research Association, New Orleans, April 24, 2000.

References

Black, P., & Wiliam, D. (1998). Inside the black box: Raising standards through classroom assessment. *Phi Delta Kappan*, 80(2), 139–148.

Bruner, J. S. (1960). *The process of education*. NY: Vintage Books.

Calfee, R. C., & Masuda, W. V. (1997). Classroom assessment as inquiry. In G. D. Phye (Ed.) *Handbook of classroom assessment: Learning, adjustment, and achievement*. NY: Academic Press.

Cizek, G. J. (1997). Learning, achievement, and assessment: Constructs at a crossroads. In G. D. Phye (Ed.) *Handbook of classroom assessment: Learning, adjustment, and achievement*. NY: Academic Press.

Code of fair testing practices in education (1988). Washington, DC: Joint Committee on Testing Practices (American Psychological Association). Available http://ericae.net/code.htm

Code of professional responsibilities in educational measurement (1995). Washington, DC: National Council on Measurement in Education. Available http://www.unl.edu/buros/article2.html

Ebel, R. L. (1962). Measurement and the teacher. *Educational Leadership*, 20, 20–24.

Farr, R., & Griffin, M. (1973). Measurement gaps in teacher education. *Journal of Research and Development in Education*, 7(1), 19–28.

Fleming, M., & Chambers, B. (1983). Teacher-made tests: Windows on the classroom. In W. E. Hathaway (Ed.), *Testing in the schools*, San Francisco: Jossey-Bass.

Gullickson, A. R. (1985). Student evaluation techniques and their relationship to grade and curriculum. *Journal of Educational Research*, 79(2), 96–100.

Gullickson, A. R. (1996). Teacher education and teacher-perceived needs in educational measurement and evaluation. *Journal of Educational Measurement*, 23(4), 347–354.

Impara, J. C., & Plake, B. S. (1996). Professional development in student assessment for educational administrators. *Educational Measurement: Issues and Practice*, 15(2), 14–19.

Mayo, S. T. (1967). Pre-service preparation of teachers in educational measurement. U.S. Department of Health, Education and Welfare. Washington, DC: Office of Education/Bureau of Research.

McMillan, J. H. (2001). *Essential assessment concepts for teachers and administrators*. Thousand Oaks, CA: Corwin Publishing Company. Available Amazon.com

McMillan, J. H., & Nash, S. (2000). Teachers' classroom assessment and grading decision making. Paper presented at the Annual Meeting of the National Council of Measurement in Education, New Orleans.

Rogosa, D. (1999). How accurate are the STAR national percentile rank scores for individual students?—An interpretive guide. Palo Alto, CA: Stanford University.

Sanders, J. R., & Vogel, S. R. (1993). The development of standards for teacher competence in educational assessment of students, in S. L. Wise (Ed.), *Teacher training in measurement and assessment skills*, Lincoln, NB: Burros Institute of Mental Measurements.

Schafer, W. D. (1991). Essential assessment skills in professional education of teachers. *Educational Measurement: Issues and Practice*, 10, (1), 3–6.

Shepard, L. A. (2000). The role of assessment in a learning culture. Paper presented at the Annual Meeting of the American Educational Research Association. Available http://www.aera.net/meeting/am2000/wrap/praddr01.htm

Standards for educational and psychological testing (1999). Washington, DC: American Educational Research Association, American Psychological Association, National Council on Measurement in Education.

Standards for teacher competence in educational assessment of students. (1990). American Federation of Teachers, National Council on Measurement in Education, National Education Association. Available: http://www.unl.edu/buros/article3.html

Stiggins, R. J. (2000). Classroom assessment: A history of neglect, a future of immense potential. Paper presented at the Annual Meeting of the American Educational Research Association.

Stiggins, R. J., & Conklin, N. F. (1992). *In teachers' hands: Investigating the practices of classroom assessment*. Albany, NY: State University of New York Press, Albany.

Wiggins, G. (1998). *Educative assessment: Designing assessments to inform and improve student performance*. San Francisco: Jossey-Bass. Available Amazon.com

Contact Information:

James H. McMillan
Box 842020
Virginia Commonwealth University
Richmond, VA 23284-2020

Teaching About Performance Assessment

How should we teach prospective teachers about performance assessment? What are the issues and concerns that new teachers will encounter as they begin their teaching careers? How can assessment and instruction be better integrated in classrooms?

Judy Arter

Northwest Regional Educational Laboratory

If there is anything definite about performance assessment, it is that experts cannot agree on a definition. Because of this, it is prudent to let readers know the definition used in the current article: Performance assessment is assessment based on observation and judgment (Airasian, 1991, p. 252; Stiggins, 1997, p. 175). One observes a performance or a product and then judges its quality. Examples abound, everything from the driver's test and Olympic judging to the multitude of formal and informal observations teachers make in the classroom: skill levels on such things as oral presentations and wrestling, quality of products such as essays and laboratory reports, and affective orientation, including level of effort and desire to learn. Although fairly broad, this definition is not intended to include *all* constructed-response-type items (especially short answer and fill in the blank), but, admittedly, the line between constructed response and performance assessment is thin. (This is probably why there are so many attempts at definition.)

Performance assessment is not new. Teachers have always observed student performances and products and made judgments about them. However, there are recent developments that highlight the current importance of teaching teachers to do performance assessment well (Herman, 1997). Although undoubtedly familiar to readers, I mention them briefly because they set up major themes for the text that follows.

1. Teachers are being asked to assist students to acquire more complex skills than ever before. Witness the content standards being developed by many states and professional organizations. Students are to read with comprehension, write well, be critical thinkers, be lifelong learners, be collaborative workers, be able to communicate their mathematical understanding, and so forth. Such complex learning targets for students require complex assessments, including performance assessments.

2. Teachers are being asked to use formal performance assessments on a daily basis, and for purposes other than grading. It is not enough to wait until the year-end, large-scale assessment to see what percentage of students meet "mastery." Continuous classroom monitoring of student progress toward important, and frequently complex, learning targets is the essence of standards-based instruction and education.

3. Since performance assessments are increasingly being used for additional purposes, some of which are high stakes, there have been many efforts to make this essentially subjective form of assessment as objective as possible. Familiar examples are standardization of tasks and criteria, careful training of those judging work, and technical work on thorny issues such as sampling and generalizability. Although the focus for this work is generally large-scale assessment, the resulting refinement of performance assessment methods has implications for improving classroom practice as well.

4. There is tantalizing preliminary evidence that performance assessments can be used for more than simply

providing information about students for decision making (as important as this is). Developing and using performance assessments can have positive impacts on instruction and student attitudes and learning, even to the point that performance assessment materials and methods can be used to help students acquire the very skills being assessed (e.g., Arter, Spandel, Cuiham, & Pollard, 1994; Borko et al., 1997; Clarke & Stephens, 1996; Khattri, 1995; Office of Educational Research and Improvement, 1997).

Because of these trends and findings, teachers need to know how to do performance assessment well (i.e., prudently, efficiently, validly, and with positive consequences for students). Yet, studies continue to show that K–12 teachers lack skill in assessing their students (Hills, 1991; Impara, Plake, & Fager, 1993; Plake, Impara, & Fager, 1993) and that they feel unprepared and uncomfortable in terms of their knowledge of assessment practices (Shafer, 1993; Wise, Lukin, & Roos, 1991; Zhang, 1997). Additionally a recent study (Fager, Plake, & Impara, 1997) found that even in those institutions where preservice course work is required or offered, there is a certain amount of feeling that it does not cover what teachers will really need to know and be able to do and that the courses are not taught by those most familiar with assessment issues and developments. Given the importance of effective assessment, we must all continue to think about and discuss what teachers need to know and be able to do with respect to classroom assessment, the best ways to assist them in learning it, and how we will know when they are competent.

Based on the experience of the Northwest Regional Educational Laboratory (NWREL) in conducting thousands of workshops for teachers on assessment and the fruitful ideas of other preservice and in-service instructors (such as Airasian, 1991; Marzano & Kendall, 1996; McTighe, 1996; and Stiggins, 1997), this article describes seven topics that should be included in a course on performance assessment and provides some ideas for teaching them. The focus is on performance assessment as practiced in the classroom; because teachers also need to know about large-scale assessments, however, this topic is discussed as well.

The following is a series of questions to consider: Do you believe that good classroom assessment can improve student achievement? Do you believe that assessing students well will make teachers' lives easier? Do you believe that it is possible to use assessment as a tool that can directly influence student learning as well as a tool for making educational decisions about students? Do you believe that assessment and instruction can be integrated? If we believe these things, then we have to be ready to demonstrate them to teachers or they will not engage in the process of learning to do classroom assessment differently. I propose that we can demonstrate all of these things with performance assessment if we approach it correctly. Not that these things cannot be demonstrated

with other forms of assessment. Rather, performance assessment especially lends itself to these ideas, can draw teachers into the topic of assessment in general, and is the focus of this article.

What Teachers Need to Know and Be Able to Do With Respect to Performance Assessment

The *Standards for Teacher Competence in Educational Assessment of Students* (American Federation of Teachers, National Council on Measurement in Education, and National Education Association, 1990) provide a good starting place for describing what teachers need to know and be able to do with respect to performance assessment. The *Standards* specify that teachers be competent in seven areas:

1. Choosing assessment methods appropriate for instructional decisions.
2. Developing assessment methods appropriate for instructional decisions.
3. Administering, scoring, and interpreting results of assessments.
4. Using assessment results when making decisions.
5. Developing valid pupil grading procedures.
6. Communicating assessment results to students and others.
7. Recognizing unethical, illegal, and inappropriate assessment methods and uses.

The *Standards* are a good place to start and provide a wealth of detail on the specific knowledge and skills teachers should have in these areas, but they do not adequately cover several important topics, those especially relevant to performance assessment.

First, the document does not mention the central necessity of having a clear conception of what is to be assessed and being sure that these targets are the best ones to shoot for. How can one assess (or teach) something if it is not clear exactly what knowledge or skills a student is to possess? Having clear targets means more than merely stating that a learning goal for students is "writing" or "problem solving." Rather, *clarity* of targets requires knowing, for example, what good writing looks like, how students develop toward this target, and what adequate (and weak) writing looks like at various grade levels.

In my work with teachers, I am becoming more and more convinced (along with others, such as Stiggins, 1997, chap. 3, and Marzano & Kendall, 1996, p. 27) that improving classroom assessment has less to do with the actual mechanism of developing assessments than with being clearer on what is to be assessed. As one reviewer of an earlier version of this article stated, "If you can hammer away on exactly what it is the teacher wants the student to be able to do, sometimes the assessment sort of pops out of the discussion." For example, in writing

Table 1

Summary of Performance Assessment Knowledge and Skills

General topic	Specific subtopics	Relationship to standards	Relationship to 3 additional topics
What performance assessment is and why we should care	Definitions Two mandatory parts to a performance assessment: tasks and criteria	Standards 1, 2	Clear targets Use a tool for learning
When to use performance assessment	Which student learning targets are best assessed with a performance assessment and which with another method Balance—performance assessment not always the answer Balance—ideal against practical	Standards 1, 2	Target-method match Use as a tool for learning
Design options	Design options for tasks Design options for criteria	Standard 2	
The nature of quality and why we should care	Quality in tasks and when to use various design options Quality in performance criteria and when to use various designs Consistency in scoring Sampling Avoiding possible sources of bias and distortion Building in features that result in positive consequences for teachers, instructions and students	Standards 1-4, 7	Clear targets Target-method match Use as a tool for learning
How to develop tasks and criteria	Practice developing tasks and criteria	Standard 2	Clear targets
Use as an instructional methodology	How to use criteria to assist students to self-assess, and features of criteria that maximize this use How to teach criteria to students The role of performance criteria in standards-based education		Clear targets Use as a tool for learning
Grading and reporting	Converting rubric scores to grades Ways to report on student progress besides grades	Standards 5, 6	

teachers need to grapple with the balance between assessing enabling skills for writing well (e.g., spelling, grammar, good sentence structure, developing a main idea with details, different ways to organize ideas) and determining whether students can use these skills in concert to actually write. Both probably need to be addressed, but exactly which skills and in what balance?

The second topic, not emphasized strongly enough in the *Standards,* is "target-method match." The *Standards* stress matching purposes with methods (see Standards 1 and 2) but not choosing the assessment method that best matches the skills and knowledge to be assessed. The

third topic not covered well in the *Standards* is the use of assessment as a tool for learning.

Keeping all of this in mind, Table 1 presents a summary of what classroom teachers need to know and be able to do with respect to performance assessment. The first column lists general topics for instruction, the second column provides subtopics, the third column cross references the topics to the *Standards for Teacher Competence,* and the final column cross references topics to the three additional areas described earlier: clear and appropriate targets, target-method match, and using assessment as a tool for learning.

Table 1 provides an outline for the remainder of the article. It is impossible in a short article to completely describe such a unit on performance assessment, including ideas on how to teach each topic. Therefore, I try here to (a) hit the high points and major things that seem to confuse teachers, (b) provide some ideas on where to begin so that the order is not only logical but immediately engaging to the adult learner, (c) describe how topics interrelate, and (d) provide references to other documents I have found to be particularly useful. I also emphasize the classroom instructional uses of performance assessment, since that topic has been less well developed by others. To avoid confusion, I refer to child learners as "students" and preservice or in-service teachers as "teachers" or "adult learners."

What Performance Assessment Is and Why We Should Care

Performance Assessment "Kick Off" Readings

Three papers useful for beginning a unit on performance assessment are those of Rudner and Boston (1994), Wiggins (1992), and Stayter and Johnston (1990). The Rudner and Boston article is a balanced overview of the rationale for performance assessment, what various groups are doing with respect to performance assessment, and current issues. (Much of this is still relevant, although descriptions of activities in specific states have changed somewhat since 1994.) The basic message of the Wiggins article is that quality matters. The point of the Stayter and Johnston chapter is that assessment affects kids; if we want it to have a positive effect, we need to pay close attention to design issues. Teachers find these articles accessible, informative, and provocative. As they read, teachers can make notes on what ideas they like, find problematic, and want to know more about. This "kick-off" activates prior knowledge, sets the tone that learning will be cooperative, provides the instructor with information about adult learners' prior knowledge and attitudes, and emphasizes the major themes of the unit.

Using Performance Assessment Definitions to Emphasize Why We Should Care

A useful way to proceed is to familiarize teachers with the definition of performance assessment and ask them to cite examples in daily life and the classroom. This provides an excellent opportunity to point out that performance assessment is not fundamentally new, to outline changes in performance assessment (as outlined in the introduction), and to emphasize the need for balance in assessment (performance assessment is simply one tool, not a cure-all). Regardless of the specific definition of performance assessment one uses, it is important to emphasize early on that there are two parts to a performance assessment: tasks and criteria. It is not assessment if it does not include both.

The Importance of Criteria. One consistently encounters "performance assessments" from supposedly reputable organizations that are simply tasks. For example, a recent Association for Supervision and Curriculum Development (ASCD) publication (Checkley, 1997) extolled the virtues of the following geography "authentic assessment." The teacher asked his students to research the name of their town. The students found other towns all across the United States with the same name. The students wrote to each of these towns and prepared a research paper and a museum display. This process purportedly assessed research skills, geographic knowledge, and communication skills. However, there were no criteria for judging the quality of student performance on any of these skills in the context of this task. So, why is this assessment? Granted, this might be a rich, "authentic," engaging task for students in which they might actually learn something about research skills, geography, and communication. But there is no way to know what, in fact, they learn.

Teachers tend to be better at developing rich, interesting tasks in which to engage students than they are at developing the criteria that describe quality performance on the task. This point is made repeatedly by those assisting teachers in developing performance assessments:

> Respondents claim that an important purpose of portfolios is valid assessment of student progress and growth, yet nowhere in the packets have we found a clear account of how achievement is to be measured. None of the portfolio guide books… [provide] help in analysis, scoring, or grading. (Calfee & Perfumo, 1993, p. 534)

> Teachers [frequently] ask the wrong question first… "What do we do?"—putting the focus immediately on designing tasks—when they need to ask, "What do we want kids to know and be able to do? How well? What does quality look like?" [We] need to ask these questions very clearly first. (Hibbard, 1996, p. 5)

In my work with teachers, it is the skill of "rubric writing" which is most elusive. Perhaps it's because we're used to assigning single grades for complex assignments, knowing what an "A" looks like in our heads, but rarely "putting it to paper" so that our students can see it as well. Perhaps the difficulty in writing scoring criteria also lies in the challenge of describing just what it really looks like to perform well, or better yet, to perform at a variety of levels of competency. Nevertheless, it is the use of rubrics as an indispensable part of the instructional process which completes the vital link between assessment and instruction. Until we invest the time discerning for ourselves what excellence in writing, or speaking, or dancing, or singing, or whatever looks like, we are unable to fully "teach" our students to achieve at these levels. (Mendel, undated)

High-quality performance criteria are essential for providing consistency between raters and for use with students as a learning tool. Good ways to illustrate the importance of criteria for these two uses are provided in the next two sections.

Using Performance Criteria to Provide Consistency Between Raters. Give adult learners a performance to assess; for example, show them a student giving an oral presentation. Ask them to evaluate the quality of performance on that task without providing them any criteria. Have them discuss their frustrations, ideas, and solutions in small groups. Then provide illustrations of good-quality performance criteria for oral presentations (Massachusetts State Department of Education, 1983; Usrey, 1998) and ask the adult learners to again evaluate performance on the task. Have them discuss the differences that good criteria make.

This activity points to the first need for criteria: to provide consistency between raters and within the same rater over time and across tasks. This activity can also lead to a good discussion of the desirability of standard criteria for use by all teachers in a grade, building, district, or department. Furthermore, it can result in a useful discussion about how high-quality criteria define complex learning targets; in fact, high-quality criteria are the final definition of complex learning targets. Teachers can then discuss how having such clear definitions might decrease their anxiety level by helping them to see desired student learning targets more clearly. Finally, the activity of scoring performance both with and without criteria can lead to a fruitful examination of the need to include the correct indicators in the criteria; the criteria must describe what we mean by quality performance. If they do not, teachers will teach to the wrong targets.

Using Performance Criteria to Improve Student Achievement. Discuss the criteria used on a driver's test. Actually contact the Department of Motor Vehicles and ask what the criteria are. (If an individual is to obtain a driver's license in the state of Washington, for example, the examiner must ultimately decide that the individual has adequate skill, has not caused congestion, and has not caused a danger.) Ask the adult learners whether it would be important for students to "know" these criteria in advance and, if so, why. The answer is typically a resounding "yes," because criteria help students know what counts so that they can practice. This decreases student anxiety levels.

Then ask the adult learners what it means to "know" criteria. Is it enough simply to hand the criteria to prospective drivers as they begin their test? (Teachers always say "no.") If students are to *know* criteria, they must be discussed beginning on the first day of class, practiced

with feedback, be illustrated with examples of good and poor performance on each important trait or dimension, modeled by the teacher, used by the students to assess their own work and that of others, and used to guide the revision of performance.

This activity points to the second major use for performance criteria: helping students understand the nature of the skills they are to master and providing a standard of comparison against which students can measure their progress. In short, performance criteria can be a tool to help students acquire the very skills assessed.

These two activities—"scoring with and without performance criteria" and "the driver's test"—begin right away to emphasize the use of performance criteria (a) to clarify the targets of instruction, (b) to track student progress toward these targets, and (c) as an instructional tool in the classroom, as noted in Table 1.

The Importance of Tasks. The other half of the performance assessment equation involves the tasks assigned to students. Tasks elicit a product or performance that can then be assessed with the criteria. Much has been written about developing rich, engaging, real-life tasks, tasks that are capable of eliciting the desired complex performances on the part of the student (e.g., McTighe, 1996). One point about performance tasks that is frequently confusing to teachers is that the task can be *any* activity during the course of which the quality of performance will be observed; it does not necessarily have to be something that occurs separately at the end of instruction. There is a place for these summative, separate assessments, but much "observation and judgment" will occur during the course of regular instruction; for example, how well is a student reading today, or how effective is group collaboration on a particular activity? The key to having daily observation be sound assessment is to have high-quality criteria that teachers have internalized to the extent that they can consistently judge performances, regardless of the context. The presence of criteria makes daily "anecdotal records" actually mean something.

When to Use Performance Assessment

Good assessment means balanced assessment: having a clear idea of what one wants to assess and then choosing the best way to assess it (target-method match; see Table 1). A rule of thumb is that simple learning targets involve simple assessment and complex learning targets involve complex assessment. For example, knowledge and simple skills (e.g., long division) can be assessed well via multiple-choice, matching, true-false, and short answer formats. However, a performance assessment is probably needed to assess writing, mathematical problem solving, science process skills, critical thinking, oral presentations, and group collaboration skills.

Good treatments of matching methods to targets can be found in Stiggins (1997, p. 81) and Marzano and Kendall (1996, p. 311). Stiggins, for example, matches meth-

Table 2

Matching Learning Targets to Assessment Methods

	Selected response	Essay	Performance assessment	Personal communication
Knowledge mastery	X	X		X
Reasoning proficiency	O	X	X	X
Skills			X	X
Ability to create products			X	
Dispositions	X	O	O	X

ods to targets as shown in Table 2. An *X* denotes a good match. An *O* denotes a partial match. A complete treatment of the reasons for the *X*s and *O*s is outside the scope of this article (and has already been done very well in the sources just cited). However, it is useful to note here that the best way to think of "good" matches is as follows: prudent, efficient, valid, and having positive consequences. Thus, although one could use performance assessment to assess all student outcomes, one probably should not because it would not be very efficient or prudent or necessarily have positive outcomes for instruction and students. It is best to save the power of performance assessment for the outcomes most needing it, especially those situations in which having written criteria for complex skills and products will help students understand the nature of the targets they are to reach.

It is useful to show adult learners examples of attempts to assess targets such as reasoning or reading comprehension in a multiple-choice format. Then show them performance assessments aimed at the same target and discuss what each format is—and is not—capable of assessing. Fixed response assessments, even when done well, tend to address decontextualized skills in isolation, while performance assessments, if done well, require students to select skills to use in concert to produce a product or perform an act. Both are useful, depending on what it is one wants to assess. It always goes back to being clear enough about the target to be assessed.

Three examples of thinking skills assessments that involve different methods and could be compared in the manner described above are: the Cornell Critical Thinking Test (multiple choice; Ennis, Millman, & Tomko, 1985), the Test on Appraising Observations (choose an answer and then justify one's choice; Norris, 1990), and performance criteria for judging the "intellectual quality" of student work (Newmann, Secada, & Wehlage, 1995).

Design Options

The tasks and performance criteria used in performance assessments vary widely. The following are the major ways in which I have seen tasks vary. (I include variations

in both stimulus and response because both represent task demands on the student; examples of these types are detailed in Regional Educational Laboratories, 1998, chap. 3.)

- A single correct answer or multiple, equally good answers
- Group work, individual work, or a combination of both
- All written versus manipulatives and equipment
- Amount of choice on how to respond (written, picture, oral, etc.)
- Format/length/complexity (on demand, project, portfolio)
- Amount of scaffolding: steps and processes spelled out or left to the student
- Student choice of which task to perform

The major ways in which performance criteria appear to vary include the following:

- Task-specific or general. Task-specific performance criteria spell out separately what responses should look like on each task; there is a separate scoring guide for each task (e.g., the open-ended math items on the Constructed Response Supplement to the Iowa Tests, 1997). In general performance criteria, the same rubric is used across similar tasks (e.g., the six-trait model for writing; see the Appendix).
- Holistic or analytic trait. In holistic performance criteria, there is one score for the overall product or performance (e.g., the math rubrics on the Constructed Response Supplement to the Iowa Tests, 1997). In analytical trait performance criteria, there are multiple scores for a single performance or product, one for each important dimension or trait (e.g., the reading rubrics used in the Oregon state assessment or the six-trait model in the Appendix).

- Number of score points. Generally there are from three (e.g., several items on the Washington Assessment of Student Learning [Washington Commission on Student Learning, 1998]) to six (e.g., Oregon state assessments [Oregon Department of Education, 1997]).
- Amount of detail used to describe each score point. Some performance criteria are extremely skimpy (e.g., Washington state's writing rubric [Washington Commission on Student Learning, 1998]), while others attempt to be extremely descriptive (e.g., the six-trait model for assessing writing; see the Appendix).
- Type of detail used to describe each score point. There are some rubrics (e.g., early attempts in Vermont [Vermont Mathematics Portfolio Project, 1991]) for which the only distinctions between score point levels are words such as *inappropriate, appropriate, workable*, and *efficient* or *rarely, sometimes, frequently*, and *extensively*. It is difficult for performance raters to know when "extensively" has occurred, which can result in low rater consistency. It is also difficult for students to understand how to improve a performance or product if they are told only that their work "rarely exhibits a sense of personal expression." Other rubrics (e.g., the six-trait model) use extensive detail to describe the specific features of work that are indicators of quality. This helps in making meaning clearer, both to raters of performance and to students trying to learn the nature of quality. (In all fairness to Vermont, the Department of Education has supplied many samples of student work to demonstrate the levels and has, through the years, worked to define the levels more thoroughly.)
- Quantitative versus qualitative descriptions of score points. A quantitative score point description might be as follows: "to get an excellent, the paper must have 10 references" (for an example, see Baker, Aschbacher, Niemi, & Sato, 1992, pp. 73–74). Although amount might sometimes be a good indicator of quality, I generally dislike this type of rubric because 3 really good references might be better than 10 bad ones.
- Presence or absence of preset performance standard. On some performance criteria, the score points represent performance standards by definition (4 = "exceeds expectations," 3 = "meets expectations," 2 = "partially meets expectations," 1 = "expectations are not met"; e.g., North Dakota Fourth Grade Writing Assessment [North Dakota Department of Public Instruction, 1998]). Developers define 3 as "meeting standards" and then go about defining characteristics of such work and finding samples to illustrate what they mean. A con-

trasting procedure is to first develop a scale that defines the range of quality products or performances (I have seen scales ranging from 3 to 6 points) and then go back and decide where on this scale performance is good enough to meet various performance standards. This is the approach taken by the Oregon Department of Education (1998). Oregon developed a 6-point scale to define the range of quality and then went back to determine where the performance standards would be. In writing, for example, performance standards range from "3" to "4" depending on grade level.

Before teachers can discuss why assessment developers make the choices they do, they need to be able to recognize variations. An instructor may ask teachers to do a type of "scavenger hunt" activity in which they look for as many examples of each variation as possible. After adult learners are able to distinguish the options, the questions to be addressed are as follows: Why do developers make these choices? What are the advantages and disadvantages of each? Choices are usually made by balancing an ideal choice (for users, uses, and learning targets) against practical considerations and throwing in technical concerns for good measure. The next two sections elaborate considerations when making choices.

The Nature of Quality and Why We Should Care

Teaching the Characteristics of Quality Performance Assessment

Many thorough lists of quality considerations for performance assessments exist (Table 3 summarizes what others have said; another good source is Herman, 1996). Note that such lists include the need for clear and appropriate learning targets, matching performance assessment choices to targets, and use as a tool for learning (see Table 1, "The nature of quality" col. 4).

Coming up with a list of quality features of performance assessment is the easy part. Teaching adult learners the nature of quality and why they should care is the tricky part. A strategy that does not seem to be effective is that of showing teachers the list of quality considerations and lecturing one's way from beginning to end. What seems to work better is to engage adult learners in a bad performance assessment and let *them* articulate what the problems are.

One example of this is a learning activity written for use by teacher trainers and instructors (Regional Educational Laboratories, 1998, Activity 1.5: Clapping Hands): In this fishbowl activity four or five teachers are the "assessees" and three to five teachers are the "assessors." Assessees are asked to perform a simple task, but each is treated differently via providing them with more infor-

Table 3
Criteria for Performance Assessments

Dimension	Yes	Somewhat	No
1. Content/skill coverage and correct method The assessment: • Clearly states skills and content to be covered • Correctly uses performance assessment to measure these skills and content • Avoids irrelevant and/or unimportant content • Deals with enduring themes or significant knowledge • Matches statements of coverage to task content and performance criteria	3	2	1
2. Performance criteria • Include everything of importance and omit irrelevant features of performance • State criteria clearly and provide samples of student work to illustrate them • Are stated generally, especially if the intent is used as an instructional tool • Are analytical traits, especially if the intent is used as an instructional tool	3	2	1
3. Performance tasks General • Elicit the desired performances or work • Recreate an "authentic" context for performance • Exemplify good instruction • Are reviewed by others (students, peers, experts) Sampling/representativeness/generalizability • Cover the content or skill area well; results can be generalized • Sample performance in a way that is representative of what a student can do Bias and distortion • Avoid factors that might get in the way of students' ability to demonstrate what they know and can do	3	2	1
4. Fairness and rater bias Performance tasks • Have content and context that are equally familiar, acceptable, and appropriate for students in all groups • Tap knowledge and skills all students have had adequate time to acquire in class • Are as free as possible of cultural, ethnic, or gender stereotypes • Are as free as possible of language barriers Performance criteria and rater training • Ensure that irrelevant features of performance do not influence how other, supposedly independent features are judged • Ensure that knowledge of the type of student does not influence judgments about performance quality • Ensure that knowledge of individual students does not affect judgements about performance quality	3	2	1
5. Consequences The assessment: • Communicates appropriate messages • Results in acceptable effects on students, teachers, and others • Is worth the instructional time devoted to it; students learn something from doing the assessment and/or using the performance criteria • Provides information relevant to the decisions being made • Is perceived by students and teachers as valid	3	2	1
6. Cost and efficiency The assessment: • Is cost efficient—the results are worth the investment • Is practical	3	2	1

Note. Copyright 1998 by Northwest Regional Educational Laboratory. Adapted with permission.

mation and help as the activity progresses. Likewise, assessors are given more information as the activity progresses. At the end, each participant describes what he or she was thinking and feeling as the activity progressed, and the entire group is invited to comment and provide examples from their own experience of occasions when they were in the position of one of the volunteers. Finally the group generates a list of what it takes to avoid the problems demonstrated in the activity: characteristics of quality tasks, performance criteria, preparation of raters, preparation of students, and reporting. Special attention is given to potential sources of bias and distortion that could lead one to draw an inappropriate conclusion about a student's achievement. These teacher-generated lists are essentially "criteria" for quality performance assessments.

A teacher more readily understands sampling, bias, unclear tasks, and unclear performance criteria when he or she personally experiences their effects. Table 4 shows a list of quality characteristics (criteria) for performance assessments generated by several teacher groups. Teachers can compare their list of criteria with that experts use for guiding the quality development of performance assessments (e.g., the list of criteria included in Table 3). In this way teachers can relate what they already know to a larger conceptual scheme.

After teachers have described for themselves what constitutes sound performance assessment, it is important for them to practice applying their criteria for quality performance assessments to actual sample assessments. It is useful to find performance assessments that are weak and strong on each dimension (trait) that is to be emphasized (e.g., tasks, criteria) and ask the teachers to critique each as a group. Then ask the adult learners what advice they would give the author of the assessment to make the assessment better on a particular trait and have them work in groups to improve the assessment using their own suggestions. It is important to focus on only a few features at a time so that teachers do not become overwhelmed with having to notice and fix everything all at once.

When the adult learners have had experience with this, have them develop their own tasks and criteria and work in peer review groups to improve their efforts. Learners could even keep a portfolio on their efforts and reflect on how their ability to develop and critique assessments has improved with time.

The interesting part of the process of (a) developing criteria for performance assessments, (b) critiquing and revising examples of anonymous performance assessments, (c) developing one's own performance assessments with peer input, and (d) keeping a portfolio is that this is exactly the same way to teach any criteria to any group of adults or students. Thus, in essence, this process models, for prospective or active teachers, what they should do with their own students in the future.

The Need to Consider Use When Determining Quality

An added complexity in discussions of quality is that use must be taken into account. Performance assessments that are adequate for one use might not be appropriate for another. For example, the features most desirable in tasks or criteria used for a large-scale, high stakes assessment might not be those most desirable in a classroom assessment that will also be used instructionally. Thus, learners will need to critique sample assessments with a specific use in mind.

As an example of how use affects assessment design, consider the various design options for performance criteria described earlier. Many large-scale performance assessment developers use task-specific, holistic criteria because (a) raters can be trained more quickly, (b) scores can be computed more quickly, and (c) it is believed that such criteria will result in higher agreement rates among raters. More useful in the classroom, however, are generalized, analytical trait criteria, which help teachers and students articulate the features of solid work that can be generalized from task to task. The value of generalized criteria for instruction has been noted in recent studies by Arter et al. (1994) and the Office of Educational Research and Improvement (1997, p. *xx*).

Consider another example of how use affects the design of performance criteria. If the purpose of the assessment is to make overall judgments about student competence, the criteria only need to be detailed enough to ensure consistent rating. If, however, the assessment is to be used to diagnose student strengths and learning needs or for instruction, all essential aspects of performance must be present, and descriptive detail is essential. Descriptive detail is important because the criteria are being used to communicate with students about the features that contribute most to the quality of a product or performance. What is left out of the criteria will be left out of the performance or product. Furthermore, this descriptive detail must be in language that students can understand, so there should be "student-friendly" versions.

An example of performance criteria that are instructionally useful (analytical trait, general, detailed, and having student-friendly versions) can be found in the six-trait model for assessing writing (NWREL, 1990, 1997; Spandel & Culham, 1998; Spandel & Stiggins, 1997). The adult version of the six-trait model is included in the Appendix.

How to Develop Performance Tasks and Criteria

A good source for assisting teachers to develop performance tasks and a variety of associated rubric types is Jay McTighe's work with the Maryland Assessment Consortium (McTighe, 1996). Here I concentrate on three ways to develop the generalized, analytical trait, detailed performance criteria that are most useful for instruction.

Table 4

Performance Assessment: The Meaning of Quality (Typical Teacher Responses)

Area	Responses
Designing tasks	Be careful of public performances; treat all students equitably; put the performance into a realistic context; be specific on instructions; open-ended; meaningful to students; consider how to handle diversity and differences (e.g., special education, cultures, gender, learning styles); the task itself is a learning experience; nonthreatening; matched to valued outcomes; equity; enough time; proper resources and equipment; can be approached by the student in a variety of ways; responses can be given in a variety of ways
Designing performance criteria	Matched to valued outcomes; clearly stated; elaboration on how to assign points; agreement on what the criteria should be; models/examples; rater buy-in; match performance criteria to task; define range of score points; covers only the important stuff; provides a "picture" of what performance would look like; has many descriptors of quality
Preparing raters	Practice; discuss differences of opinion; have models/examples of different score points; have the raters do the assessment themselves; have raters explain their ratings; calibrate the raters; check consistency over time
Preparing students	Share criteria well ahead; give students the opportunity to add to criteria; train students on what the criteria mean and how it looks when performance is good or poor; use models; do formative assessments with feedback; make the assessment purpose clear; students must have prerequisite skills; students need to trust the raters; self-assessment using the criteria
Reporting results	Make sure the scores have meaning; treat students equitably; be specific and descriptive; provide evidence; allow time for discussion; emphasize what students can do, not what they can't do; nonthreatening; meaningful to students or parents
Overall	Avoid potential sources of bias and distortion: bias in tasks, criteria, or administration; criteria that don't cover the right "stuff"; poor training of raters; poor student preparation; tasks that don't elicit the right performance; sampling inadequacy; student personality; embarrassment with regard to being compared with others; changing criteria; scheduling the assessment at bad times; fatigue of raters or students; poor student or rater motivation; lack of teacher, student, or rater buy-in; rater bias; developmentally inappropriate tasks or criteria; the tendency for raters to score toward the center of the scale; examinee manipulation of the situation or raters; testwiseness; students not knowing the criteria for success; student anxiety; too much teacher help; negative teacher attitude toward the assessment; readability of assessment materials; distractions during assessment; cultural inappropriateness of tasks

First, given sufficient expertise on the skills for which criteria are being developed, a person can sometimes just sit down and write out the criteria. This process can be illustrated with many common everyday situations. For example, most adults have fun developing criteria for effective whining, room cleaning, or restaurants. In education, most of us are familiar enough with oral presentations that we stand a chance of articulating and writing out decent criteria. And measurement experts usually can write out the criteria for a good-quality performance assessment.

These "off the top of my head" criteria, however, need to be subjected to a reality test. After the criteria have been written down, it is always a good idea to gather samples of the performance under consideration and try to rate them according to one's criteria. This process helps one notice important aspects of performance one has forgotten, borderline cases that need to be clarified through refined statements in the criteria, the need to more clearly specify levels of performance with indicators of quality and so forth. (Note that the criteria for a high-quality performance assessment included in Table 3 do not have levels defined.)

The second way to develop general performance criteria is to simply start with the student work, and this is actually where most teachers begin. Obtain sets of student work that illustrate various levels of quality on the skill in question: writing, communicating mathematical understanding, critical thinking, and so forth. Ask adult learners to sort the work into three performance stacks: strong, medium, and weak. Then have them describe the differences among the stacks (this method is illustrated in detail in Regional Educational Laboratories, 1998, Activity 2.1: Sorting Student Work).

The main problem teachers run into when sorting and describing is using descriptors that are too general. For example, when generating criteria for math problem solving, teachers want to say that one feature of a strong student response is that it is "logical." The challenge is to dig beneath the general descriptor to find the specific characteristics of the work that make one believe it is logical. I usually ask teachers to find a piece they think is logical and point out the aspects that made them think so. They usually mention things such as the following: The student chose the correct information to use, went through from beginning to end without any sidesteps, chose a procedure that would lead to a correct solution, used a problem representation (visual or mathematical) that helped clarify the problem's meaning, restated the problem accurately in his or her own words, seemed to know which representations were right for the problem, and knew when and where to make connections with other knowledge in order to proceed. If such statements can then be connected to actual samples of student work, it provides a powerful instructional tool for teachers and a powerful learning tool for students.

If adult learners have trouble sorting work, they might not have enough of an idea of the construct in question to have formed even intuitive criteria. This leads to the third approach for helping adult learners define performance criteria: They need to read the literature in the content area in question. This frequently occurs, for example, when teachers are attempting to develop criteria for critical thinking. Defining the construct and collecting relevant samples of student work to sort provides a way to profitably interact with preservice content area courses.

Even though developing criteria is a good exercise, it is fortunate that teachers do not always have to start from scratch. There are many good sources of criteria and rubrics. One of my favorites is Perlman (1994). The 70 or so rubrics in this collection provide a good opportunity for adult learners to practice distinguishing good criteria from weak ones and to practice distinguishing criteria that might work for large-scale assessment from those that might be most useful in the classroom.

Use of Criteria as an Instructional Methodology

There are two steps involved in making performance criteria work as tools for learning in the classroom: having a clear notion in one's own mind of what the criteria are and then teaching them to students. The first step was described in the previous section on developing performance criteria. The second step in making performance criteria work as instructional tools in the classroom is to teach them to students. My colleagues have developed seven strategies for teaching criteria to students (Spandel & Culham, 1998; Spandel & Stiggins, 1997). These strategies were developed in the context of writing, but several of them transfer easily to other performances and products.

The first strategy is to *teach students the vocabulary they need to think and speak like writers, communicators, and problem solvers.* Help students understand the nature of quality through engaging them in the kinds of sorting and descriptive activities described earlier. In other words, engage students in developing criteria for quality. Students need to have versions of criteria written in language they can understand (i.e., "student-friendly" rubrics). For example, the six-trait model has student-friendly versions available for primary elementary and secondary students (Regional Educational Laboratories, 1998). I have also seen student-friendly versions of mathematics problem-solving rubrics produced by the Oregon Department of Education and Washington State's Central Kitsap District (1997).

The second strategy is to *read, discuss, and score anonymous samples of student work.* Once criteria are in place, students need to practice using them, noting what is strong and weak in work. They need to not only judge the quality of work but articulate the reasons for their judgment; there is no such thing as a "correct" score, only a justifiable score. To justify their scores, students are asked to find the words in the rubric that describe the work under consideration.

The third strategy is to *practice focused revision*. In addition to being able to notice what is strong or weak in work, students need to know how to fix that which is weak. One procedure is to ask students to give advice to the author and then work in groups to improve the sample performance using the advice given. For example, when working on ideas in writing, students might note that the paper is weak because it is unfocused, emphasizes irrelevant details, or does not include enough descriptive detail to make a point (all descriptors in the trait of "ideas" in the Appendix). The students might advise the author to narrow the topic by selecting one potentially interesting point and elaborating on it using relevant details and anecdotes. Students would then revise the writing using their own advice.

The fourth strategy is to *use reallife samples to illustrate criteria*. In terms of writing, this can be done with various published items (stories, picture books, manuals, instructions, etc.). In helping students learn, for example, the concept of "voice" in writing, one might ask them to match text to authors (Mark Twain, Nathaniel Hawthorne, etc.). Or one could have students compare different writing styles.

The fifth strategy is to *have students help the teacher revise the teacher's products or performances using the criteria for quality*. For example, you could ask your adult learners to critique the performance assessments you use in your class, give you advice on how to improve them, and help you revise them. In K–12, a teacher could ask students to help revise his or her own writing. Sometimes students are amazed to see that writing does not simply emerge full blown from the pen during the first draft.

The sixth strategy is to *allow students opportunities to articulate their emerging notion of quality*. In writing, for example, students could write letters to authors describing why, using the language of the performance criteria, they like the work, or students could describe their progress to parents using the language of the performance criteria.

The final strategy is to *teach minilessons*. For writing, this means organizing regular instructional lessons by trait: ideas, organization, voice, word choice, sentence fluency and conventions. If the criteria really do describe what we mean by quality, why not teach directly to them? Teachers already teach the traits of good writing. What is often lacking is the conscious link between what is being taught and the standards being developed.

Two papers that articulate well the power of using general performance criteria to help students learn are those of Spandel (1996) and Arter (1996).

I have begun asking participants in my workshops (teachers, administrators, and others) to state the most salient characteristics of "standards-based instruction" as

they currently understand it. Admittedly an unscientific sample, here is the essence of what they have said.

- There are clearly stated long-term learning targets for students (content standards): what we want students to know and be able to do when they leave K–12 education.
- There are benchmarks along the way so that we know whether we are on track in terms of guiding students to the ultimate level of competency.
- These learning targets are connected to the real world.
- Instruction and assessment are aimed at these important targets and aligned across grade levels to reduce duplication and make it clear how the skills and understandings developed one year will be built upon the next year.
- Standards-referenced descriptions of student learning are used rather than norm-referenced or self-referenced; we define the nature of quality and match student achievement to it in order to judge achievement.
- Everybody—students, teachers, parents, community members — is aware of the nature of excellence and what it takes to succeed. Students can see where they are. Teachers can tell parents at any time how their children are progressing toward "proficiency."

The performance criteria associated with performance assessments can be a prime example of such standards-based instruction.

- Performance criteria help define standards; they are the final definition.
- Developing performance criteria is more than assessment; it helps instruction.
- Performance criteria make standards clear to students (and teachers).
- Teaching criteria to students improves the very skills being assessed.

Grading and Reporting

Grading and reporting is the final topic in Table 1 that should be covered in a course on performance assessment. This topic is covered more thoroughly in the article by Susan Brookhart and so is not discussed at length here. Let me mention, however, that the most frequent question from teachers relating to performance assessment and grading is "How do I convert rubric scores to grades?" Any instruction on performance assessment would be incomplete without helping teachers think about this question. This question is tricky because the purpose of using rubrics to begin with (to help students learn) can be at odds with the purpose of grading (to report student progress or to discipline or reward students), and frequently rubric scores need to be combined with scores from other types of assessment to arrive at a final grade. As pointed out by many authors (e.g., Association for Supervision and Curriculum Development, 1996; Kohn, 1994), teachers need to first think about the purposes for grading: Who are the users? What are the uses? What is grading supposed to accomplish? From this reflection, a method for combining rubric scores with other measures of student achievement to arrive at a "grade" sometimes emerges. One way to involve teachers in this discussion is provided in Activities 4.2 (Putting Grading and Reporting Questions in Perspective) and 4.6 (How to Convert Rubric Scores to Grades) in Regional Educational Laboratories (1998).

Conclusion

Teachers need to know how to construct, administer, score, and use the results from good-quality performance assessments. They need to know these things not just to grade or satisfy some external mandate (although the current climate demands this), but because expertise in performance assessment can make instruction faster, easier, and better. To help teachers see this, instruction on performance assessment must include building the vision of performance assessment as a tool for learning as well as a tool for tracking student progress. There is also a certain immediacy to teachers' need to know about assessment; they literally need information they can use on Monday morning. If we, as preservice and in-service instructors, cannot capture teachers' attention right away and give them something to use immediately, learning to be good assessors will take a back seat to other topics that vie for teacher attention.

What features of performance assessments make them most useful in the classroom as instructional tools? What is the impact on student achievement of using performance assessment in this manner? What approaches to teaching assessment motivate teachers to want to learn more? These are profitable areas for continuing inquiry and research.

Appendix
The Six-Trait Model for
Assessing Student Writing

Note. Copyright 1998 by Northwest Regional Educational Laboratory. Adapted with permission.

Ideas and Content (Development)

Level 5: *This paper is clear and focused. It holds the reader's attention. Relevant anecdotes and details enrich the central theme.*

a. The topic is narrow and manageable.

b. Relevant, telling, quality details give the reader important information that goes beyond the obvious or predictable.

c. Reasonably accurate details are present to support the main ideas.

d. The writer seems to be writing from knowledge or experience; the ideas are fresh and original.

e. The reader's questions are anticipated and answered.

f. Insight—an understanding of life and a knack for picking out what is significant—is an indicator of high-level performance, though not required.

Level 3: *The writer is beginning to define the topic, even though development is still basic or general.*

a. The topic is fairly broad; however, you can see where the writer is headed.

b. Support is attempted but doesn't go far enough yet in fleshing out the key issues or story line.

c. Ideas are reasonably clear, though they may not be detailed, personalized, accurate, or expanded enough to show in-depth understanding or a strong sense of purpose.

d. The writer seems to be drawing on knowledge or experience but has difficulty going from general observations to specifics.

e. The reader is left with questions. More information is needed to "fill in the blanks."

f. The writer generally stays on the topic but does not develop a clear theme. The writer has not yet focused the topic past the obvious.

Level 1: *As yet, the paper has no clear sense of purpose or central theme. To extract meaning from the text, the reader must make inferences based on sketchy or missing details. The writing reflects more than one of these problems:*

a. The writer is still in search of a topic, brainstorming, or has not yet decided what the main idea of the piece will be.

b. Information is limited or unclear or the length is not adequate for development.

c. The idea is a simple restatement of the topic or an answer to the question with little or no attention to detail.

d. The writer has not begun to define the topic in a meaningful, personal way.

e. Everything seems as important as everything else; the reader has a hard time sifting out what is important.

f. The text may be repetitious, or may read like a collection of disconnected, random thoughts with no discernible point.

Organization

Level 5: *The organization enhances and showcases the central idea or theme. The order, structure, or presentation of information is compelling and moves the reader through the text.*

a. An inviting introduction draws the reader in; a satisfying conclusion leaves the reader with a sense of closure and resolution.

b. Thoughtful transitions clearly show how ideas connect.

c. Details seem to fit where they're placed; sequencing is logical and effective.

d. Pacing is well controlled; the writer knows when to slow down and elaborate and when to pick up the pace and move on.

e. The title, if desired, is original and captures the central theme of the piece.

f. Organization flows so smoothly the reader hardly thinks about it; the choice of structure matches the purpose and audience.

Level 3: *The organizational structure is strong enough to move the reader through the text without too much confusion.*

a. The paper has a recognizable introduction and conclusion. The introduction may not create a strong sense of anticipation; the conclusion may not tie up all loose ends.

b. Transitions often work well; at other times, connections between ideas are fuzzy.

c. Sequencing shows some logic, but not under control enough that it consistently supports the ideas. In fact, sometimes it is so predictable and rehearsed that the structure takes attention away from the content.

d. Pacing is fairly well controlled, though the writer sometimes lunges ahead too quickly or spends too much time on details that do not matter.

e. A title (if desired) is present, although it may be uninspired or an obvious restatement of the prompt or topic.

f. The organization sometimes supports the main point or story line; at other times, the reader feels an urge to slip in a transition or move things around.

Level 1: *The writing lacks a clear sense of direction. Ideas, details, or events seem strung together in a loose or random fashion; there is no identifiable internal structure. The writing reflects more than one of these problems:*

a. There is no real lead to set up what follows, no real conclusion to wrap things up.

b. Connections between ideas are confusing or not even present.

c. Sequencing needs lots and lots of work.

d. Pacing feels awkward; the writer slows to a crawl when the reader wants to get on with it, and vice versa.

e. No title is present (if requested), or if present, does not match well with the content.

f. Problems with organization make it hard for the reader to get a grip on the main point or story line.

Voice

Level 5: *The writer speaks directly to the reader in a way that is individual, compelling, and engaging. The writer "aches with caring," yet is aware and respectful of the audience and the purpose for writing.*

a. The reader feels a strong interaction with the writer, sensing the person behind the words.

b. The writer takes a risk by revealing who he/she is and what he/she thinks.

c. The tone and voice give flavor and texture to the message and are appropriate for the purpose and audience.

d. Narrative writing seems honest, personal, and written from the heart. Expository or persuasive writing reflects a strong commitment to the topic by showing why the reader needs to know this and why they should care.

e. This piece screams to be read aloud, shared, and talked about. The writing makes you think about and react to the author's point of view.

Level 3: *The writer seems sincere, but not fully engaged or involved. The result is pleasant or even personable, but not compelling.*

a. The writing communicates in an earnest, pleasing manner.

b. Only one or two moments here or there surprise, delight, or move the reader.

c. The writer seems aware of an audience but weighs ideas carefully and discards personal insights in favor of safe generalities.

d. Narrative writing seems sincere, but not passionate; expository or persuasive writing lacks consistent engagement with the topic to build credibility.

e. The writer's willingness to share his/her point of view may emerge strongly at some places, but is often obscured behind vague generalities.

f.

Level 1: *The writer seems indifferent, uninvolved, or distanced from the topic and/or the audience. As a result, the paper reflects more than one of the following problems:*

a. The writer speaks in a kind of monotone that flattens all potential highs or lows of the message.

b. The writing is humdrum and "risk free."

c. The writer is not concerned with the audience, or the writer's style is a complete mismatch for the intended reader.

d. The writing is lifeless or mechanical; depending on the topic, it may be overly technical or jargonistic.

e. No point of view is reflected in the writing.

Word Choice

Level 5: *Words convey the intended message in a precise, interesting, and natural way. The words are powerful and engaging.*

a. Words are specific and accurate; it is easy to understand just what the writer means.

b. The words and phrases create pictures and linger in your mind.

c. The language is natural and never overdone; both words and phrases are individual and effective.

d. Striking words and phrases often catch the reader's eye—and linger in the reader's mind. (You can recall a handful as you reflect on the paper.)

e. Lively verbs energize the writing. Precise nouns and modifiers add depth and specificity.

f. Precision is obvious. The writer has taken care to put just the right word or phrase in just the right spot.

Level 3: *The language is functional, even if it lacks much energy. It is easy to figure out the writer's meaning on a general level.*

a. Words are adequate and correct in a general sense; they simply lack much flair and originality.

b. Familiar words and phrases communicate, but rarely capture the reader's imagination. Still, the paper may have one or two fine moments.

c. Attempts at colorful language show a willinguess to stretch and grow, but sometimes it goes too far (thesaurus overload!).

d. The writing is marked by passive verbs, everyday nouns and adjectives, and lack of interesting adverbs.

e. The words are only occasionally refined; it's more often "the first thing that popped into my mind."

f. The words and phrases are functional—with only a moment or two of sparkle.

Level 1: *The writer struggles with a limited vocabulary, searching for words to convey meaning. The writing reflects more than one of these problems:*

a. Language is so vague that only a limited message comes through.

b. "Blah, blah, blah" is all that the reader reads and hears.

c. Words are used incorrectly, making the message secondary to the misfires with the words.

d. Limited vocabulary and/or frequent misuse of parts of speech impair understanding.

e. Jargon or cliches distract or mislead. Persistent redundancy distracts the reader.

f. Problems with language leave the reader wondering what the writer is trying to say. The words just don't work in this piece.

Sentence Fluency

Level 5: *The writing has an easy flow, rhythm, and cadence. Sentences are well built, with strong and varied structure that invites expressive oral reading.*

a. Sentences are constructed in a way that underscores and enhances the meaning.

b. Sentences vary in length as well as structure. Fragments, if used, add style. Dialogue, if present, sounds natural.

c. Purposeful and varied sentence beginnings add variety and energy.

d. The use of creative and appropriate connectives between sentences and thoughts shows how each relates to and builds upon the one before it.

e. The writing has cadence; the writer has thought about the sound of the words as well as the meaning. The first time you read it aloud is a breeze.

Level 3: *The text hums along with a steady beat, but tends to be more pleasant or businesslike than musical, more mechanical than fluid.*

a. Although sentences may not seem artfully crafted or musical, they get the job done in a routine fashion.

b. Sentences are usually constructed correctly; they hang together; they are sound.

c. Sentence beginnings are not all alike; some variety is attempted.

d. The reader sometimes has to hunt for clues (e.g., connecting words and phrases like *however, therefore, naturally, after a while, on the other hand, to be specific, for example, next, first of all, later, but as it turned out, although,* etc.) that show how sentences interrelate.

e. Parts of the text invite expressive oral reading; others may be stiff, awkward, choppy or gangly.

Level 1: *The reader has to practice quite a bit in order to give this paper a fair interpretive reading. The writing reflects more than one of the following problems:*

a. Sentences are choppy, incomplete, rambling, or awkward; they need work. Phrasing does not sound natural. The patterns may create a sing-song rhythm or a chop-chop cadence that lulls the reader to sleep.

b. There is little or no "sentence sense" present. Even if this piece were flawlessly edited, the sentences would not hang together.

c. Many sentences begin the same way—and may follow the same patterns (e.g., subject-verb-object).

d. Endless connectives (*and, and so, but then, because, and then,* etc.) or a complete lack of connectives create a massive jumble of language.

e. The text does not invite expressive oral reading.

Conventions

Level 5: *The writer demonstrates a good grasp of standard writing conventions (e.g., spelling, punctuation, capitalization, grammar, usage, paragraphing) and uses conventions effectively to enhance readability. Errors tend to be so few that just minor touch-ups would get this piece ready to publish.*

a. Spelling is generally correct, even on more difficult words.

b. The punctuation is accurate, even creative, and guides the reader through the text.

c. A thorough understanding and consistent application of capitalization skills are present.

d. Grammar and usage are correct and contribute to clarity and style.

e. Paragraphing tends to be sound and reinforces the organizational structure.

f. The writer may manipulate conventions for stylistic effect—and it works! The piece is very close to being ready to publish.

Note: Grades 7 and up only—The writing is sufficiently complex to allow the writer to show skill in using a wide range of conventions. For writers at younger ages, the writing shows control over those conventions that are grade/age appropriate.

Level 3: *The writer shows reasonable control over a limited range of standard writing conventions. Conventions are sometimes handled well and enhance readability; at other times, errors are distracting and impair readability.*

a. Spelling is usually correct or reasonably phonetic on common words, but more difficult words are problematic.

b. End punctuation is usually correct; internal punctuation (commas, apostrophes, semicolons, dashes, colons, parentheses) is sometimes missing/wrong.

c. Most words are capitalized correctly; control over more sophisticated capitalization skills may be spotty.

d. Paragraphing is attempted but may run together or begin in the wrong places.

e. Problems with grammar or usage are not serious enough to distort meaning but may not be correct or accurately applied all of the time.

f. Moderate (a little of this, a little of that) editing would be required to polish the text for publication.

Level 1: *Errors in spelling, punctuation, capitalization, usage and grammar, and/or paragraphing repeatedly distract the*

reader and make the text difficult to read. The writing reflects more than one of these problems:

a. Spelling errors are frequent, even on common words.

b. Punctuation (including terminal punctuation) is often missing or incorrect.

c. Capitalization is random, and only the easiest rules show awareness of correct use.

d. Errors in grammar or usage are very noticeable, frequent, and affect meaning.

e. Paragraphing is missing, irregular, or so frequent (every sentence) that it has no relationship to the organizational structure of the text.

f. The reader must read once to decode, then again for meaning. Extensive editing (virtually every line) would be required to polish the text for publication.

References

Airasian, P. W. (1991). *Classroom assessment.* New York: McGraw-Hill.

American Federation of Teachers, National Council on Measurement in Education, and National Education Association. (1990). *Standards for teacher competence in educational assessments of students.* Washington, DC: Authors.

Arter, J. (1996). Using assessment as a tool for learning. In R. Blum & J. Arter (Eds.), *Student performance assessment in an era of restructuring.* Alexandria, VA: Association for Supervision and Curriculum Development.

Arter, J., Spandel, V., Culham, R., & Pollard, J. (1994). *The impact of training students to be self-assessors of writing.* Paper presented at the annual meeting of the American Educational Research Association, New Orleans, LA.

Association for Supervision and Curriculum Development. (1996). *Communicating student learning* (T. Guskey, Ed.). Alexandria, VA: Author.

Baker, E. L., Aschbacher, P. R., Niemi, D., & Sato, E. (1992). *CRESST performance assessment models: Assessing content area explanations.* Los Angeles: CRESST.

Borko, H., Mayfield, V., Marion, S., et al. (1997). Teachers' developing ideas and practices about mathematics performance assessment: Successes, stumbling blocks, and implications for professional development. *Teaching and Teacher Education, 13,* 259–278.

Calfee, R., & Perfumo, P. (1993). Student portfolios: Opportunities for a revolution in assessment. *Journal of Reading, 36,* 534.

Central Kitsap School District. (1997). *The student friendly guide to mathematics problem solving.* Silverdale, WA: Author.

Checkley, K. (1997). Assessment that serves instruction. *Education Update, 39*(4), 1.

Clarke, D., & Stephens, M. (1996). The ripple effect: The instructional impact of the systemic introduction of performance assessment in mathematics. In M. Birenbaum & F. Dochy (Eds.), *Alternatives in assessment of achievements, learning processes and prior knowledge.* Norwell, MA: Kluwer Academic.

Constructed Response Supplement to the Iowa Tests. (1997). Itaska, IL: Riverside.

Ennis, R. H., Millman, J., & Tomko, T. (1985). *Cornell Critical Thinking Tests* (3rd ed.). Pacific Grove, CA: Midwest.

Fager, J. J., Plake, B. S., & Impara, J. C. (1997). *Examining teacher educators' knowledge of classroom assessment: A pilot study.*

Paper presented at the NCME national conference, Chicago, IL.

Herman, J. (1996). Technical quality matters. In R. Blum & J. Arter (Eds.), *Student performance assessment in an era of restructuring*. Alexandria, VA: Association for Supervision and Curriculum Development.

Herman, J. (1997). *Assessing new assessments: How do they measure up?* Los Angeles: Graduate School of Education and Information Studies, University of California, Los Angeles.

Hibbard, M. (1996). *Education Update, 38*(4), p. 5.

Hills, J. R. (1991). Apathy concerning grading and testing. *Phi Delta Kappan, 72,* 540–545.

Impara, J. C., Plake, B. S., & Fager, J. J. (1993). Teachers' assessment background and attitudes toward testing. *Theory into Practice, 32,* 113–117.

Khattri, N. (1995). *Performance assessments: Observed impacts on teaching and learning*. Washington, DC: Pelavin Associates.

Kohn, A. (1994, October). Grading: The issue is not how but why. *Educational Leadership*, pp. 38–41.

Marzano, R. J., & Kendall, J. S. (1996). *Designing standards-based districts, schools and classrooms*. Aurora, CO: Mid-Continent Regional Educational Laboratory.

Massachusetts State Department of Education. (1983). *Development of the state speaking assessment instrument: Reliability and feasibility*. Malden, MA: Author.

McTighe, J. (1996). Performance-based assessment in the classroom: A planning framework. In R. Blum & J. Arter (Eds.), *Student performance assessment in an era of restructuring*. Alexandria, VA: Association for Supervision and Curriculum Development.

Mendel, S. (undated). *Creating portraits of performance*. Aurora, CO: Peakview Elementary School.

Newmann, F., Secada, W., & Weblage, G. (1995). *A guide to authentic instruction and assessment*. Madison: School of Education, University of Wisconsin.

Norris, S. P (1990). *Test on Appraising Observations*. St. John's, Newfoundland: Memorial University of Newfoundland.

North Dakota Department of Public Instruction. (1998). *North Dakota fourth grade writing calibration packet*. Bismarck, ND: Author.

Northwest Regional Educational Laboratory. (1990). *Writing assessment: Training in analytical scoring* [video]. Los Angeles: lOX.

Northwest Regional Educational Laboratory. (1997). *Seeing with new eyes* [video]. Los Angeles: lOX.

Office of Educational Research and Improvement. (1997). *Studies of education reform: Assessment of student performance*. Washington, DC: Author.

Oregon Department of Education. (1997). *Read Informative and Literary Texts—Official scoring guides*. Salem, OR: Author.

Oregon Department of Education (1998). *Performance standards*. Available: http://www.open.k12.or.us/jitt/standards/perform.htm

Perlman, C. (1994). *The CPS performance assessment idea book*. Chicago: Chicago Public Schools.

Plake, B. S., Impara, J. C., & Fager, J. J. (1993). Assessment competencies of teachers: A national survey. *Educational Measurement: Issues and Practice, 12*(4), 10–12, 39.

Regional Educational Laboratories. (1998). *Improving classroom assessment: A toolkit for professional developers* (2nd ed.). Portland, OR: Northwest Regional Educational Laboratory.

Rudner, L., & Boston, C. (1994). Performance assessment. *ERIC Review, 3*(1), 2–12.

Shafer, W. D. (1993). Assessment in teacher education. *Theory into Practice, 32,* 118–126.

Spandel, V. (1996, January). Criteria: The power behind revision. *Writing Teacher*, pp. 9–25.

Spandel, V., & Culham, R. (1998). *Writing workshop materials*. Portland, OR: Northwest Regional Educational Laboratory.

Spandel, V., & Stiggins, R. J. (1997). *Creating writers: Linking writing assessment and instruction*. New York: Longman.

Stayter, F., & Johnston, P. (1990). Evaluating the teaching and learning of literacy. In T. Shanahan (Ed.), *Reading and writing together: New perspectives for the classroom*. Norwood, MA: Christopher-Gordon.

Stiggins, R. J. (1997). *Student-centered classroom assessment* (2nd ed.). Columbus, OH: Merrill.

Usrey, P (1998). *The traits of a competent oral communicator*. Portland, OR: Northwest Regional Educational Laboratory.

Vermont Mathematics Portfolio Project. (1991). *Resource book*. Montpelier: Vermont Department of Education.

Washington Commission on Student Learning. (1998). *Assessment sampler Grade 7*. Olympia, WA: Author.

Wiggins, G. (1992, May). Creating tests worth taking. *Educational Leadership*, pp. 26–33.

Wise, S. L., Lukin, L. E., & Roos, L. L. (1991). Teacher beliefs about training in testing and measurement. *Journal of Teacher Education, 42,* 37–42.

Zhang, Z. (1997). *Assessment Practices Inventory: A multivariate analysis of teachers' perceived assessment competency*. Paper presented at the NCME national conference, Chicago, IL.

Judy Arter is Assessment Unit Manager, Northwest Regional Educational Laboratory, 101 SW Main Street, Suite 500, Portland, OR 97204. Her specializations are classroom assessment and performance assessment.

From [&em]Educational Measurement: Issues and Practices[&stop], Summer 1999, pp. 30-44. © 2000 by the National Council on Measurement in Education. Reprinted by permission of the publisher.

Fighting the Tests

A Practical Guide to Rescuing Our Schools

Mr. Kohn urges us to make the fight against standardized tests our top priority because, until we have chased this monster from the schools, it will be difficult, perhaps even impossible, to pursue the kinds of reforms that can truly improve teaching and learning.

BY ALFIE KOHN

DON'T LET anyone tell you that standardized tests are not accurate measures. The truth of the matter is that they offer a remarkably precise method for gauging the size of the houses near the school where the test was administered. Every empirical investigation of this question has found that socioeconomic status (SES) in all its particulars accounts for an overwhelming proportion of the variance in test scores when different schools, towns, or states are compared.[1] Ignorance would therefore be the most charitable explanation for the practice of publishing charts that rank schools (or towns or states) by these scores—or for using those rankings to draw conclusions about classroom quality.

However, if this were the only problem with standardized tests, we probably would not have sufficient reason to work for their elimination. After all, when evaluating test results, one could factor in SES to determine a "true" score. And one could track a given school's (or district's) results over time; assuming no major demographic changes, a statistically significant shift in scores would then seem to be

meaningful. But here's the problem: even results corrected for SES are not very useful because the tests themselves are inherently flawed.[2] This assessment is borne out by research that finds a statistical association between high scores on standardized tests and relatively shallow thinking. One such study classified elementary school students as "actively" engaged in learning if they went back over things they didn't understand, asked questions of themselves as they read, and tried to connect what they were doing to what they had already learned. Students were classified as "superficially" engaged if they just copied down answers, guessed a lot, and skipped the hard parts. It turned out that the superficial style was positively correlated with high scores on the Comprehensive Tests of Basic Skills (CTBS) and the Metropolitan Achievement Test (MAT).[3] Similar findings have emerged from studies of middle school and high school students.[4] These are only statistical relationships, of course—significant correlations, but not absolute correspondences. Many students think deeply *and* score well on tests, while

many others do neither. But, as a rule, better standardized exam results are more likely to go hand-in-hand with a shallow approach to learning than with deep understanding.

What is true of a student's thinking is also true of a teacher's instruction. A rise in scores may be worse than meaningless: it may actually be reason for concern. What matters is how that change was brought about and what had to be sacrificed to make it happen. Across the nation, schools under intense pressure to show better test results have allowed those tests to cannibalize the curriculum. Administrators have cut back or even eliminated vital parts of schooling: programs in the arts, recess for young children, electives for high schoolers, class meetings (and other activities intended to promote social and moral learning), discussions about current events (since that material will not appear on the test), the use of literature in the early grades (if the tests are focused narrowly on decoding skills), and entire subject areas, such as science (if the tests cover only language arts and math). When students will be judged on the basis of a multiple-choice test, teachers may use multiple-choice exercises and in-class tests beforehand. (This has aptly been called the "dumbing down" of instruction, although curiously not by the conservative critics with whom that phrase is normally associated.) Teachers may even place all instruction on hold and spend time administering and reviewing practice tests.

WE MUST DO OUR BEST IN THE SHORT TERM TO PROTECT CURRENT STUDENTS FROM THE WORST EFFECTS OF A GIVEN POLICY, BUT WE MUST ALSO WORK TO CHANGE OR ELIMINATE THAT POLICY.

In my experience, the people who work most closely with kids are those most likely to understand how harmful standardized testing is. Many teachers—particularly those who are very talented—have what might be described as a dislike/hate relationship with these exams. Support for such testing seems to grow as you move further from the students, going from teacher to principal to central office administrator to school board member to state board member, state legislator, and governor. Those for whom classroom visits are occasional photo opportunities are most likely to be big fans of testing and to offer self-congratulatory sound bites about the need for "tougher standards" and "accountability." The more that parents and other members of the community learn about these tests, the more critical of them—if not appalled by them—they tend to become.[5]

There is much more to be said about how standardized tests measure what matters least, about their psychometric deficiencies and pedagogical consequences. But a good deal of this has already been said—by me[6] and by others.[7] *Kappan* readers may have come to the same conclusions based on their own experience.

Even someone who does not have to be convinced of the merit of the arguments, however, may need to be reminded of their cumulative significance. It is this: As the year 2001 begins, we are facing an educational emergency in this country. The intellectual life is being squeezed out of our schools as they are transformed into what are essentially giant test-prep centers. The situation is most egregious, and the damage most pronounced, where high stakes are attached to the tests—for example, where money is dangled in front of teachers, principals, and schools if they manage to raise the scores or where students are actually forced to repeat a grade or denied a diploma on the basis of their performance on a single test.

Most of us have pet projects, favorite causes, practices and policies about which we care deeply. These include such issues as multiple intelligences, multi-age classrooms, or multicultural curricula; cooperative learning, character education, or the creation of caring communities in schools; teaching for understanding, developmentally appropriate practice, or alternative assessment; the integration of writing or the arts into the curriculum; project- or problem-based learning, discovery-oriented science, or whole language; giving teachers or students more autonomy, or working with administrators to help them make lasting change. But every one of these priorities is gravely threatened by the top-down, heavy-handed, corporate-style, standardized version of school reform that is driven by testing. That's why all of us, despite our disparate agendas, need to make common cause. We must make the fight against standardized tests our top priority because, until we have chased this monster from the schools, it will be difficult, perhaps even impossible, to pursue the kinds of reforms that can truly improve teaching and learning.

W HENEVER something in the schools is amiss, it makes sense for us to work on two tracks at once. We must do our best in the short term to protect current students from the worst effects of a given policy, but we must also work to change or eliminate that policy. If we overlook the need to minimize the harm of what is currently taking place, then we do a disservice to children in the here and now. But (and this is by far the more common error) if we overlook the need to alter the current reality, then we are condemning our children's children to having to make the best of the

same unacceptable situation because it will still exist.

Standardized testing is a case in point. So let me begin by offering some short-term responses.

First, if you are a teacher, you should do what is necessary to prepare students for the tests—and then get back to the *real* learning. Never forget the difference between these two objectives. Be clear about it in your own mind, and, whenever possible, help others to understand the distinction. For example, you might send a letter to parents explaining what you are doing and why. ("Before we can design rigorous and exciting experiments in class, which I hope will have the effect of helping your child learn to think like a scientist, we're going to have to spend some time getting ready for the standardized tests being given next month. I hope we'll be able to return before too long to what research suggests is a more effective kind of instruction.") If you're lucky, parents will call you, indignantly demanding to know why their kids aren't able to pursue the more effective kind of instruction all the time. "Excellent question!" you'll reply, as you hand over a sheet containing the addresses and phone numbers of the local school board, the state board of education, legislators, and the governor.

Second, do no more test preparation than is absolutely necessary. Some experts have argued that a relatively short period of introducing students to the content and format of the tests is sufficient to produce scores equivalent to those obtained by students who have spent the entire year in test-prep mode. "You don't need to study only the test and distort your entire curriculum eight hours a day, 180 days a year, for 12 years," says Harvey Daniels, who specializes in literacy education. "We've got very interesting studies where teachers do 35 or 38 weeks of what they think is best for kids, and then they'll give them three weeks of test cramming just before the test. And the kids do just as well as kids who have 40 weeks of test-driven curriculum."[8] This is corroborated by some research that found that a one-hour intensive reading readiness tutorial for young children produced test results equivalent to *two years* of skills-oriented direct instruction.[9] Of course, such outcomes will vary depending on the child and the nature of the test.

Or consider compromises such as this:

One first-grade teacher in Kentucky helped her students develop their own reading program, which moves them faster and more effectively through (and beyond) the district's reading program objectives than the basal. Even so, she is required by her school's administration to put her class through a basal reader program on a prescribed weekly schedule. The solution, quickly evolved by the class: They do each week's work in the basal on Monday, with little effort, then work on the meaningful curriculum—theirs—Tuesday through Friday.[10]

Third, whatever time is spent on test preparation should be as creative and worthwhile as possible. Avoid traditional drilling whenever you can. Several educators have figured out how to turn some of these tests into a kind of puzzle that children can play an active role in solving. The idea is to help students become adept at the particular skill called test-taking, so they will be able to show what they already know.[11]

Fourth, administrators and other school officials should never brag about high (or rising) test scores. To do so is not only misleading but also serves to legitimate the tests. In fact, people associated with high-scoring schools or districts have a unique opportunity to make an impact. It's easy for critics of tests to be dismissed with a "sour grapes" argument: "You're just opposed to standardized testing because it makes you look bad." But administrators and school board members in high-scoring areas can say, "Actually, our students happen to do well on these tests, but that's nothing to be proud of. We value great teaching and learning, which is precisely what suffers when people become preoccupied with test scores. Please join us in phasing them out."

Finally, whatever your position on the food chain of American education, one of your primary obligations is to be a buffer—to absorb as much pressure as possible from those above you without passing it on to those below. If you are a superintendent or assistant superintendent and must face school board members who want to see higher test scores, the most constructive thing you can do is to protect principals from these ill-conceived demands—to the best of your ability and without losing your job in the process. If you are a building administrator, on the receiving end of test-related missives from the central office, your challenge is to shield teachers from this pressure—and, indeed, to help them pursue meaningful learning in their classrooms. If you are a

teacher unlucky enough to work for an administrator who hasn't read this paragraph, your job is to minimize the impact on students. Try to educate those above you whenever it seems possible to do so, but cushion those below you every day. Otherwise you become part of the problem.

AS IMPORTANT as I believe these suggestions to be, it is also critical to recognize their limits. There is only so much creativity that can be infused into preparing students for bad tests. There is only so much buffering that can be done in a high-stakes environment. These recommendations merely try to make the best of a bad thing. Ultimately, we need to work to end that bad thing, to move beyond stopgap measures and take on the system itself.

Unfortunately, even some well-intentioned educators who understand the threat posed by testing never get to that point. Consider some of the justifications they offer for their inaction.

• *Just teach well, and the tests will take care of themselves.* This may be true in some subject areas, or in some states, or in some neighborhoods. But it is often a convenient delusion. Especially in science and social studies, to prepare students for the tests in the most effective way may well be to teach badly—to fill them full of dates and definitions and cover a huge amount of material in a superficial fashion. Conversely, to teach in a way that helps students understand (and become enthusiastic about) ideas may actually lower their scores. Linda McNeil's description of the choice faced by Texas educators will be instantly and painfully familiar to teachers across the country—but may come as news to some parents, school board members, politicians, and reporters:

The myth of the proficiencies [that is, the standards] was that because they were aimed at minimum skills, they would change only the weakest teaching. The "good" teachers would as a matter of course "already be covering" this material and so would not have to make adjustments. In fact, the transformation of the curriculum into received knowledge, to be assessed by students' selection of one answer among four provided on a computer-scored test, undermined both the quality and quantity that "good teachers" could present to their students.... [Thus] teachers faced serious ethical dilemmas. They could teach to the proficiencies and assure high test scores for their students. Or they

could teach the curricula they had been developing (and wanted to continue to develop) and teach not only a richer subject matter but also one that was aimed at students' understanding and their long-term learning, not the short-term goals inherent in the district testing of memorized fragments. This was not an easy choice.[12]

Nor is the dilemma likely to be painlessly resolved by consultants who tell us we need only adopt a specific instructional reform to have the best of both worlds: an intellectually impressive classroom that will help students meet the state standards. The degree of standardization in most accountability-based systems is so high—and the quality of the tests is so low—that the proposed reform either will not raise the scores or isn't particularly impressive after all. That's why we should react with caution, if not alarm, to the word *alignment*. The dictates to which we are supposed to be aligning the curriculum are often pedagogically suspect, and the motive for doing so often may have more to do with compliance than with what is in the best interests of children. Moreover, even if their objectives and our motives were defensible, the process of alignment typically requires a degree of uniformity—and is undertaken with a degree of rigidity—that ought to raise concerns about the whole enterprise.

• *This too shall pass.* Education has always had its fads, and standards on steroids may be one of them. But there is no guarantee that high-stakes testing will fade away on its own. Too much is invested by now and too many powerful interest groups are backing high-stakes testing for us to assume it will simply fall of its own weight. In any case, too many children will be sacrificed in the meantime if we don't take action to expedite its demise.

• *My job is to teach, not to get involved in political disputes.* When 7-year-olds can't read good books because they are being drilled on what Jonathan Kozol calls "those obsessively enumerated particles of amputated skill associated with upcoming state exams,"[13] the schools have already been politicized. The only question is whether we will become involved on the other side—that is, on the side of real learning. In particular, much depends on whether those teachers and administrators who already harbor (and privately acknowledge) concerns about testing are willing to go public, to take a stand, to say, "This is bad for kids." To paraphrase a famous quotation, all that is necessary for the triumph of damaging educational policies is that good educators keep silent.

• *The standards and tests are here to stay; we might as well get used to them.* Here we have the inverse of "This too shall pass." Yet, paradoxically, both attitudes lead to the identical inaction. Real children in real classrooms suffer from this kind of defeatism, which can quickly become a self-fulfilling prophecy: assume something is inevitable, and it becomes so precisely because we do not challenge it. The fact of the matter is that standardized tests are not like the weather, something to which we must resign ourselves. They haven't always existed, and they don't exist in most parts of the world. What we are facing is not a force of nature but a force of politics, and political decisions can be questioned, challenged, and ultimately reversed.

Hᴏᴡ WE take on the tests may depend partly on such practical considerations as where we can have the greatest impact. Those of us who see little benefit at all from standardized tests in their current forms need to remember that ours is not an all-or-nothing crusade but a movement that can proceed incrementally. One way to begin is by fighting for the principles most likely to generate widespread support.

WHETHER YOU JOIN AN EXISTING ORGANI-ZATION OR HELP TO FORM A NEW ONE, BEGIN BY LEARNING ALL YOU CAN ABOUT THE TESTS USED IN YOUR STATE AS WELL AS ABOUT MORE GENERIC TESTING ISSUES.

For example, even *Education Week*, known for its relentless advocacy of the standards-and-testing agenda, has acknowledged that there is "virtually unanimous agreement among experts that no single measure should decide a student's academic fate."[14] This is certainly true. The prestigious National Research Council came to that conclusion,[15] as have most other professional organizations (e.g., the American Educational Research Association and the American Psychological Association), the generally pro-testing American Federation of Teachers, and even the companies that manufacture and sell the tests. To make students repeat a grade or to deny them diplomas on the basis of a single exam is unconscionable. Yet, at this writing, about half of the states are either doing so or planning to do so. This issue is not a bad point of entry for potential activists. It may be persuasive even to politicians who have not thought much about these matters and who otherwise accept the slogans of standards and accountability.[16]

Similarly, even people who are unwilling to dispense with standardized testing altogether may be open to persuasion that these tests

• should not be the only means by which students or schools are evaluated, inasmuch as they miss (or misrepresent) many aspects of student learning that ought to be assessed some other way;

• should not, in any case, be imposed by fiat on all schools in the state, with the result that communities are prevented from making their own decisions;[17]

• should not be administered too often;

• are inappropriate for young children; and

• should be used only to rate, never to rank (since the goal is to derive useful information, not to create winners and losers and thereby discourage schools from working together).

This is not to say that we shouldn't also be inviting people to question ideological assumptions that are harder to dislodge—to consider, for example, that a preoccupation with results and achievement can in itself interfere with learning[18] or that educational progress need not (and, to some extent, cannot) be reduced to numbers. But even someone who resists those ideas may agree that it is wrong to make a student's future hinge on a single standardized test. (Needless to say, allowing students several chances to retake the same test does little to address the problem. Besides, many students are likely to give up and drop out after the first or second failure.)

Some of the ideas that follow can be pursued individually, but most depend on working with others. Thus the first suggestion is to *organize*. Find people in your area who share your concerns so you can have a more powerful impact together. You are not alone in opposing standard-ized testing, but without collective action, you might as well be. So work with friends, neighbors, and colleagues to set up study groups, committees, phone trees, websites, and listservs. Give yourselves an organizational name, print up some letterhead, and instantly you gain credibility. (Now you're not just a bunch of rebels. You're the "[name of area] Educators Opposing Excessive Testing.") Every person who seems interested in becoming involved should be asked to find 10 more potential recruits, and each of those recruits should be asked to do the same. Even as you engage in the activities listed below, you should be continuing to bring others into the effort.[19]

There is no reason, however, to waste time duplicating someone else's endeavors. You may want to begin by joining an existing network if one is already active in your area. One way to do so is to visit my website (www.alfiekohn.org), click on "Standards and Testing," and follow the links or visit the website of FairTest (www.fairtest.org), the nation's leading organization challenging standardized testing. This group also has a quarterly newsletter, a storehouse of useful documents, and a listserv called the Assessment Reform Network (ARN).

Whether you join an existing organization or help to form a new one, begin by learning all you can about the tests used in your state as well as about more generic testing issues. Then you can take a number of actions.

1. Talk to friends and neighbors at every opportunity—in line at the supermarket, in the dentist's waiting room, on airplanes, at the hairdresser's, at the playground, at dinner parties, and at children's birthday parties. Help people in your community understand that, if a local official boasts about rising test scores, they should consider responding, "You know, if that's what you're mostly concerned about, then I'm worried about the quality of my child's schooling."

2. Get in the habit of attending—and speaking out at—school board meetings and other events dealing with education policy.

3. Let parents know they can write a letter to school administrators or board members expressing concern that test preparation is eclipsing more important learning activities. Here is a sample, provided by James Popham:

Dear ____:

I want to register my concern that there seems to be an excessive emphasis in our school on getting students ready for the standardized achievement tests scheduled for administration during (*give the month of the upcoming test-administration*). The reason I'm concerned is that I'm fearful the teaching staff's preoccupation with raising scores on those tests may be preventing the teachers from covering other important skills and knowledge that the school's students need.

I realize that you and your teaching staff are under considerable pressure to "raise test scores" because it is widely believed that students' scores on standardized achievement tests reflect the quality of a teaching staff and, by implication, the quality of the school's principal.

I've been doing some reading on that topic, and I understand why it is that students' standardized test scores do not provide an appropriate indication of a teaching staff's competence. Scores on those tests are more a reflection of the student population served by a school than an indication of the skill of the school's educators.

I hope that you and your staff will address this test-preparation issue in the near future. Parents want the school's children to get the very best education possible. I'm sure you do too. That will not happen, however, if our school's heavy emphasis on test-preparation deflects the school's teachers from dealing with the curricular content our children need.

Sincerely,
[Your Name][20]

4. Write to—or, better yet, pull together a delegation of concerned citizens and visit—your state legislators and other public officials. This is the sort of familiar and predictable recommendation that you may be tempted to skip over, but you really ought to take it seriously. Politicians respond to pointed and persistent lobbying, and, as a rule, they haven't heard nearly enough from those of us who feel strongly about this issue. Your goal may be simply to educate policy makers about the effects of testing, or it may be to encourage them to oppose (or support) specific policies and legislation.

5. Write letters to the editor—or, better yet, op-ed articles—for your local newspaper.

6. Organize a delegation of educators and parents and request a meeting with the education reporter and top editors of your local paper. Help them to see the problems inherent in citing rising or falling test scores as an indication of educational quality. Explain to them that most experts in the field oppose high-stakes testing. And tell them: "Every time you publish a chart that ranks schools on the basis of test scores, our children's learning suffers. Here's why…"

7. Sponsor a forum or teach-in on testing. Invite the media. Sign up new volunteers. Such a meeting might carry a provocative title to attract those already on your side (e.g., "Standardized Testing: Waste of Time or Menace to Children?"), but then again it might be promoted in more neutral terms ("Rethinking Standardized Testing") to attract more people. Those responsible for the tests can be invited to appear and respond to questions.

8. Print some bumper stickers with slogans such as "Standardized Testing Is Dumbing Down Our Schools." Here, it is definitely appropriate to be provocative.[21]

9. Participate in—and help ensure press coverage of—some form of protest. This might include marches and demonstrations, as well as other, more targeted activities that are already taking place in some areas. Some of these are described below.

10. For every workshop or inservice training event offered by educational service agencies, universities, and administrators that provides advice on raising test scores and teaching to the standards, three should be offered that encourage teachers to *challenge* the standards and tests—or at least help them think about how to protect their students from the damaging effects.

11. Invite researchers in the area to conduct a survey. When it's completed, release the results at a press conference. One group of investigators suggested including these questions:

Do the tests improve students' motivation? Do parents understand the results? Do teachers think that the tests measure the curriculum fairly? Do administrators use the results wisely? How much money is spent on assessment and related services? How much time do teachers spend preparing students for various tests? Do the media report the data accurately and thoroughly? Our surveys suggest that many districts will be shocked to discover the degree of dissatisfaction among stakeholders.[22]

12. Challenge politicians, corporate executives, and others who talk piously about the need to "raise the bar," impose "tougher standards," ensure "accountability," and so on to take the tests themselves. This is especially important in the case of high-stakes exit exams, which are increasingly being used to deny diplomas to students who don't pass them. In many states, the reality is that few adults could pass these tests.

There are two ways to issue such an invitation to decision makers: as a private opportunity for them to learn more about (and, perhaps, understand the absurdity of) the exam, or as a public challenge for them to take the test and agree to have their scores published in the newspaper. The first approach was used in West Bend, Wisconsin, where about 30 business leaders took a short version of the state's proposed graduation exam. They "had so much trouble with it that some wonder[ed] whether it truly will measure the quality of future employees." One bank executive—presumably a supporter of testing in the abstract until he encountered the actual test—remarked, "I think it's good to challenge students, but not like this."[23]

The second approach was taken by the *St. Petersburg Times* when it "challenged several top elected officials to join 735,000 Florida schoolchildren… by taking the rigorous Florida Comprehensive Assessment Test. They declined. Some did so with a sense of humor. Some admitted the math might give them fits. Others were unamused by the entire exercise. All said no."[24] Educators and parents might consider holding a press conference to issue such a public challenge, arguing that, if officials fear they won't be able to pass the test, they should be prepared to justify requiring teenagers to do something that they, themselves, cannot. If they refuse the challenge, they should be called on to defend their refusal.

13. Consider filing a lawsuit against the tests, which are potentially vulnerable in many ways. They may be inherently discriminatory. They may be used despite the absence of evidence that they are statistically valid measurement instruments. They may be inconsistent with the state's own standards, or they may require students to know things they haven't yet been taught.

14. Investigate whether your state has an "opt-out" clause that allows parents to exempt their children from testing just by notifying the authorities. These clauses are not widely known—indeed, even some activists are not always aware of their existence in their own states—but they ought to be publicized if they are on the books where you live.

15. Perhaps the most extreme—but, in the opinion of a growing number of people, well justified—strategy is to boycott

the tests even where there is no opt-out provision. If that suggestion seems drastic, I can only respond that desperate circumstances call for drastic action. Punitive consequences are being meted out on the basis of manifestly inadequate and inappropriate exams. Children are literally becoming sick with fear over their scores. We are facing the prospect that massive numbers of students—particularly low-income and minority students—will be pushed out of school altogether.[25]

In short, more and more people believe that writing letters to the editor isn't enough, that a line has been crossed such that we can no longer justify our participation in—and thus tacit support of—these testing programs. One kind of boycott involves students who, on their own or at their parents' behest, refuse to show up for tests and make it clear why they are doing so. There are various ways in which educators can support such an action: by making sure that students and parents know that boycotts are already taking place elsewhere, by speaking out in support of those who decide to do this, by teaching students about the theory and practice of civil disobedience, by suggesting alternative educational activities in which boycotters can participate on test day, and by lobbying local officials to make sure that boycotting students are not punished. (Of course, educators who are also parents can invite their own children to consider being part of such a protest.)

In another kind of boycott, teachers and administrators themselves refuse to be part of the testing program. Like Bartleby in Melville's short story, who created an uproar when, "in a singularly mild, firm voice, [he] replied, 'I would prefer not to,'" they declare that they simply cannot in good conscience break the shrink-wrap on those exams and thereby become part of something they believe is bad for children. It takes considerable courage to put one's job on the line. Yet that courage has already been displayed, with striking results, in other countries. "Elementary [school] achievement is high" in Japan, for example, partly because teachers in that country "are free from the pressure to teach to standardized tests." It is important to understand why there are no such tests in that country (with the exception of an infamous university admission exam): it is because Japanese teachers collectively refused to administer them. For many years now, they have successfully prevented the government from doing to their children what our government is doing to our children.[26]

Similarly, in the early 1990s, teachers in England and Wales basically stopped the new national testing program in its tracks, at least for a while, by a comparable act of civil disobedience. What began there "as an unfocused mishmash of voices became a united boycott involving all teacher unions, a large number of governing bodies, and mass parental support." Teachers made it clear that their action was taken on behalf of their students, based on the teachers' recognition that "to teach well for the tests was in effect to teach badly."[27]

In 1999, Jim Bougas, a middle school teacher in a small town in Massachusetts, noticed that the history portion of the MCAS exam required students to answer questions about the Civil War even though the state's own guidelines called for that topic to be covered at the end of the year, after the test was administered. For him, this was the last straw with respect to a testing system that was already geared toward memorization and was forcing instruction to become more superficial. Bougas, a soft-spoken man who had been teaching for 28 years, informed his principal that he would not administer the test. He was reassigned to the library during that period, and a stern letter of reprimand was placed in his personnel file along with a warning not to repeat his protest. The next year, following a denial of his request to be reassigned to other duties when the test was to be administered, he agonized about what to do. Finally, he decided that, if the test was just as unfair and destructive in 2000 as it had been in 1999, his response could not be any different—even at the risk of suspension or dismissal. Besides, as he told a reporter, "If the MCAS continues, I have no job because they've taken it away from me as long as I have to spend my time teaching to the test. I can't do that anymore. So I have nothing to lose."[28]

Such a protest is not only inspirational to many of us but an invitation to ponder the infinitely greater impact of *collective* action. Imagine, for example, that a teacher at any given school in your area quietly approached each person on the staff in turn and asked: "If __ percent of the teachers at this school pledged to boycott the next round of testing, would you join them?" (The specific percentage would depend on what seemed realistic and yet might signify sufficient participation to offer some protection for those involved.) Then, if the designated number of boycotters is reached, each teacher would be invited to take part in what would be a powerful act of civil disobedience. Press coverage would doubtless be substantial, and

despairing-but-cowed teachers in other schools might be encouraged to follow suit.

Without question, this is a risky undertaking. Theoretically, even an entire school faculty could be fired. But the more who participate and the more careful they are about soliciting support from parents and other members of the community beforehand, the more difficult it would be for administrators to respond harshly. (Of course, some administrators are as frustrated with the testing as teachers are.) Participants would have to be politically savvy, building alliances and offering a coherent, quotable rationale for their action. They would need to make it clear—at a press conference and in other forums—that they were taking this action not because they are unwilling to do more work or are afraid of being held accountable, but because these tests lower the quality of learning and do a serious injustice to the children in the community.

The bottom line is that standardized testing can continue only with the consent and cooperation of the educators who allow the tests to be distributed in their schools—and of the parents who permit their children to take them. If we withhold that consent, if we refuse to cooperate, then the testing process grinds to a halt. That is what happened in Japan. That is what can happen in the United States if we understand the urgency of the situation. Discuss it with your university students, your staff, your colleagues. Ask yourself and others, What if they gave a test and nobody came?

MOST OF these suggestions—along with other acts of resistance—spring not from someone's imagination but from real activities being undertaken around the country. Parents in Wisconsin successfully lobbied their state legislators to prevent a high school exit exam from being the sole determinant of whether students are permitted to graduate—a stinging defeat for Gov. Tommy Thompson. In Florida, where schools are graded on the basis of test scores and successful schools receive more money while the least successful schools are threatened with a loss of funding, a group of teachers and their principal at Gulf Gate Elementary, an "A" school, publicly refused to accept their bonuses. In a similar protest in North Carolina, teachers at East Chapel Hill High School pooled their state bonus checks and formed a foundation to send grants to the state's poorer schools.

Parents and teachers have taken to the streets in Colorado and Ohio. Lawsuits have been filed in Louisiana, Indiana, and Nevada to challenge the legality of high-stakes tests. (The first case to go to trial, in Texas, was decided in favor of the state.) Petitions are being circulated, locally and nationally; legislators are being lobbied; websites are being set up in several states to help testing opponents coordinate their efforts.[29] And individuals are courageously challenging the system in a variety of ways. In early 1999, George Schmidt, a veteran Chicago high school teacher, published some of that city's tests (after students had already taken them) in a small independent newspaper so that the public could evaluate the validity and value of the questions. He was promptly charged with "gross disruption of the educational process," suspended without pay, and sued for $1.4 million.

Eugene Garcia, dean of the school of education at the University of California, Berkeley, resigned his position on an advisory committee to the state board of education. He did so to protest—and draw attention to—the board's decision to require students with limited proficiency in English to take tests on which they are certain to do poorly simply because they don't speak the language. He then called for parents of such students to decline to participate in the testing program, thereby increasing the number of English-speaking students who would score below the median (since the state's high-stakes test, incredibly, is norm referenced). These results, he speculated, might shock some of these families into opposing the tests.

Most impressive, and most dramatic, has been the growing number of boycotts all across the nation. Parents have said, in effect, "Not with my child you don't!" and have refused to allow their children to take the tests. At first in scattered fashion—reflecting the lack of coordination among people who had independently decided that the tests were destructive—students either declined to take the tests or failed them on purpose. This happened as long ago as 1989 in Torrance, California, and two years later in a parent-led protest involving several Colorado districts. Then, in 1998–99, parents across Michigan exempted 22.5% of that state's students from the high school proficiency portion of the Michigan Educational Assessment Program (MEAP). Some districts had up to 90% of their students waived from taking the test, suggesting a "grassroots revolt by parents and students."[30] The following year, high school students walked out on a test in Marin County, California, calling it unjust that non-English-speaking students would have to take an English-language test, while students at the Whitney Young Magnet School in Chicago deliberately flunked the Illinois exam, saying they "refused to feed this test-taking frenzy." That same year, there were protests in Merton, Wisconsin, and in Danvers, Cambridge, and Newton, Massachusetts. And last spring, a genuine boycott movement spread across Massachusetts, with hundreds of students sitting out that state's required tests as the result of a student-led campaign. Something similar happened in Illinois.

Boycotters and other protesters are disturbed not only by the tests themselves but by the profoundly undemocratic nature of what passes for school reform today: a one-size-fits-all set of standards and assessments handed down from the state capital and imposed with the force of law. Thus individual schools or districts may devise thoughtful criteria for awarding a high school diploma, perhaps using what the Coalition of Essential Schools calls "exhibitions" of mastery—only to have the state's education czar brush aside such alternatives and declare that nothing will count except a student's score on a uniform set of pencil-and-paper tests. This is precisely what has happened in New York, and it has recently led to an intriguing and constructive form of rebellion. A group of superintendents in Monroe County (whose students happen to do quite well on the state's Regents Exams) are in the early stages of creating an independent local board that will issue a diploma to students "who meet a set of validated criteria based on multiple assessments and multiple forms of assessment," according to William Cala, the superintendent of Fairport Schools. Representatives of business and higher education will help to formulate these criteria and then oversee administration of the diplomas. The participation of these groups will ensure that receiving a county rather than a state-sanctioned diploma will not put students at a disadvantage. Indeed, a document that certifies the ability to think deeply in different ways, using a variety of formats—and to apply knowledge in realistic situations—ultimately may be worth more than a diploma certifying the ability to take standardized tests well. Moreover, the schooling that *precedes* graduation may be far more worthwhile than the sort held hostage to conventional exit exams. In any event, the idea of creating a legally valid, practically useful, locally devised diploma neatly neutralizes the standards-and-accountability autocracy. What state authorities are doing already lacks logic and the support of research. Now they may be stripped of the one thing they do possess: the power to compel compliance.

Less because of such protests than because decision makers are starting to realize the catastrophic effects of high-stakes testing, there has been some tinkering with the tests. It appears that more states will step back from the brink, particularly when it becomes clear that affluent white students may be affected. Some test backers grudgingly concede that they may have moved a little too quickly, and now we are witnessing a delay of implementation here, a lower passing grade there, some sanctions waived and some expectations softened. This tentative response has already begun to generate a counterreaction from hard-core pundits and politicians who affect a macho tone and taunt those responsible for watering down the tests and giving in to pressure groups (such as alarmed parents). As a harsh, punitive approach begins to reveal itself as counterproductive, this contingent has responded by demanding an even harsher, more punitive response.

In fact, though, the problem with this backpedaling is that it doesn't go nearly far enough. Those who understand the weaknesses of standardized tests—and, indeed, the deficiencies of the whole tougher standards sensibility—will derive scant comfort from efforts to adjust the scores required for passing or to tinker with the applications of rewards and punishments. These minor repairs don't address the underlying problems with using such exams to judge students and educators, much less to bully them into higher scores. Those of us in the resistance movement are not quibbling about how high or how fast; we are calling the whole enterprise into question. We are not proposing to make school easier, but to make it better—and that requires rethinking standardized testing itself.

NOTES

1. A study of math scores on the 1992 National Assessment of Educational Progress found that a combination of four variables unrelated to instruction (number of parents living at home, parents' educational background, type of community, and state poverty rate) explained a whopping 89% of the differences in state scores. In fact, one of those

variables, the number of students who had one parent living at home, accounted for 71% of the variance all by itself. See Glen E. Robinson and David P. Brandon, *NAEP Test Scores: Should They Be Used to Compare and Rank State Educational Quality?* (Arlington, Va.: Educational Research Service, 1994). The same pattern holds within states. In Massachusetts, five factors explained 90% of the variance in scores on the Massachusetts Comprehensive Assessment System (MCAS) exam, leading a researcher to conclude that students' performance "has almost everything to do with parental socioeconomic backgrounds and less to do with teachers, curricula, or what the children learned in the classroom." See Kevin J. Clancy, "Making More Sense of MCAS Scores," *Boston Globe*, 24 April 2000, p. A-19. Another study looked just at the poverty level in each of 593 districts in Ohio and found a .80 correlation with 1997 scores on that state's proficiency test, meaning that this measure alone explained nearly two-thirds of the differences in test results. See Randy L. Hoover, "Forces and Factors Affecting Ohio Proficiency Test Performance," available at http://cc.ysu.edu/~rlhoover/OPT. Even a quick look at the grades given to Florida schools under that state's new rating system found that "no school where less than 10% of the students qualify for free lunch scored below a C, and no school where more than 80% of the students qualify scored above a C." See Jodi Wilgoren, "Florida's Vouchers a Spur to Two Schools Left Behind," *New York Times*, 14 March 2000, p. A-18. Then there is the SAT, which, far from being a measure of merit (sometimes pointedly contrasted with affirmative action criteria), is largely a measure of family income. Break down the test-takers by income, measured in $10,000 increments, and without exception the scores rise with each jump in parents' earnings. See "1999 College Bound Seniors' Test Scores: SAT," *FairTest Examiner*, Fall 1999, p. 13; the information is also available at www.collegeboard.org.

2. The nature and extent of those flaws vary with the nature of the testing program, of course. Exams that are norm-referenced, timed, composed largely of multiple-choice questions, given to young children, or designed to measure the short-term acquisition of isolated facts and skills are particularly unhelpful.

3. See Judith L. Meece, Phyllis C. Blumenfeld, and Rick H. Hoyle, "Students' Goal Orientations and Cognitive Engagement in Classroom Activities," *Journal of Educational Psychology*, vol. 80, 1988, pp. 514–23. The correlation was .28, significant at $p < .001$.

4. The middle school students "who value literacy activities and who are task-focused toward literacy activities" got lower scores on the CTBS reading test. See Eric M. Anderman, "Motivation and Cognitive Strategy Use in Reading and Writing," paper presented at the National Reading Conference, San Antonio, December 1992. The same pattern showed up with high school students taking the SAT. Researchers classified students' approaches to studying as "surface" (doing as little as possible and sticking to rote memorization), "deep" (understanding ideas and connecting new material to existing knowledge), or "achieving" (trying to get good grades and beat everyone else, without interest in what was being learned). It turned out that those who adopted a surface or achieving style did the best on the SAT. SAT scores were negatively correlated with a deep approach to learning. See Cathy W. Hall, Larry M. Bolen, and Robert H. Gupton, Jr., "Predictive Validity of the Study Process Questionnaire for Undergraduate Students," *College Student Journal*, vol. 29, 1995, pp. 234–39.

5. It would be instructive to see a poll that measured familiarity with the tests as well as attitudes about testing and then looked at the interaction between the two. But we do not have to speculate about the effect of becoming familiar with *alternatives* to standardized tests. A survey of parents of third-graders in an ethnically diverse, working-class district near Denver found higher levels of support for performance assessments than for standardized tests, once the former option was presented and explained. Parents in this study were shown examples of standardized test questions such as "How much change will you get if you have $6.55 and spend $4.32? a) $2.23 b) $2.43 c) $3.23 d) $10.87" as well as performance assessment questions such as "Suppose you couldn't remember what 8 x 7 is. How could you figure it out?" A large majority of respondents preferred performance assessments. Indeed, many remarked that the latter were more challenging and gave teachers more insight into what the students understood and where they were struggling. The researchers admitted being "surprised that parents rated informal sources of information—talking to the teacher and seeing graded samples of their child's work—as more useful than standardized tests for learning about their 'child's progress in school' and even for judging the 'quality of education provided at their child's school.'" Clearly, they concluded, "parents' favorable ratings of standardized national tests do not imply a preference for such measures over other less formal sources of information." See Lorrie A. Shepard and Carribeth L. Bliem, "Parents' Thinking About Standardized Tests and Performance Assessments," *Educational Researcher*, November 1995, pp. 25–32.

6. See Alfie Kohn, *The Case Against Standardized Testing: Raising the Scores, Ruining the Schools* (Portsmouth, N.H.: Heinemann, 2000) or chapter 4 of The Schools Our Children Deserve (Boston: Houghton Mifflin, 1999), from which much of the former book was adapted.

7. See, for example, Peter Sacks, *Standardized Minds* (Cambridge, Mass.: Perseus, 1999); and Kathy Swope and Barbara Miner, eds., *Failing Our Kids: Why the Testing Craze Won't Fix Our Schools* (Milwaukee: Rethinking Schools, 2000). For background information about these tests, see Gerald W. Bracey, *Put to the Test: An Educator's and Consumer's Guide to Standardized Testing* (Bloomington, Ind.: Phi Delta Kappa International, 1998); and any of several publications by W. James Popham.

8. Harvey Daniels, "Whole Language: What's the Fuss?," *Rethinking Schools*, Winter 1993, p. 5.

9. See Merle B. Karnes, Allan M. Shwedel, and Mark B. Williams, "A Comparison of Five Approaches for Educating Young Children from Low-Income Homes," in The Consortium for Longitudinal Studies, ed., *As the Twig Is Bent...: Lasting Effects of Preschool Programs* (Hillsdale, N.J.: Erlbaum, 1983), pp. 133–69.

10. Hilton Smith, "Foxfire Teachers' Networks," in John M. Novak, ed., *Democratic Teacher Education: Programs, Processes, Problems, and Prospects* (Albany: State University of New York Press, 1994), p. 29.

11. See Kathe Taylor and Sherry Walton, *Children at the Center: A Workshop Approach to Standardized Test Prepara-*

tion, K–8 (Portsmouth, N.H.: Heinemann, 1998); and Lucy Calkins, Kate Montgomery, and Donna Santman, *A Teacher's Guide to Standardized Reading Tests: Knowledge Is Power* (Portsmouth, N.H.: Heinemann, 1998). Several articles in the December 1996/January 1997 issue of *Educational Leadership* are also relevant.

12. Linda M. McNeil, *Contradictions of School Reform: Educational Costs of Standardized Testing* (New York: Routledge, 2000), pp. 204, 203.

13. Jonathan Kozol, Foreword to Deborah Meier, *Will Standards Save Public Education?* (Boston: Beacon, 2000), p. x.

14. Lynn Olson, "Worries of a Standards 'Backlash' Grow," *Education Week*, 5 April 2000, p. 12. Note that even the headline of this article assumes that a backlash against the standards-and-testing movement is something one should worry about rather than welcome—a bias reflected in most coverage of the issue.

15. "No single test score can be considered a definitive measure of a student's knowledge," so "an educational decision that will have a major impact on a test taker should not be made solely or automatically on the basis of a single test score. Other relevant information about the student's knowledge and skills should also be taken into account," according to Jay P. Heubert and Robert M. Hauser, eds., *High Stakes: Testing for Tracking, Promotion, and Graduation* (Washington, D.C.: National Academy Press, 1999).

16. For example, one Republican state legislator in Delaware announced: "I cannot support, under any circumstances, a test that will be the be-all and end-all of a student's [getting a diploma]. So why don't we just remove that? How have we ever got to the point where we allow one test to determine our children's future?" At that point in the debate, according to a newspaper account, "several in the chamber spoke of how they had successfully moved from high school through college to even advanced degrees without having to pass a single, difficult, standardized test. Others recalled conversations with teachers who admitted they would not be successful taking the tests themselves. 'It seems like we're trying to treat the symptom instead of the disease,'" remarked another Republican representative, adding, "The problem is the testing." See Tom Elder, "Education Bill Passes Dela-

ware House," *Delaware State News*, 17 March 2000. Similarly, Pennsylvania's state board of education ruled out a test to determine whether students would receive a diploma, with one board member commenting, "I couldn't sit here in this seat and take that kind of decision out of the hands of teachers who had worked hard with the students for 13 years." See Christopher Newton, "State Education Board Rules Out High School Test," *Philadelphia Inquirer*, 20 April 2000.

17. This argument in particular resonates with people across the political spectrum.

18. For more on this point, see *The Schools Our Children Deserve*, chap. 2.

19. For further thoughts on helping educators to become more adept at political organizing, see Ellen H. Brinkley and Constance Weaver, "Organizing for Political Action: Suggestions from Experience," in Kenneth S. Goodman, ed., *In Defense of Good Teaching: What Teachers Need to Know About the "Reading Wars"* (Portsmouth, N.H.: Heinemann, 1998), pp. 183–90.

20. This letter appears in W. James Popham, *Testing! Testing!: What Every Parent Should Know About School Tests* (Boston: Allyn and Bacon, 2000), p. 284.

21. One rather tentative bumper sticker now being circulated asks, "Is Standardized Testing Hurting Our Kids?" A more decisive one features the initials of the state's test in a circle with a red diagonal slash running through them, followed by: "These Tests Hurt Kids!" Meanwhile, some educators have printed up t-shirts that read, "High Stakes Are for Tomatoes."

22. Scott G. Paris et al., "A Developmental Perspective on Standardized Achievement Testing," *Educational Researcher*, June/July 1991, p. 17.

23. Anne Davis, "Executives in West Bend Struggle with Sample of State Graduation Test," *Milwaukee Journal Sentinel*, 20 January 1999.

24. Stephen Hegarty, "Officials Dodge FCAT Dare," *St. Petersburg Times*, 13 February 2000.

25. On the respects in which standardized testing is most damaging to low-income and minority students, see Kohn, *The Case Against Standardized Testing*, chap. 4; idem, "Standardized Testing and Its Victims," *Education Week*, 27 September 2000, pp. 60, 46, 47; Swope and Miner; and McNeil.

26. See Catherine C. Lewis, *Educating Hearts and Minds: Reflections on Japanese Preschool and Elementary Education* (Cambridge: Cambridge University Press, 1995), pp. 201, 16.

27. Jane Coles, "Enough Was Enough: The Teachers' Boycott of National Curriculum Testing," *Changing English*, vol. 1, no. 2, 1994, pp. 16, 23.

28. This account is based on Robin Lord, "Harwich Teacher Refused to Hand Out MCAS Test," *Cape Cod Times*, 3 June 1999; Ed Hayward, "MCAS Opponents Hold Rally in Hub," *Boston Herald*, 16 May 2000; and personal communications. Bougas received a two-week suspension without pay in May 2000, but, at this writing, still has his job. Several other Massachusetts teachers have also refused to administer the MCAS, so far without repercussions.

29. For example, www.stopopts.org in Ohio; http://personal.cfw.com/~dday/VASOLs.html in Virginia; www.xfcat.com in Florida; www.geocities.com/nccds/index.html in North Carolina; www.taasblues.com in Texas; www.castausa.com in Nevada; www.cpog.org in Georgia; www.fairtest.org/arn/masspage.html in Massachusetts; www.pipeline.com/~rgibson/meap.html in Michigan; and www.stopAIMSnow.org in Arizona.

30. Tracy Van Moorlehem, "Students, Parents Rebel Against State Test," *Detroit Free Press*, 29 April 1998, p. 1-A. Overall, "those opting out of the test tend to be average or above-average students," some of whom wore t-shirts that urged their peers to "just say no" to the test, Moorlehem reports. In response to the students' actions, state officials did not reconsider the value of the tests but began offering students substantial scholarships for high scores.

ALFIE KOHN is the author of eight books, including The Schools Our Children Deserve: Moving Beyond Traditional Classrooms and "Tougher Standards" (*Houghton Mifflin, 1999*) *and* The Case Against Standardized Testing: Raising the Scores, Ruining the Schools (*Heinemann, 2000*), *from which this article is adapted. His five previous* Kappan *articles are available at www.alfiekohn.org. © 2001, Alfie Kohn.*

From *Phi Delta Kappan,* January 2001, Vol. 82, No. 5, pp. 348-357. © 2001 by Phi Delta Kappan. Reprinted by permission of the magazine and the author.

Helping Standards Make the
GRADE

*When reporting on student work, educators need a clear,
comprehensive grading system that shows how students
are measuring up to standards.*

Thomas R. Guskey

The issue of grading looms on the horizon for standards-based education. With standards and assessments now in place, educators face the daunting task of how best to grade and report student learning in terms of those standards. Most educators recognize the inadequacies of their current grading and reporting methods (Marzano, 2000). Few, however, have found alternatives that satisfy the diverse needs of students, parents, teachers, school administrators, and community members.

Standards don't lessen the responsibility of educators to evaluate the performance of students and to report the results. Nevertheless, the focus on standards poses unique challenges in grading and reporting. What are those challenges, and how can educators develop standards-based grading and reports that are accurate, honest, and fair?

Criterion-Referenced Standards

The first challenge is moving from norm-referenced to criterion-referenced grading standards. *Norm-referenced* standards compare each students's performance to that of other students in the group or class. Teachers first rank students on some measure of their achievement or performance. They assign a set percentage of top-ranked students (usually 10 to 20 percent) the highest grade, a second set percentage (perhaps 20 to 30 percent) the second highest grade, and so on. The percentages

typically correspond to an approximation of the bell-shaped, normal probability curve, hence the expression "grading on the curve." Most adults experienced this type of grading during their school days.

Criterion-referenced standards, in contrast, compare each student's performance to clearly stated performance descriptions that differentiate levels of quality. Teachers judge students' performance by what each student does, regardless of how well or poorly their classmates perform.

Using the normal probability curve as a basis for assigning grades yields highly consistent grade distributions from one teacher to the next. All teachers' classes have essentially the same percentages of *A*s, *B*s, and *C*s. But the consequences for students are overwhelmingly negative. Learning becomes highly competitive because students must compete against one another for the new high grades that the teacher distributes. Under these conditions, students see that helping others threatens their own chances for success. Because students do not achieve high grades by performing well, but rather by doing better than their classmates, learning becomes a game of winners and losers, and because teachers keep the number of rewards arbitrarily small, most students must be losers (Haladyna, 1999; Johnson & Johnson, 1989). Strong evidence shows that "grading on the curve" is detrimental to relationships—both among students and among teachers and students (Krumboltz & Yeh, 1996).

In a standards-based system, grading and reporting must be criterion-referenced. Teachers at all levels must identify what they want their students to learn and be able to do and what evidence they will use to judge that achievement or performance. Grades based on clearly stated learning criteria have direct meaning and communicate that meaning.

Differentiating Grading Criteria

A second challenge is to differentiate the types of grading criteria that teachers will use. Although teachers and students generally consider criterion-referenced grading to be more fair and equitable (Kovas, 1993), the specific grading criteria that teachers use may be very diverse. We can classify these criteria into three broad categories: *product, process,* and *progress* (Guskey, 1996).

Standards don't lessen the responsibility of educators to evaluate the performance of students and to report the results.

Product criteria relate to students' specific achievements or levels of performance. They describe what students know and are able to do at a particular point in time. Advocates of standards generally favor product criteria. Teachers using product criteria base students' grades or reports exclusively on final examination scores; final products, such as reports, projects, or portfolios; overall assessments of performance; and other culminating demonstrations of learning.

Process criteria relate not to the final results, but to how students got there. Educators who believe that product criteria do not provide a complete picture of student learning generally favor process criteria. For example, teachers who consider student effort, class behavior, or work habits are using process criteria. So are those who count daily work, regular classroom quizzes, homework, class participation, punctuality of assignments, or attendance in determining students' grades.

Progress criteria relate to how much students actually gain from their learning experiences. Other terms include learning gain, improvement grading, value-added grading, and educational growth. Teachers who use progress criteria typically look at how far students have come rather than where students are. Others attempt to judge students' progress in terms of their "learning potential." As a result, progress grading criteria are often highly individualized among students.

Because they are concerned about student motivation, self-esteem, and the social consequences of grading, few teachers today use product criteria solely in determining grades. Instead, most base their grading on some combination of criteria, especially when a student

receives only a single grade in a subject area (Brookhart, 1993; Frary, Cross, & Weber, 1993). The majority of teachers also vary the criteria they use from student to student, taking into account individual circumstances (Truog & Friedman, 1996). Although teachers do so in an effort to be fair, the result is often a hodgepodge grade that includes elements of achievement, effort, and improvement (Brookhart, 1991). Interpreting the grade or report thus becomes difficult for parents, administrators, community members, and even the students (Friedman & Frisbie, 1995). An *A*, for example, may mean that the student knew what the teacher expected before instruction began (product), didn't learn as well as expected but tried very hard (process), or simply made significant improvement (progress).

Measurement experts generally recommend using product criteria exclusively in determining students' grades. They point out that the more process and progress criteria come into play, the more subjective and biased grades are likely to be (O'Connor, 1999; Ornstein, 1994). How can a teacher know, for example, how difficult a task was for students or how hard they worked to complete it?

Many teachers, however, point out that if they use product criteria exclusively, some high-ability students receive high grades with little effort, whereas the hard work of less-talented students is seldom acknowledged. Others say that if teachers consider only product criteria, low-ability students and those who are disadvantaged—students who must work the hardest—have the least incentive to do so. These students find the relationship between high effort and low grades unacceptable and, as a result, often express their displeasure with indifference, deception, or disruption (Tomlinson, 1992).

A practical solution to this problem, and one that increasing numbers of teachers and schools are using, is to establish clear indicators of product, process, and progress, and then to report each separately (Stiggins, 2001; Wiggins, 1996). Teachers separate grades or marks for learning skills, effort, work habits, or progress from grades for achievement and performance. Parents generally prefer this approach because it gives them more detailed and prescriptive information. It also simplifies reporting for teachers because they no longer have to combine so many diverse types of information into a single grade. The key to success, however, rests in the clear specification of those indicators and the criteria to which they relate. This means that teachers must describe how they plan to evaluate students' achievement, effort, work habits, and progress, and then must communicate these plans directly to students, parents, and others.

Reporting Tools

A third challenge for standards-based education is clarifying the purpose of each reporting tool. Although report cards are the primary method, most schools today use a variety of reporting devices: weekly or monthly progress reports, open-house meetings, newsletters, evaluated projects or assignments, school Web pages, parent-teacher conferences, and student-led conferences (Guskey & Bailey, 2001). Each reporting tool must fulfill a specific purpose, which requires considering three vital aspects of communication:

- What information do we want to communicate?
- Who is the primary audience for that information?
- How would we like that information to be used?

Many educators make the mistake of choosing their reporting tools first, without giving careful attention to the purpose. For example, some charge headlong into developing a standards-based report card without first addressing core questions about why they are doing it. Their efforts often encounter unexpected resistance and rarely bring positive results. Both parents and teachers perceive the change as a newfangled fad that presents no real advantage over traditional reporting methods. As a result, the majority of these efforts become short-lived experiments and are abandoned after a few troubled years of implementation.

Efforts that begin by clarifying the purpose, however, make intentions clear from the start. If, for instance, the purpose of the report card is to communicate to parents the achievement status of students, then parents must understand the information on the report card and know how to use it. This means that educators should include parents on report card committees and give their input careful consideration. This not only helps mobilize everyone in the reporting process, it also keeps efforts on track. The famous adage that guides architecture also applies to grading and reporting: *Form follows function.* Once the purpose of functions is clear, teachers can address more easily questions regarding form or method (Guskey & Bailey, 2001).

Developing a Reporting Form

The fourth challenge for standards-based education is developing the centerpiece of a standards-based reporting system: the report card. This typically involves a four-step process. First, teams of educators identify the major learning goals or standards that students are expected to achieve at each grade level or course of study. Second, educators establish performance indicators for those learning goals or standards. In other words, educators decide what evidence best illustrates students' attainment of each goal or standard. Third, they determine graduated levels of quality for assessing student performance. This step involves identifying incremental levels of attainment, sometimes referred to as benchmarks, as students progress toward the learning goals or standards (Andrade, 2000; Wiggins & McTighe, 1998). Finally, educators, often in collaboration with

parents, develop a reporting form that communicates teachers' judgments of students' progress and achievement in relation to the learning goals or standards.

Many parents initially respond to a standards-based reporting form with, "This is great. But tell me, how is my child doing *really*?"

Identifying Reporting Standards

Identifying the specific learning goals or standards on which to base grades is probably the most important, but also the most challenging, aspect of standards-based grading. These learning goals or standards should stipulate precisely what students should know and be able to do as a result of their learning experiences. In earlier times, we might have referred to cognitive skills, learning competencies, or performance outcomes (Guskey, 1999). Teachers frequently list these learning goals in their lesson plans, make note of them on assignments and performance tasks, and include them in monthly or weekly progress reports that go home to parents.

A crucial consideration in identifying learning goals or standards is determining the degree of specificity. Standards that are too specific make supporting forms cumbersome to use and difficult to understand. Standards that are too broad or general, however, make it hard to identify students' unique strengths and weaknesses. Most state-level standards, for example, tend to be broad and need to be broken down or "unpacked" into homogeneous categories or topics (Marzano, 1999). For grading and reporting purposes, educators must seek a balance. The standards must be broad enough to allow for efficient communication of student learning, yet specific enough to be useful (see Gronlund, 2000; Marzano & Kendall, 1995; Wiggins & McTighe, 1998).

Another issue is the differentiation of standards across marking periods or grade levels. Most schools using standards-based grading develop reporting forms that are based on grade-level learning goals or standards. Each standard has one level of complexity set for each grade that students were expected to meet before the end of the academic year. Most parents, however, are accustomed to grading systems in which learning standards become increasingly complex with each marking period. If the standard states "Students will write clearly and effectively," for example, many parents believe that their children should do this each marking period, not simply move toward doing so by the end of the academic year. This is especially true of parents who encourage their children to attain the highest mark possible in all subject areas every marking period.

To educators using such forms, students who receive *1* or *2* on a 4-point grading scale during the first or second marking period are making appropriate progress and are on track for their grade level. For parents, however, a report card filled with *1s* and *2s* when the highest mark is a *4*, causes great concern. They think that their children are failing. Although including a statement on the reporting form, such as "Marks indicate progress toward end-of-the-year learning standards," is helpful, it may not alleviate parents' concerns.

Example of a Double-Mark, Standards-Based Reporting Form

Elementary Progress Report

Reading	1st	2nd	3rd	4th
Understands and uses different skills and strategies	1+	2++		
Understands the meaning of what is read	1++	2+		
Reads different materials for a variety of purposes	1-	2-		
Reading level		1++	2+	
Work habits	S	S		
Writing	1st	2nd	3rd	4th
Writes clearly and effectively	1+	2++		
Understands and uses the steps in the writing process	1++	2++		
Writes in a variety of forms for different audiences and purposes	1+	2-		
Analyzes and evaluates the effectiveness of written work	N	1+		
Understands and uses the conventions of writing: punctuation, capitalization, spelling, and legibility	1-	2-		
Work habits	S	S		
Communication	1st	2nd	3rd	4th
Uses listening and observational skills to gain understanding	1+	2-		
Communicates ideas clearly and effectively (formal communication)	1-	2+		
Uses communication strategies and skills to work effectively with others (informal communication)	N	1+		
Work habits	U	S		

This report is based on grade-level standards established for each subject area. The ratings indicate your student's progress in relation to the year-end standard.

Evaluation Marks

4 = Exceptional
3 = Meets standard
2 = Approaches standard
1 = Beginning standard
N = Not applicable

Level Expectation Marks

++ = Advanced
+ = On level
− = Below level

Social Learning Skills & Effort Marks

E = Exceptional
S = Satisfactory
U = Unsatisfactory

Facilitating Interpretation

Many parents initially respond to a standards-based reporting form with, "This is great. But tell me, how is my child doing *really?*" Or they ask, "How is my child doing compared to the other children in the class?" They ask these questions because they don't know how to interpret the information. Further, most parents had comparative, norm-based reporting systems when they were in school and are more familiar with reports that compare students to their classmates. Above all, parents want to make sense of the reporting form. Their fear is that their children will reach the end of the school year and won't have made sufficient progress to be promoted to the next grade.

To ensure more accurate interpretations, several schools use a two-part marking system with their standards-based reporting form (see example). Every marking period, each student receives two marks for each standard. The first mark indicates the student's level of progress with regard to the standard—a *1, 2, 3,* or *4,* indicating *beginning, progressing, proficient,* or *exceptional.* The second mark indicates the relation of that level of progress to established expectations at this point in the school year. For example, a ++ might indicate *advanced for grade-level expectations,* a + might indicate *on target* or *meeting grade-level expectations,* and a – would indicate *below grade-level expectations* or *needs improvement.*

The advantage of this two-part marking system is that it helps parents make sense of the reporting form each marking period. It also helps alleviate their concerns about what seem like low grades and lets them know whether their children are progressing at an appropriate rate. Further, it helps parents take a standards-based perspective in viewing their children's performances. Their question is no longer "Where is my child in comparison to his or her classmates?" but "Where is my child in relation to the grade-level learning goals and expectations?"

The one drawback of the two-part marking system is that expectations must take into account individual differences in students' development of cognitive skills. Because students in any classroom differ in age and cognitive development, some might not meet the specified criteria during a particular marking period— even though they will likely do so before the end of the year. This is especially common in kindergarten and the early primary grades, when students tend to vary widely in their entry-level skills but can make rapid learning progress (Shuster, Lemma, Lynch, & Nadeau, 1996). Educators must take these developmental differences into consideration and must explain them to parents.

Choosing Performance-Level Descriptors

Standards-based reporting forms that use numerical grading scales also require a key or legend that explains the meaning of each numeral. These descriptors help parents and others understand what each numeral means.

A common set of descriptors matches performance levels *1, 2, 3,* and *4* with the achievement labels *beginning, progressing, proficient,* and *exceptional.* If the standards reflect behavioral aspects of students' performance, then teachers more commonly use such descriptors as *seldom, sometimes, usually,* and *consistently/independently.* These labels are preferable to *above average, average,* and *below average,* which reflect norm-referenced comparisons rather than criterion-referenced standards.

Such achievement descriptors as *exceptional* or *advanced* are also preferable to *exceeds standard* or *extending* to designate the highest level of performance. Educators can usually articulate specific performance criteria for an *exceptional* or *advanced* level of achievement or performance. *Exceeds standard* or *extending,* however, are much less precise and may leave students and parents wondering just what they need to do to exceed or extend. Descriptors should be clear, concise, and directly interpretable.

Many reporting forms include a fifth level of *not applicable* or *not evaluated* to designate standards that have not yet been addressed or were not assessed during that particular marking period. Including these labels is preferable to leaving the marking spaces blank because parents often interpret a blank space as an item that the teacher missed or neglected.

Maintaining Consistency

A final challenge is consistency. To communicate with parents, most schools and school districts involved in standards-based grading try to maintain a similar reporting format across grade levels. Most also use the same performance-level indicators at all grade levels so that parents don't have to learn a new set of procedures for interpreting the reporting form each year as their children move from one grade level to the next. Many parents also see consistency as an extension of a well-designed curriculum. The standards at each grade level build on and extend those from earlier levels.

While maintaining a similar format across grade levels, however, most schools and school districts list different standards on the reporting form for each level. Although the reporting format and performance indicators remain the same, the standards on the 1st grade reporting form are different from those on the 2nd grade form, and so on. This gives parents a clear picture of the increasing complexity of the standards at each subsequent grade level.

An alternative approach is to develop one form that lists the same broad standards for multiple grades. To clarify the difference at each grade level, a curriculum guidebook describing precisely what the standard means and what criteria are used in evaluating the standard at each grade level usually accompanies the form. Most reporting forms of this type also include a narrative section, in which teachers offer additional explanations. Although this approach to standards-based grading simplifies the reporting form, it also requires significant parent training and a close working relationship among parents, teachers, and school and district leaders (Guskey & Bailey, 2001).

Advantages and Shortcomings

When we establish clear learning goals or standards, standards-based grading offers important information about students' achievement and performance. If sufficiently detailed, the information is useful for both diagnostic and prescriptive purposes. For these reasons, standards-based grading facilitates teaching and learning better than almost any other grading method.

At the same time, standards-based grading has shortcomings. First and foremost, it takes a lot of work. Not only must educators identify the learning goals or standards on which grades will be based, but they also must decide what evidence best illustrates students' attainment or each goal or standard, identify graduated levels of quality for assessing students' performance, and develop reporting tools that communicate teachers' judgements of learning progress. These tasks may add considerably to the workload of teachers and school leaders.

A second shortcoming is that the reporting forms are sometimes too complicated for parents to understand. In their efforts to provide parents with rich information, educators can go overboard and describe learning goals in unnecessary detail. As a result, reporting forms become cumbersome and time-consuming for teachers to complete and difficult for parents to understand. We must seek a crucial balance in identifying standards that are specific enough to provide parents with useful, prescriptive information, but broad enough to allow for efficient communication between educators and parents.

A third shortcoming is that the report may not communicate the appropriateness of students' progress. Simply reporting a student's level of proficiency with regard to a particular standard communicates nothing about the adequacy of that level of achievement or performance. To make sense of the information, parents need to know how that level of achievement or performance compares to the established learning expectations for that particular grade level.

Finally, although teachers can use standards-based grading at any grade level and in any course of study, most current applications are restricted to the elementary level where there is little curriculum differentiation. In the middle grades and at the secondary level, students usually pursue more diverse courses of study. Because of these curricular differences, standards-based reporting forms as the middle and secondary levels must vary from student to student. The marks need to relate to each student's achievement and performance in his or her particular courses or academic program. Although advances in technology, such as computerized reporting forms, allow educators to provide such individualized reports, relatively few middle and high school educators have taken up the challenge.

The standards must be broad enough to allow for efficient communication of student learning, yet specific enough to be useful.

New Standards for Grading

As educators clarify student learning goals and standards, the advantages of standards-based grading become increasingly evident. Although it makes reporting forms more detailed and complex, most parents value the richness of the information when the reports are expressed in terms that they can understand and use. Reporting forms that use a two-part marking system show particular promise—but such a system may require additional explanation to parents. Teachers must also set expectations for learning progress not just at the grade level, but also for each marking period.

Successfully implementing standards-based grading and reporting demands a close working relationship among teachers, parents, and school and district leaders. To accurately interpret the reporting form, parents need to know precisely what the standards mean and how to make sense of the various levels of achievement or performance in relation to those standards. Educators must ensure, therefore, that parents are familiar with the language and terminology. Only when all groups understand what grades mean and how they are used to improve student learning will we realize the true value of a standards-based approach to education.

References

Andrade, H. G. (2000). Using rubrics to promote thinking and learning. *Educational Leadership, 57*(5), 13–18.

Brookhart, S. M. (1991). Grading practices and validity. *Educational Measurement: Issues and Practice, 10*(1), 35–36.

Brookhart, S. M. (1993). Teachers' grading practices: Meaning and values. *Journal of Educational Measurement, 30*(2), 123–142.

Frary, R. B., Cross, L. H., & Weber, L. J. (1993). Testing and grading practices and opinions of secondary teachers of academic subjects: Implications for instruction in measurement. *Educational Measurement: Issues and Practice, 12*(3), 23–30.

Friedman, S. J., & Frisbie, D. A. (1995). The influence of report cards on the validity of grades reported to parents. *Educational and Psychological Measurement, 55*(1), 5–26.

Gronlund, N. E. (2000). *How to write and use instructional objective's* (6th ed.). Upper Saddle River, NJ: Merrill.

Guskey, T. R. (1996). Reporting on student learning: Lessons from the past—Prescriptions for the future. In T. R. Guskey (Ed.), *Communicating student learning: 1996 Yearbook of the Association for Supervision and Curriculum Development* (pp. 13–24). Alexandria, VA: ASCD.

Guskey, T. R. (1999). Making standards work. *The School Administrator, 56*(9), 44.

Guskey, T. R., & Bailey, J. M. (2001). *Developing grading and reporting systems for student learning*. Thousand Oaks, CA: Corwin Press.

Haladyna, T. M. ('1999). *A complete guide to student grading*. Boston: Allyn & Bacon.

Johnson, D. W., & Johnson, R. T. (1989). *Cooperation and competition: Theory and research*. Endina, MN: Interaction.

Kendall, J. S., & Marzano, R. J. (1995). *The systematic identification and articulation of content standards and benchmarks: Update*. Aurora, CO: McREL.

Kovas, M. A. (1993). Make your grading motivating: Keys to performance-based evaluation. *Quill and Scroll, 68*(1), 10–11.

Krumboltz, J. D., & Yeh, C. J. (1996). Competitive grading sabotages good teaching. *Phi Delta Kappan, 78*(4), 324–326.

Marzano, R. J. (1999). Building curriculum and assessment around standards. *The High School Magazine, 6*(5), 14–19.

Marzano, R. J. (2000). *Transforming classroom grading*. Alexandria, VA: ASCD.

O'Connor, K. (1999). *How to grade for learning*. Arlington Heights, IL: Skylight.

Ornstein, A. C. (1994). Grading practices and policies: An overview and some suggestions. *NASSP Bulletin, 78*(559), 55–64.

Shuster, C., Lemma, P., Lynch, T., & Nadeau, K. (1996). A *study of kindergarten and 1st grade report cards: What are young children expected to learn?* Paper presented at the annual meeting of the American Educational Research Association, New York.

Stiggins, R. J. (2001). *Student-involved classroom assessment* (3rd ed.). Upper Saddle River, NJ: Merrill/Prentice Hall.

Tomlinson, T. (1992). *Hard work and high expectations: Motivating students to learn*. Washington, DC: Office of Educational Research and Improvement, U.S. Department of Education.

Truog, A. L., & Friedman, S. J. (1996). *Evaluating high school teachers' written grading policies from a measurement perspective*. Paper presented at the annual meeting of the National Council on Measurement in Education, New York.

Wiggins, G. (1996). Honesty and fairness: Toward better grading and reporting. In T. R. Guskey (Ed.), *Communicating student learning: 1996 Yearbook of the Association for Supervision and Curriculum Development* (pp. 141–176). Alexandria, VA: ASCD.

Wiggins, G., & McTighe, J. (1998). *Understanding by design*. Alexandria, VA: ASCD.

Thomas R. Guskey is Professor of Educational Policy Studies and Evaluation, College of Education, University of Kentucky, Lexington, KY 40506; guskey@pop.uky.edu.

From *Educational Leadership,* September 2001, pp. 20-27. Reprinted with permission of the Association for Supervision and Curriculum Development (ASCD). © 2001 by ASCD. All rights reserved.

Index

Index

Howard, Barbara, 31
hyperactivity, as a characteristic of ADHD, 46, 47

I

ideal teachers, 8, 10
identification, extrinsic motivation and, 136
imaginational overexcitability, 55
immigrants, new, and multicultural education, 65–66
impulsivity, as a characteristic of ADHD, 46
inappropriate practices, DAP guidelines and, 155
inattention, as a characteristic of ADHD, 46
inclusion, children with special needs and, 50–52, 154
individualized education plan (IEP), 155
Inspiration®, 108, 109–112, 114
integrated regulation, extrinsic motivation and, 136
integration, extrinsic motivation and, 134–137
intellectual overexcitability, 55
intelligence(s), 87–91, 96
interactive learning, 127–129
internalization, extrinsic motivation and, 134–137
Internet, 126–127
intrinsic motivation, 132, 133; versus extrinsic motivation, 139–142; reinforcers and, 159
introjected regulation, extrinsic motivation and, 136

K

Kamins, Melissa, 92, 94
Kemple, Kristen, 163, 165–166
knowledge, 90; of infants, 26–28
knowledge representation, concept mapping and, 106
Kohlberg, Lawrence, 32
Korea, babies of, 27
Kosslyn, Stephen, 76
Kozol, Jonathan, 205
Kreidler, William, 177

L

language diversity, 70–71
learning skills, 90
learning strategies, concept mapping and, 109–112
learning strategies, self-efficacy and, 146
learning-profile differentiation, 119
LeDoux, Joseph, 75, 83
left hemisphere, 75–77
Lerner, Barbara, 103
list learning strategies, cognitive psychology and, 5

M

Mackenzie, R. J., 167
mathematics, cognitive psychology and learning, 4–5
"maximal selfs," 103

McNeil, Linda, 205
Meltzoff, Andrew, 26, 27
memory, 85–86
mental subcomponents, 76
Merzenich, Michael, 84
metacognitive skills, 90
middle schools, 33–38; gifted education in, 39–43; helping students cope with phases of death in, 17
mindtools, concept mapping and, 106–115
morally accountable, children as, 31
morals, of children, 31–32
motivation, 90, 96; assessment and, 183; extrinsic, 132, 135–137; intrinsic, 132, 133–134; intrinsic versus extrinsic, 139–142; self-efficacy and academic, 145–146
Mueller, Claudia, 92, 93
multicultural education, 65–66, 67–69, 70–71
multiple-modality instruction, 14
Myth of the First Three Years, The (Bruer), 83

N

National Board of Professional Teaching Standards, teacher competence and, 9
negative effects, of praising, 94
neuroscience, 74, 76–80; controversy over use of, research in education and cognitive science, 82–86
Next Generation, 126–129
norm-referenced standards, 212

O

"on-task" data, 149, 150
"opt-out" clauses, standardized tests and, 207
Organismic Integration Theory (OIT), 135–136
outcome expectancies, self-efficacy, 144
overexcitability, 54–55
overjustification effect, 140

P

"parallel partner," 119
perceived control, self-efficacy and, 144
performance assessment, teaching about, 186–201
performance expectations, self-efficacy and, 144
persuasion, self-efficacy and verbal, 146
PET scans, 78–79
phonemes, controversy over neuroscience versus cognitive science and, 84–85
phonological awareness, 4
physiological reactions, self-efficacy and, 146
pictures, social problem-solving model and, 177
Pinter, Steven, 84
"planned ignoring," 172
plasticity, of the brain, 84–85
play, 29–30
polarization, 21

positive reinforcement, as strategy, of behavior, 156
posters, social problem-solving model and, 177
praise, 173–174; dangers of, 92–96
Praxis teacher competency test, 9
"problem puppets," social problem-solving model and, 177
problem solving: cognitive psychology and strategies for, 5; conflict resolution and social, 175–179
problem-based learning, 98
procedural knowledge, concept mapping and, 106–107
process criteria, criterion-referenced standards and, 213
product criteria, criterion-referenced standards and, 213
progress criteria, criterion-referenced standards and, 213
project-based learning, 101
propositional knowledge, concept mapping and, 106–107
propositional networks, concept mapping and, 106, 110
proximity control, classroom behavior and, 173
psychomotor overexcitability, 55
puppet role-plays, social problem-solving model and, 176–177

R

readiness differentiation, 118–119
reading, learning to, and cognitive psychology, 3–4, 5
reflective teachers, 9, 10
reinforcement: in early childhood settings, 155–156, 163–166; strategies of, 153–161
reporting forms, standards-based assessment and, 214
reporting standards, standards-based assessment and, 214–215
reporting tools, standards-based assessment and, 213–214
respected teachers, 10
Restak, Richard, 84
rewards. *See* extrinsic rewards
right hemisphere, 75–77
Ritalin, as a treatment for ADHD, 47
Robinson's SQ3R method, 49
role playing, social problem-solving model and, 176–177
Rosenfeld, Alvin, 31
rules. *See* classroom rules

S

SAT (Scholastic Aptitude Test), 89
satisfying teachers, 9–10, 11
Schacter, Daniel, 86
schema activation, cognitive psychology and, 5
schema, propositions and, 106
Sejnowski, Terry, 84
self-concept, self-efficacy and, 144

Test Your Knowledge Form

We encourage you to photocopy and use this page as a tool to assess how the articles in *Annual Editions* expand on the information in your textbook. By reflecting on the articles you will gain enhanced text information. You can also access this useful form on a product's book support Web site at *http://www.dushkin.com/online/*.

NAME: _____   DATE: _____

TITLE AND NUMBER OF ARTICLE: _____

BRIEFLY STATE THE MAIN IDEA OF THIS ARTICLE: _____

_____

LIST THREE IMPORTANT FACTS THAT THE AUTHOR USES TO SUPPORT THE MAIN IDEA:

_____

WHAT INFORMATION OR IDEAS DISCUSSED IN THIS ARTICLE ARE ALSO DISCUSSED IN YOUR TEXTBOOK OR OTHER READINGS THAT YOU HAVE DONE? LIST THE TEXTBOOK CHAPTERS AND PAGE NUMBERS:

_____

LIST ANY EXAMPLES OF BIAS OR FAULTY REASONING THAT YOU FOUND IN THE ARTICLE:

_____

LIST ANY NEW TERMS/CONCEPTS THAT WERE DISCUSSED IN THE ARTICLE, AND WRITE A SHORT DEFINITION:

We Want Your Advice

ANNUAL EDITIONS revisions depend on two major opinion sources: one is our Advisory Board, listed in the front of this volume, which works with us in scanning the thousands of articles published in the public press each year; the other is you—the person actually using the book. Please help us and the users of the next edition by completing the prepaid article rating form on this page and returning it to us. Thank you for your help!

ANNUAL EDITIONS: Educational Psychology 02/03

ARTICLE RATING FORM

Here is an opportunity for you to have direct input into the next revision of this volume.
We would like you to rate each of the articles listed below, using the following scale:

1. **Excellent: should definitely be retained**
2. **Above average: should probably be retained**
3. **Below average: should probably be deleted**
4. **Poor: should definitely be deleted**

Your ratings will play a vital part in the next revision.
Please mail this prepaid form to us as soon as possible.
Thanks for your help!

RATING	ARTICLE
_____	1. What Good Is Educational Psychology? The Case of Cognition and Instruction
_____	2. Good Teachers, Plural
_____	3. What I Hope for in My Children's Teachers: A Parent's Perspective
_____	4. Helping Children Cope with Loss, Death and Grief: Response to a National Tragedy
_____	5. The Standards Juggernaut
_____	6. Wired for Thought
_____	7. Play an Endangered Species
_____	8. Raising a Moral Child
_____	9. The School and the Child and the Child in the School
_____	10. Differing Perspectives, Common Ground: The Middle School and Gifted Education Relationship
_____	11. Chaos in the Classroom: Looking at ADHD
_____	12. The Oppression of Inclusion
_____	13. Challenges of Identifying and Serving Gifted Children With ADHD
_____	14. Gifted Students Need an Education, Too
_____	15. Teaching the New Immigrants: How "Multicultural" an Educator Are You Prepared to Be?
_____	16. Celebrate Diversity!
_____	17. Cultural and Language Diversity in the Middle Grades
_____	18. In Search of … Brain-Based Education
_____	19. Educators Need to Know About the Human Brain
_____	20. Ability and Expertise: It's Time to Replace the Current Model of Intelligence
_____	21. Caution—Praise Can Be Dangerous
_____	22. The Challenges of Sustaining a Constructivist Classroom Culture
_____	23. The Tyranny of Self-Oriented Self-Esteem
_____	24. Concept Mapping as a Mindtool for Critical Thinking
_____	25. Mapping a Route Toward Differentiated Instruction
_____	26. Reconcilable Differences? Standards-Based Teaching and Differentiation
_____	27. Educating the Net Generation
_____	28. Intrinsic and Extrinsic Motivations: Classic Definitions and New Directions

RATING	ARTICLE
_____	29. Intrinsic Versus Extrinsic Motivation in Schools: A Reconciliation
_____	30. Self-Efficacy: An Essential Motive to Learn
_____	31. Teaching Students to Regulate Their Own Behavior
_____	32. Reinforcement in Developmentally Appropriate Early Childhood Classrooms
_____	33. Another View on "Reinforcement in Developmentally Appropriate Early Childhood Classrooms"
_____	34. Using Classroom Rules to Construct Behavior
_____	35. "I Had It First": Teaching Young Children to Solve Problems Peacefully
_____	36. Fundamental Assesment Principles for Teachers and School Administrators
_____	37. Teaching About Performance Assessment
_____	38. Fighting the Tests: A Practical Guide to Rescuing Our Schools
_____	39. Helping Standards Make the Grade

(Continued on next page)

BUSINESS REPLY MAIL
FIRST-CLASS MAIL PERMIT NO. 84 GUILFORD CT

POSTAGE WILL BE PAID BY ADDRESSEE

McGraw-Hill/Dushkin
530 Old Whitfield Street
Guilford, Ct 06437-9989

ABOUT YOU

Name

Date

Are you a teacher? ☐   A student? ☐
Your school's name

Department

Address   City   State   Zip

School telephone #

YOUR COMMENTS ARE IMPORTANT TO US!

Please fill in the following information:
For which course did you use this book?

Did you use a text with this ANNUAL EDITION?   ☐ yes ☐ no
What was the title of the text?

What are your general reactions to the *Annual Editions* concept?

Have you read any pertinent articles recently that you think should be included in the next edition? Explain.

Are there any articles that you feel should be replaced in the next edition? Why?

Are there any World Wide Web sites that you feel should be included in the next edition? Please annotate.

May we contact you for editorial input?   ☐ yes ☐ no
May we quote your comments?   ☐ yes ☐ no